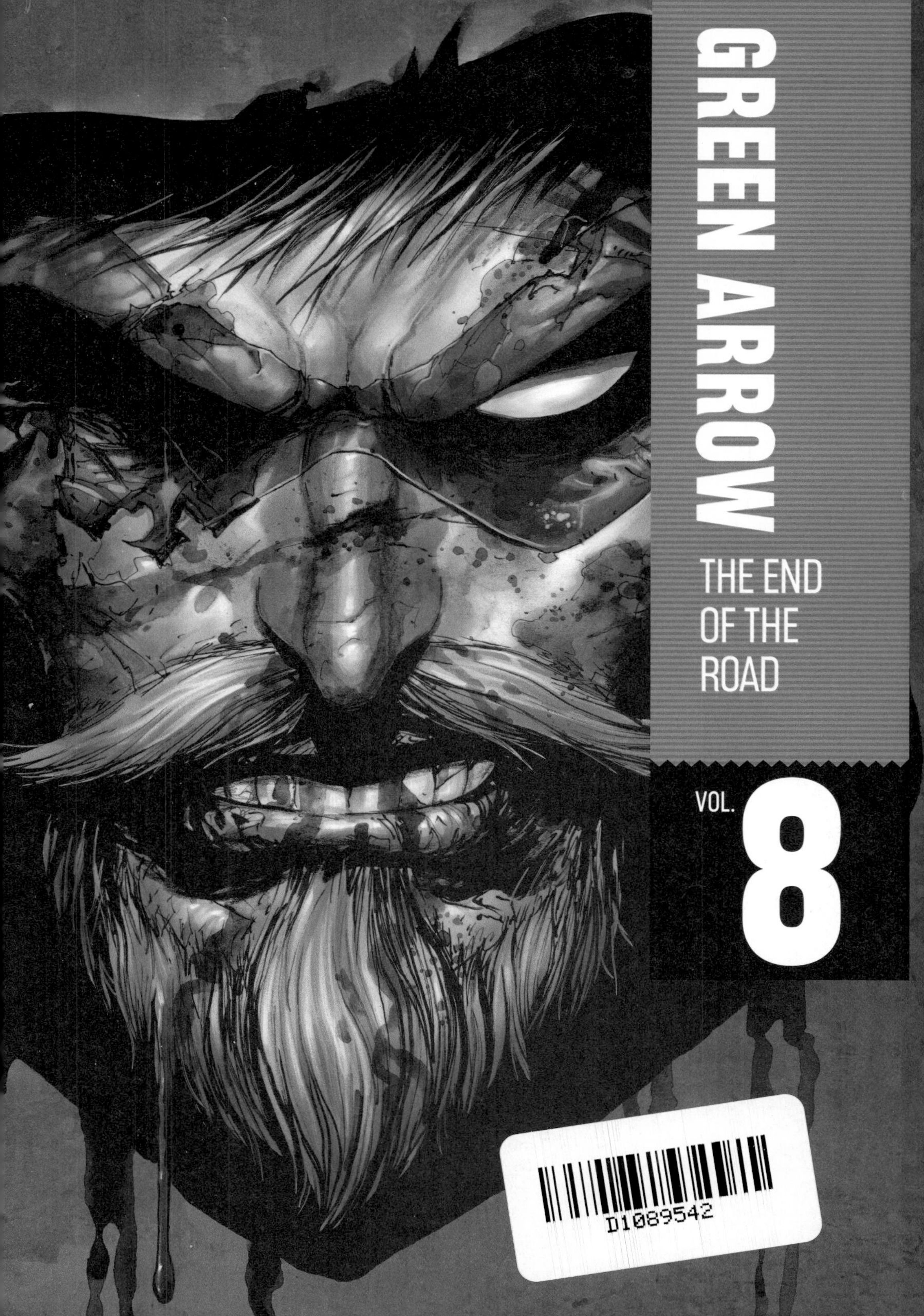

# GREEN ARROW

## THE END OF THE ROAD

VOL. 8

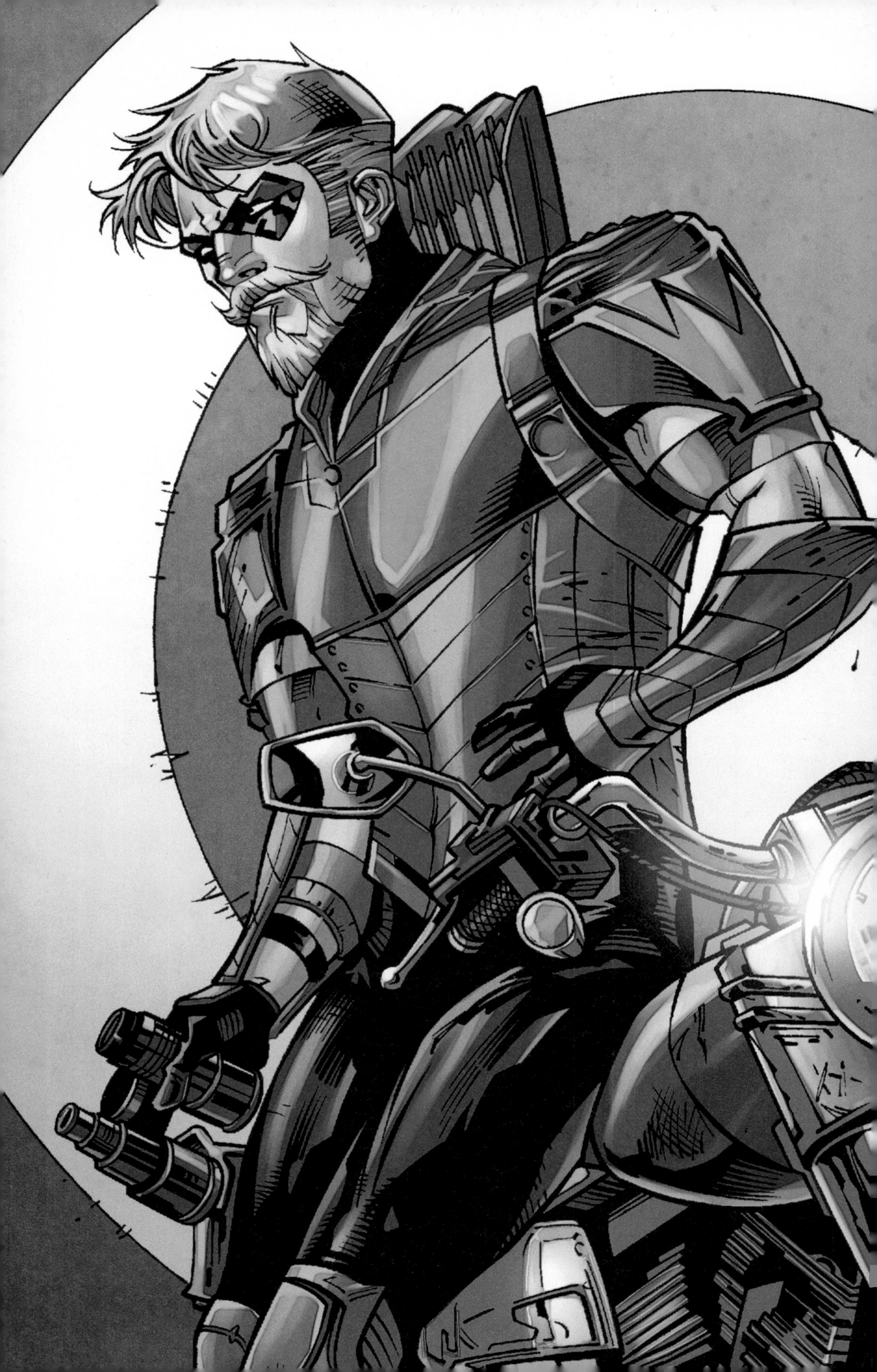

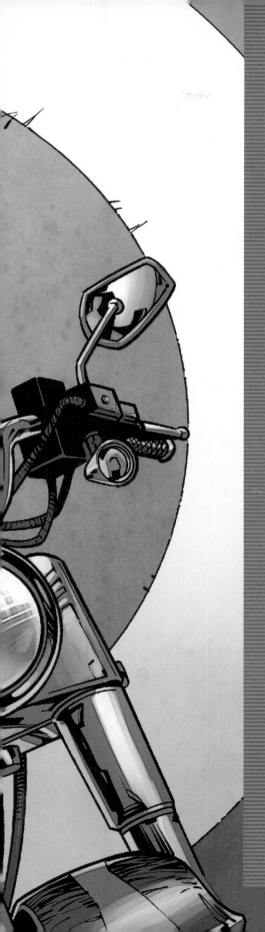

# GREEN ARROW

### THE END OF THE ROAD

writers
**JACKSON LANZING**
**COLLIN KELLY**
**MAIRGHREAD SCOTT**

pencillers
**JAVIER FERNANDEZ**
**MATTHEW CLARK**
**MARCIO TAKARA**

inkers
**JAVIER FERNANDEZ**
**SEAN PARSONS**
**MARCIO TAKARA**

colorists
**JOHN KALISZ**
**MARCELO MAIOLO**
**JASON WRIGHT**

letterer
**ANDWORLD DESIGN**

collection cover artist
**KEVIN NOWLAN**

VOL. **8**

ALEX ANTONE
KATIE KUBERT            Editors – Original Series
DAVE WIELGOSZ          Assistant Editor – Original Series
JEB WOODARD            Group Editor – Collected Editions
ERIKA ROTHBERG         Editor – Collected Edition
STEVE COOK             Design Director – Books
CURTIS KING JR.        Publication Design
TOM VALENTE            Publication Production

BOB HARRAS             Senior VP – Editor-in-Chief, DC Comics
PAT McCALLUM           Executive Editor, DC Comics

DAN DiDIO              Publisher
JIM LEE                Publisher & Chief Creative Officer
BOBBIE CHASE           VP – New Publishing Initiatives & Talent Development
DON FALLETTI           VP – Manufacturing Operations & Workflow Management
LAWRENCE GANEM         VP – Talent Services
ALISON GILL            Senior VP – Manufacturing & Operations
HANK KANALZ            Senior VP – Publishing Strategy & Support Services
DAN MIRON              VP – Publishing Operations
NICK J. NAPOLITANO     VP – Manufacturing Administration & Design
NANCY SPEARS           VP – Sales
MICHELE R. WELLS       VP & Executive Editor, Young Reader

**GREEN ARROW VOL. 8: THE END OF THE ROAD**

Published by DC Comics. Compilation and all new material Copyright © 2020 DC Comics. All Rights Reserved.
Originally published in single magazine form in Green Arrow 39-42, 48-50. Copyright © 2018, 2019 DC Comics.
All Rights Reserved. All characters, their distinctive likenesses, and related elements featured in this
publication are trademarks of DC Comics. The stories, characters, and incidents featured in this publication
are entirely fictional. DC Comics does not read or accept unsolicited submissions of ideas, stories, or artwork.
DC – A WarnerMedia Company.

DC Comics, 2900 West Alameda Ave., Burbank, CA 91505
Printed by LSC Communications, Owensville, MO, USA. 1/3/20. First Printing.
ISBN: 978-1-4012-9899-9

Library of Congress Cataloging-in-Publication Data is available.

**PEFC Certified**
This product is from
sustainably managed
forests and controlled
sources
PEFC/29-31-337    www.pefc.org

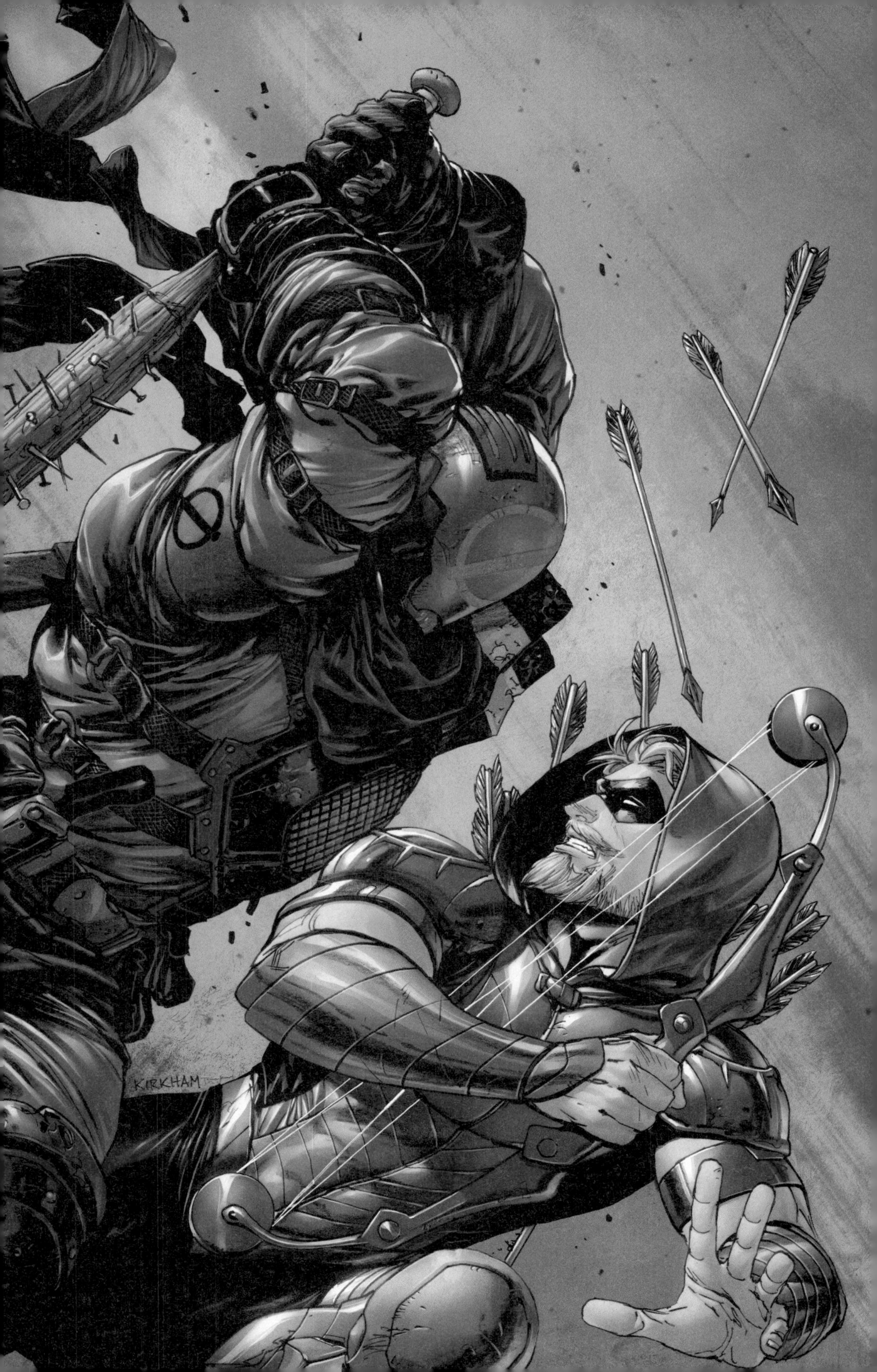
KIRKHAM

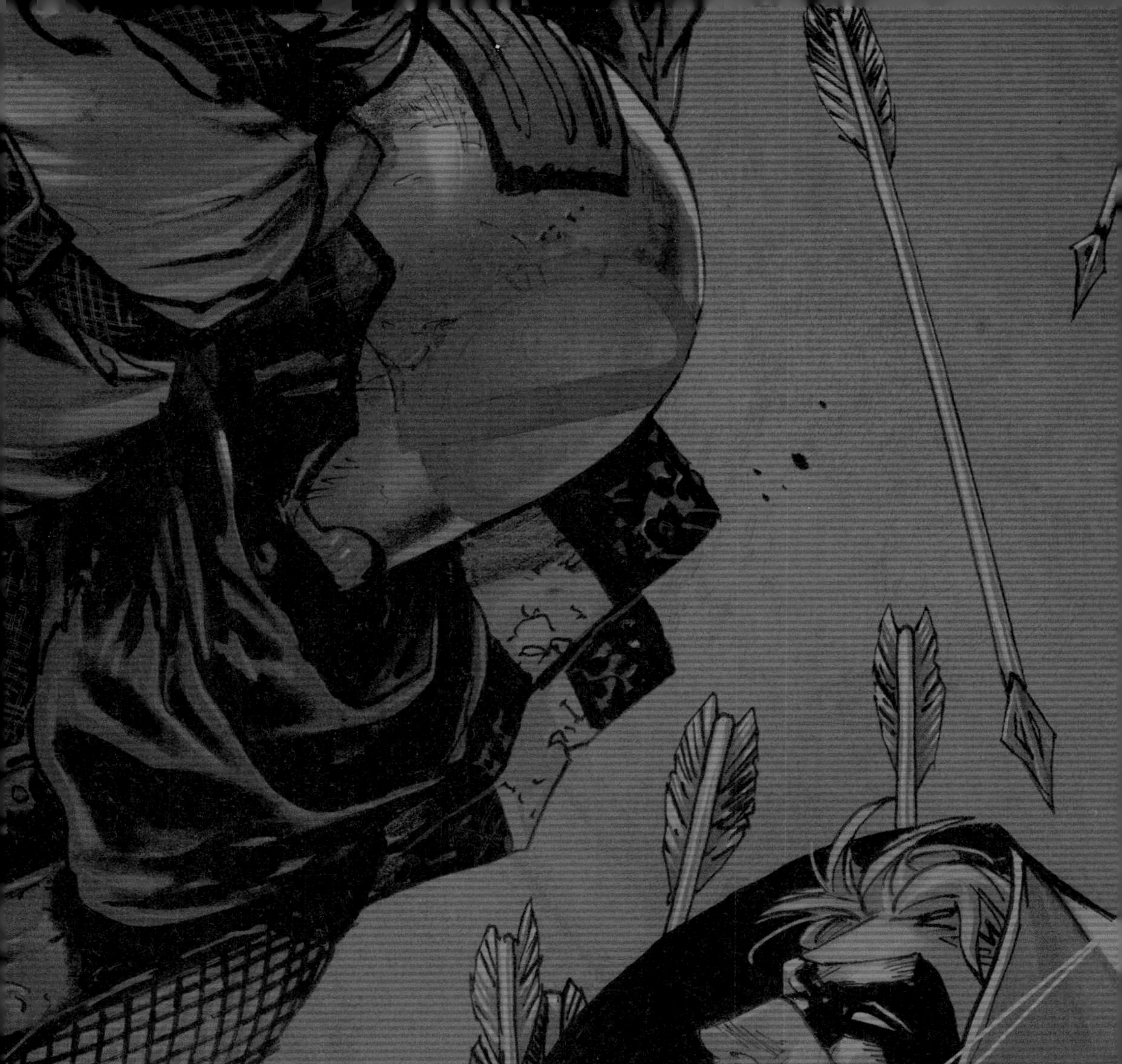

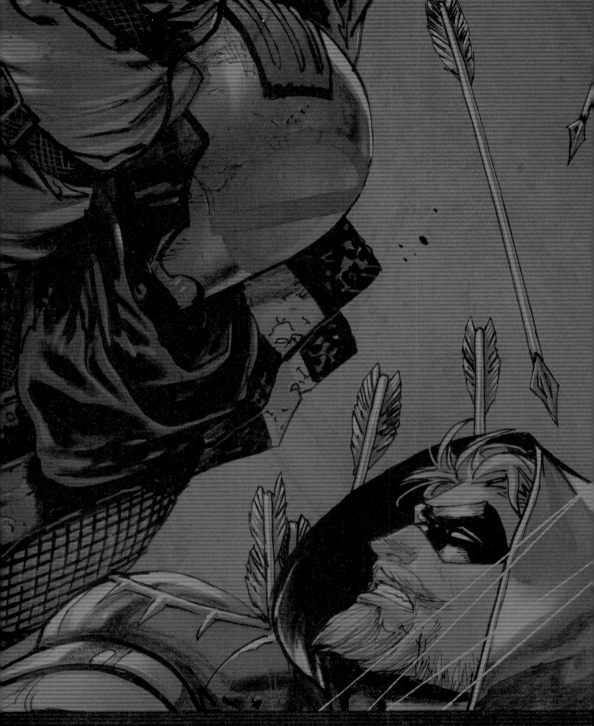

# GREEN ARROW
#39

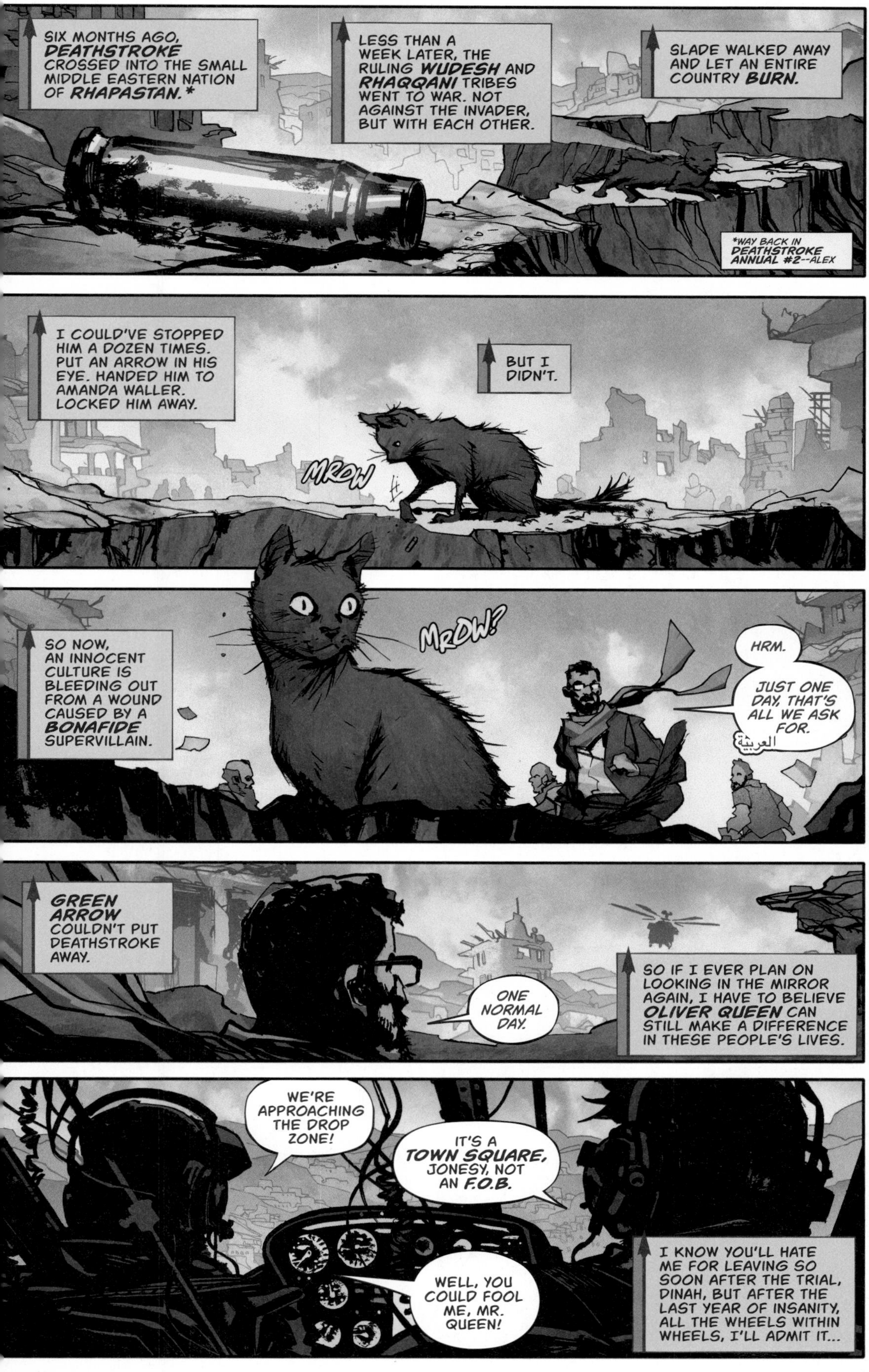
SIX MONTHS AGO, DEATHSTROKE CROSSED INTO THE SMALL MIDDLE EASTERN NATION OF RHAPASTAN.*
LESS THAN A WEEK LATER, THE RULING WUDESH AND RHAQQANI TRIBES WENT TO WAR. NOT AGAINST THE INVADER, BUT WITH EACH OTHER.
SLADE WALKED AWAY AND LET AN ENTIRE COUNTRY BURN.
*WAY BACK IN DEATHSTROKE ANNUAL #2--ALEX
I COULD'VE STOPPED HIM A DOZEN TIMES. PUT AN ARROW IN HIS EYE. HANDED HIM TO AMANDA WALLER. LOCKED HIM AWAY.
BUT I DIDN'T.
MROW
SO NOW, AN INNOCENT CULTURE IS BLEEDING OUT FROM A WOUND CAUSED BY A BONAFIDE SUPERVILLAIN.
MROW?
HRM.
JUST ONE DAY, THAT'S ALL WE ASK FOR.
العربية
GREEN ARROW COULDN'T PUT DEATHSTROKE AWAY.
ONE NORMAL DAY.
SO IF I EVER PLAN ON LOOKING IN THE MIRROR AGAIN, I HAVE TO BELIEVE OLIVER QUEEN CAN STILL MAKE A DIFFERENCE IN THESE PEOPLE'S LIVES.
WE'RE APPROACHING THE DROP ZONE!
IT'S A TOWN SQUARE, JONESY, NOT AN F.O.B.
WELL, YOU COULD FOOL ME, MR. QUEEN!
I KNOW YOU'LL HATE ME FOR LEAVING SO SOON AFTER THE TRIAL, DINAH, BUT AFTER THE LAST YEAR OF INSANITY, ALL THE WHEELS WITHIN WHEELS, I'LL ADMIT IT...

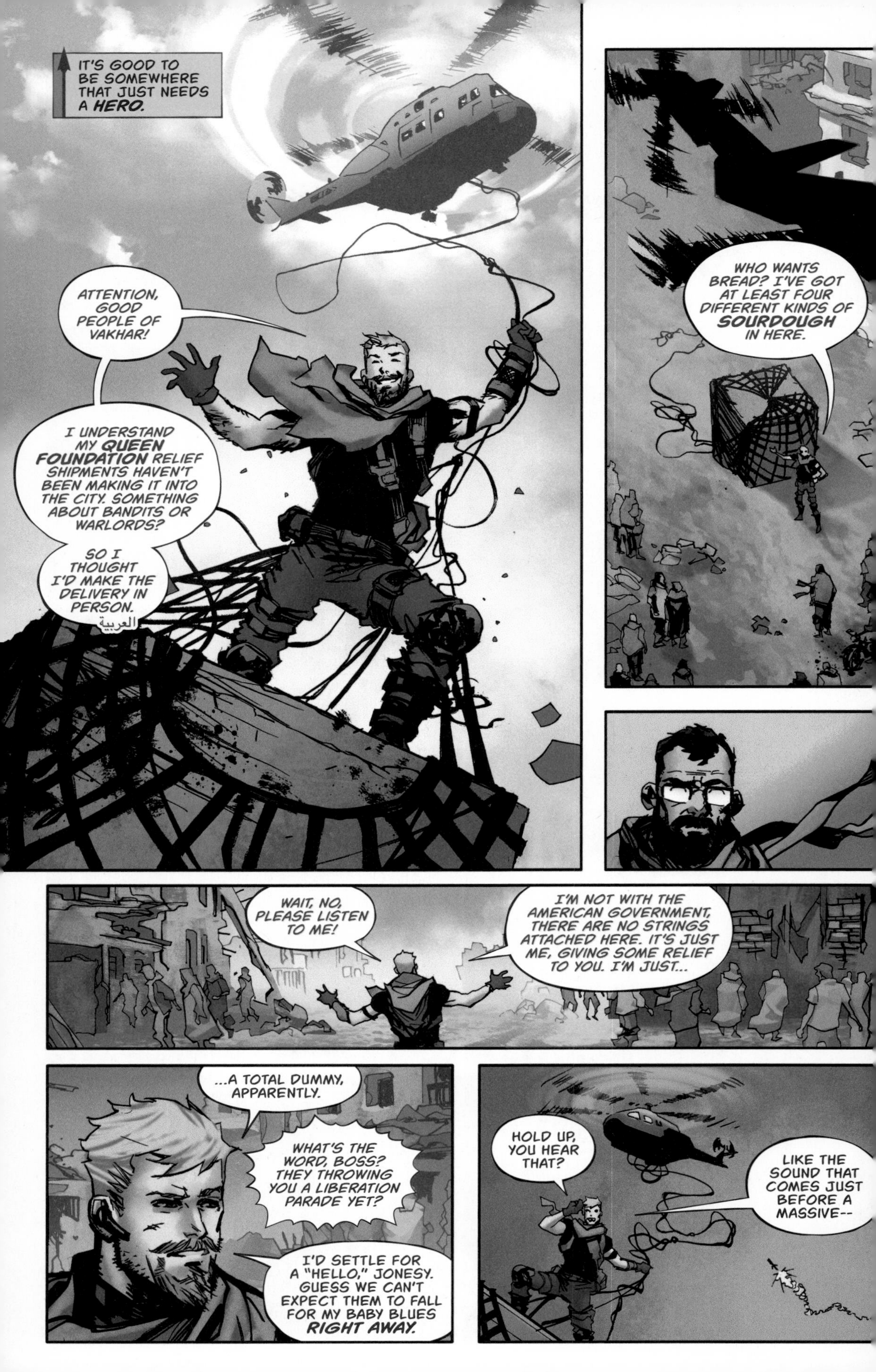
IT'S GOOD TO BE SOMEWHERE THAT JUST NEEDS A HERO.
ATTENTION, GOOD PEOPLE OF VAKHAR!
I UNDERSTAND MY QUEEN FOUNDATION RELIEF SHIPMENTS HAVEN'T BEEN MAKING IT INTO THE CITY. SOMETHING ABOUT BANDITS OR WARLORDS?
SO I THOUGHT I'D MAKE THE DELIVERY IN PERSON.
العربية
WHO WANTS BREAD? I'VE GOT AT LEAST FOUR DIFFERENT KINDS OF SOURDOUGH IN HERE.
WAIT, NO, PLEASE LISTEN TO ME!
I'M NOT WITH THE AMERICAN GOVERNMENT, THERE ARE NO STRINGS ATTACHED HERE. IT'S JUST ME, GIVING SOME RELIEF TO YOU. I'M JUST...
...A TOTAL DUMMY, APPARENTLY.
WHAT'S THE WORD, BOSS? THEY THROWING YOU A LIBERATION PARADE YET?
I'D SETTLE FOR A "HELLO," JONESY. GUESS WE CAN'T EXPECT THEM TO FALL FOR MY BABY BLUES RIGHT AWAY.
HOLD UP, YOU HEAR THAT?
LIKE THE SOUND THAT COMES JUST BEFORE A MASSIVE--

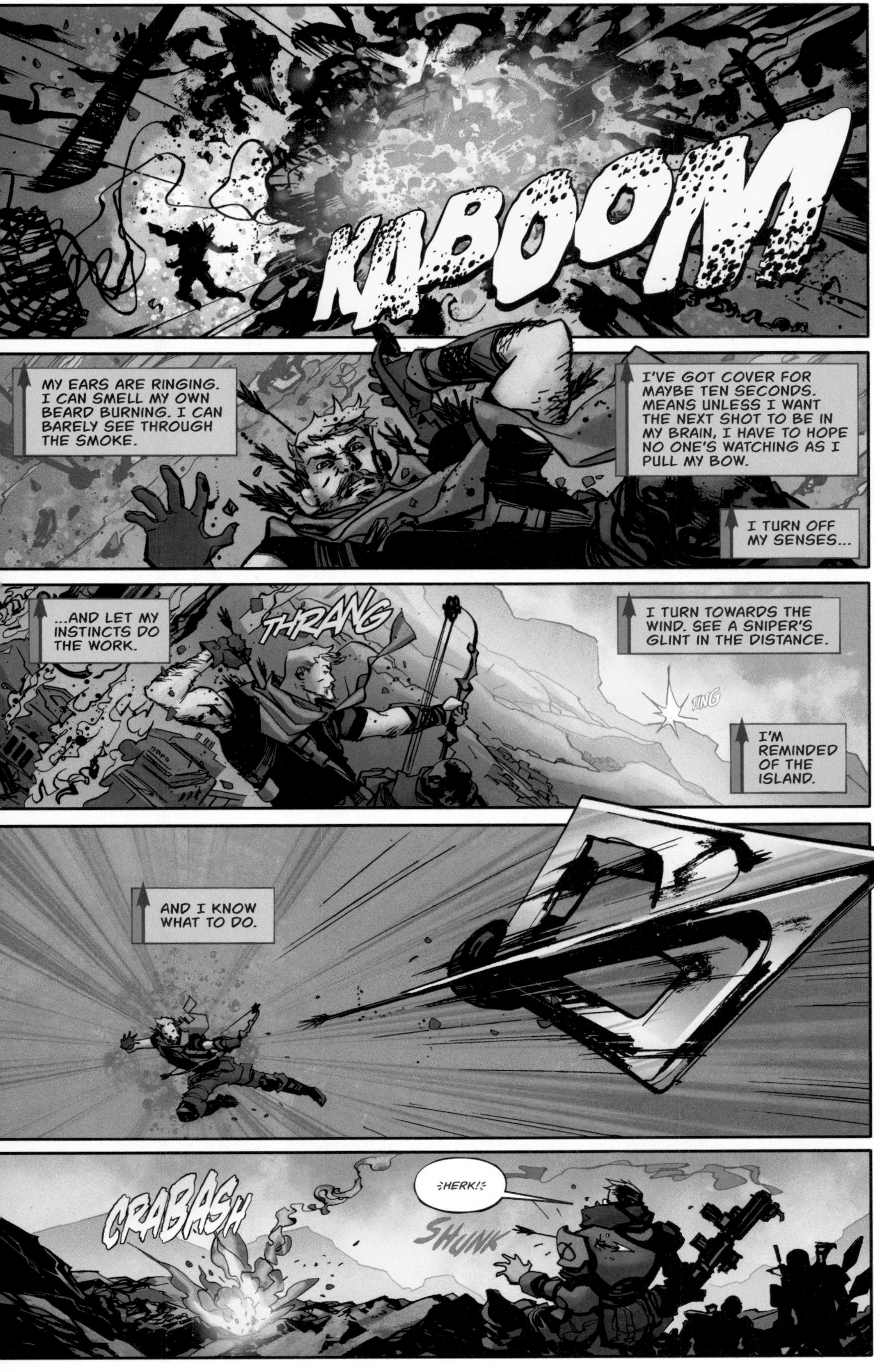
KABOOM!
MY EARS ARE RINGING. I CAN SMELL MY OWN BEARD BURNING. I CAN BARELY SEE THROUGH THE SMOKE.
I'VE GOT COVER FOR MAYBE TEN SECONDS. MEANS UNLESS I WANT THE NEXT SHOT TO BE IN MY BRAIN, I HAVE TO HOPE NO ONE'S WATCHING AS I PULL MY BOW.
I TURN OFF MY SENSES...
...AND LET MY INSTINCTS DO THE WORK.
THRANG
I TURN TOWARDS THE WIND. SEE A SNIPER'S GLINT IN THE DISTANCE.
TING
I'M REMINDED OF THE ISLAND.
AND I KNOW WHAT TO DO.
CRABASH
HERK!
SHUNK

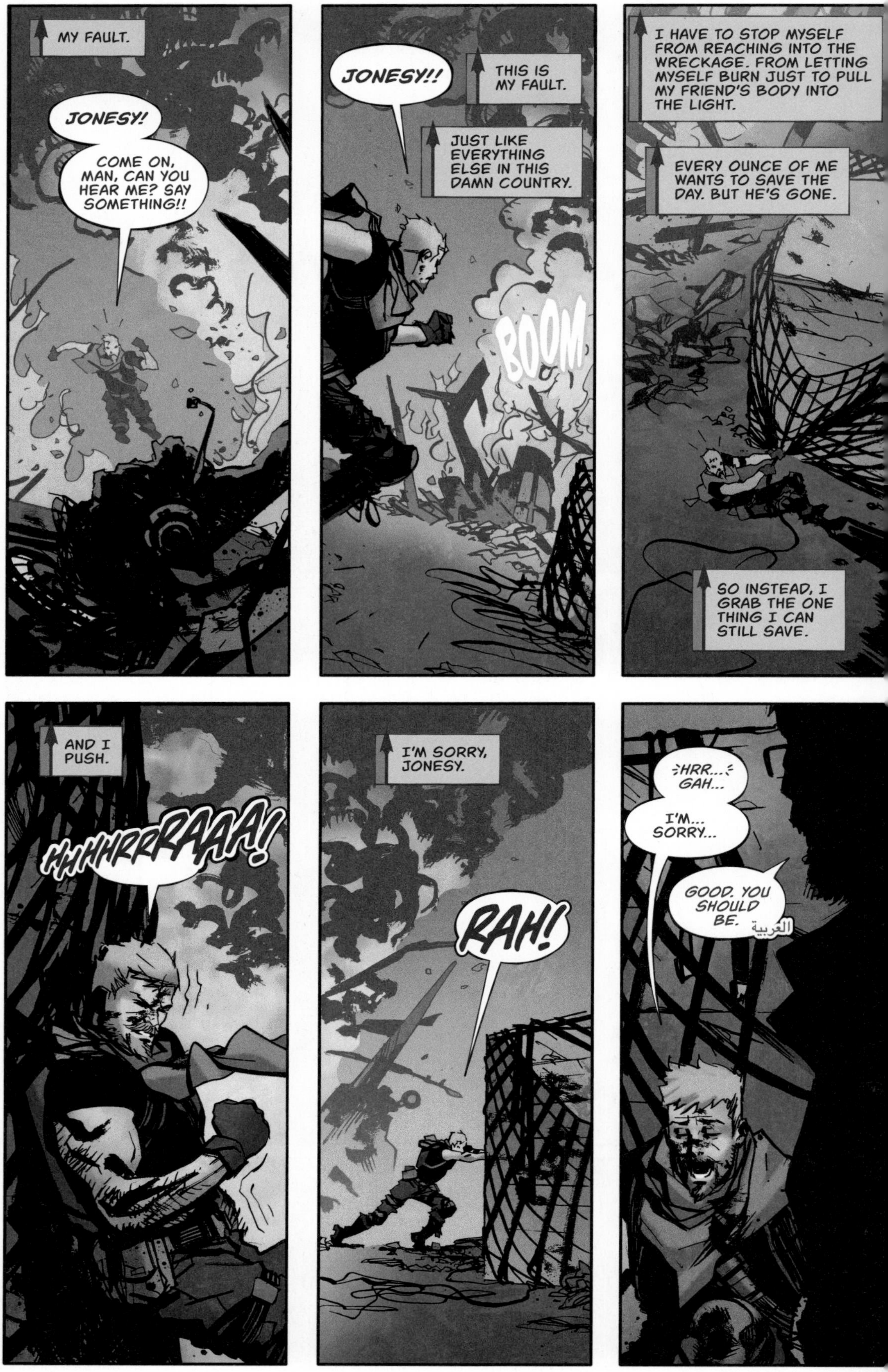
MY FAULT.
JONESY!
COME ON, MAN, CAN YOU HEAR ME? SAY SOMETHING!!
JONESY!!
THIS IS MY FAULT.
JUST LIKE EVERYTHING ELSE IN THIS DAMN COUNTRY.
BOOM
I HAVE TO STOP MYSELF FROM REACHING INTO THE WRECKAGE. FROM LETTING MYSELF BURN JUST TO PULL MY FRIEND'S BODY INTO THE LIGHT.
EVERY OUNCE OF ME WANTS TO SAVE THE DAY. BUT HE'S GONE.
SO INSTEAD, I GRAB THE ONE THING I CAN STILL SAVE.
AND I PUSH.
HHHHRRRAAAA!
I'M SORRY, JONESY.
RAH!
HRR... GAH...
I'M... SORRY...
GOOD. YOU SHOULD BE. العربية

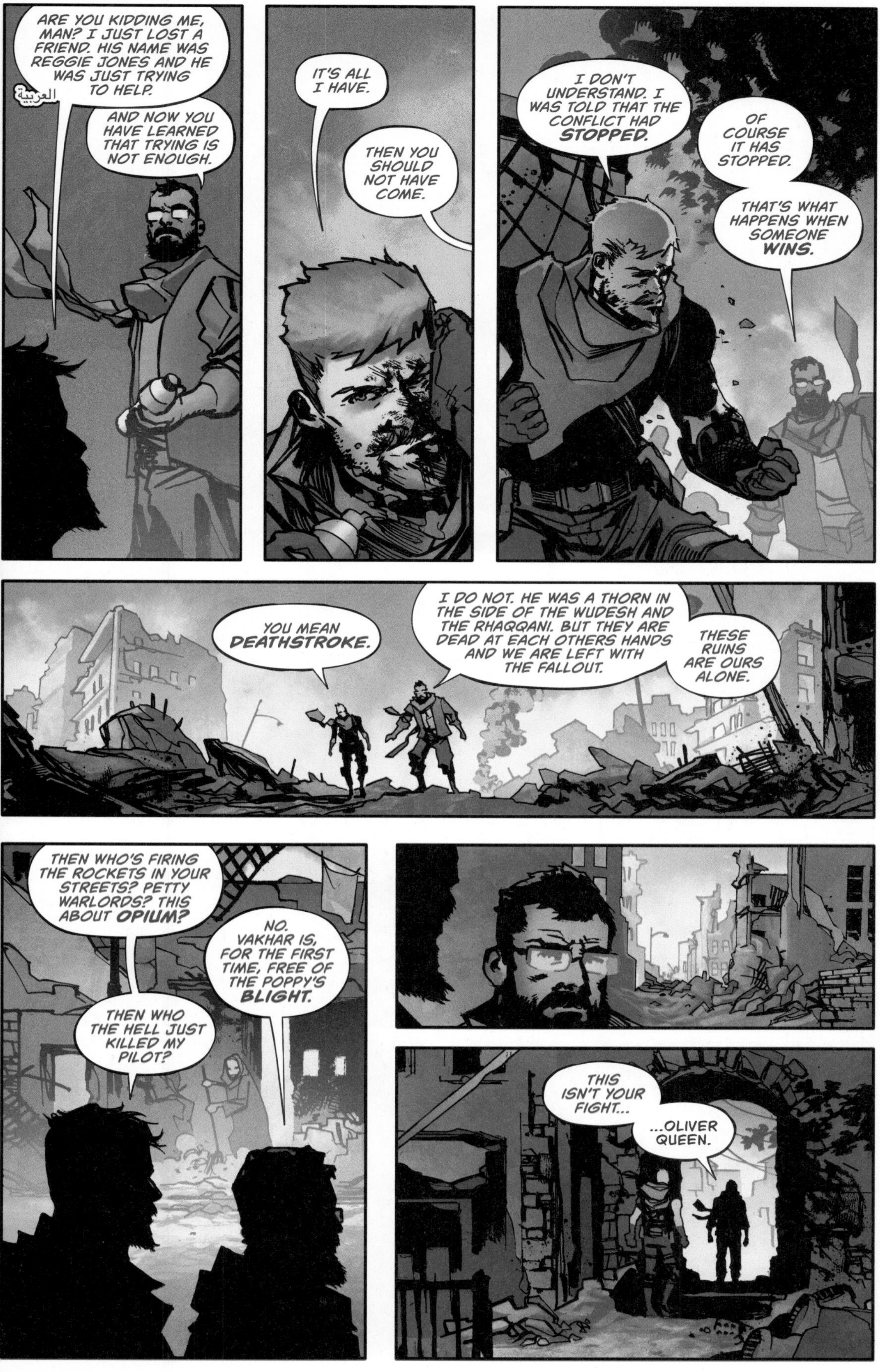
ARE YOU KIDDING ME, MAN? I JUST LOST A FRIEND. HIS NAME WAS REGGIE JONES AND HE WAS JUST TRYING TO HELP.
العربية
AND NOW YOU HAVE LEARNED THAT TRYING IS NOT ENOUGH.
IT'S ALL I HAVE.
THEN YOU SHOULD NOT HAVE COME.
I DON'T UNDERSTAND. I WAS TOLD THAT THE CONFLICT HAD STOPPED.
OF COURSE IT HAS STOPPED.
THAT'S WHAT HAPPENS WHEN SOMEONE WINS.
YOU MEAN DEATHSTROKE.
I DO NOT. HE WAS A THORN IN THE SIDE OF THE WUDESH AND THE RHAQQANI. BUT THEY ARE DEAD AT EACH OTHERS HANDS AND WE ARE LEFT WITH THE FALLOUT.
THESE RUINS ARE OURS ALONE.
THEN WHO'S FIRING THE ROCKETS IN YOUR STREETS? PETTY WARLORDS? THIS ABOUT OPIUM?
NO. VAKHAR IS, FOR THE FIRST TIME, FREE OF THE POPPY'S BLIGHT.
THEN WHO THE HELL JUST KILLED MY PILOT?
THIS ISN'T YOUR FIGHT...
...OLIVER QUEEN.

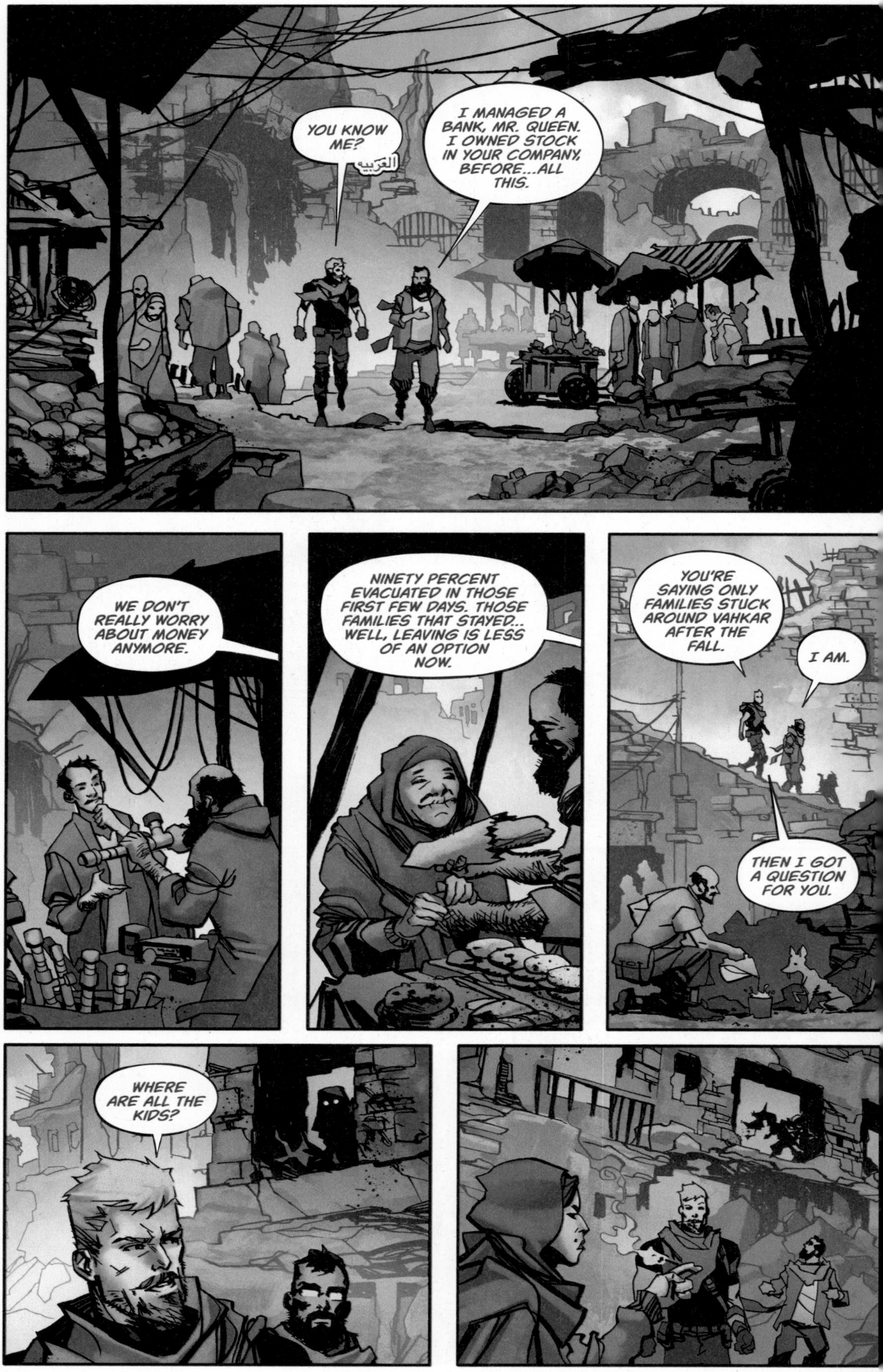
YOU KNOW ME?
العربية
I MANAGED A BANK, MR. QUEEN. I OWNED STOCK IN YOUR COMPANY, BEFORE...ALL THIS.
WE DON'T REALLY WORRY ABOUT MONEY ANYMORE.
NINETY PERCENT EVACUATED IN THOSE FIRST FEW DAYS. THOSE FAMILIES THAT STAYED... WELL, LEAVING IS LESS OF AN OPTION NOW.
YOU'RE SAYING ONLY FAMILIES STUCK AROUND VAHKAR AFTER THE FALL.
I AM.
THEN I GOT A QUESTION FOR YOU.
WHERE ARE ALL THE KIDS?

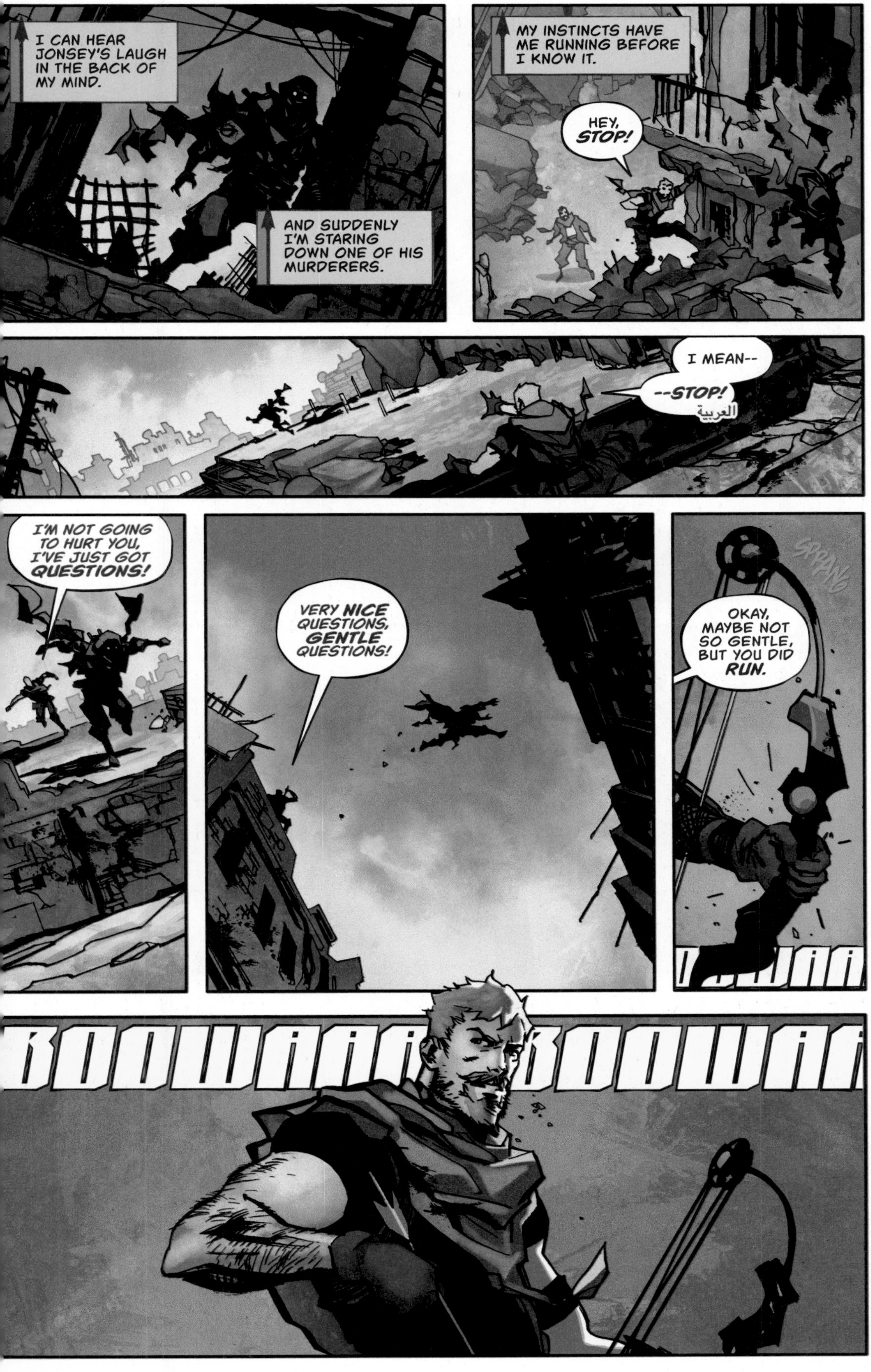

I CAN HEAR JONSEY'S LAUGH IN THE BACK OF MY MIND.
AND SUDDENLY I'M STARING DOWN ONE OF HIS MURDERERS.
MY INSTINCTS HAVE ME RUNNING BEFORE I KNOW IT.
HEY, STOP!
I MEAN--
--STOP!
العربية
I'M NOT GOING TO HURT YOU, I'VE JUST GOT QUESTIONS!
VERY NICE QUESTIONS, GENTLE QUESTIONS!
SPRANG
OKAY, MAYBE NOT SO GENTLE, BUT YOU DID RUN.

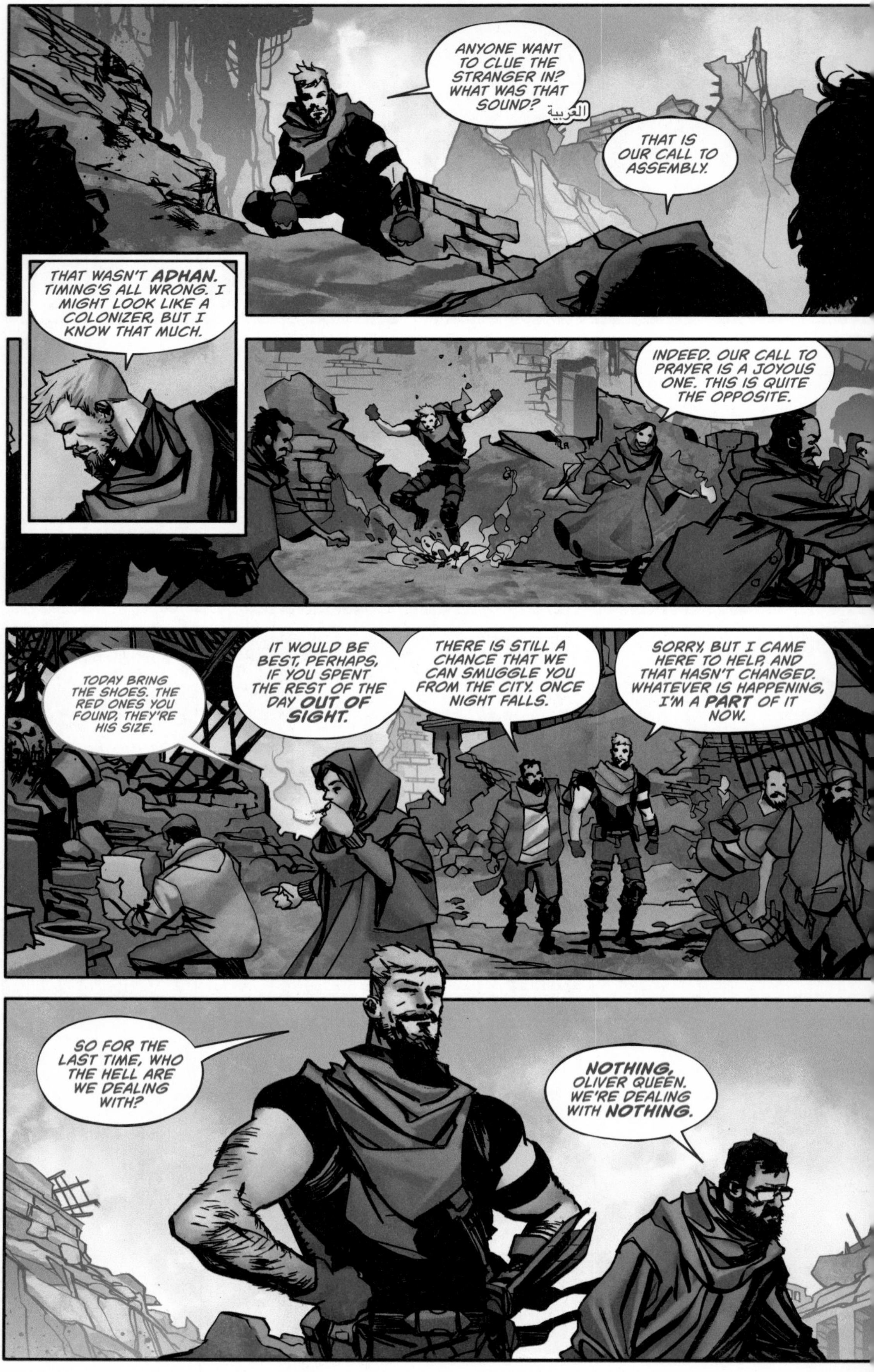
ANYONE WANT TO CLUE THE STRANGER IN? WHAT WAS THAT SOUND?
العربية
THAT IS OUR CALL TO ASSEMBLY.
THAT WASN'T ADHAN. TIMING'S ALL WRONG. I MIGHT LOOK LIKE A COLONIZER, BUT I KNOW THAT MUCH.
INDEED. OUR CALL TO PRAYER IS A JOYOUS ONE. THIS IS QUITE THE OPPOSITE.
TODAY BRING THE SHOES. THE RED ONES YOU FOUND, THEY'RE HIS SIZE.
IT WOULD BE BEST, PERHAPS, IF YOU SPENT THE REST OF THE DAY OUT OF SIGHT.
THERE IS STILL A CHANCE THAT WE CAN SMUGGLE YOU FROM THE CITY. ONCE NIGHT FALLS.
SORRY, BUT I CAME HERE TO HELP, AND THAT HASN'T CHANGED. WHATEVER IS HAPPENING, I'M A PART OF IT NOW.
SO FOR THE LAST TIME, WHO THE HELL ARE WE DEALING WITH?
NOTHING, OLIVER QUEEN. WE'RE DEALING WITH NOTHING.

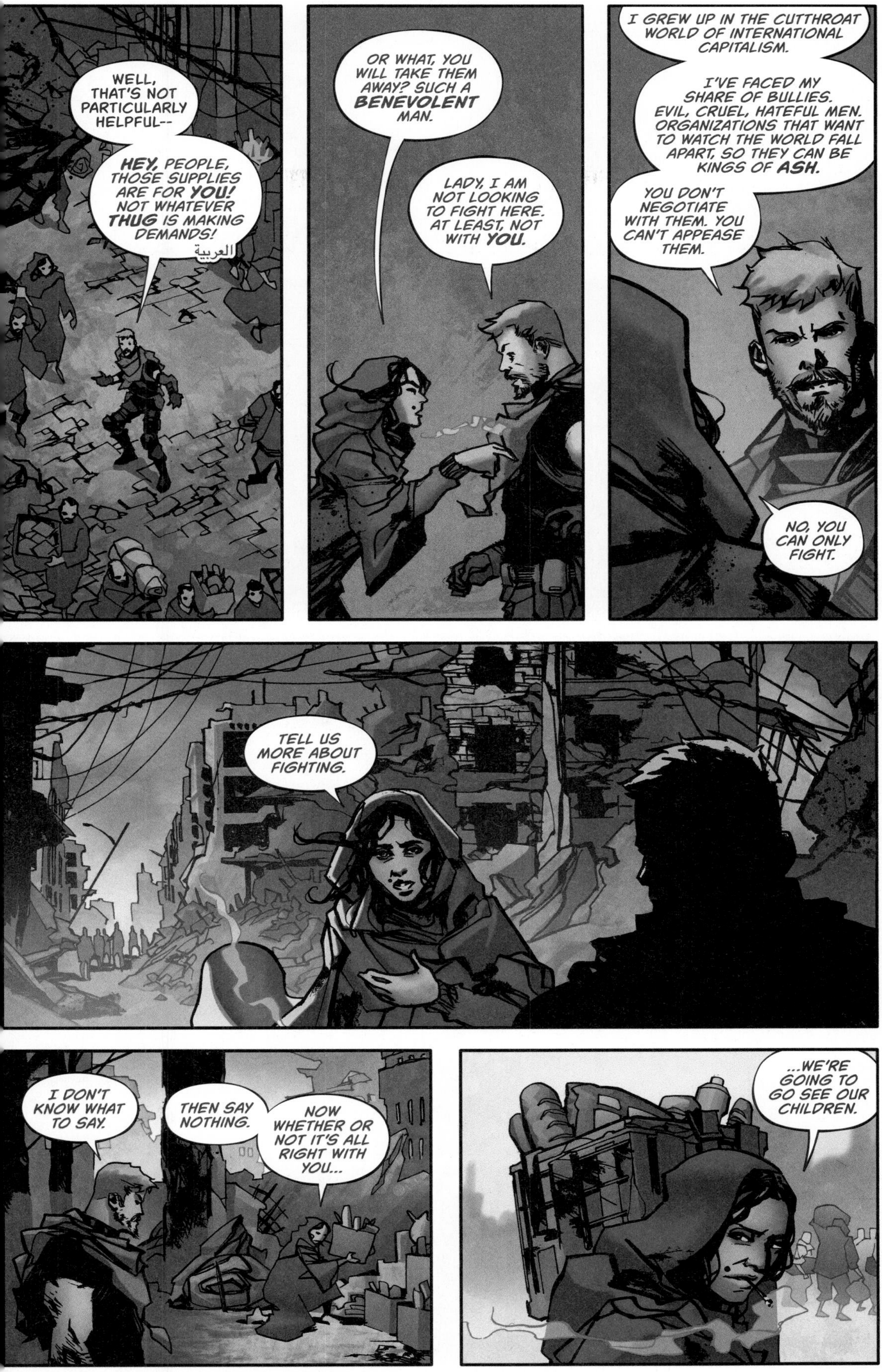
WELL, THAT'S NOT PARTICULARLY HELPFUL--
HEY, PEOPLE, THOSE SUPPLIES ARE FOR YOU! NOT WHATEVER THUG IS MAKING DEMANDS!
العربية
OR WHAT, YOU WILL TAKE THEM AWAY? SUCH A BENEVOLENT MAN.
LADY, I AM NOT LOOKING TO FIGHT HERE. AT LEAST, NOT WITH YOU.
I GREW UP IN THE CUTTHROAT WORLD OF INTERNATIONAL CAPITALISM.
I'VE FACED MY SHARE OF BULLIES. EVIL, CRUEL, HATEFUL MEN. ORGANIZATIONS THAT WANT TO WATCH THE WORLD FALL APART, SO THEY CAN BE KINGS OF ASH.
YOU DON'T NEGOTIATE WITH THEM. YOU CAN'T APPEASE THEM.
NO, YOU CAN ONLY FIGHT.
TELL US MORE ABOUT FIGHTING.
I DON'T KNOW WHAT TO SAY.
THEN SAY NOTHING.
NOW WHETHER OR NOT IT'S ALL RIGHT WITH YOU...
...WE'RE GOING TO GO SEE OUR CHILDREN.

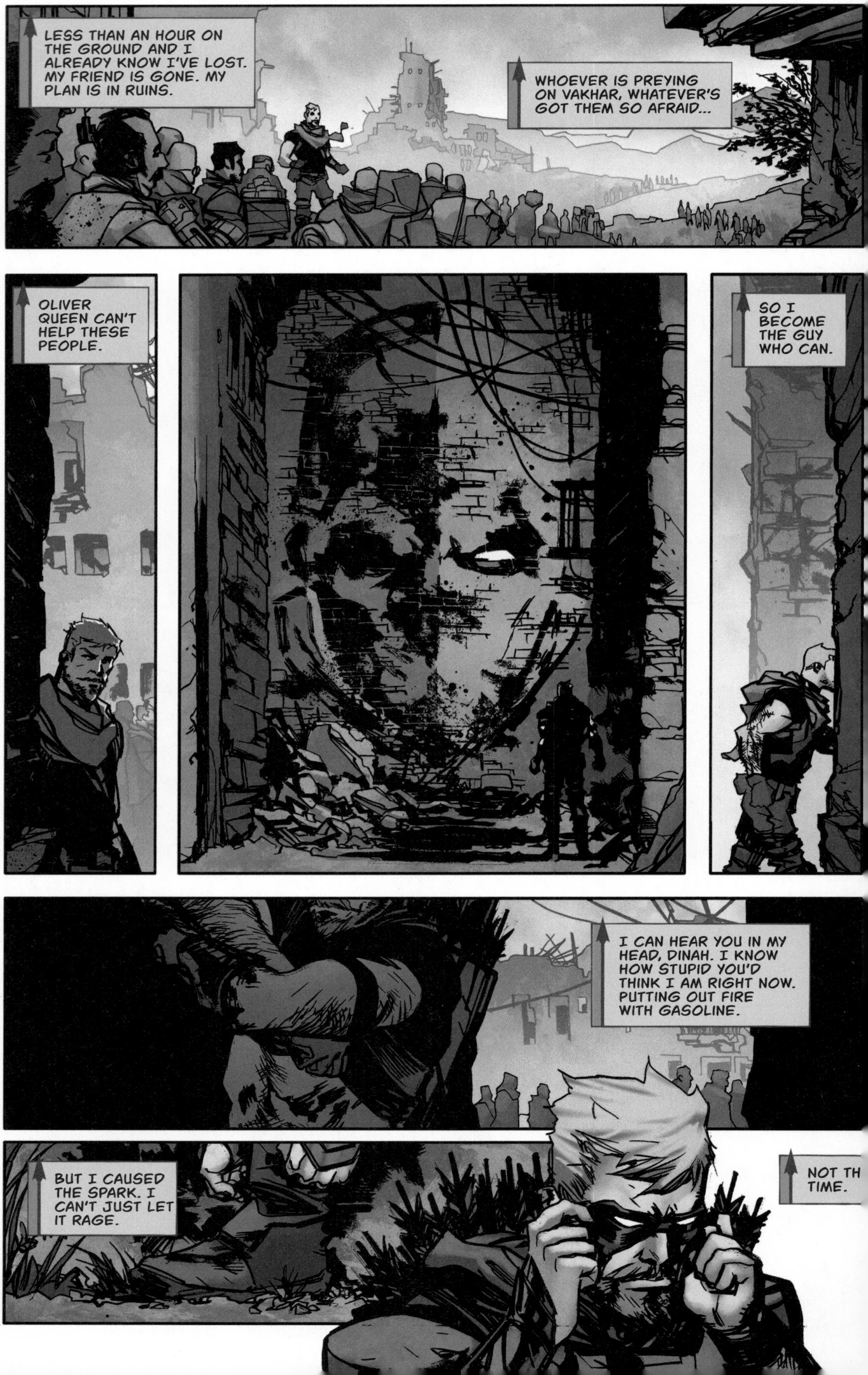
LESS THAN AN HOUR ON THE GROUND AND I ALREADY KNOW I'VE LOST. MY FRIEND IS GONE. MY PLAN IS IN RUINS.
WHOEVER IS PREYING ON VAKHAR, WHATEVER'S GOT THEM SO AFRAID...
OLIVER QUEEN CAN'T HELP THESE PEOPLE.
SO I BECOME THE GUY WHO CAN.
I CAN HEAR YOU IN MY HEAD, DINAH. I KNOW HOW STUPID YOU'D THINK I AM RIGHT NOW. PUTTING OUT FIRE WITH GASOLINE.
BUT I CAUSED THE SPARK. I CAN'T JUST LET IT RAGE.
NOT TH
TIME.

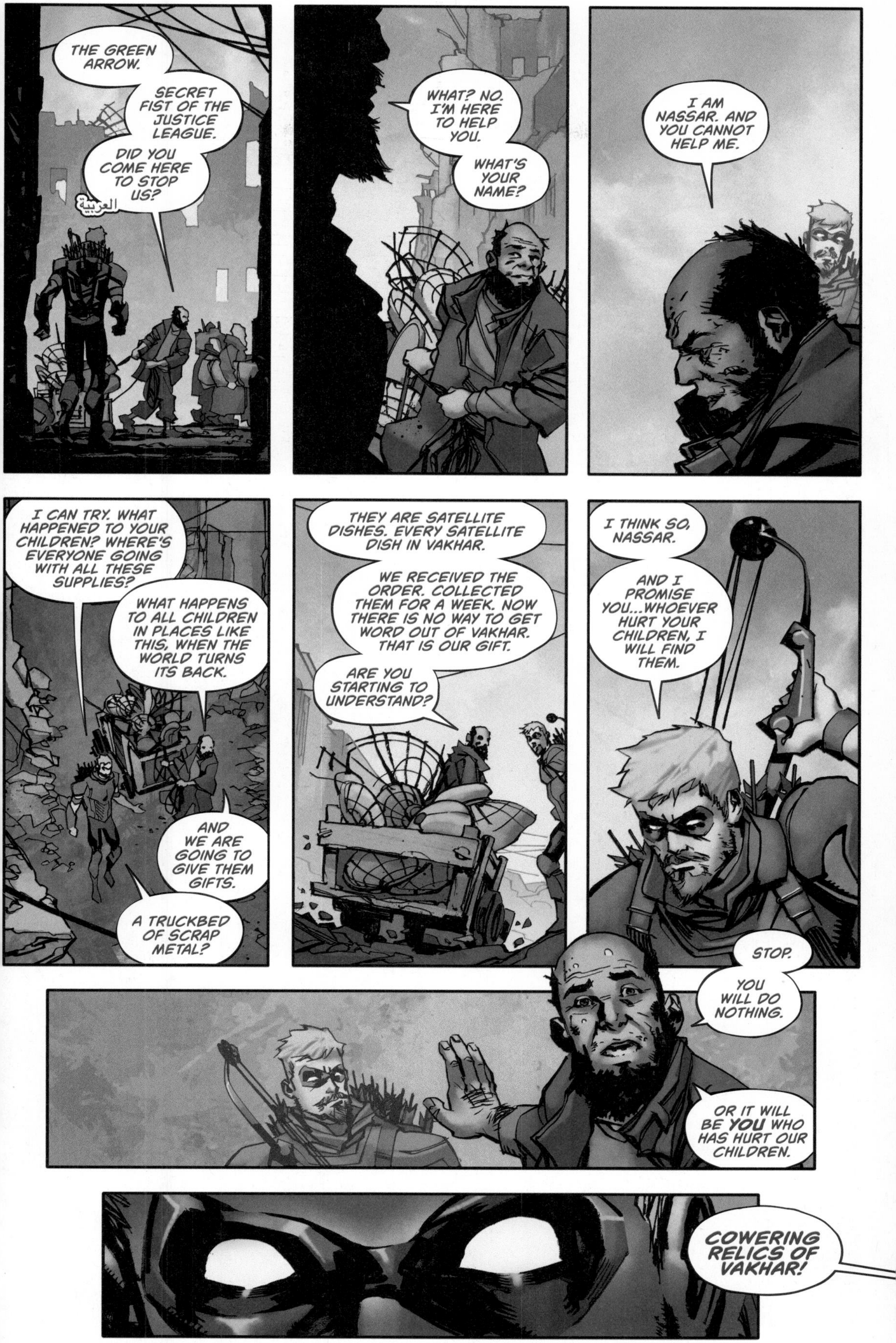
THE GREEN ARROW.
SECRET FIST OF THE JUSTICE LEAGUE.
DID YOU COME HERE TO STOP US?
العربية
WHAT? NO. I'M HERE TO HELP YOU.
WHAT'S YOUR NAME?
I AM NASSAR. AND YOU CANNOT HELP ME.
I CAN TRY. WHAT HAPPENED TO YOUR CHILDREN? WHERE'S EVERYONE GOING WITH ALL THESE SUPPLIES?
WHAT HAPPENS TO ALL CHILDREN IN PLACES LIKE THIS, WHEN THE WORLD TURNS ITS BACK.
AND WE ARE GOING TO GIVE THEM GIFTS.
A TRUCKBED OF SCRAP METAL?
THEY ARE SATELLITE DISHES. EVERY SATELLITE DISH IN VAKHAR.
WE RECEIVED THE ORDER. COLLECTED THEM FOR A WEEK. NOW THERE IS NO WAY TO GET WORD OUT OF VAKHAR. THAT IS OUR GIFT.
ARE YOU STARTING TO UNDERSTAND?
I THINK SO, NASSAR.
AND I PROMISE YOU...WHOEVER HURT YOUR CHILDREN, I WILL FIND THEM.
STOP.
YOU WILL DO NOTHING.
OR IT WILL BE YOU WHO HAS HURT OUR CHILDREN.
COWERING RELICS OF VAKHAR!

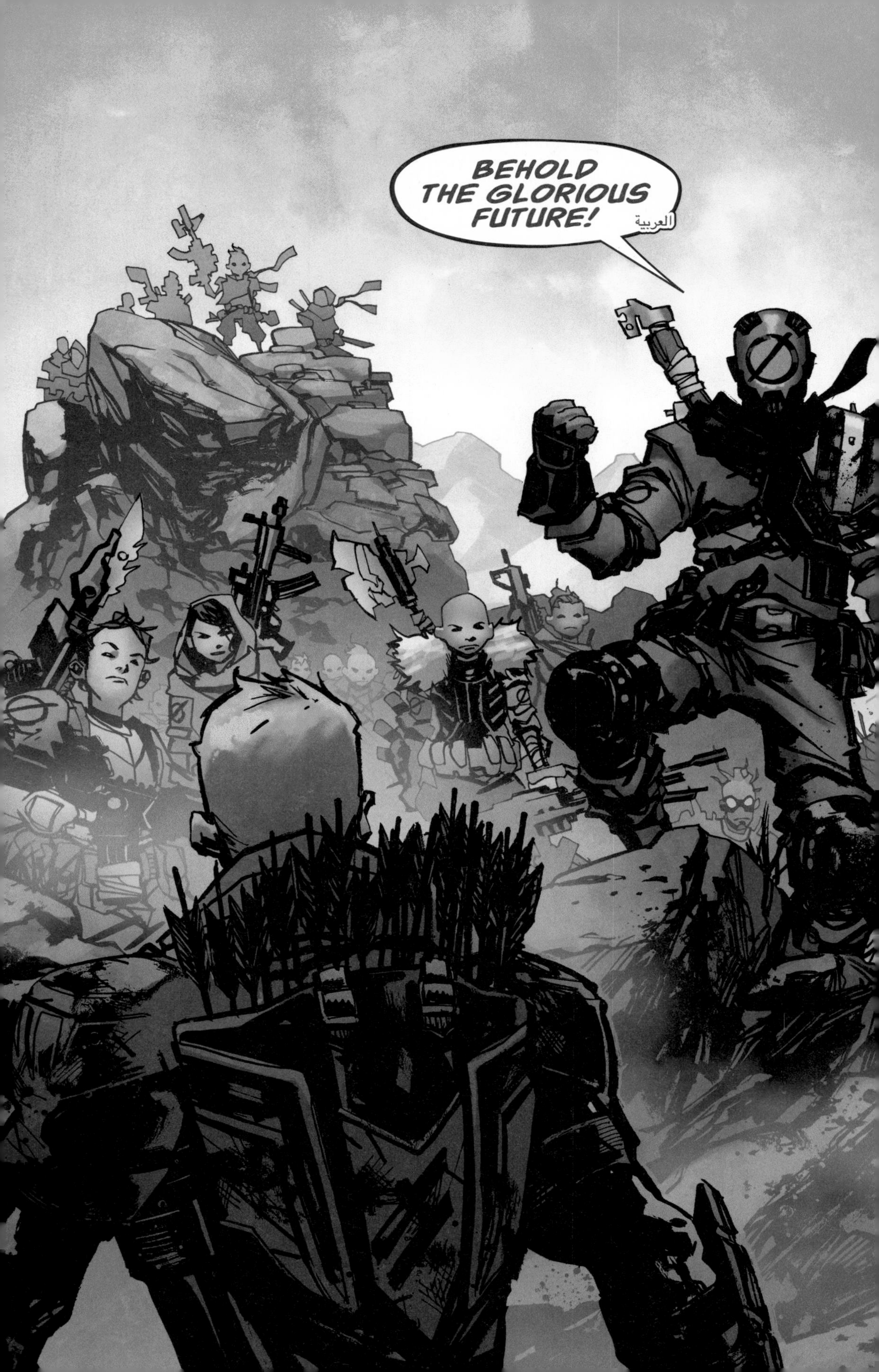
BEHOLD THE GLORIOUS FUTURE!
العربية

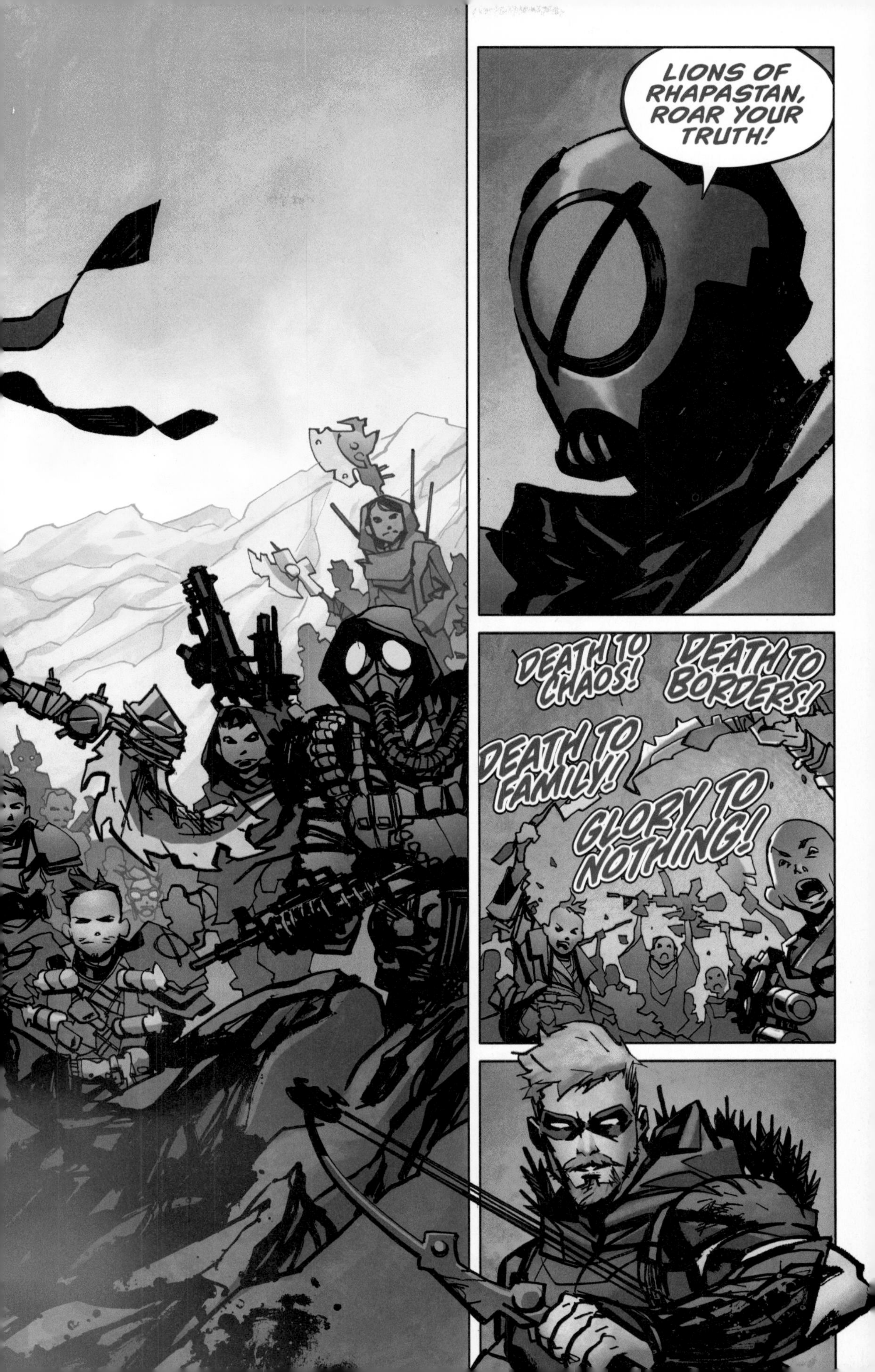
LIONS OF RHAPASTAN, ROAR YOUR TRUTH!
DEATH TO CHAOS!
DEATH TO BORDERS!
DEATH TO FAMILY!
GLORY TO NOTHING!

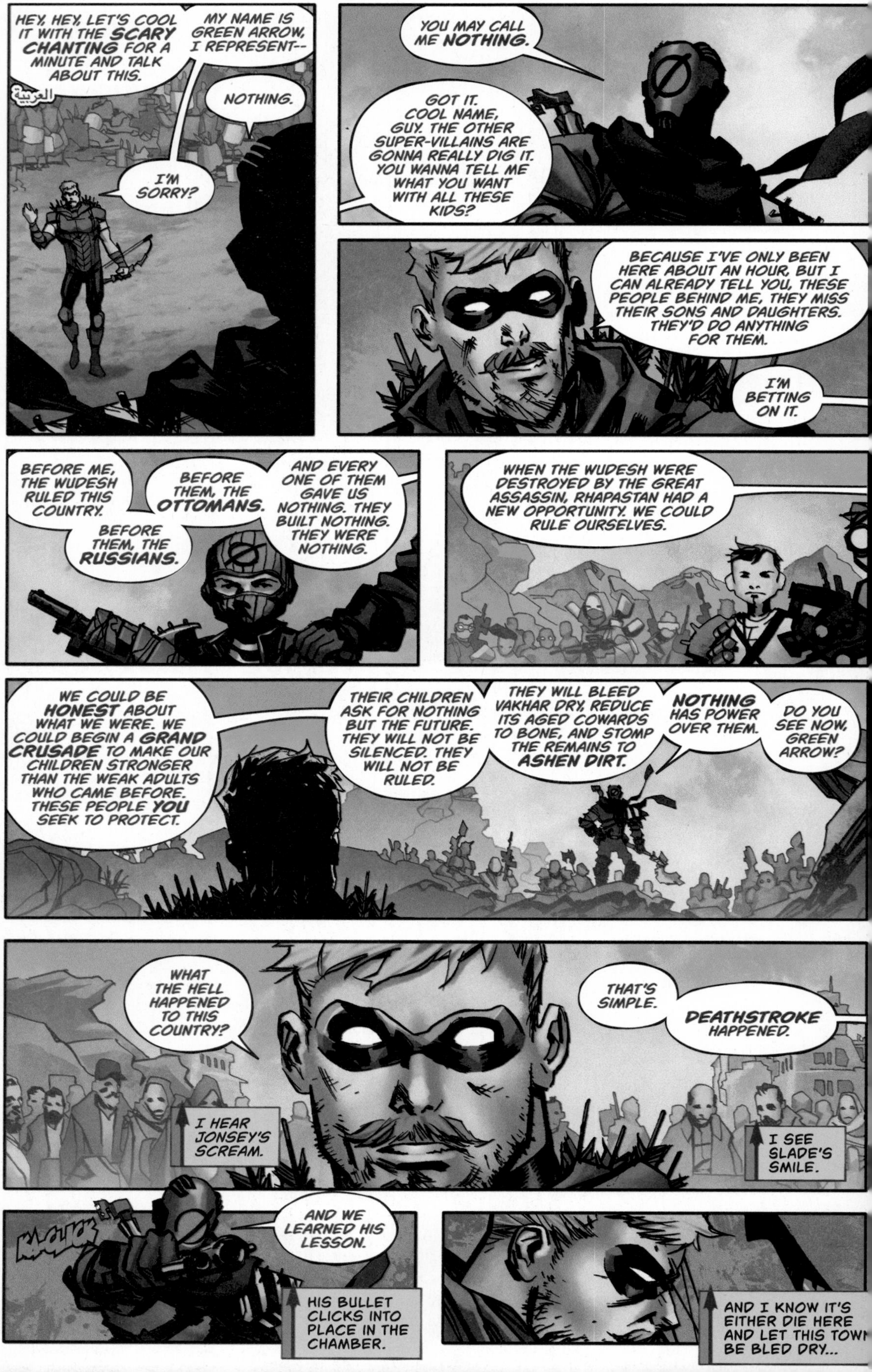

HEY, HEY, LET'S COOL IT WITH THE SCARY CHANTING FOR A MINUTE AND TALK ABOUT THIS.
العربية
MY NAME IS GREEN ARROW, I REPRESENT--
NOTHING.
I'M SORRY?
YOU MAY CALL ME NOTHING.
GOT IT. COOL NAME, GUY. THE OTHER SUPER-VILLAINS ARE GONNA REALLY DIG IT. YOU WANNA TELL ME WHAT YOU WANT WITH ALL THESE KIDS?
BECAUSE I'VE ONLY BEEN HERE ABOUT AN HOUR, BUT I CAN ALREADY TELL YOU, THESE PEOPLE BEHIND ME, THEY MISS THEIR SONS AND DAUGHTERS. THEY'D DO ANYTHING FOR THEM.
I'M BETTING ON IT.
BEFORE ME, THE WUDESH RULED THIS COUNTRY.
BEFORE THEM, THE RUSSIANS.
BEFORE THEM, THE OTTOMANS.
AND EVERY ONE OF THEM GAVE US NOTHING. THEY BUILT NOTHING. THEY WERE NOTHING.
WHEN THE WUDESH WERE DESTROYED BY THE GREAT ASSASSIN, RHAPASTAN HAD A NEW OPPORTUNITY. WE COULD RULE OURSELVES.
WE COULD BE HONEST ABOUT WHAT WE WERE. WE COULD BEGIN A GRAND CRUSADE TO MAKE OUR CHILDREN STRONGER THAN THE WEAK ADULTS WHO CAME BEFORE. THESE PEOPLE YOU SEEK TO PROTECT.
THEIR CHILDREN ASK FOR NOTHING BUT THE FUTURE. THEY WILL NOT BE SILENCED. THEY WILL NOT BE RULED.
THEY WILL BLEED VAKHAR DRY, REDUCE ITS AGED COWARDS TO BONE, AND STOMP THE REMAINS TO ASHEN DIRT.
NOTHING HAS POWER OVER THEM.
DO YOU SEE NOW, GREEN ARROW?
WHAT THE HELL HAPPENED TO THIS COUNTRY?
THAT'S SIMPLE.
DEATHSTROKE HAPPENED.
I HEAR JONSEY'S SCREAM.
I SEE SLADE'S SMILE.
KA-CLICK
AND WE LEARNED HIS LESSON.
HIS BULLET CLICKS INTO PLACE IN THE CHAMBER.
AND I KNOW IT'S EITHER DIE HERE AND LET THIS TOWN BE BLED DRY...

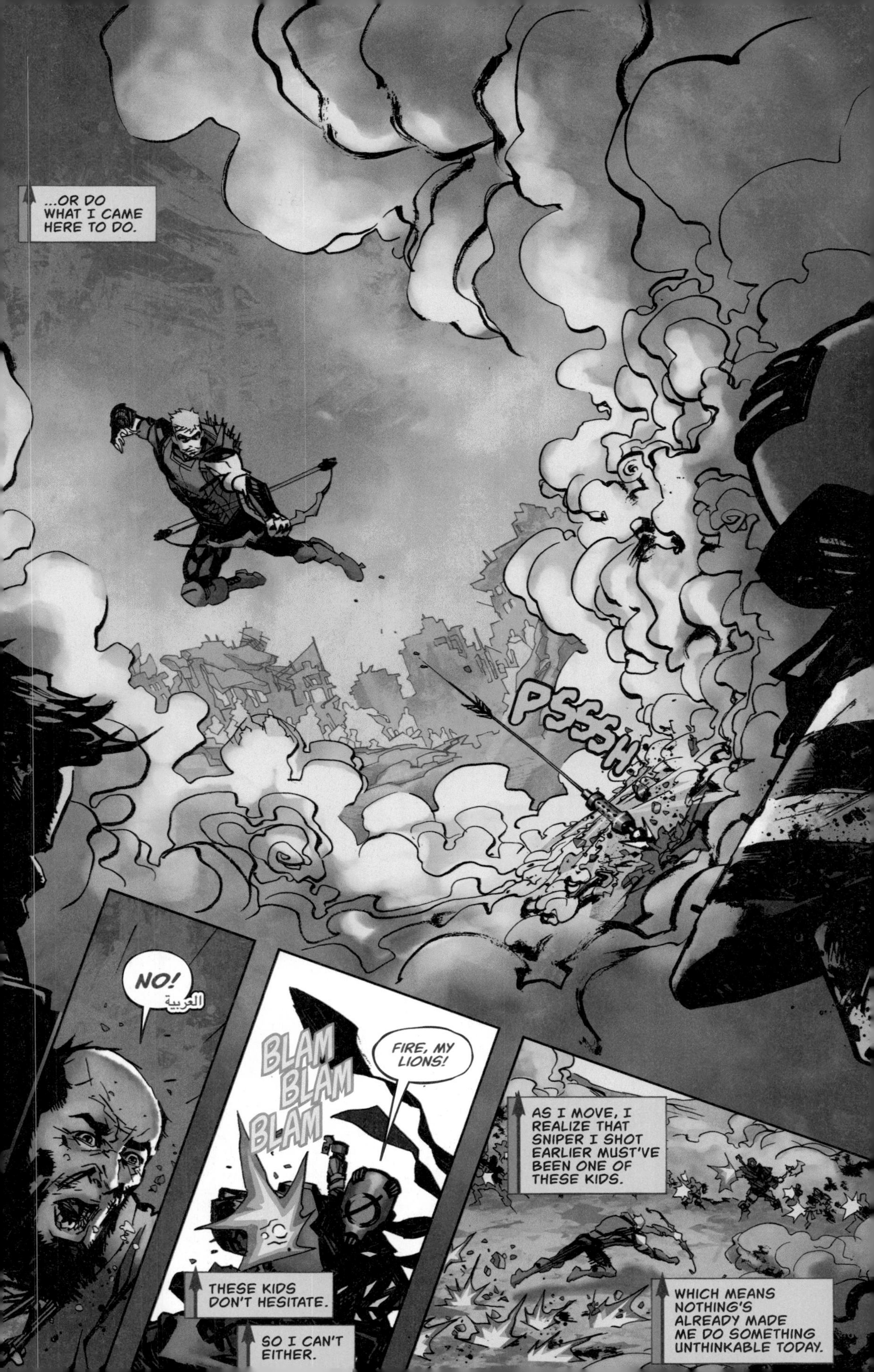
...OR DO WHAT I CAME HERE TO DO.
PSSSH
NO!
العربية
BLAM BLAM BLAM
FIRE, MY LIONS!
THESE KIDS DON'T HESITATE.
SO I CAN'T EITHER.
AS I MOVE, I REALIZE THAT SNIPER I SHOT EARLIER MUST'VE BEEN ONE OF THESE KIDS.
WHICH MEANS NOTHING'S ALREADY MADE ME DO SOMETHING UNTHINKABLE TODAY.

IT WON'T HAPPEN AGAIN.

RIOT CONTROL ARROW.

NON-LETHAL, WIDE-RANGING. MAXIMUM IMPACT WITH MINIMAL PAIN.

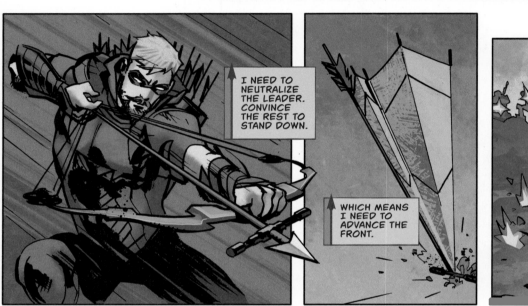

I NEED TO NEUTRALIZE THE LEADER. CONVINCE THE REST TO STAND DOWN.

WHICH MEANS I NEED TO ADVANCE THE FRONT.

SO I FIRE THE BIGGEST MAGNET I HAVE.

AND BRING THE NUMBERS BACK TO EVEN.

HEY, NOTHING! TELL ME AGAIN ABOUT YOUR GLORIOUS FUTURE.

العربية

IT STILL HURTS TO SEE IT USED AGAINST KIDS.

GOOD THING I BROUGHT A TRENCH.

BUT NOTHING'S FORCE IS STILL OVERWHELMING. MY EARS COUNT AT LEAST TWENTY ASSAULT RIFLES.

ALL OF WHICH ARE MADE OF METAL.

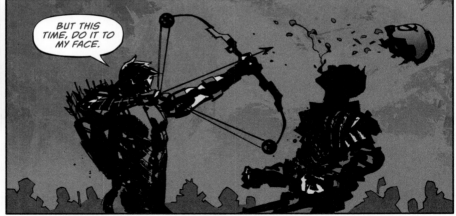

BUT THIS TIME, DO IT TO MY FACE.

DO IT. FIRE!

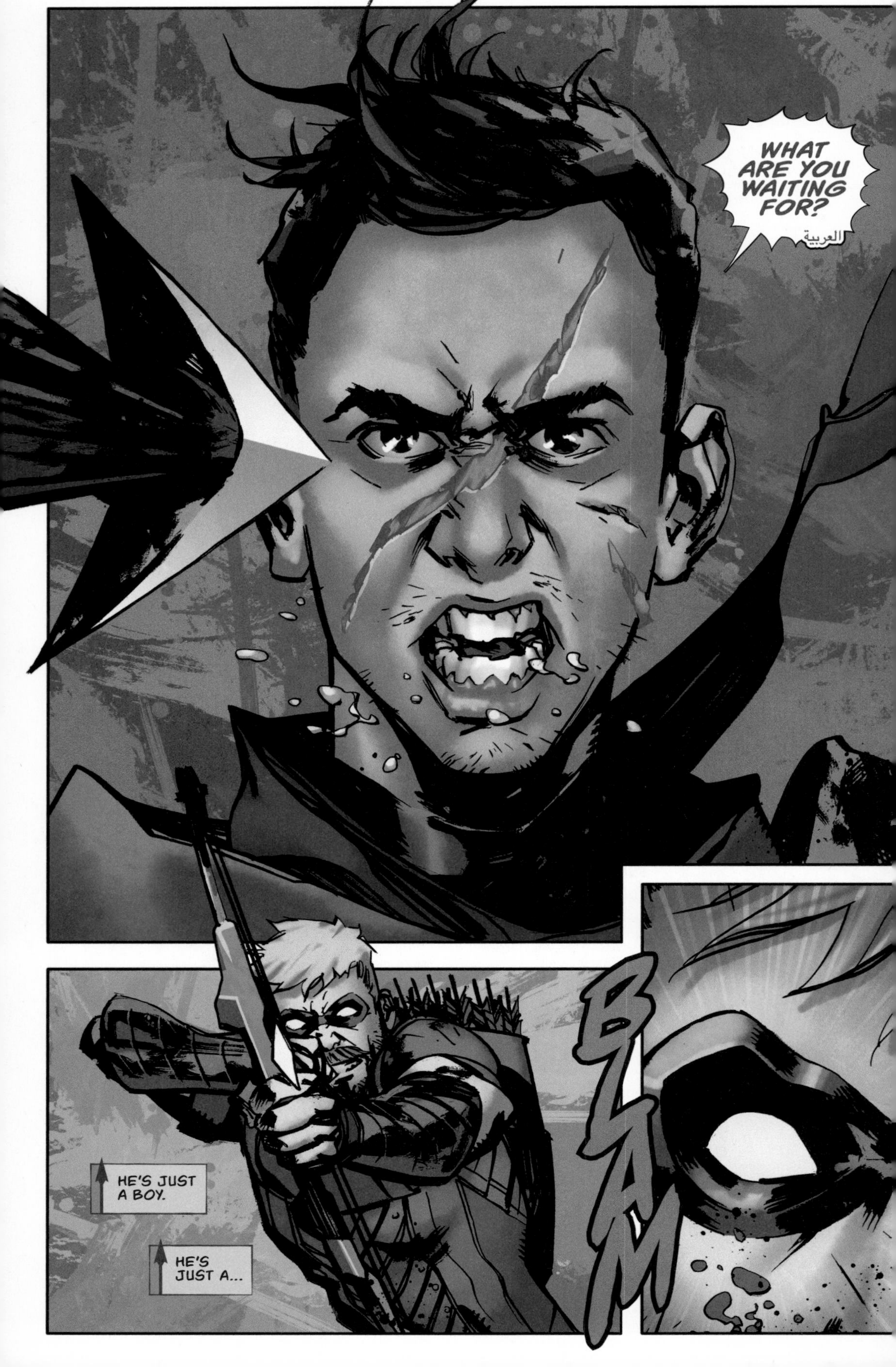
WHAT ARE YOU WAITING FOR?
العربية
HE'S JUST A BOY.
HE'S JUST A...
BLAM

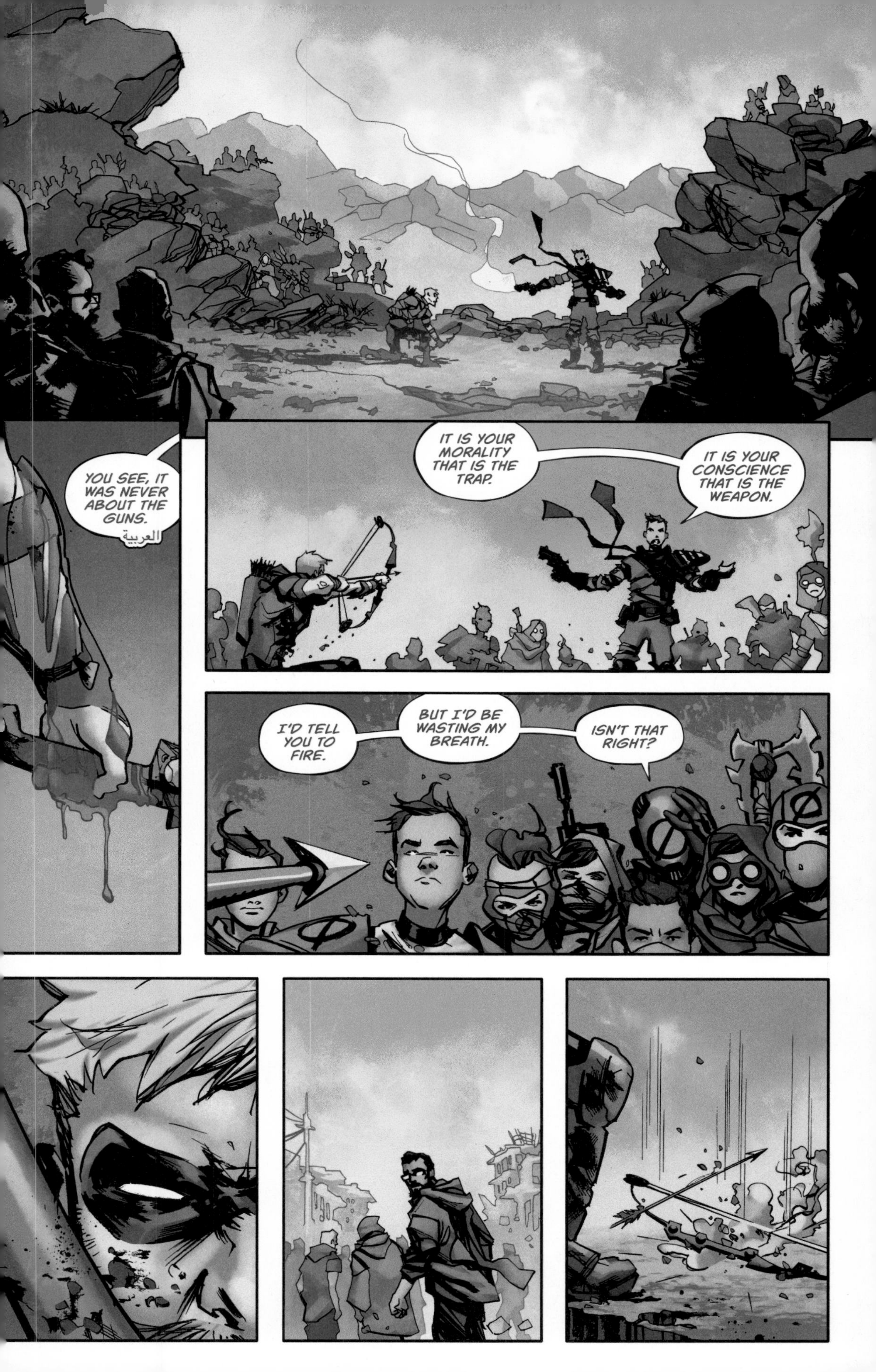
YOU SEE, IT WAS NEVER ABOUT THE GUNS.
العربية
IT IS YOUR MORALITY THAT IS THE TRAP.
IT IS YOUR CONSCIENCE THAT IS THE WEAPON.
I'D TELL YOU TO FIRE.
BUT I'D BE WASTING MY BREATH.
ISN'T THAT RIGHT?

The Children of Vakhar pa
on
JACKSON LANZING & COLLIN KELLY Writers MARCIO TAKARA Artist MARCELO MAIOLO Colors DERON BENNETT Letters
TYLER KIRKHAM & TOMEU MOREY Cover
DAVE WIELGOSZ Asst. Editor ALEX ANTONE Editor JAMIE S. RICH Group Editor
WELCOME TO RHAPASTAN, GREEN ARROW.
THIS IS NO PLACE FOR HEROES.
العربية

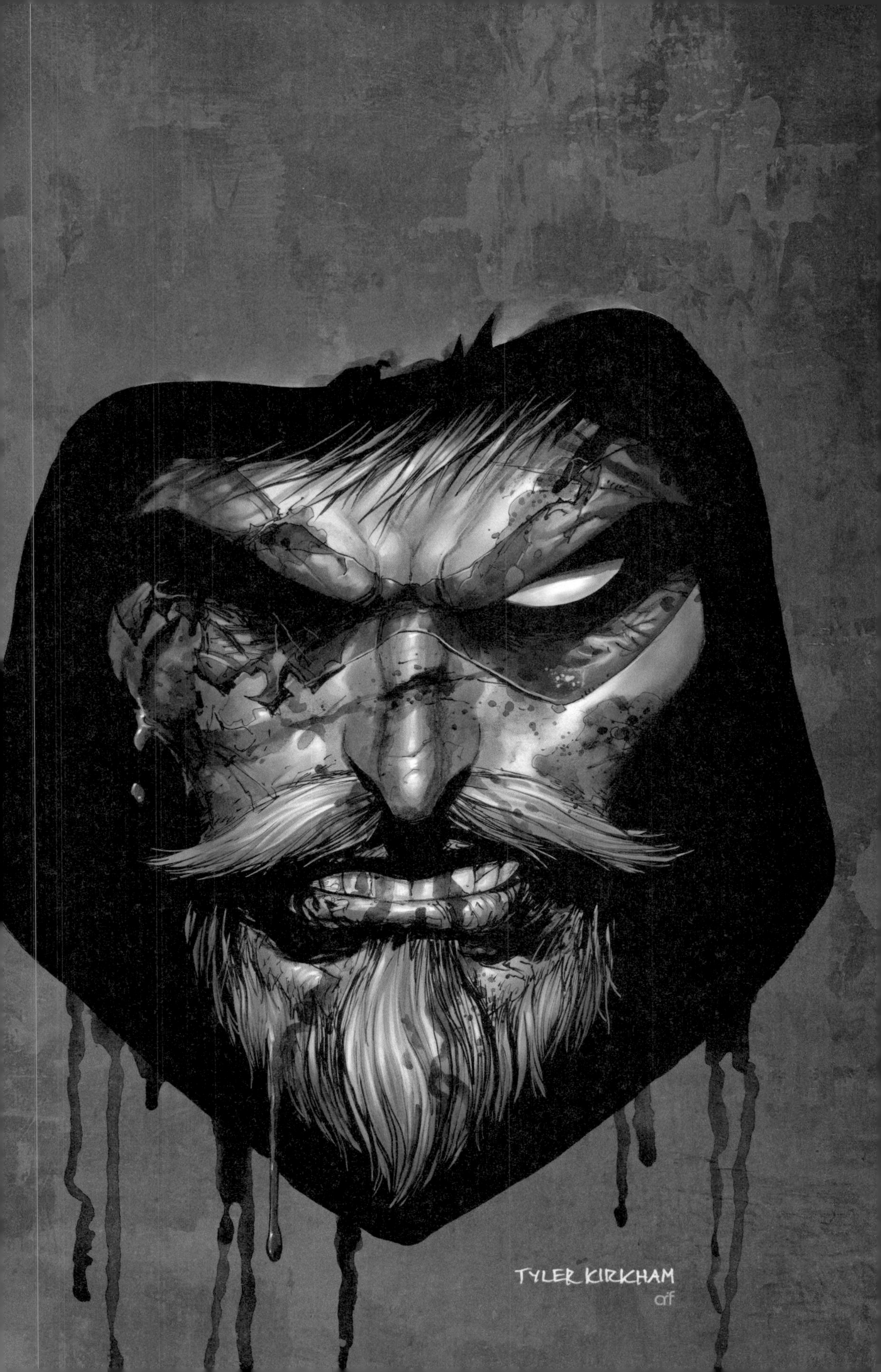
TYLER KIRKHAM
art

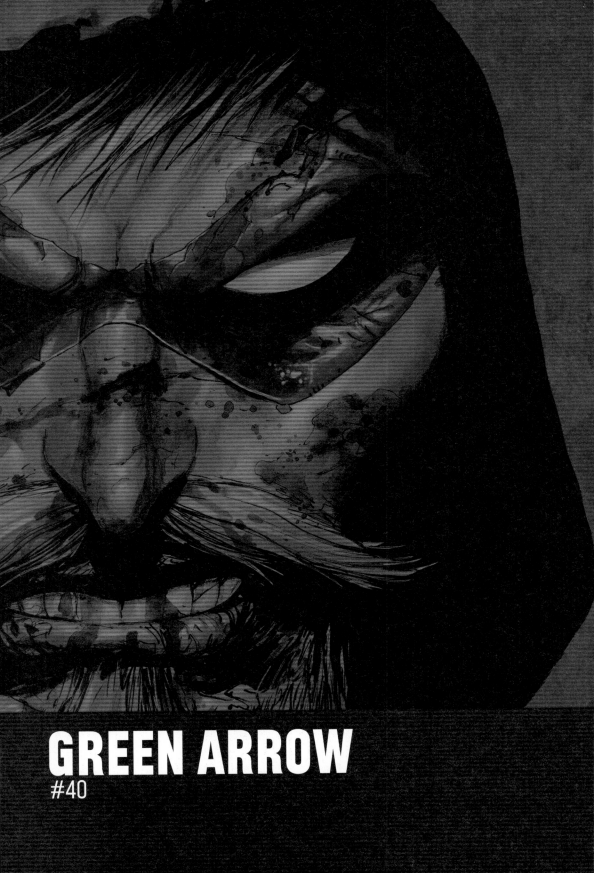

# GREEN ARROW
#40

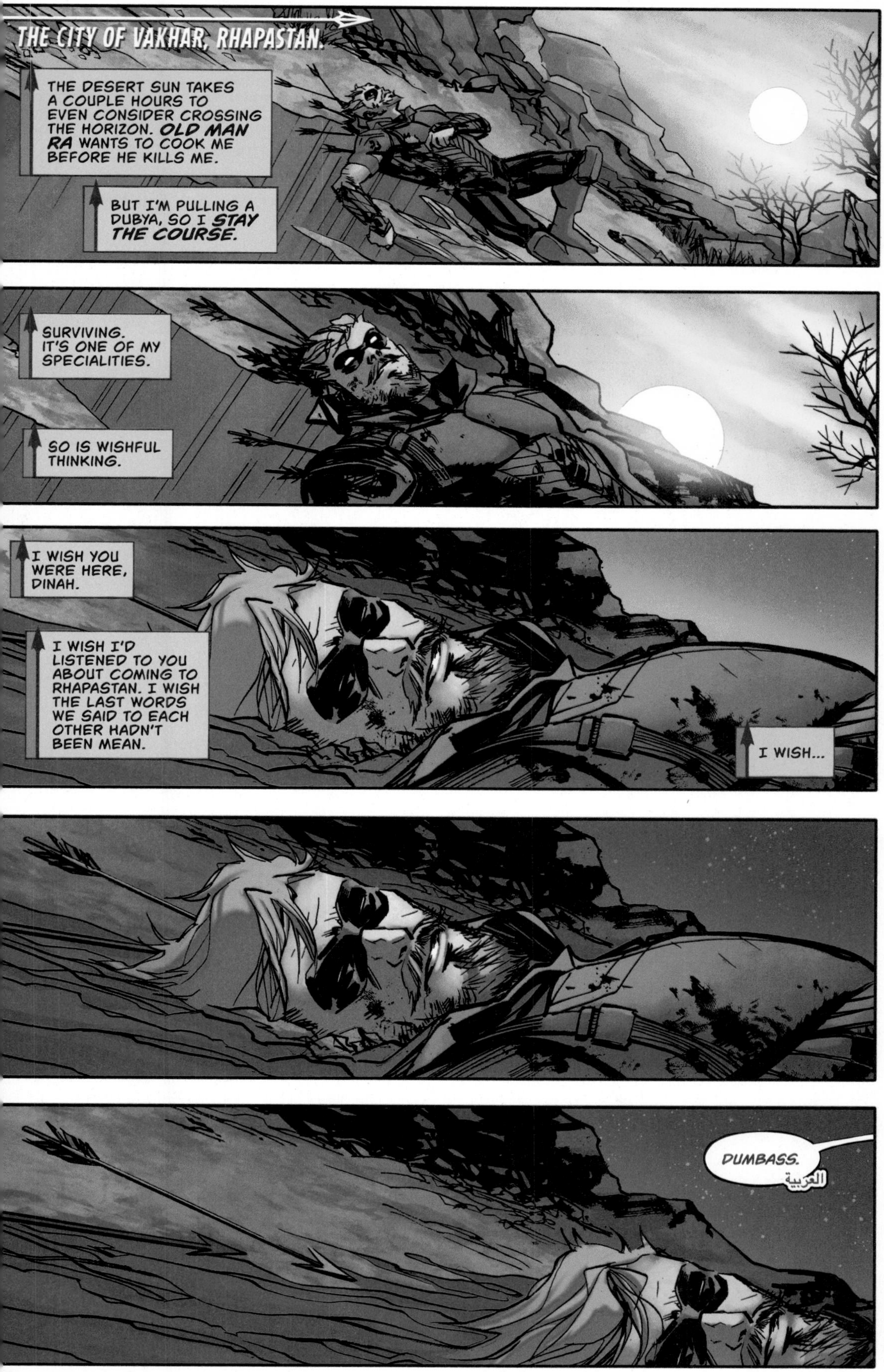
THE CITY OF VAKHAR, RHAPASTAN.
THE DESERT SUN TAKES A COUPLE HOURS TO EVEN CONSIDER CROSSING THE HORIZON. OLD MAN RA WANTS TO COOK ME BEFORE HE KILLS ME.
BUT I'M PULLING A DUBYA, SO I STAY THE COURSE.
SURVIVING. IT'S ONE OF MY SPECIALITIES.
SO IS WISHFUL THINKING.
I WISH YOU WERE HERE, DINAH.
I WISH I'D LISTENED TO YOU ABOUT COMING TO RHAPASTAN. I WISH THE LAST WORDS WE SAID TO EACH OTHER HADN'T BEEN MEAN.
I WISH...
DUMBASS.
العربية

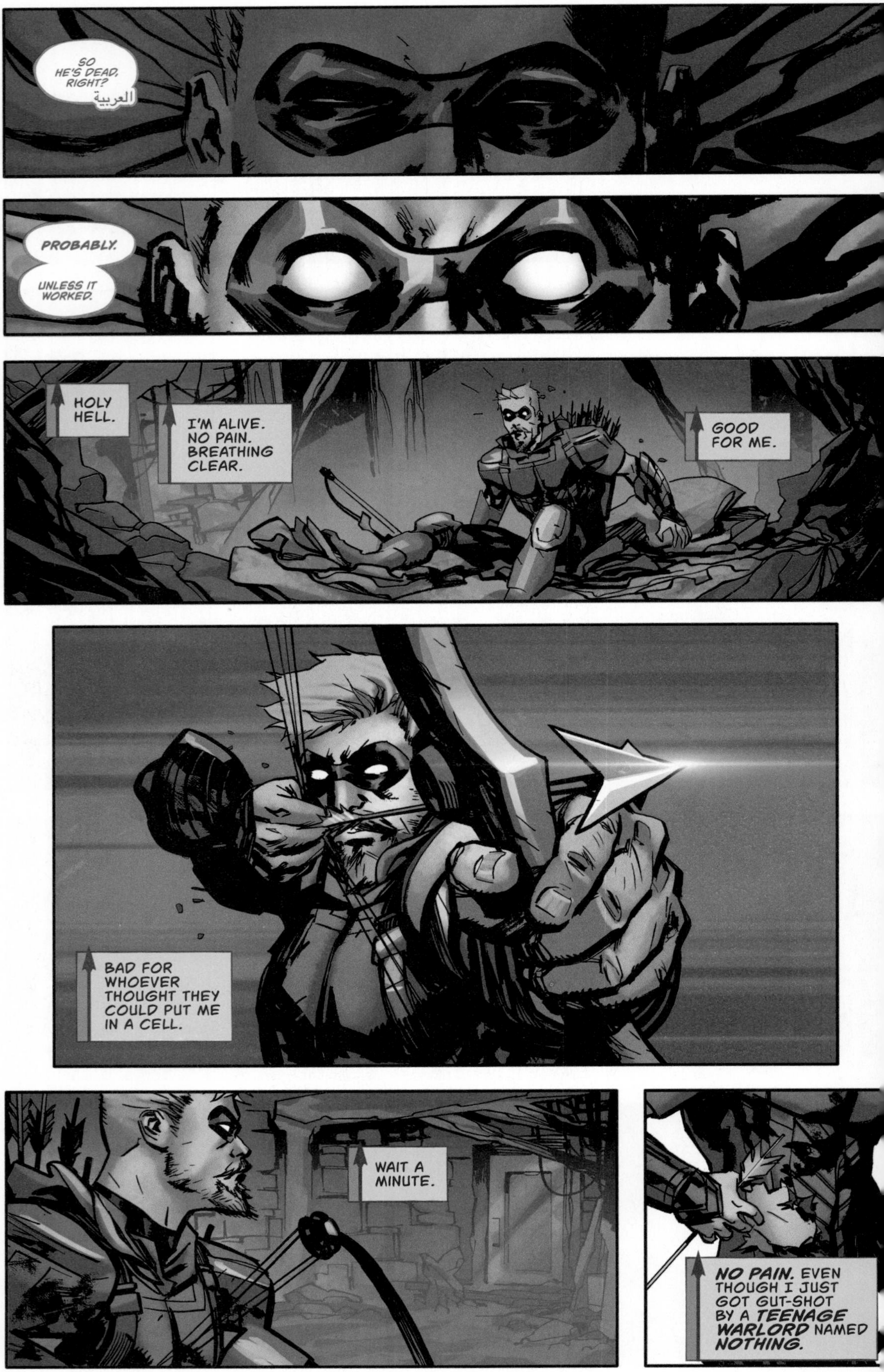

SO HE'S DEAD, RIGHT?
العربية
PROBABLY.
UNLESS IT WORKED.
HOLY HELL.
I'M ALIVE. NO PAIN. BREATHING CLEAR.
GOOD FOR ME.
BAD FOR WHOEVER THOUGHT THEY COULD PUT ME IN A CELL.
WAIT A MINUTE.
NO PAIN. EVEN THOUGH I JUST GOT GUT-SHOT BY A TEENAGE WARLORD NAMED NOTHING.

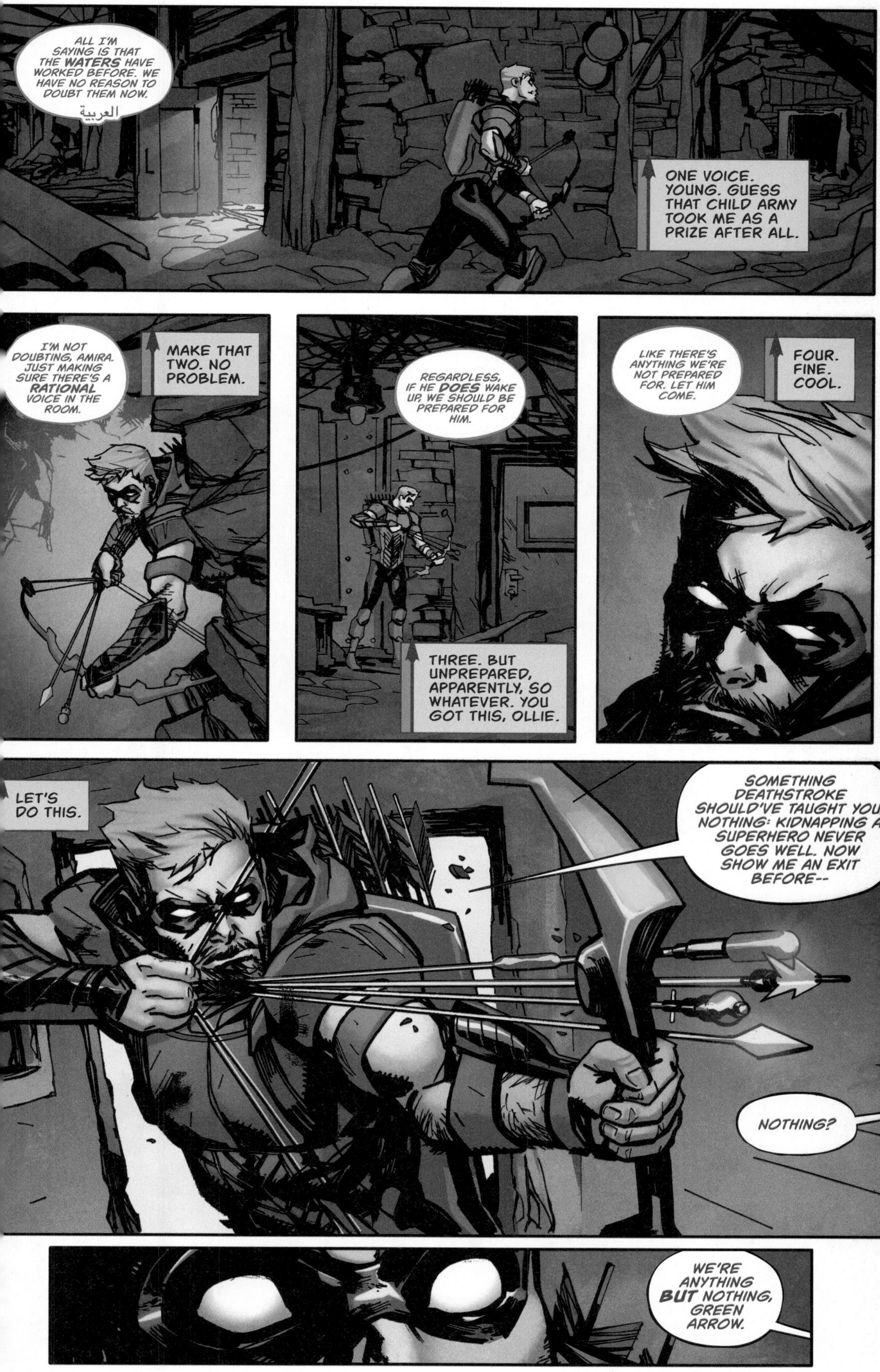
ALL I'M SAYING IS THAT THE WATERS HAVE WORKED BEFORE. WE HAVE NO REASON TO DOUBT THEM NOW.
العربية
ONE VOICE. YOUNG. GUESS THAT CHILD ARMY TOOK ME AS A PRIZE AFTER ALL.
I'M NOT DOUBTING, AMIRA. JUST MAKING SURE THERE'S A RATIONAL VOICE IN THE ROOM.
MAKE THAT TWO. NO PROBLEM.
REGARDLESS, IF HE DOES WAKE UP, WE SHOULD BE PREPARED FOR HIM.
THREE. BUT UNPREPARED, APPARENTLY, SO WHATEVER. YOU GOT THIS, OLLIE.
LIKE THERE'S ANYTHING WE'RE NOT PREPARED FOR. LET HIM COME.
FOUR. FINE. COOL.
LET'S DO THIS.
SOMETHING DEATHSTROKE SHOULD'VE TAUGHT YOU, NOTHING: KIDNAPPING A SUPERHERO NEVER GOES WELL. NOW SHOW ME AN EXIT BEFORE--
NOTHING?
WE'RE ANYTHING BUT NOTHING, GREEN ARROW.

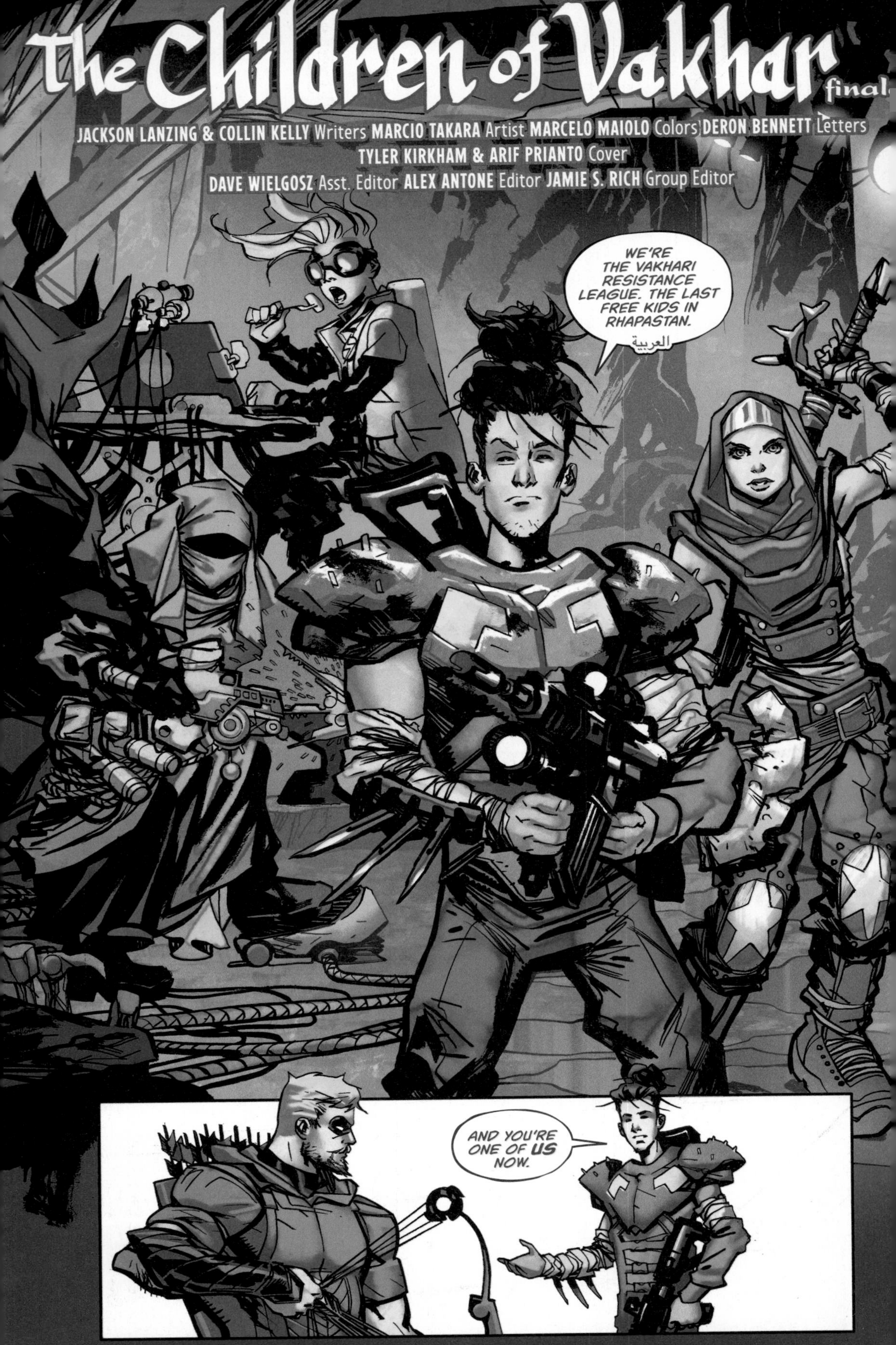
The Children of Vakhar final
JACKSON LANZING & COLLIN KELLY Writers MARCIO TAKARA Artist MARCELO MAIOLO Colors DERON BENNETT Letters
TYLER KIRKHAM & ARIF PRIANTO Cover
DAVE WIELGOSZ Asst. Editor ALEX ANTONE Editor JAMIE S. RICH Group Editor
WE'RE THE VAKHARI RESISTANCE LEAGUE. THE LAST FREE KIDS IN RHAPASTAN. العربية
AND YOU'RE ONE OF US NOW.

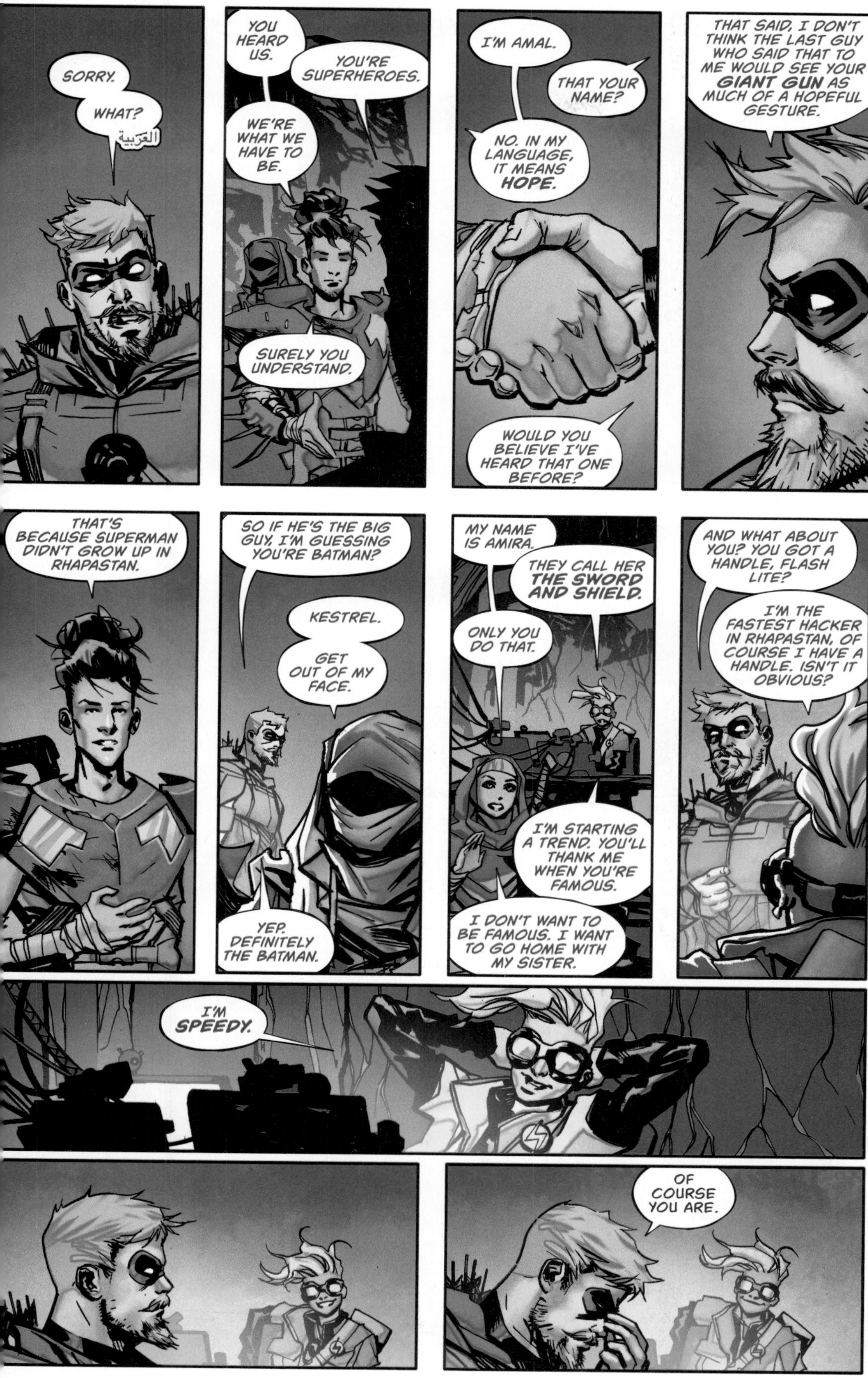
SORRY.
WHAT?
العربية
YOU HEARD US.
YOU'RE SUPERHEROES.
WE'RE WHAT WE HAVE TO BE.
SURELY YOU UNDERSTAND.
I'M AMAL.
THAT YOUR NAME?
NO. IN MY LANGUAGE, IT MEANS HOPE.
WOULD YOU BELIEVE I'VE HEARD THAT ONE BEFORE?
THAT SAID, I DON'T THINK THE LAST GUY WHO SAID THAT TO ME WOULD SEE YOUR GIANT GUN AS MUCH OF A HOPEFUL GESTURE.
THAT'S BECAUSE SUPERMAN DIDN'T GROW UP IN RHAPASTAN.
SO IF HE'S THE BIG GUY, I'M GUESSING YOU'RE BATMAN?
KESTREL.
GET OUT OF MY FACE.
YEP. DEFINITELY THE BATMAN.
MY NAME IS AMIRA.
THEY CALL HER THE SWORD AND SHIELD.
ONLY YOU DO THAT.
I'M STARTING A TREND. YOU'LL THANK ME WHEN YOU'RE FAMOUS.
I DON'T WANT TO BE FAMOUS. I WANT TO GO HOME WITH MY SISTER.
AND WHAT ABOUT YOU? YOU GOT A HANDLE, FLASH LITE?
I'M THE FASTEST HACKER IN RHAPASTAN, OF COURSE I HAVE A HANDLE. ISN'T IT OBVIOUS?
I'M SPEEDY.
OF COURSE YOU ARE.

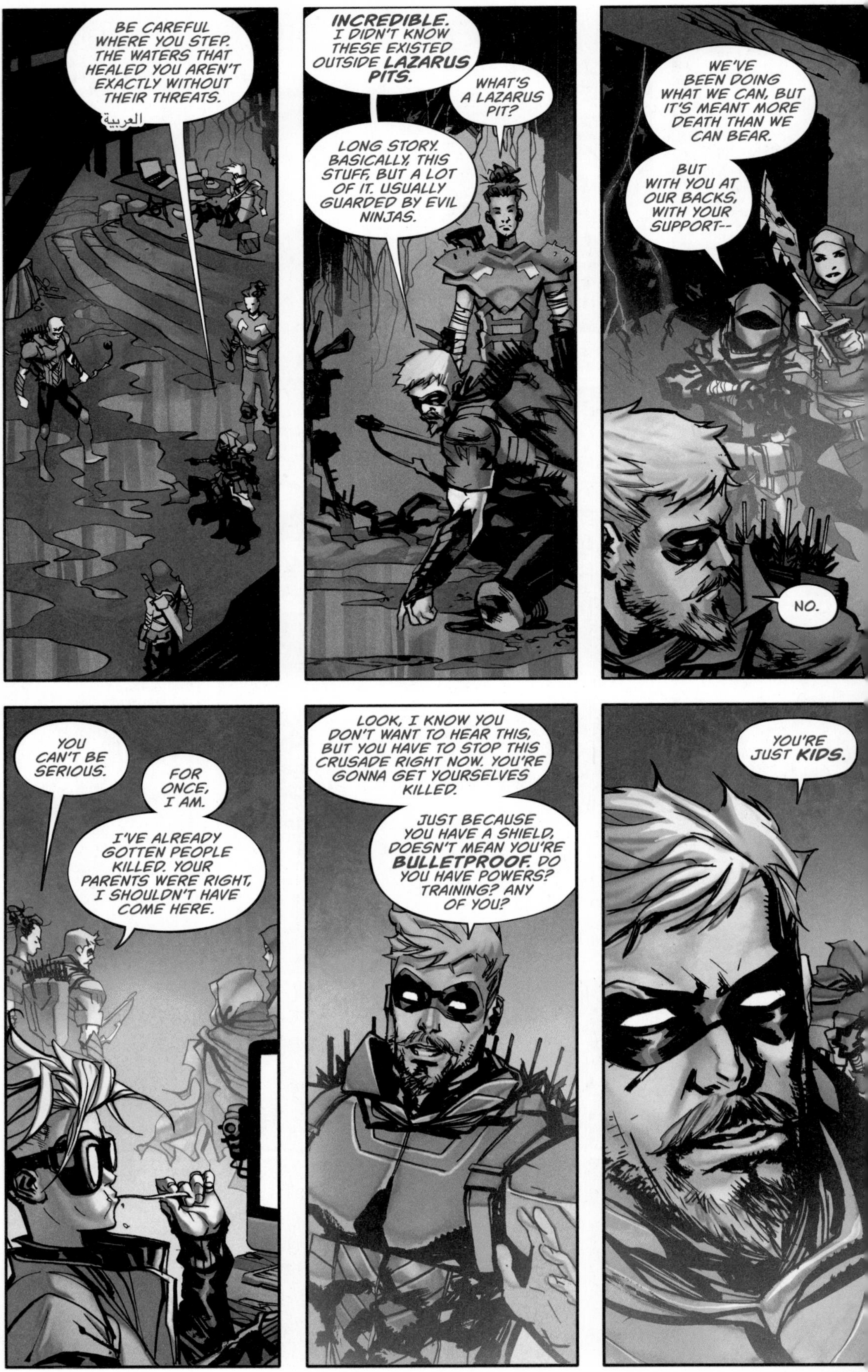
BE CAREFUL WHERE YOU STEP. THE WATERS THAT HEALED YOU AREN'T EXACTLY WITHOUT THEIR THREATS.
العربية
INCREDIBLE. I DIDN'T KNOW THESE EXISTED OUTSIDE LAZARUS PITS.
WHAT'S A LAZARUS PIT?
LONG STORY. BASICALLY, THIS STUFF, BUT A LOT OF IT. USUALLY GUARDED BY EVIL NINJAS.
WE'VE BEEN DOING WHAT WE CAN, BUT IT'S MEANT MORE DEATH THAN WE CAN BEAR.
BUT WITH YOU AT OUR BACKS, WITH YOUR SUPPORT--
NO.
YOU CAN'T BE SERIOUS.
FOR ONCE, I AM.
I'VE ALREADY GOTTEN PEOPLE KILLED. YOUR PARENTS WERE RIGHT, I SHOULDN'T HAVE COME HERE.
LOOK, I KNOW YOU DON'T WANT TO HEAR THIS, BUT YOU HAVE TO STOP THIS CRUSADE RIGHT NOW. YOU'RE GONNA GET YOURSELVES KILLED.
JUST BECAUSE YOU HAVE A SHIELD, DOESN'T MEAN YOU'RE BULLETPROOF. DO YOU HAVE POWERS? TRAINING? ANY OF YOU?
YOU'RE JUST KIDS.

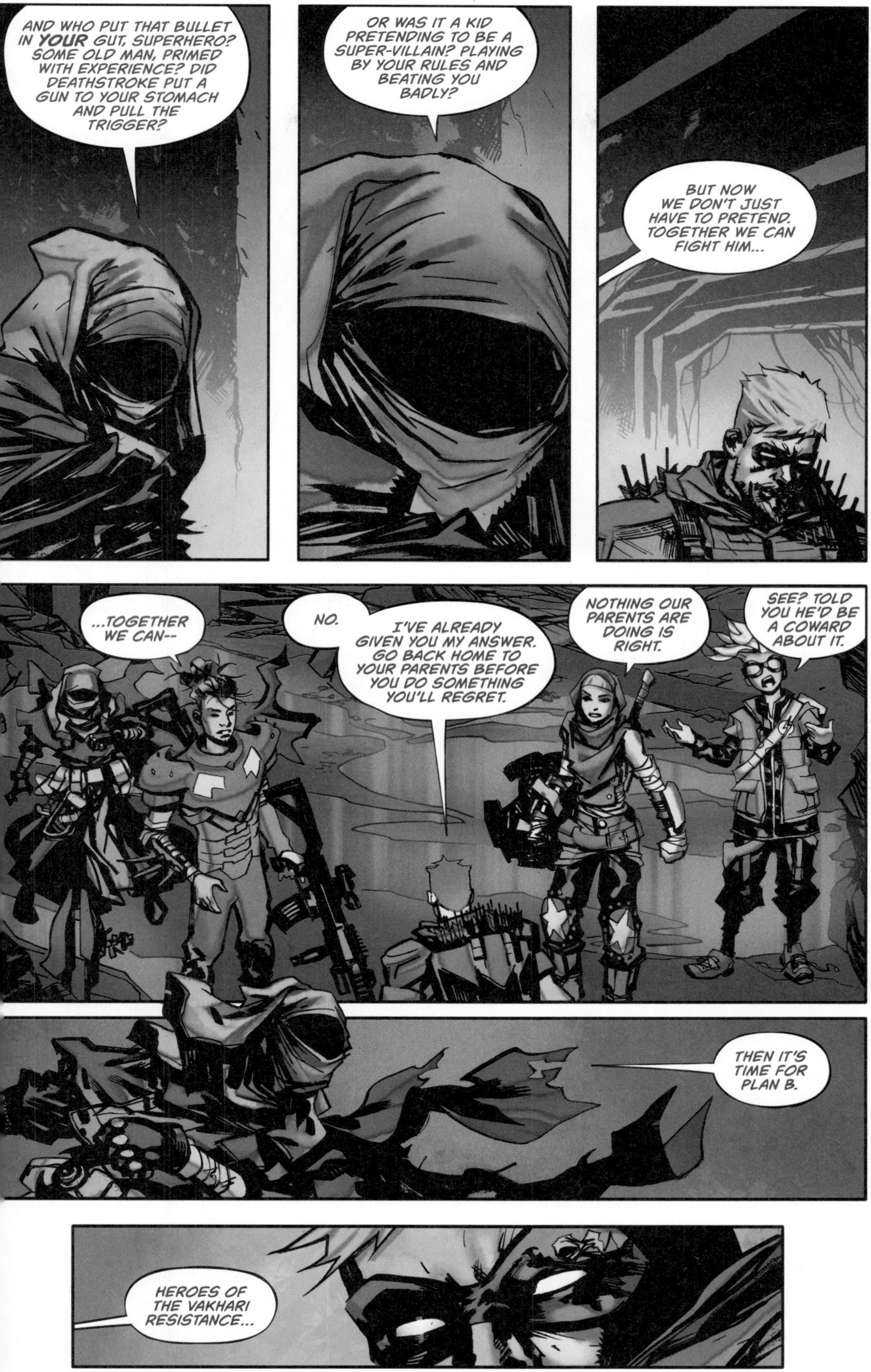
AND WHO PUT THAT BULLET IN YOUR GUT, SUPERHERO? SOME OLD MAN, PRIMED WITH EXPERIENCE? DID DEATHSTROKE PUT A GUN TO YOUR STOMACH AND PULL THE TRIGGER?
OR WAS IT A KID PRETENDING TO BE A SUPER-VILLAIN? PLAYING BY YOUR RULES AND BEATING YOU BADLY?
BUT NOW WE DON'T JUST HAVE TO PRETEND. TOGETHER WE CAN FIGHT HIM...
...TOGETHER WE CAN--
NO.
I'VE ALREADY GIVEN YOU MY ANSWER. GO BACK HOME TO YOUR PARENTS BEFORE YOU DO SOMETHING YOU'LL REGRET.
NOTHING OUR PARENTS ARE DOING IS RIGHT.
SEE? TOLD YOU HE'D BE A COWARD ABOUT IT.
THEN IT'S TIME FOR PLAN B.
HEROES OF THE VAKHARI RESISTANCE...

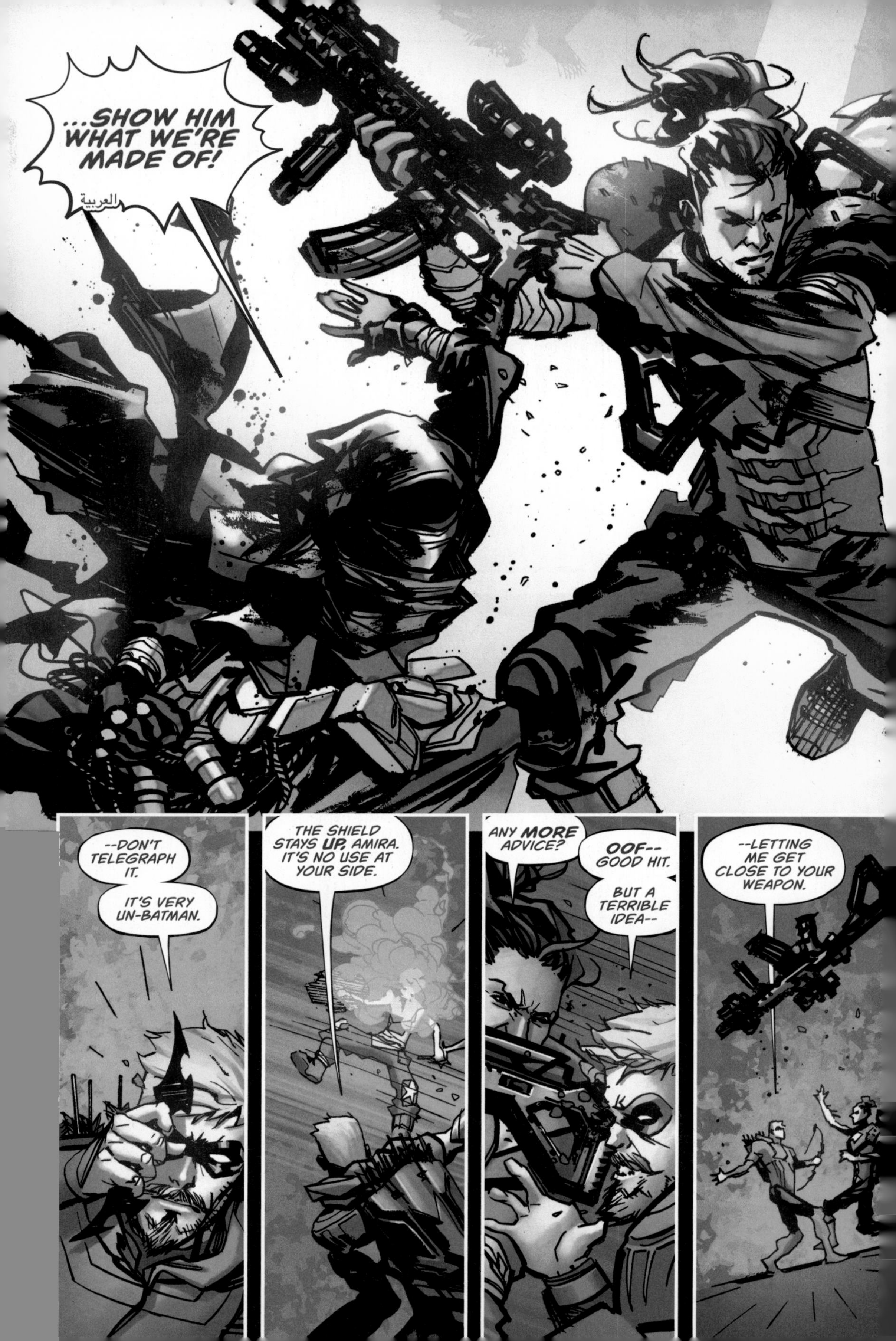
العربية
...SHOW HIM WHAT WE'RE MADE OF!
--DON'T TELEGRAPH IT.
IT'S VERY UN-BATMAN.
THE SHIELD STAYS UP, AMIRA. IT'S NO USE AT YOUR SIDE.
ANY MORE ADVICE?
OOF-- GOOD HIT.
BUT A TERRIBLE IDEA--
--LETTING ME GET CLOSE TO YOUR WEAPON.

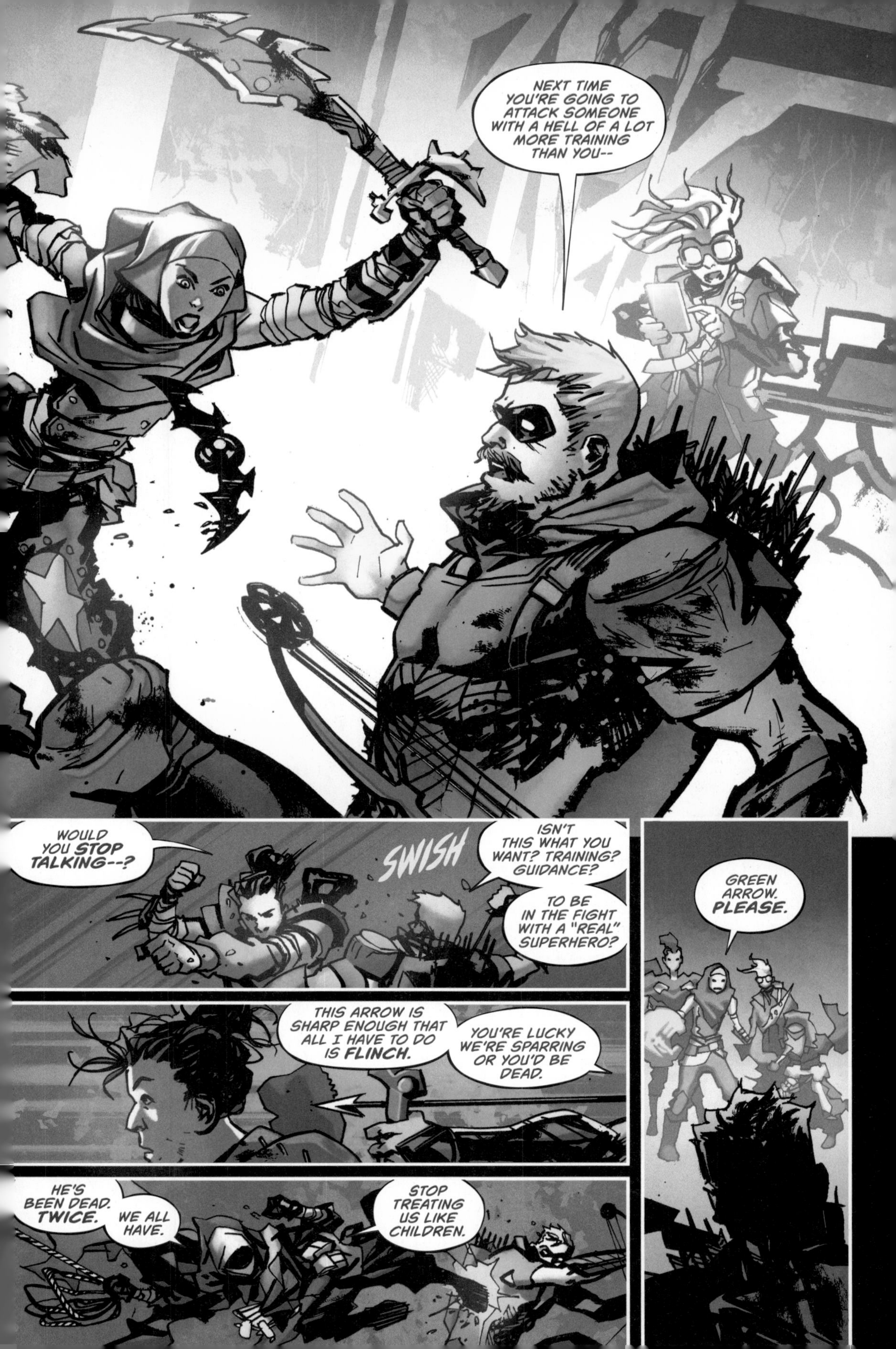
NEXT TIME YOU'RE GOING TO ATTACK SOMEONE WITH A HELL OF A LOT MORE TRAINING THAN YOU--
WOULD YOU STOP TALKING--?
SWISH
ISN'T THIS WHAT YOU WANT? TRAINING? GUIDANCE?
TO BE IN THE FIGHT WITH A "REAL" SUPERHERO?
THIS ARROW IS SHARP ENOUGH THAT ALL I HAVE TO DO IS FLINCH.
YOU'RE LUCKY WE'RE SPARRING OR YOU'D BE DEAD.
HE'S BEEN DEAD. TWICE.
WE ALL HAVE.
STOP TREATING US LIKE CHILDREN.
GREEN ARROW. PLEASE.

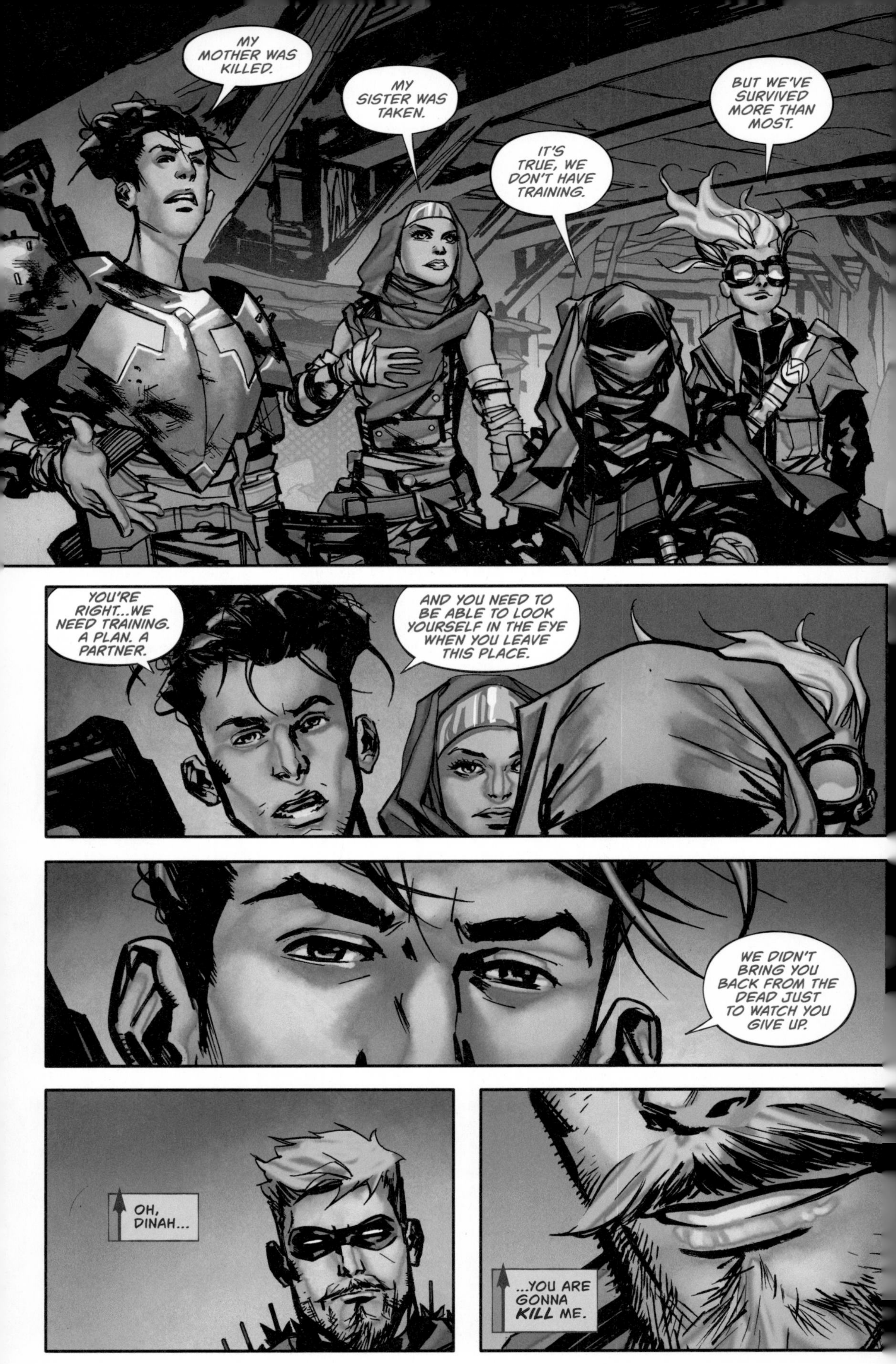
MY MOTHER WAS KILLED.
MY SISTER WAS TAKEN.
IT'S TRUE, WE DON'T HAVE TRAINING.
BUT WE'VE SURVIVED MORE THAN MOST.
YOU'RE RIGHT...WE NEED TRAINING. A PLAN. A PARTNER.
AND YOU NEED TO BE ABLE TO LOOK YOURSELF IN THE EYE WHEN YOU LEAVE THIS PLACE.
WE DIDN'T BRING YOU BACK FROM THE DEAD JUST TO WATCH YOU GIVE UP.
OH, DINAH...
...YOU ARE GONNA **KILL** ME.

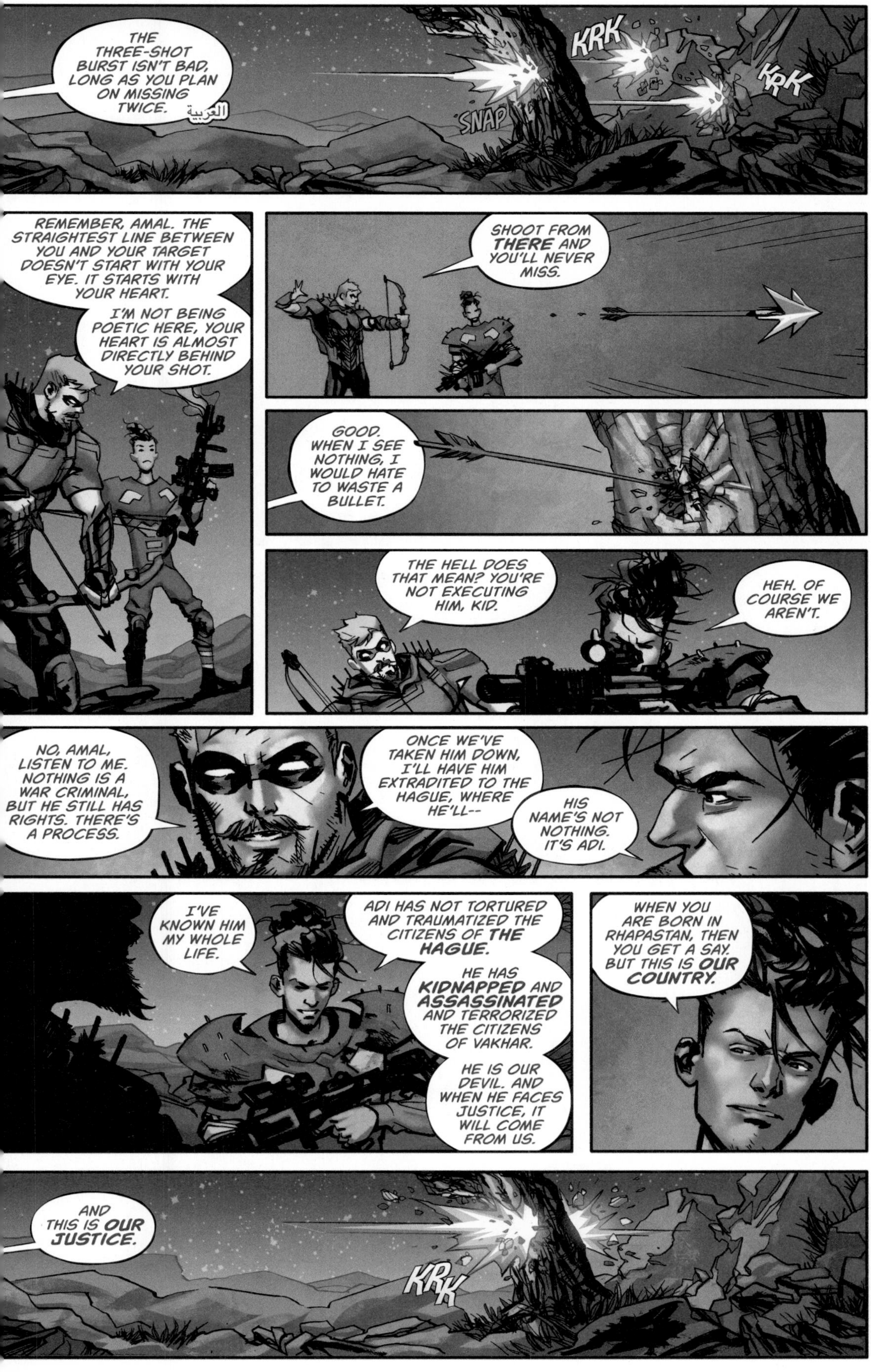

THE THREE-SHOT BURST ISN'T BAD, LONG AS YOU PLAN ON MISSING TWICE. العربية
SNAP
KRK
KRK
REMEMBER, AMAL. THE STRAIGHTEST LINE BETWEEN YOU AND YOUR TARGET DOESN'T START WITH YOUR EYE. IT STARTS WITH YOUR HEART.
I'M NOT BEING POETIC HERE, YOUR HEART IS ALMOST DIRECTLY BEHIND YOUR SHOT.
SHOOT FROM THERE AND YOU'LL NEVER MISS.
GOOD. WHEN I SEE NOTHING, I WOULD HATE TO WASTE A BULLET.
THE HELL DOES THAT MEAN? YOU'RE NOT EXECUTING HIM, KID.
HEH. OF COURSE WE AREN'T.
NO, AMAL, LISTEN TO ME. NOTHING IS A WAR CRIMINAL, BUT HE STILL HAS RIGHTS. THERE'S A PROCESS.
ONCE WE'VE TAKEN HIM DOWN, I'LL HAVE HIM EXTRADITED TO THE HAGUE, WHERE HE'LL--
HIS NAME'S NOT NOTHING. IT'S ADI.
I'VE KNOWN HIM MY WHOLE LIFE.
ADI HAS NOT TORTURED AND TRAUMATIZED THE CITIZENS OF THE HAGUE.
HE HAS KIDNAPPED AND ASSASSINATED AND TERRORIZED THE CITIZENS OF VAKHAR.
HE IS OUR DEVIL. AND WHEN HE FACES JUSTICE, IT WILL COME FROM US.
WHEN YOU ARE BORN IN RHAPASTAN, THEN YOU GET A SAY. BUT THIS IS OUR COUNTRY.
AND THIS IS OUR JUSTICE.
KRK

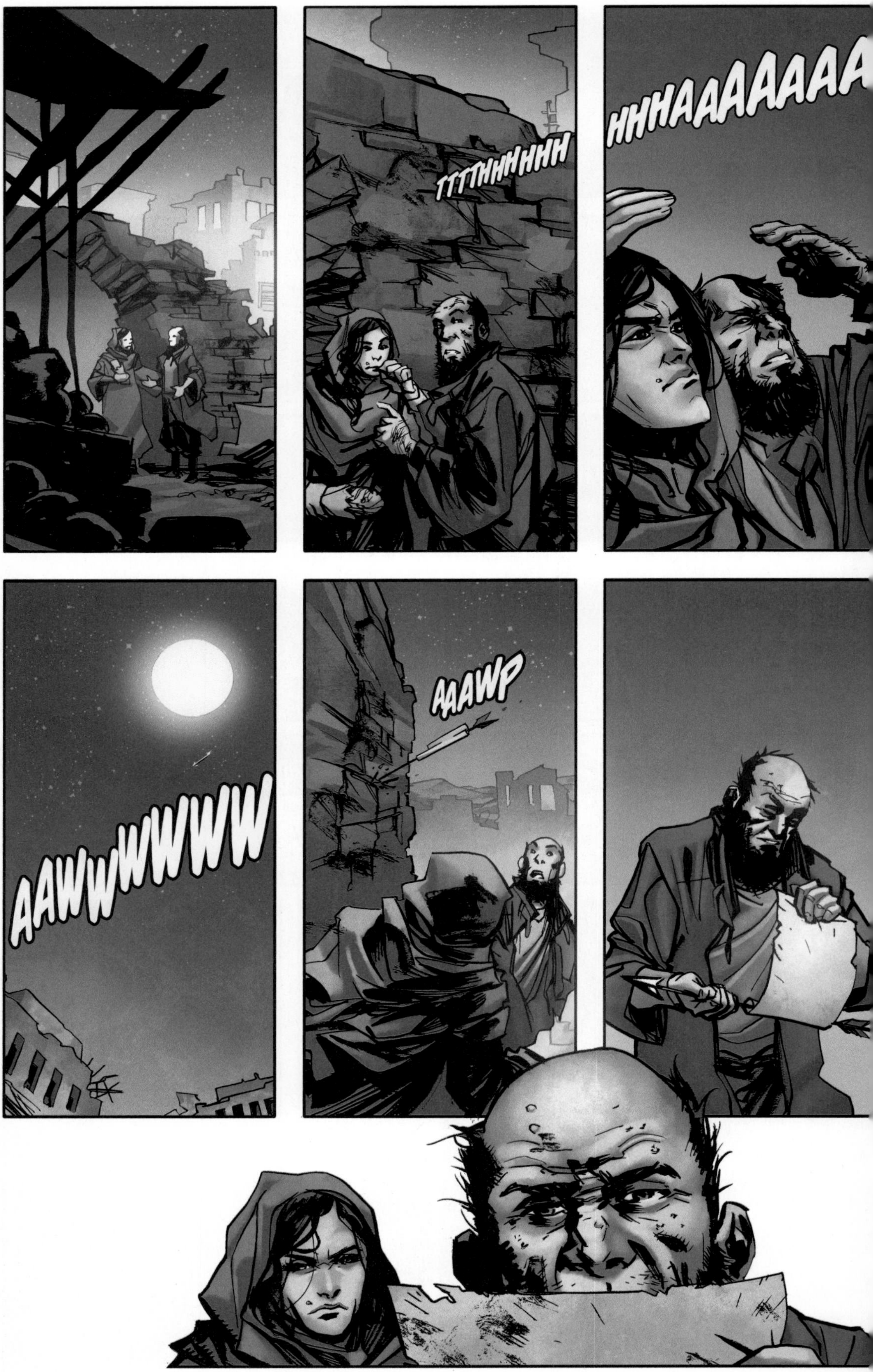
TTTTHHHHHH
HHHAAAAAAAA
AAWWWWWW
AAAWP

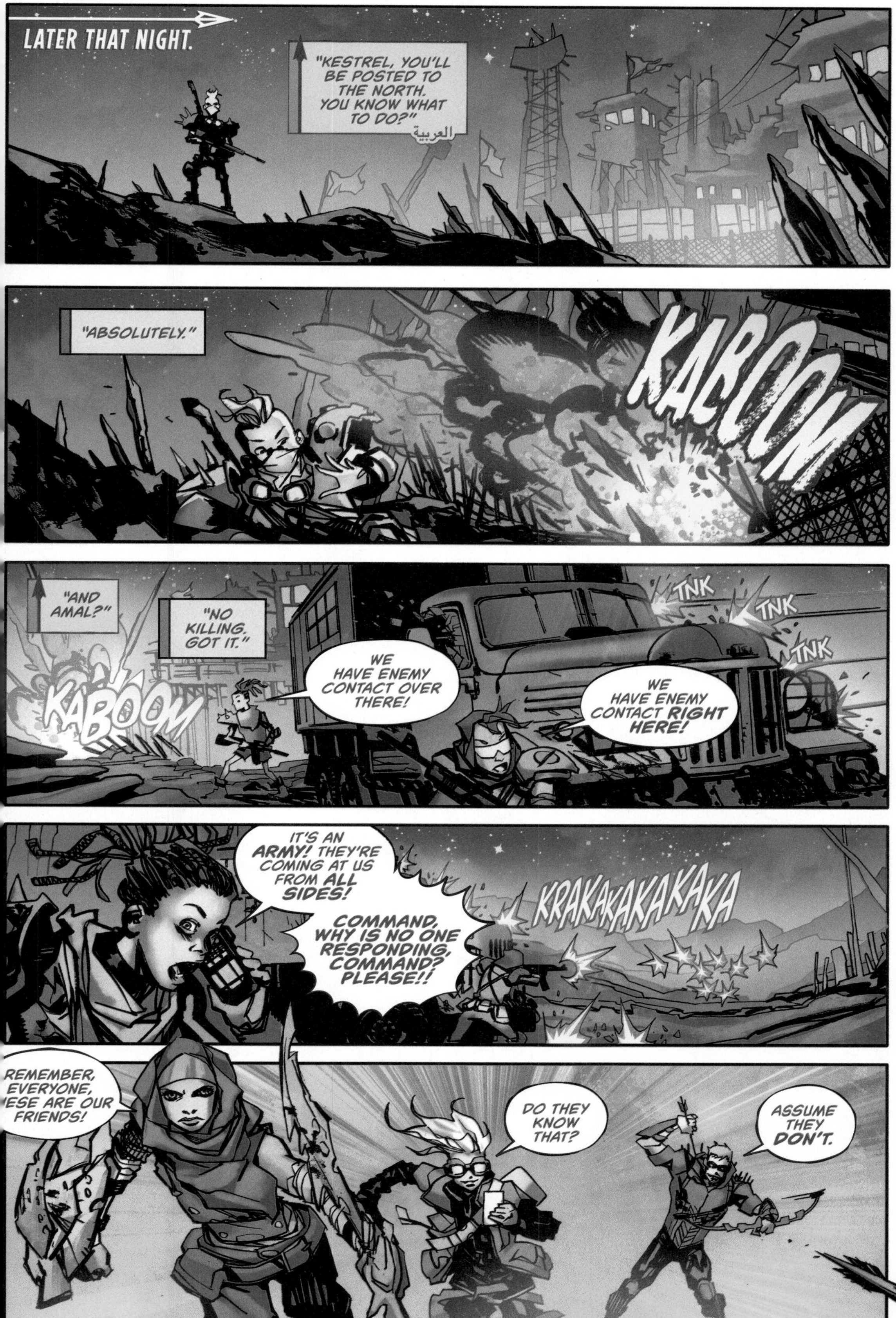
LATER THAT NIGHT.
"KESTREL, YOU'LL BE POSTED TO THE NORTH. YOU KNOW WHAT TO DO?" العربية
"ABSOLUTELY."
KABOOM
"AND AMAL?"
"NO KILLING. GOT IT."
KABOOM
WE HAVE ENEMY CONTACT OVER THERE!
TNK
TNK
TNK
WE HAVE ENEMY CONTACT RIGHT HERE!
IT'S AN ARMY! THEY'RE COMING AT US FROM ALL SIDES!
COMMAND, WHY IS NO ONE RESPONDING, COMMAND? PLEASE!!
KRAKAKAKAKAKAKA
REMEMBER, EVERYONE, ESE ARE OUR FRIENDS!
DO THEY KNOW THAT?
ASSUME THEY DON'T.

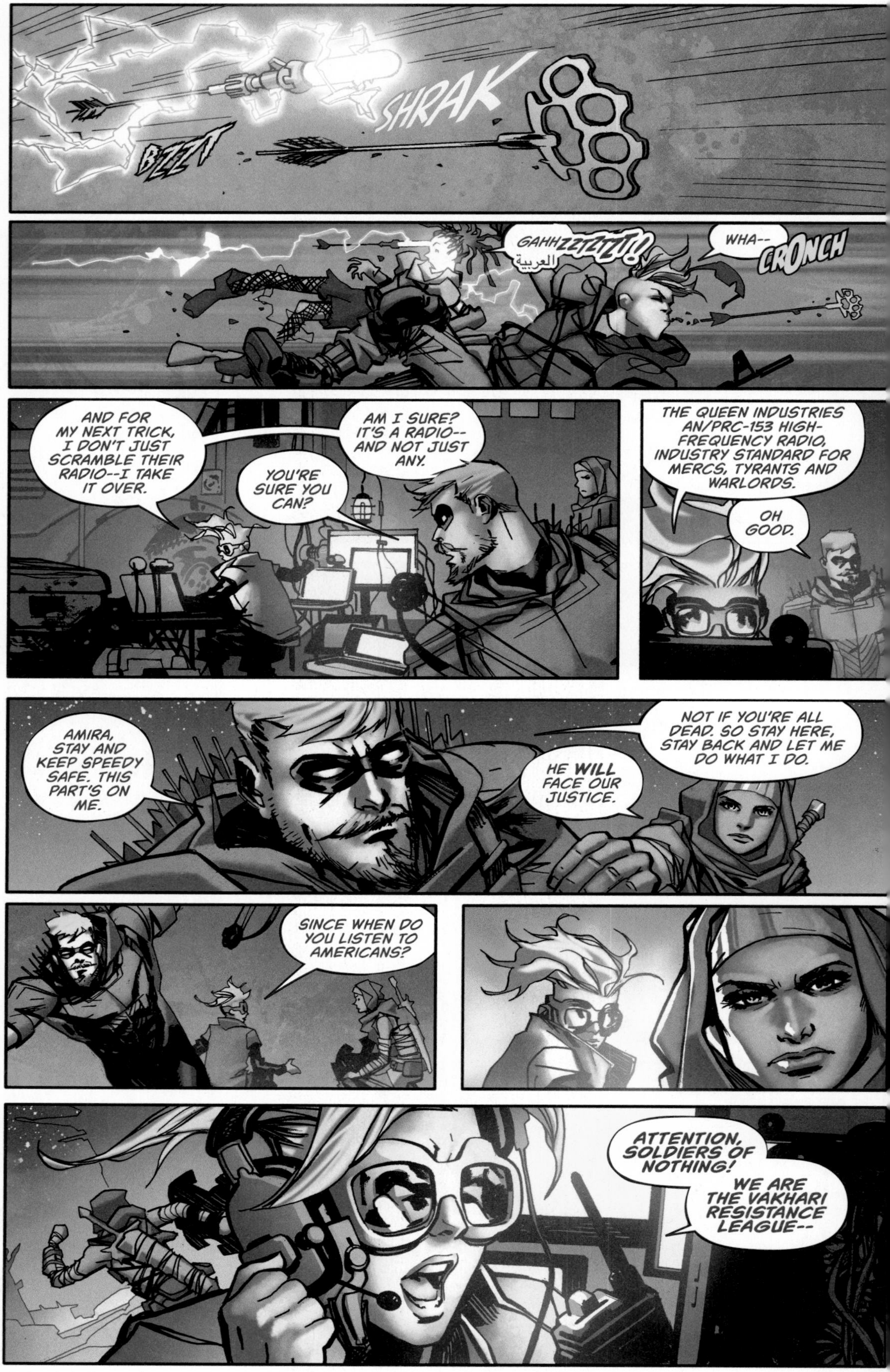
BZZZT
SHRAK
GAHHZZZZZZT!
العربية
WHA--
CRONCH
AND FOR MY NEXT TRICK, I DON'T JUST SCRAMBLE THEIR RADIO--I TAKE IT OVER.
YOU'RE SURE YOU CAN?
AM I SURE? IT'S A RADIO-- AND NOT JUST ANY.
THE QUEEN INDUSTRIES AN/PRC-153 HIGH-FREQUENCY RADIO, INDUSTRY STANDARD FOR MERCS, TYRANTS AND WARLORDS.
OH GOOD.
AMIRA, STAY AND KEEP SPEEDY SAFE. THIS PART'S ON ME.
HE WILL FACE OUR JUSTICE.
NOT IF YOU'RE ALL DEAD. SO STAY HERE, STAY BACK AND LET ME DO WHAT I DO.
SINCE WHEN DO YOU LISTEN TO AMERICANS?
ATTENTION, SOLDIERS OF NOTHING!
WE ARE THE VAKHARI RESISTANCE LEAGUE--

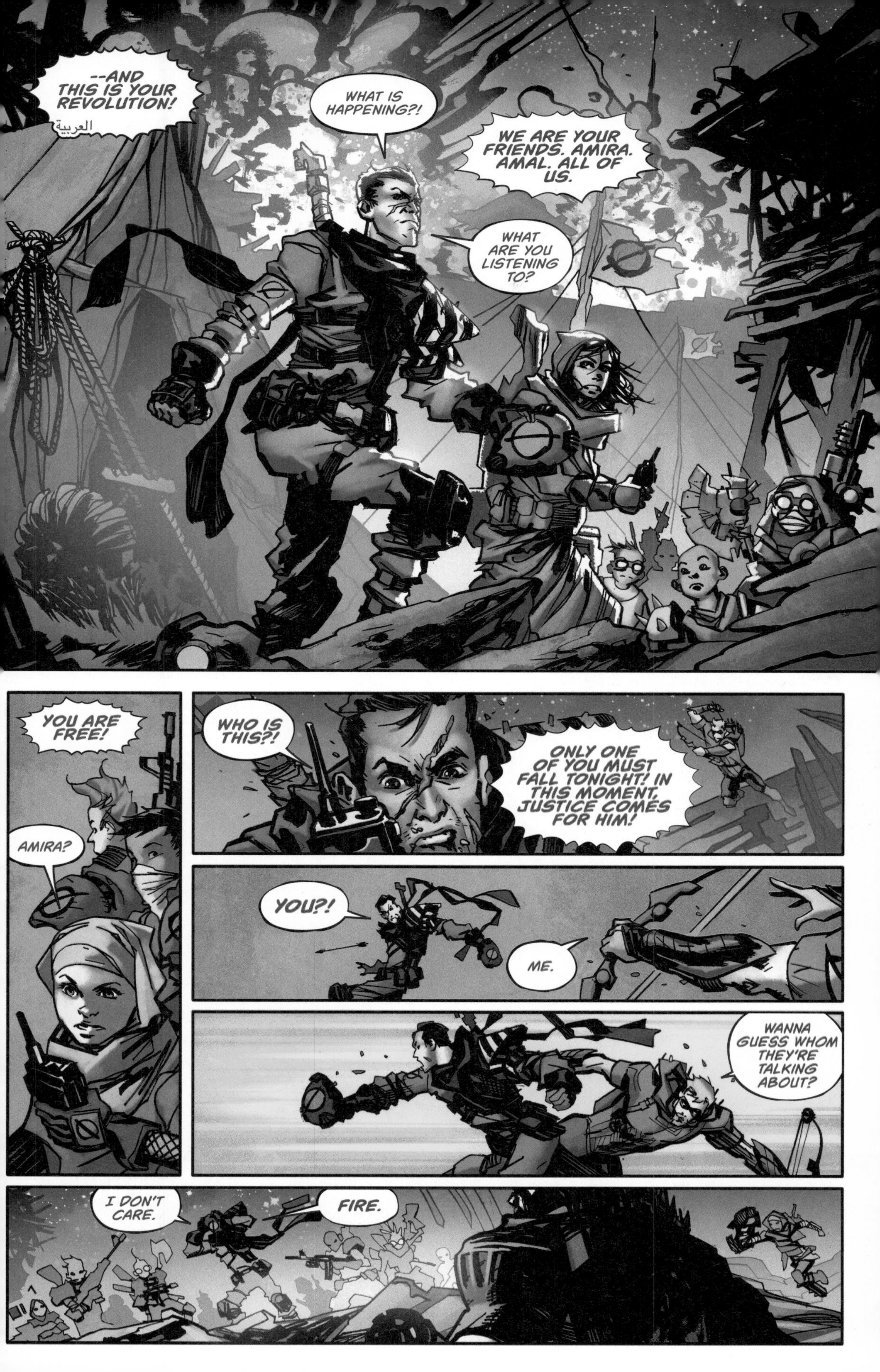
--AND THIS IS YOUR REVOLUTION!
العربية
WHAT IS HAPPENING?!
WE ARE YOUR FRIENDS. AMIRA. AMAL. ALL OF US.
WHAT ARE YOU LISTENING TO?
YOU ARE FREE!
AMIRA?
WHO IS THIS?!
ONLY ONE OF YOU MUST FALL TONIGHT! IN THIS MOMENT, JUSTICE COMES FOR HIM!
YOU?!
ME.
WANNA GUESS WHOM THEY'RE TALKING ABOUT?
I DON'T CARE.
FIRE.

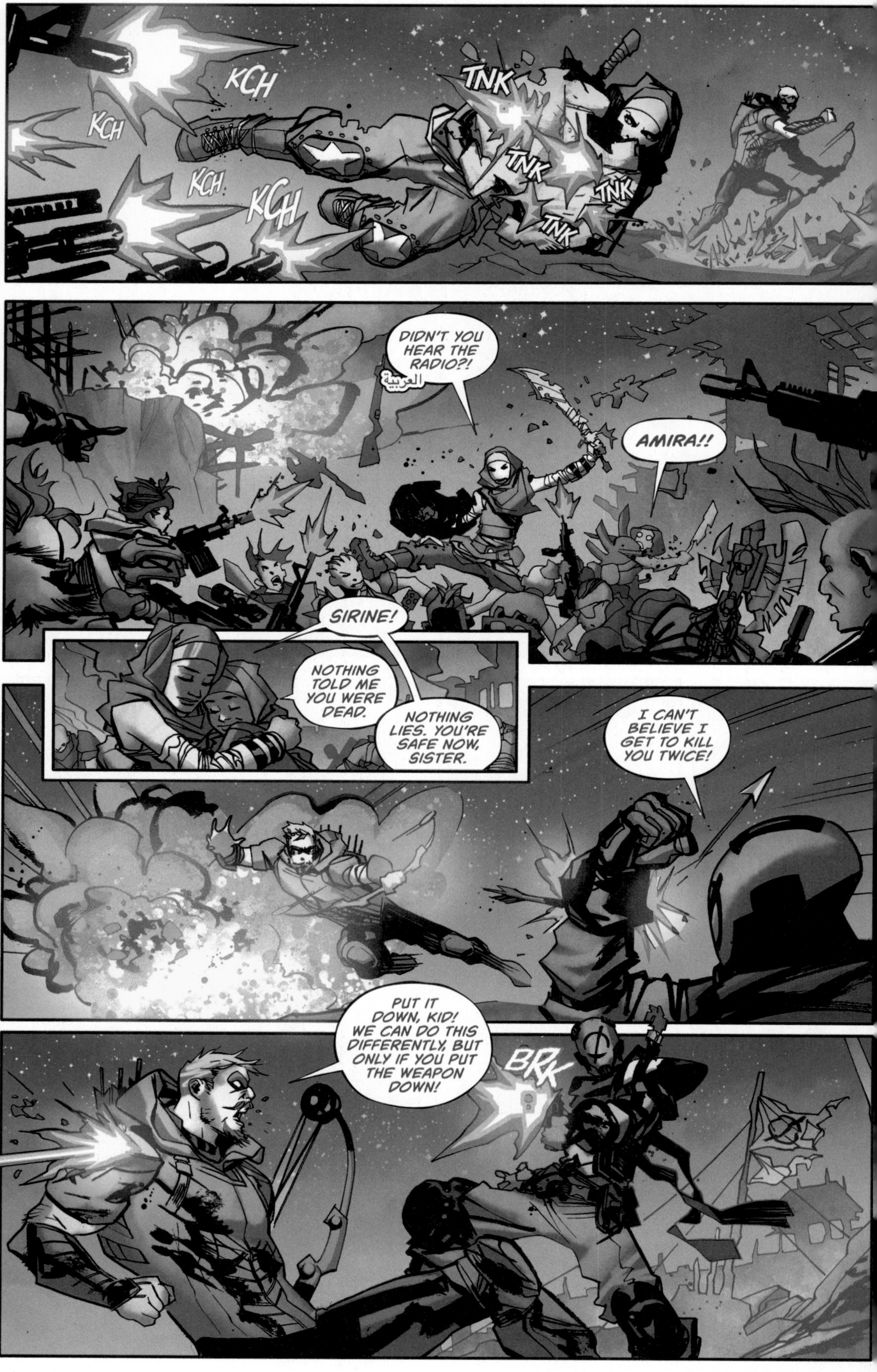

KCH
KCH
KCH
KCH
TNK
TNK
TNK
TNK
DIDN'T YOU HEAR THE RADIO?!
العربية
AMIRA!!
SIRINE!
NOTHING TOLD ME YOU WERE DEAD.
NOTHING LIES. YOU'RE SAFE NOW, SISTER.
I CAN'T BELIEVE I GET TO KILL YOU TWICE!
PUT IT DOWN, KID! WE CAN DO THIS DIFFERENTLY, BUT ONLY IF YOU PUT THE WEAPON DOWN!
BRRK

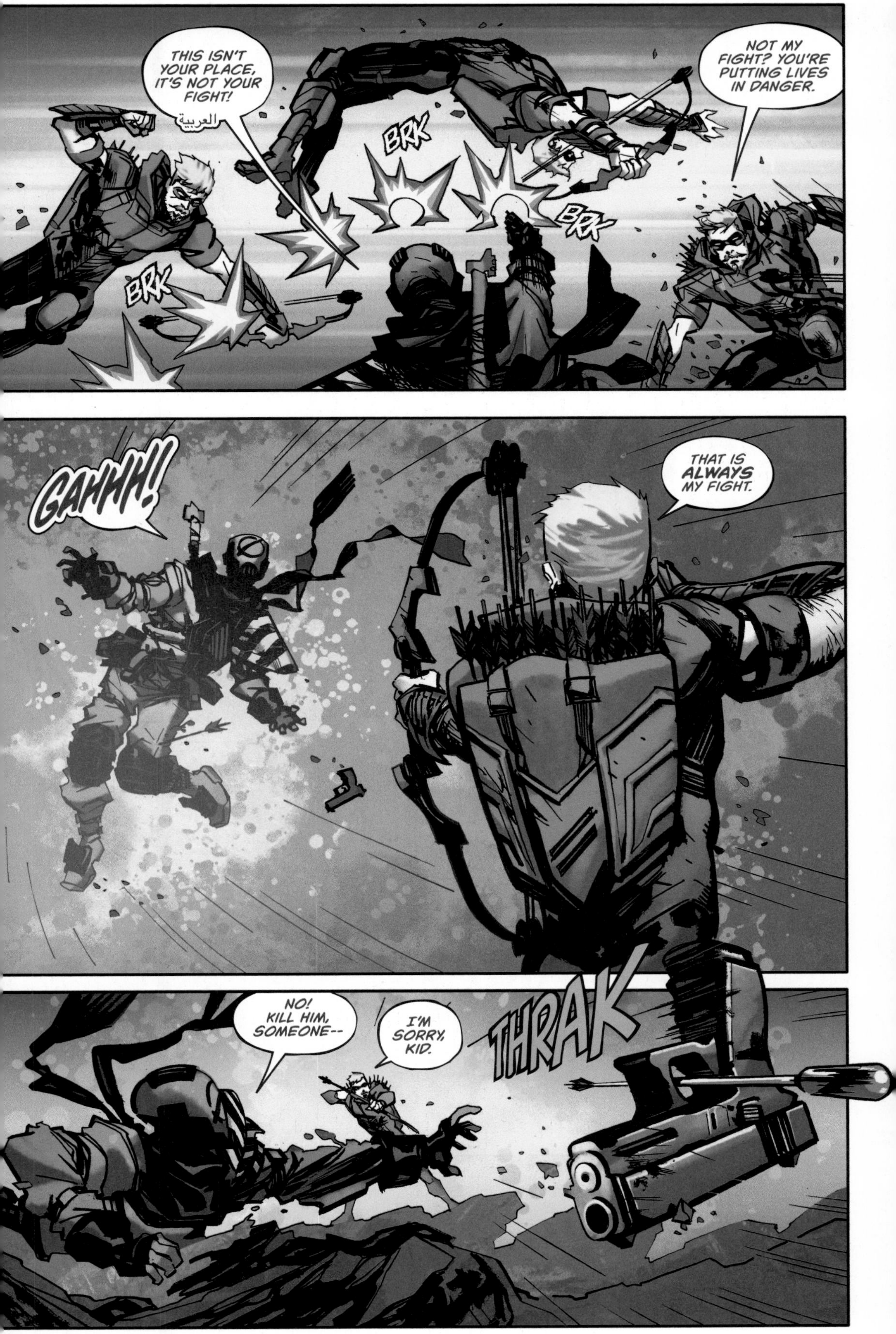

THIS ISN'T YOUR PLACE, IT'S NOT YOUR FIGHT!
العربية
NOT MY FIGHT? YOU'RE PUTTING LIVES IN DANGER.
BRK
BRK
BRK
GAHHH!!
THAT IS ALWAYS MY FIGHT.
NO! KILL HIM, SOMEONE--
I'M SORRY, KID.
THRAK

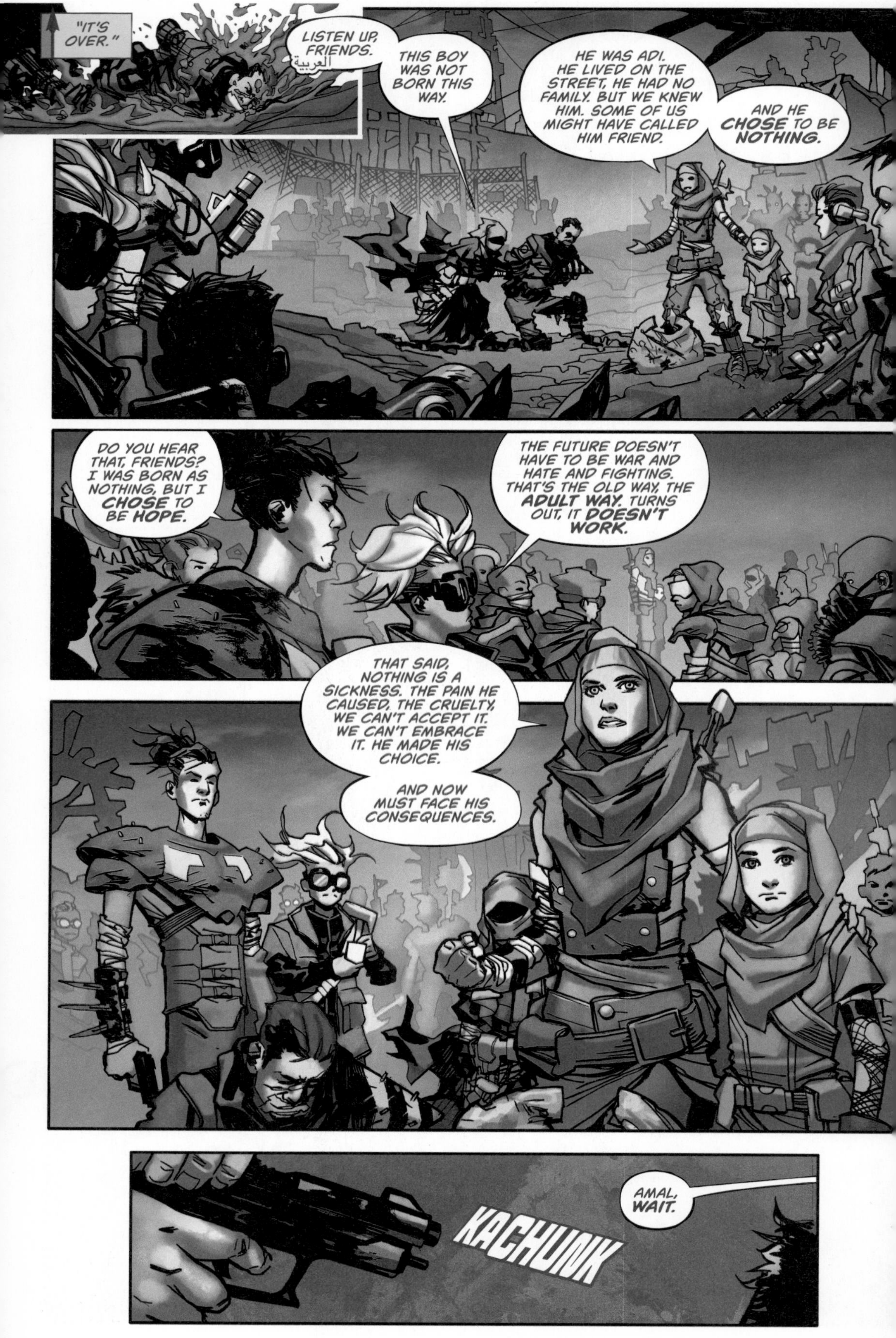

"IT'S OVER."
LISTEN UP, FRIENDS.
العربية
THIS BOY WAS NOT BORN THIS WAY.
HE WAS ADI. HE LIVED ON THE STREET, HE HAD NO FAMILY. BUT WE KNEW HIM. SOME OF US MIGHT HAVE CALLED HIM FRIEND.
AND HE CHOSE TO BE NOTHING.
DO YOU HEAR THAT, FRIENDS? I WAS BORN AS NOTHING, BUT I CHOSE TO BE HOPE.
THE FUTURE DOESN'T HAVE TO BE WAR AND HATE AND FIGHTING. THAT'S THE OLD WAY, THE ADULT WAY. TURNS OUT, IT DOESN'T WORK.
THAT SAID, NOTHING IS A SICKNESS. THE PAIN HE CAUSED, THE CRUELTY, WE CAN'T ACCEPT IT. WE CAN'T EMBRACE IT. HE MADE HIS CHOICE.
AND NOW MUST FACE HIS CONSEQUENCES.
KACHUNK
AMAL, WAIT.

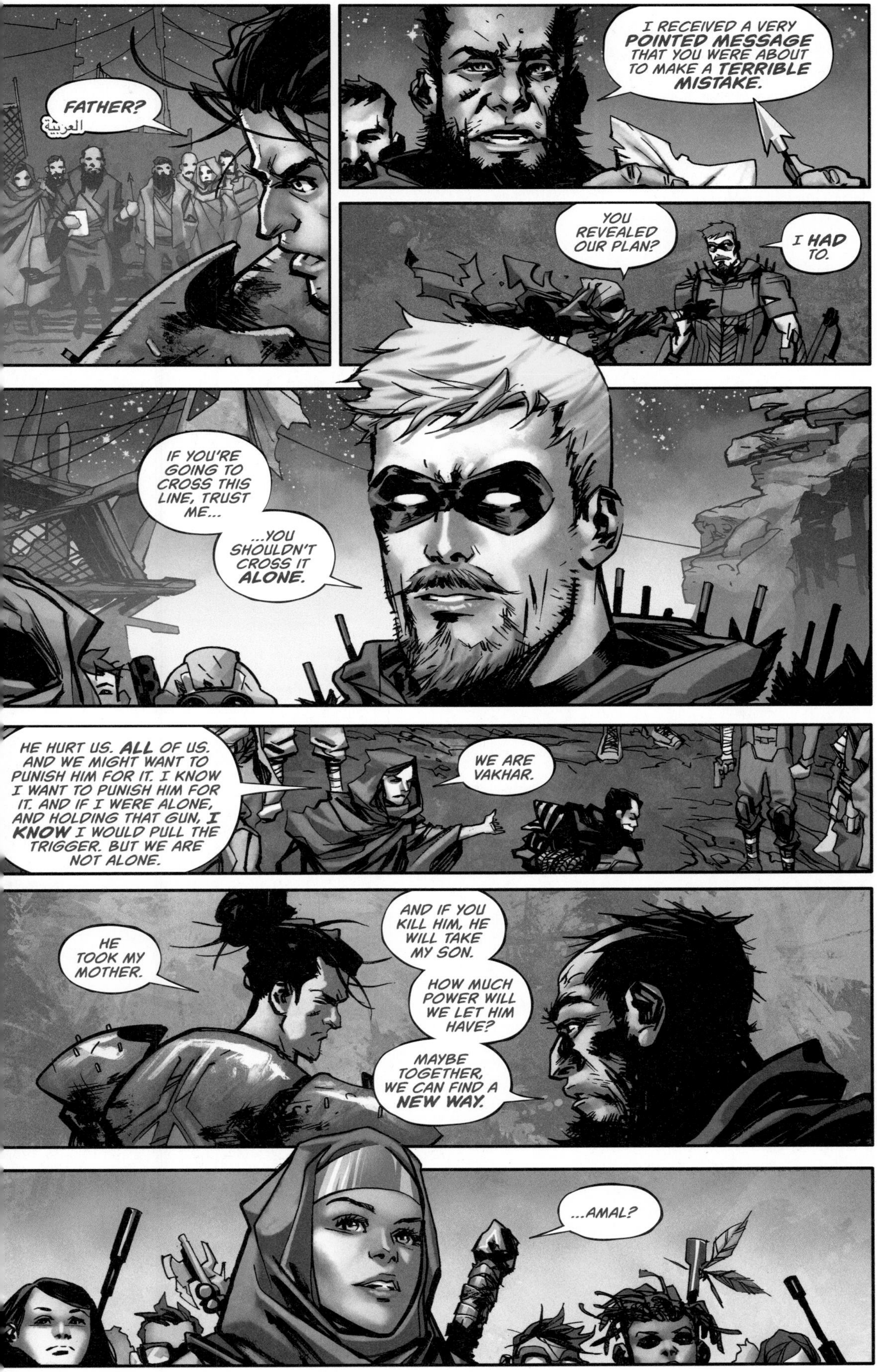
FATHER?
العربية
I RECEIVED A VERY POINTED MESSAGE THAT YOU WERE ABOUT TO MAKE A TERRIBLE MISTAKE.
YOU REVEALED OUR PLAN?
I HAD TO.
IF YOU'RE GOING TO CROSS THIS LINE, TRUST ME...
...YOU SHOULDN'T CROSS IT ALONE.
HE HURT US. ALL OF US. AND WE MIGHT WANT TO PUNISH HIM FOR IT. I KNOW I WANT TO PUNISH HIM FOR IT. AND IF I WERE ALONE, AND HOLDING THAT GUN, I KNOW I WOULD PULL THE TRIGGER. BUT WE ARE NOT ALONE.
WE ARE VAKHAR.
HE TOOK MY MOTHER.
AND IF YOU KILL HIM, HE WILL TAKE MY SON.
HOW MUCH POWER WILL WE LET HIM HAVE?
MAYBE TOGETHER, WE CAN FIND A NEW WAY.
...AMAL?

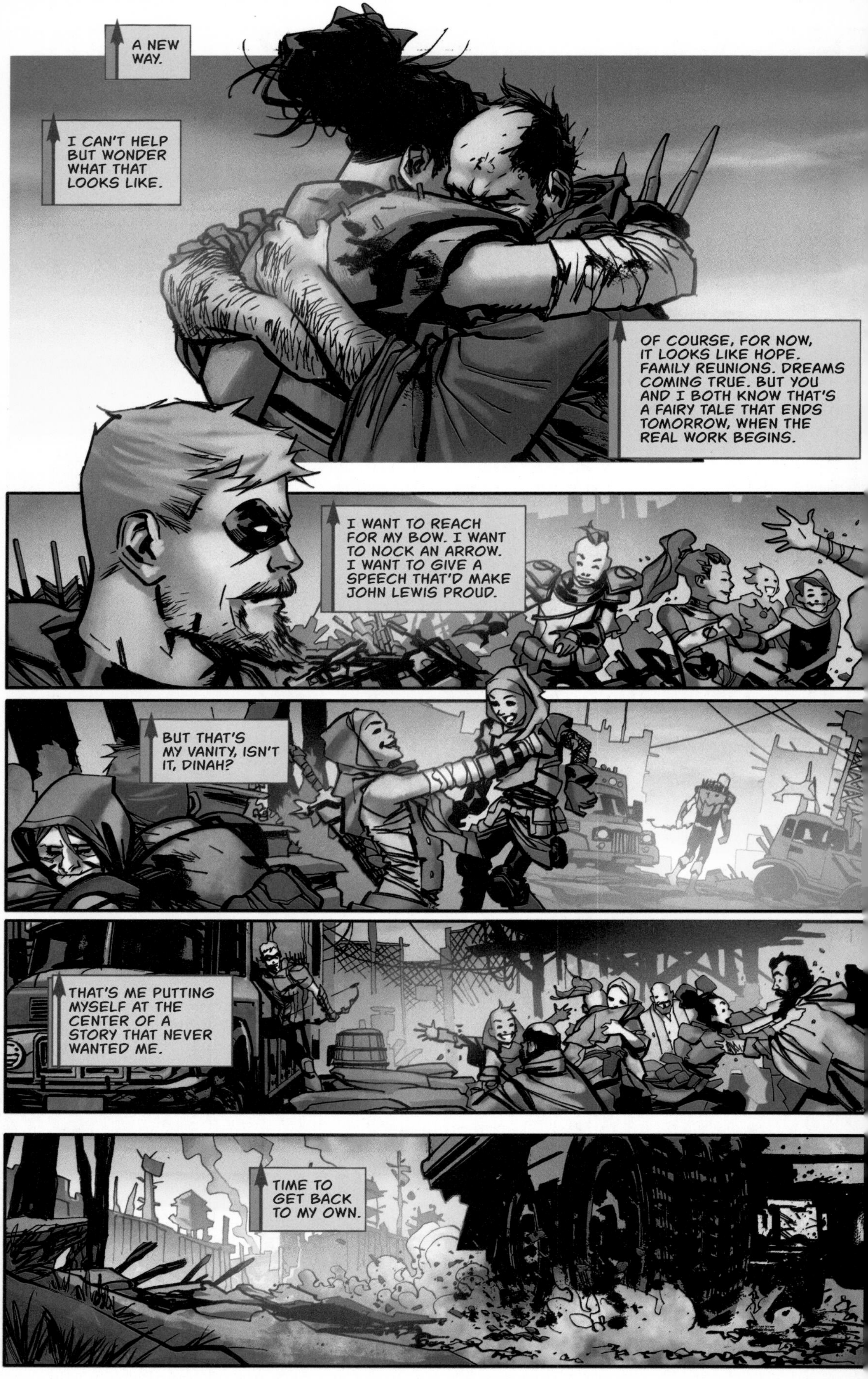
A NEW WAY.
I CAN'T HELP BUT WONDER WHAT THAT LOOKS LIKE.
OF COURSE, FOR NOW, IT LOOKS LIKE HOPE. FAMILY REUNIONS. DREAMS COMING TRUE. BUT YOU AND I BOTH KNOW THAT'S A FAIRY TALE THAT ENDS TOMORROW, WHEN THE REAL WORK BEGINS.
I WANT TO REACH FOR MY BOW. I WANT TO NOCK AN ARROW. I WANT TO GIVE A SPEECH THAT'D MAKE JOHN LEWIS PROUD.
BUT THAT'S MY VANITY, ISN'T IT, DINAH?
THAT'S ME PUTTING MYSELF AT THE CENTER OF A STORY THAT NEVER WANTED ME.
TIME TO GET BACK TO MY OWN.

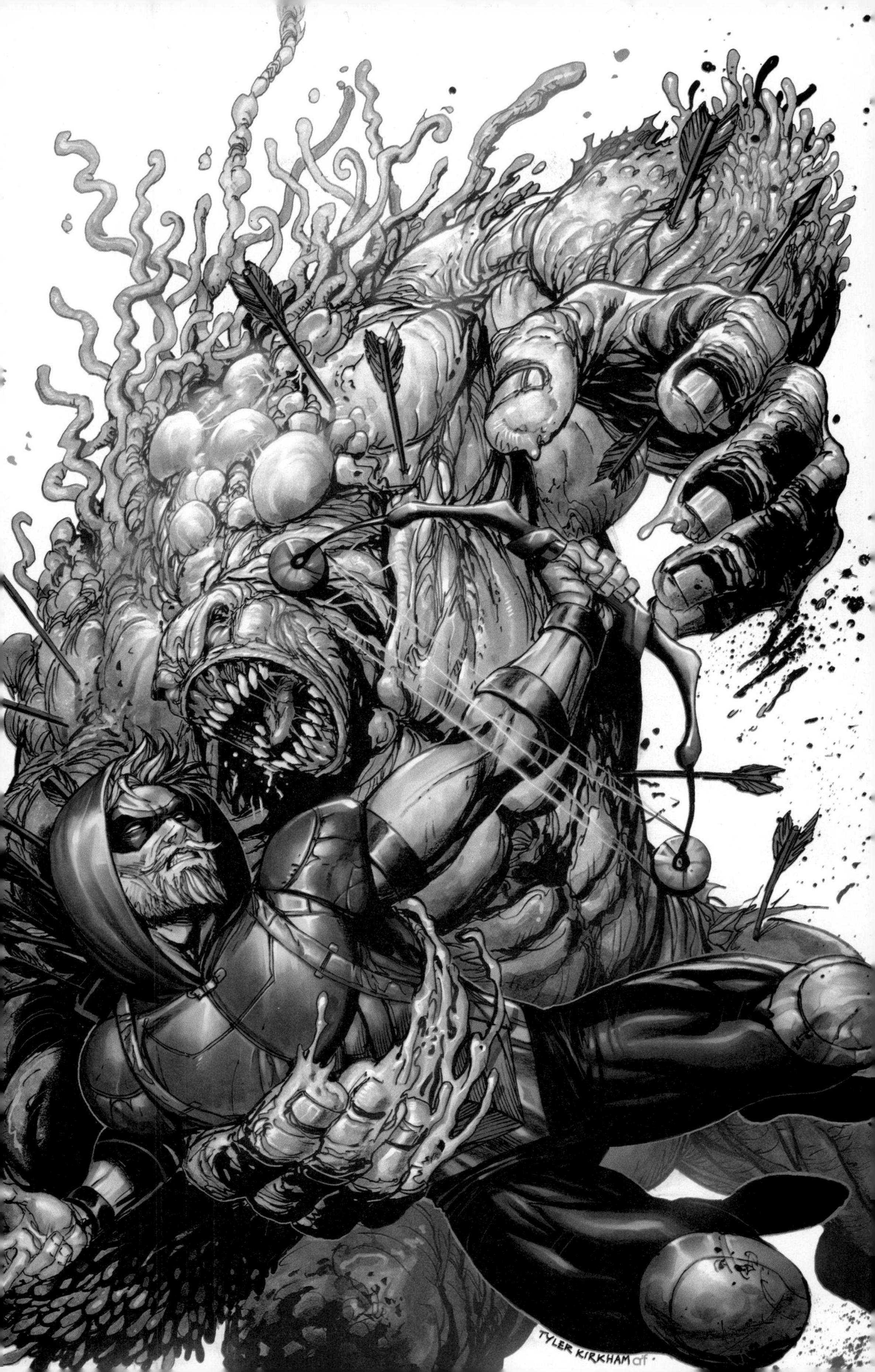
TYLER KIRKHAM

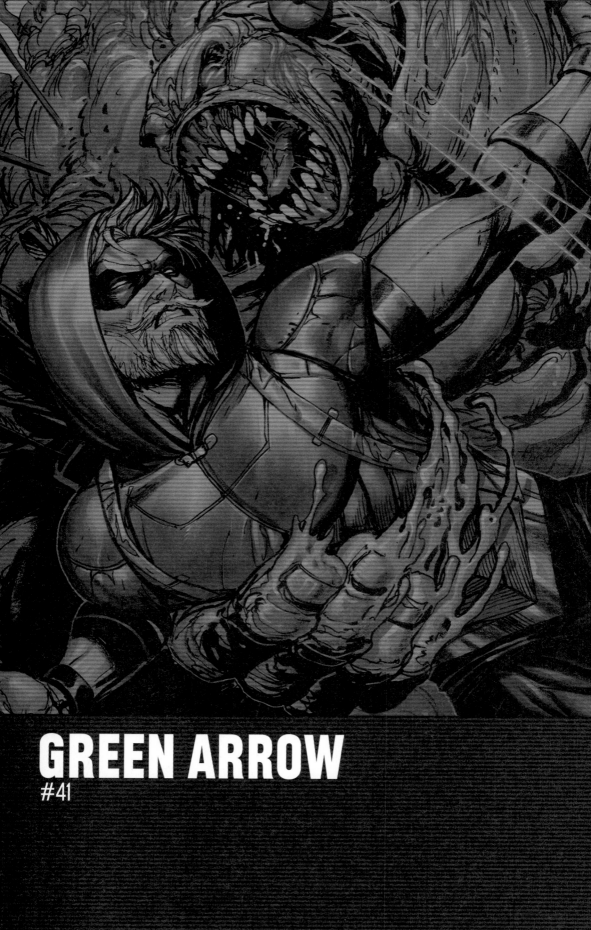

# GREEN ARROW
#41

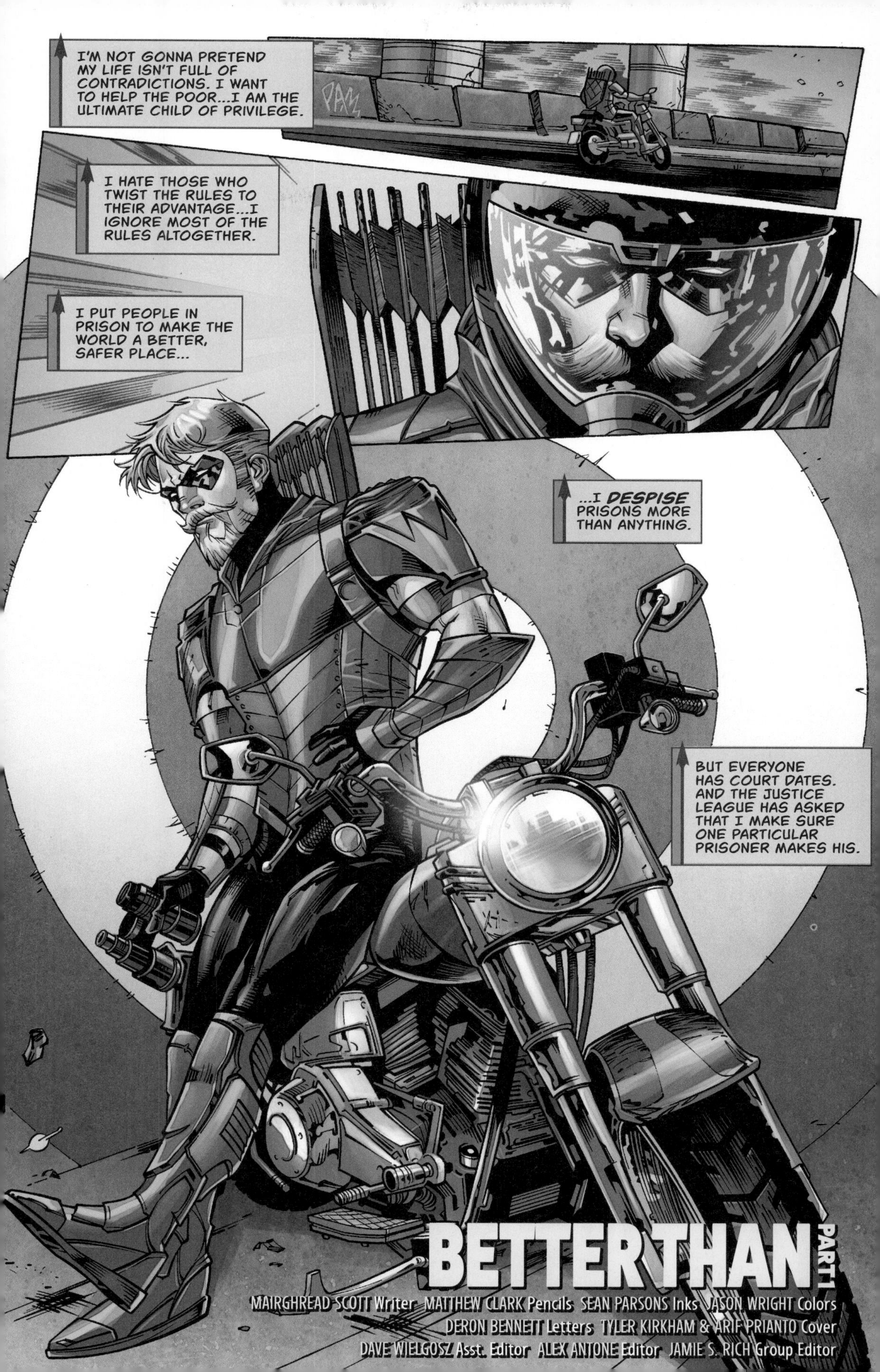

I'M NOT GONNA PRETEND MY LIFE ISN'T FULL OF CONTRADICTIONS. I WANT TO HELP THE POOR...I AM THE ULTIMATE CHILD OF PRIVILEGE.
I HATE THOSE WHO TWIST THE RULES TO THEIR ADVANTAGE...I IGNORE MOST OF THE RULES ALTOGETHER.
I PUT PEOPLE IN PRISON TO MAKE THE WORLD A BETTER, SAFER PLACE...
...I DESPISE PRISONS MORE THAN ANYTHING.
BUT EVERYONE HAS COURT DATES. AND THE JUSTICE LEAGUE HAS ASKED THAT I MAKE SURE ONE PARTICULAR PRISONER MAKES HIS.
BETTER THAN PART 1
MAIRGHREAD SCOTT Writer MATTHEW CLARK Pencils SEAN PARSONS Inks JASON WRIGHT Colors
DERON BENNETT Letters TYLER KIRKHAM & ARIF PRIANTO Cover
DAVE WIELGOSZ Asst. Editor ALEX ANTONE Editor JAMIE S. RICH Group Editor

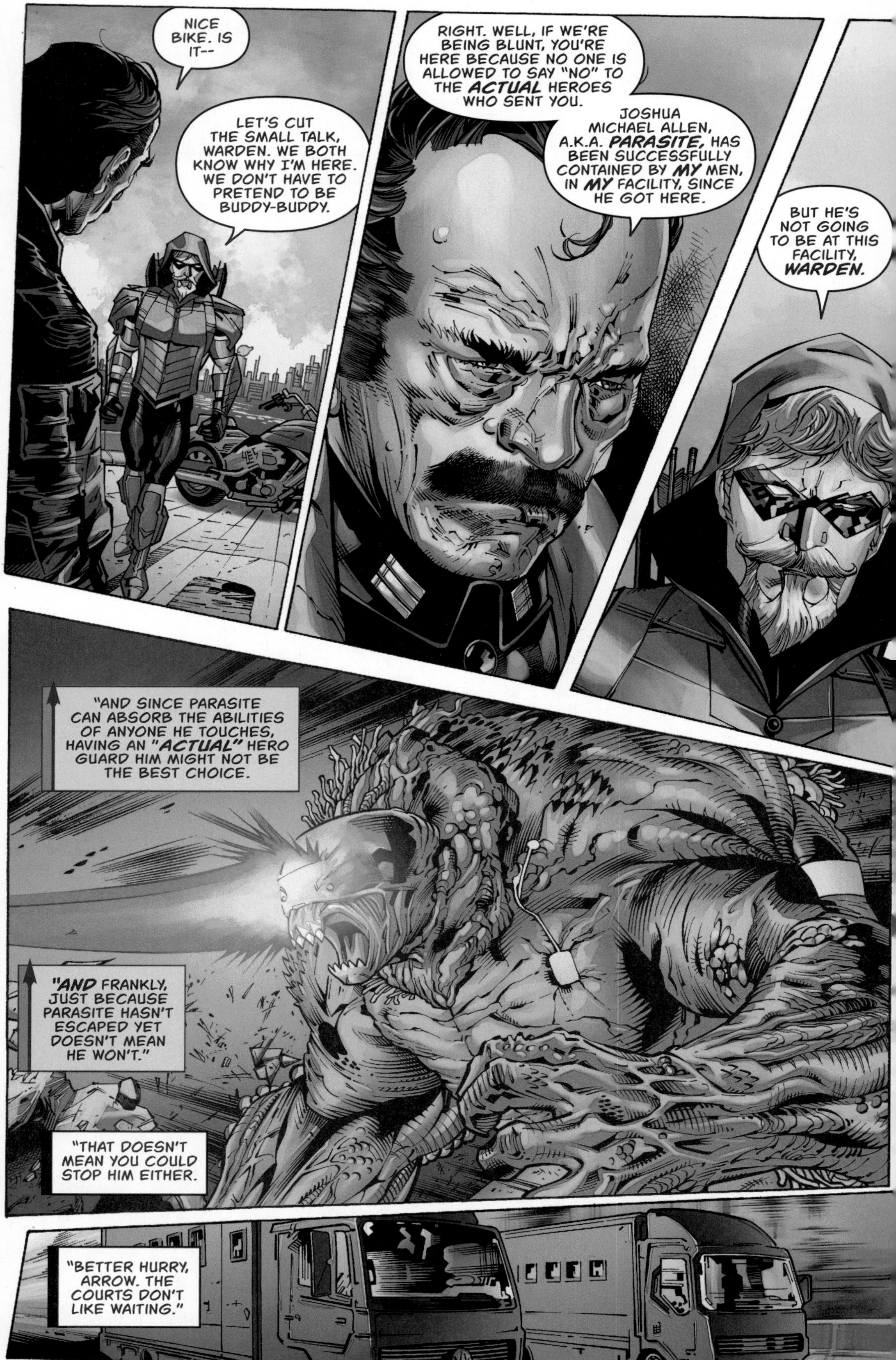
NICE BIKE. IS IT--
LET'S CUT THE SMALL TALK, WARDEN. WE BOTH KNOW WHY I'M HERE. WE DON'T HAVE TO PRETEND TO BE BUDDY-BUDDY.
RIGHT. WELL, IF WE'RE BEING BLUNT, YOU'RE HERE BECAUSE NO ONE IS ALLOWED TO SAY "NO" TO THE ACTUAL HEROES WHO SENT YOU.
JOSHUA MICHAEL ALLEN, A.K.A. PARASITE, HAS BEEN SUCCESSFULLY CONTAINED BY MY MEN, IN MY FACILITY, SINCE HE GOT HERE.
BUT HE'S NOT GOING TO BE AT THIS FACILITY, WARDEN.
"AND SINCE PARASITE CAN ABSORB THE ABILITIES OF ANYONE HE TOUCHES, HAVING AN "ACTUAL" HERO GUARD HIM MIGHT NOT BE THE BEST CHOICE.
"AND FRANKLY, JUST BECAUSE PARASITE HASN'T ESCAPED YET DOESN'T MEAN HE WON'T."
"THAT DOESN'T MEAN YOU COULD STOP HIM EITHER.
"BETTER HURRY, ARROW. THE COURTS DON'T LIKE WAITING."

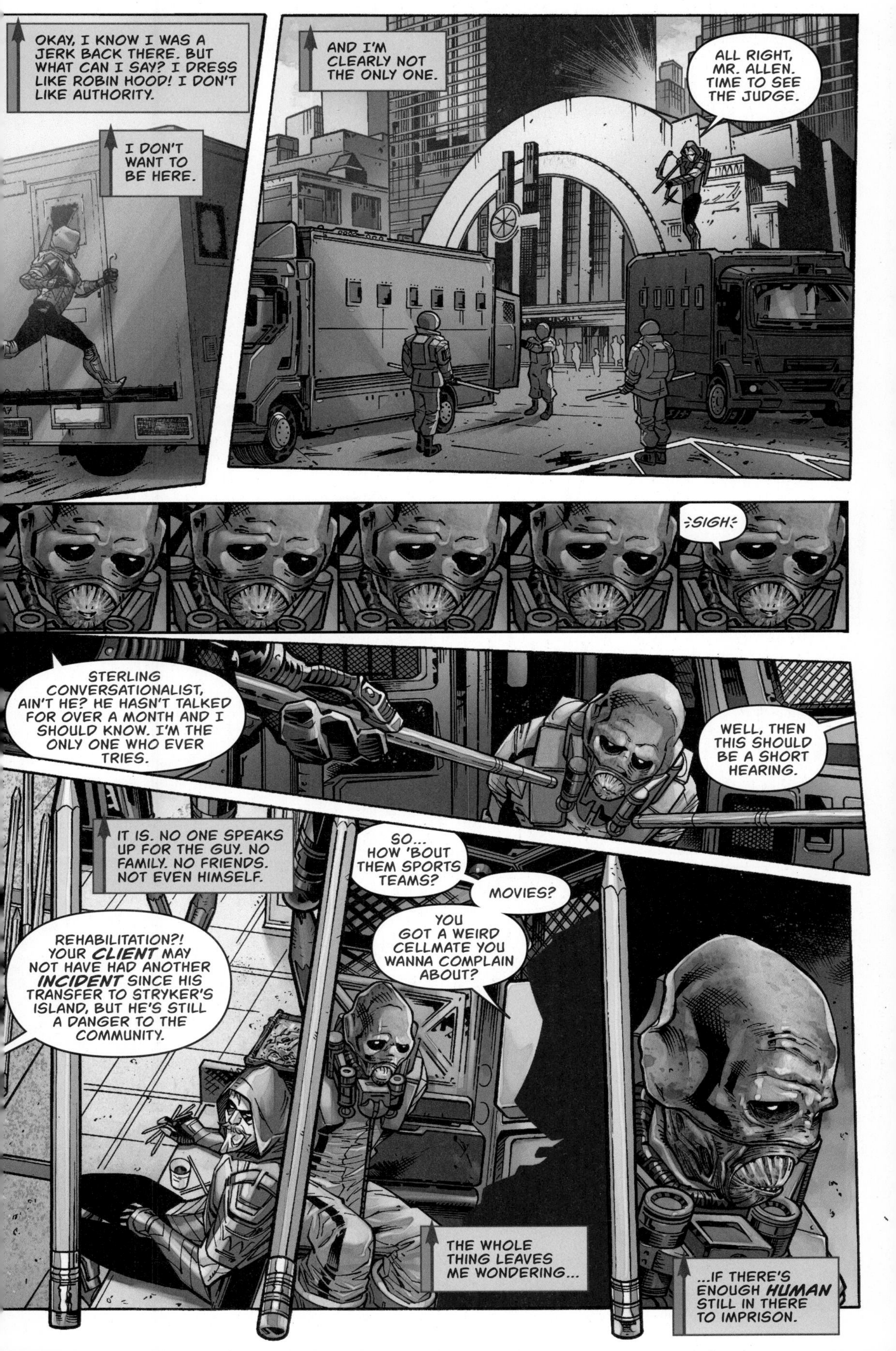
OKAY, I KNOW I WAS A JERK BACK THERE. BUT WHAT CAN I SAY? I DRESS LIKE ROBIN HOOD! I DON'T LIKE AUTHORITY.
I DON'T WANT TO BE HERE.
AND I'M CLEARLY NOT THE ONLY ONE.
ALL RIGHT, MR. ALLEN. TIME TO SEE THE JUDGE.
SIGH
STERLING CONVERSATIONALIST, AIN'T HE? HE HASN'T TALKED FOR OVER A MONTH AND I SHOULD KNOW. I'M THE ONLY ONE WHO EVER TRIES.
WELL, THEN THIS SHOULD BE A SHORT HEARING.
IT IS. NO ONE SPEAKS UP FOR THE GUY. NO FAMILY. NO FRIENDS. NOT EVEN HIMSELF.
SO... HOW 'BOUT THEM SPORTS TEAMS?
MOVIES?
YOU GOT A WEIRD CELLMATE YOU WANNA COMPLAIN ABOUT?
REHABILITATION?! YOUR CLIENT MAY NOT HAVE HAD ANOTHER INCIDENT SINCE HIS TRANSFER TO STRYKER'S ISLAND, BUT HE'S STILL A DANGER TO THE COMMUNITY.
THE WHOLE THING LEAVES ME WONDERING...
...IF THERE'S ENOUGH HUMAN STILL IN THERE TO IMPRISON.

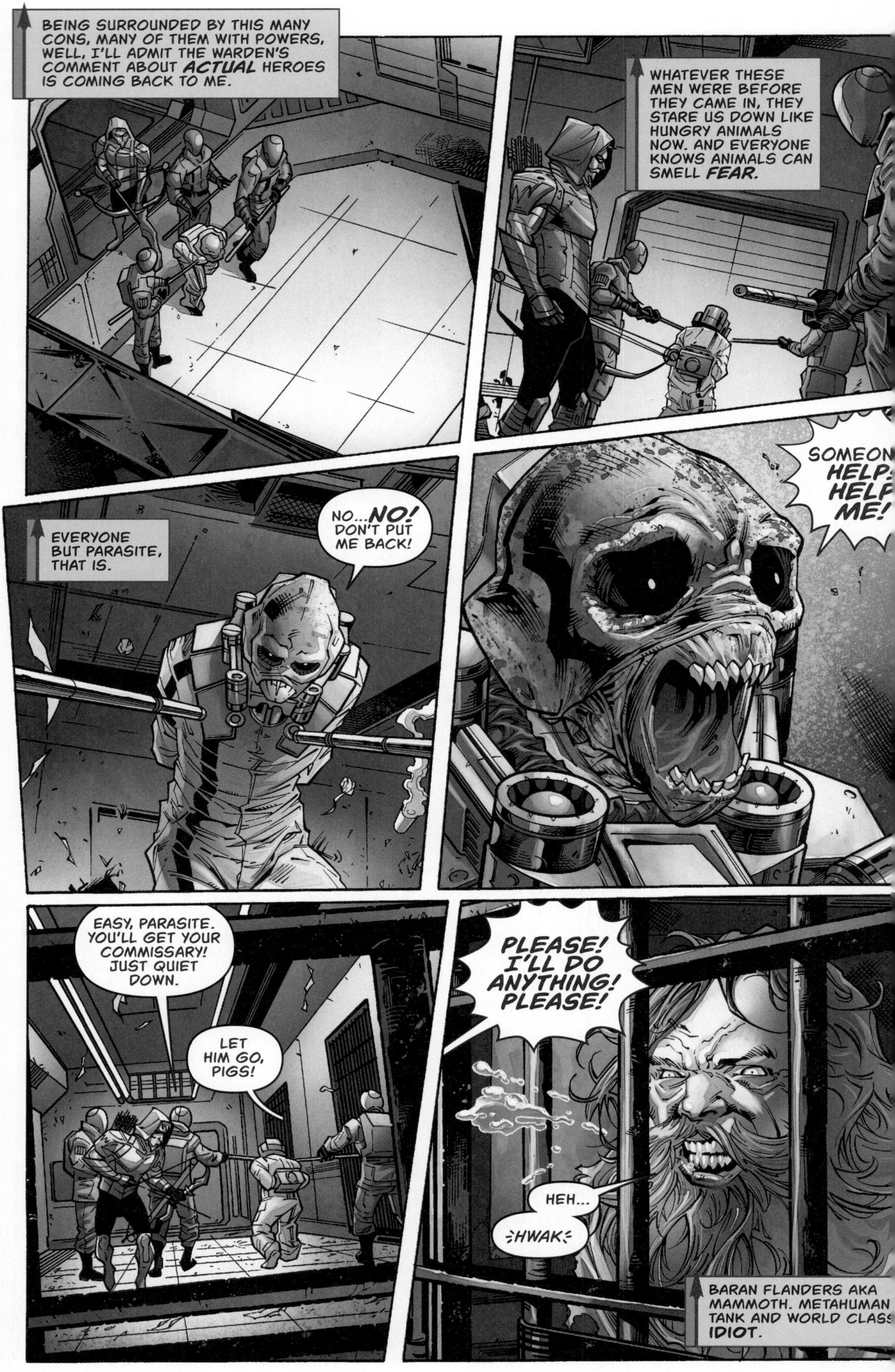
BEING SURROUNDED BY THIS MANY CONS, MANY OF THEM WITH POWERS, WELL, I'LL ADMIT THE WARDEN'S COMMENT ABOUT ACTUAL HEROES IS COMING BACK TO ME.
WHATEVER THESE MEN WERE BEFORE THEY CAME IN, THEY STARE US DOWN LIKE HUNGRY ANIMALS NOW. AND EVERYONE KNOWS ANIMALS CAN SMELL FEAR.
EVERYONE BUT PARASITE, THAT IS.
NO...NO! DON'T PUT ME BACK!
EASY, PARASITE. YOU'LL GET YOUR COMMISSARY! JUST QUIET DOWN.
LET HIM GO, PIGS!
PLEASE! I'LL DO ANYTHING! PLEASE!
HEH...
HWAK
BARAN FLANDERS AKA MAMMOTH. METAHUMAN TANK AND WORLD CLASS IDIOT.

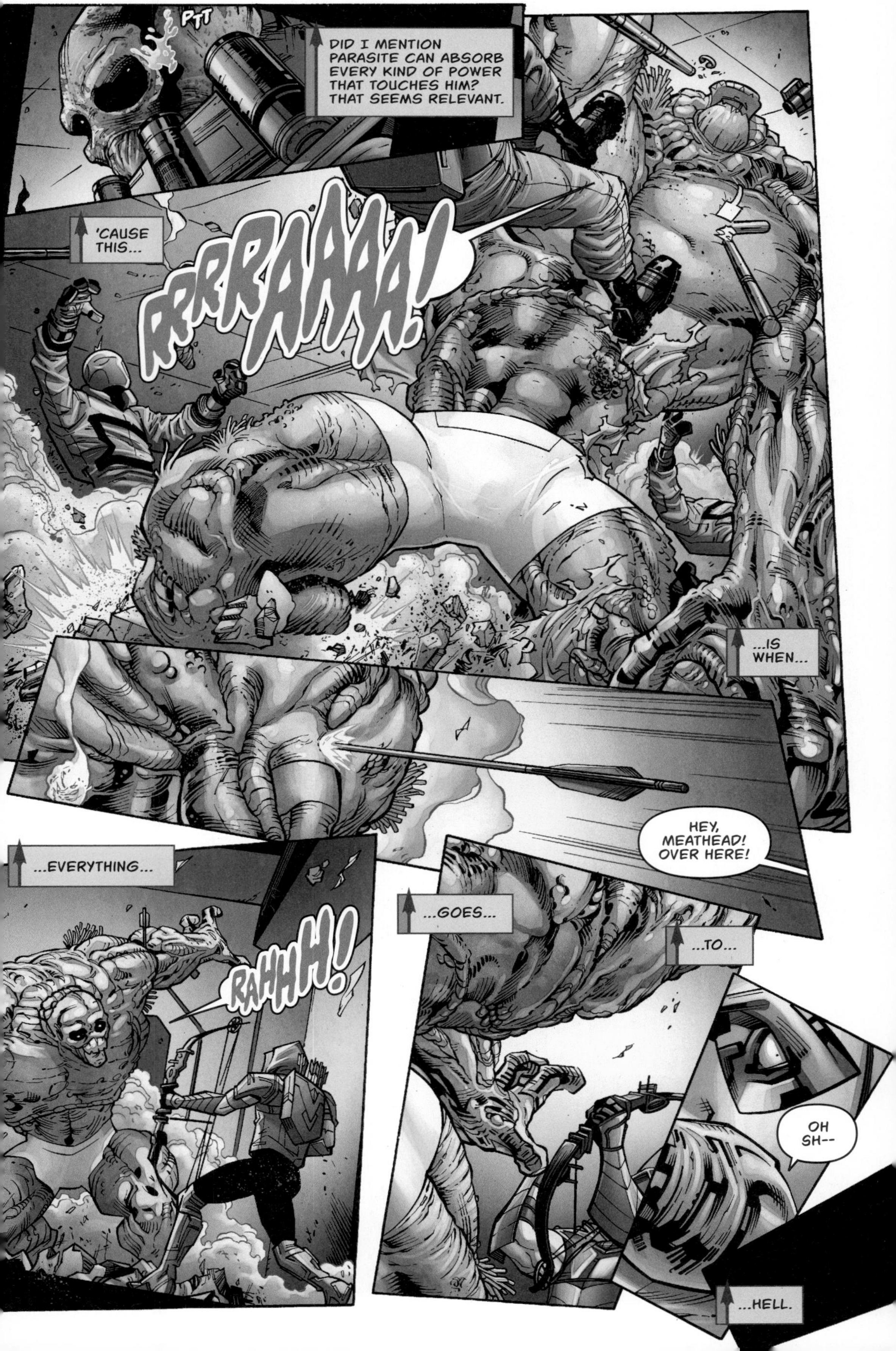
PTT
DID I MENTION PARASITE CAN ABSORB EVERY KIND OF POWER THAT TOUCHES HIM? THAT SEEMS RELEVANT.
'CAUSE THIS...
RRRRAAAA!
...IS WHEN...
HEY, MEATHEAD! OVER HERE!
...EVERYTHING...
RAHHH!
...GOES...
...TO...
OH SH--
...HELL.

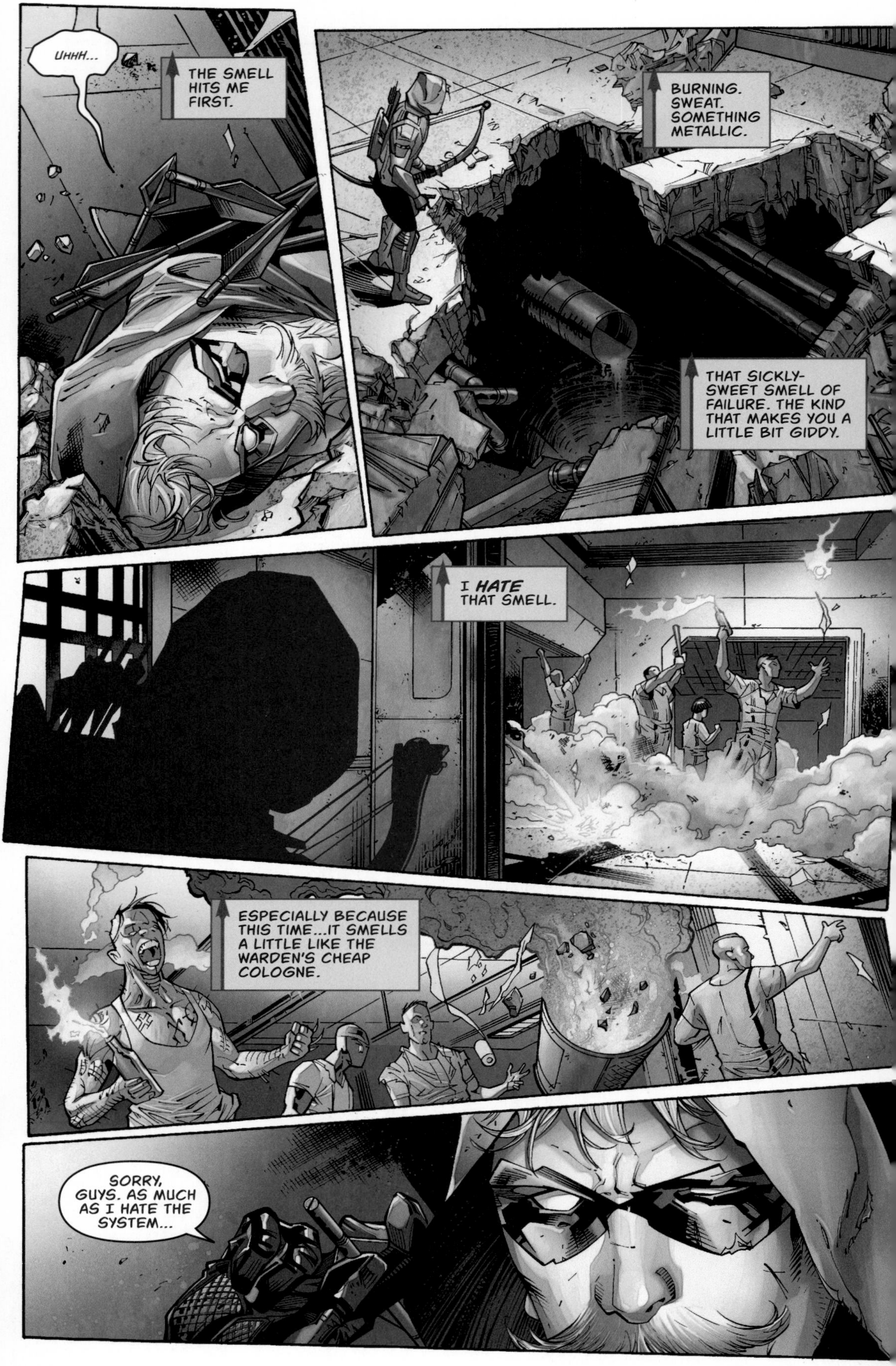
UHHH...
THE SMELL HITS ME FIRST.
BURNING. SWEAT. SOMETHING METALLIC.
THAT SICKLY-SWEET SMELL OF FAILURE. THE KIND THAT MAKES YOU A LITTLE BIT GIDDY.
I HATE THAT SMELL.
ESPECIALLY BECAUSE THIS TIME...IT SMELLS A LITTLE LIKE THE WARDEN'S CHEAP COLOGNE.
SORRY, GUYS. AS MUCH AS I HATE THE SYSTEM...

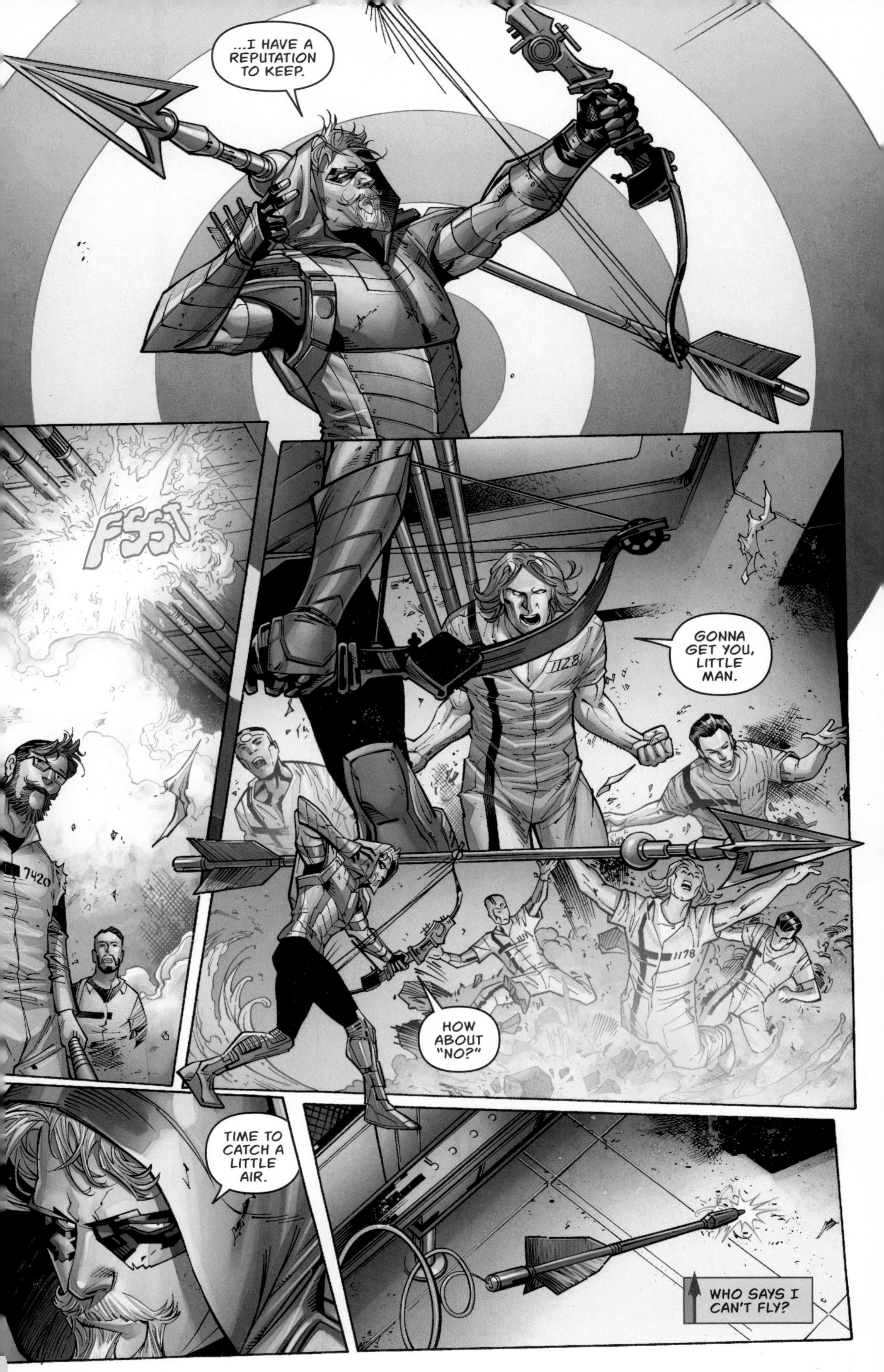
...I HAVE A REPUTATION TO KEEP.
FSST
GONNA GET YOU, LITTLE MAN.
HOW ABOUT "NO?"
TIME TO CATCH A LITTLE AIR.
WHO SAYS I CAN'T FLY?

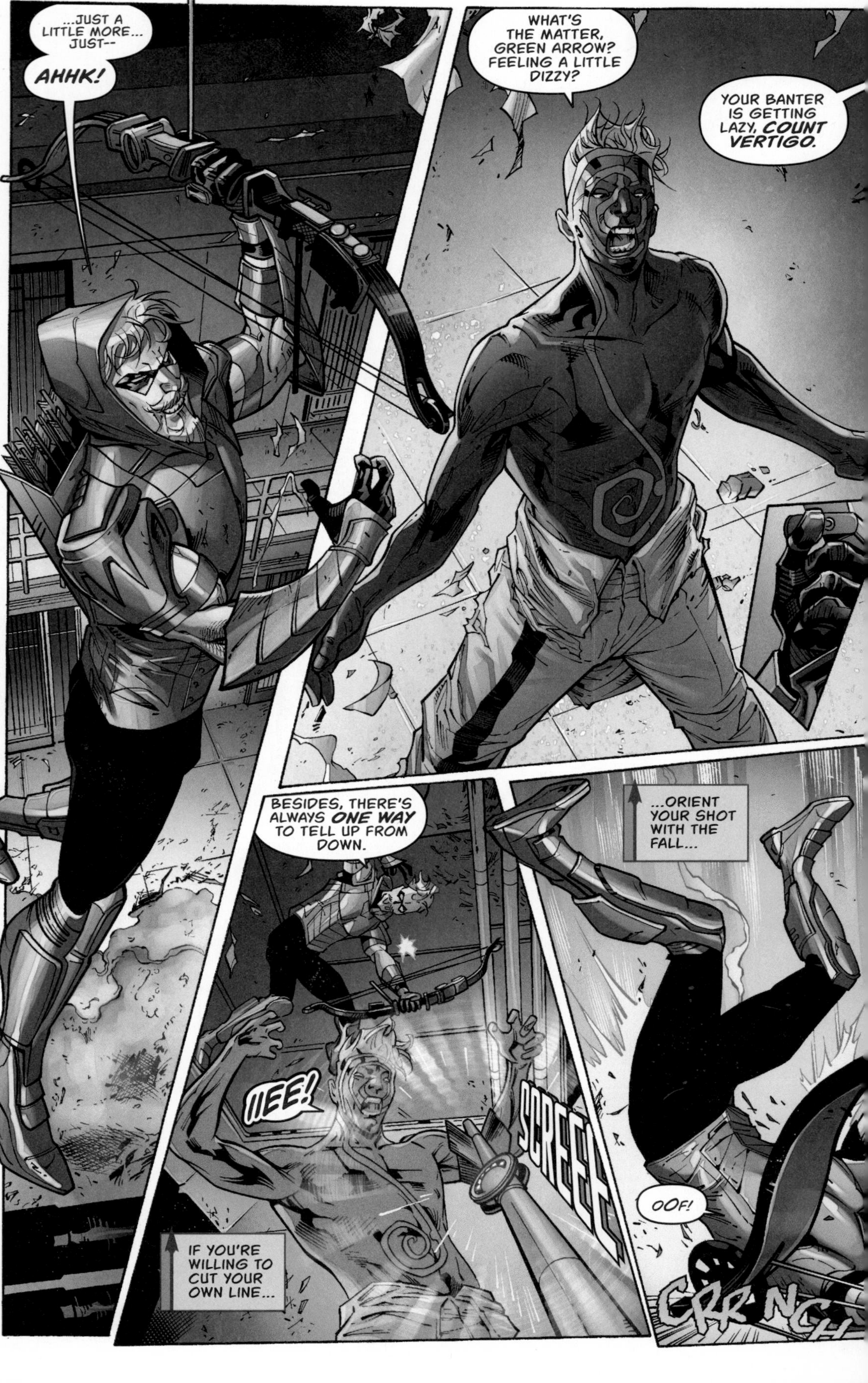

...JUST A LITTLE MORE... JUST--
AHHK!
WHAT'S THE MATTER, GREEN ARROW? FEELING A LITTLE DIZZY?
YOUR BANTER IS GETTING LAZY, COUNT VERTIGO.
BESIDES, THERE'S ALWAYS ONE WAY TO TELL UP FROM DOWN.
IIEE!
SCREEEE
IF YOU'RE WILLING TO CUT YOUR OWN LINE...
...ORIENT YOUR SHOT WITH THE FALL...
OOF!
CRRNCH

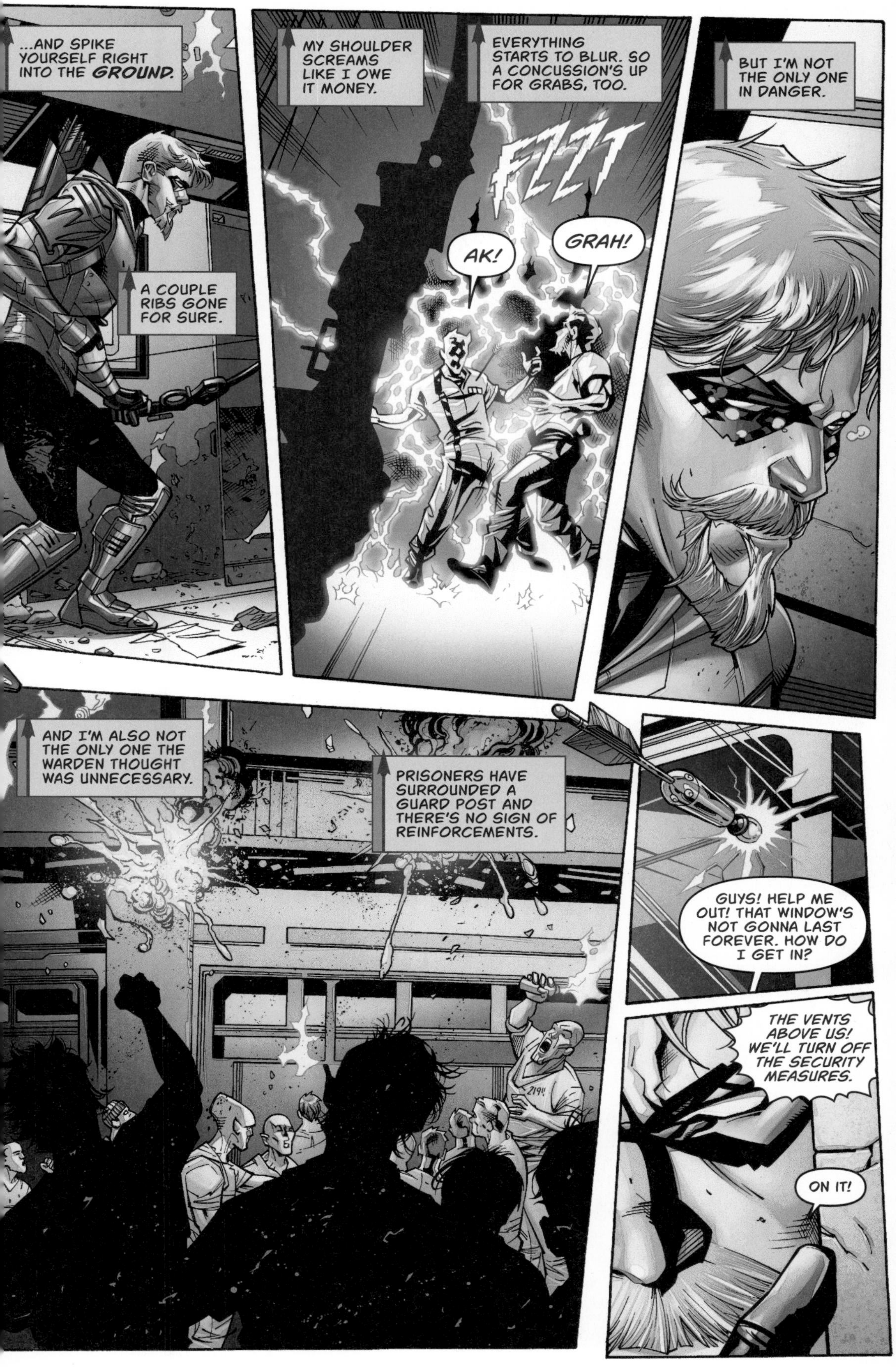
...AND SPIKE YOURSELF RIGHT INTO THE GROUND.
A COUPLE RIBS GONE FOR SURE.
MY SHOULDER SCREAMS LIKE I OWE IT MONEY.
EVERYTHING STARTS TO BLUR. SO A CONCUSSION'S UP FOR GRABS, TOO.
FZZT
AK!
GRAH!
BUT I'M NOT THE ONLY ONE IN DANGER.
AND I'M ALSO NOT THE ONLY ONE THE WARDEN THOUGHT WAS UNNECESSARY.
PRISONERS HAVE SURROUNDED A GUARD POST AND THERE'S NO SIGN OF REINFORCEMENTS.
GUYS! HELP ME OUT! THAT WINDOW'S NOT GONNA LAST FOREVER. HOW DO I GET IN?
THE VENTS ABOVE US! WE'LL TURN OFF THE SECURITY MEASURES.
ON IT!

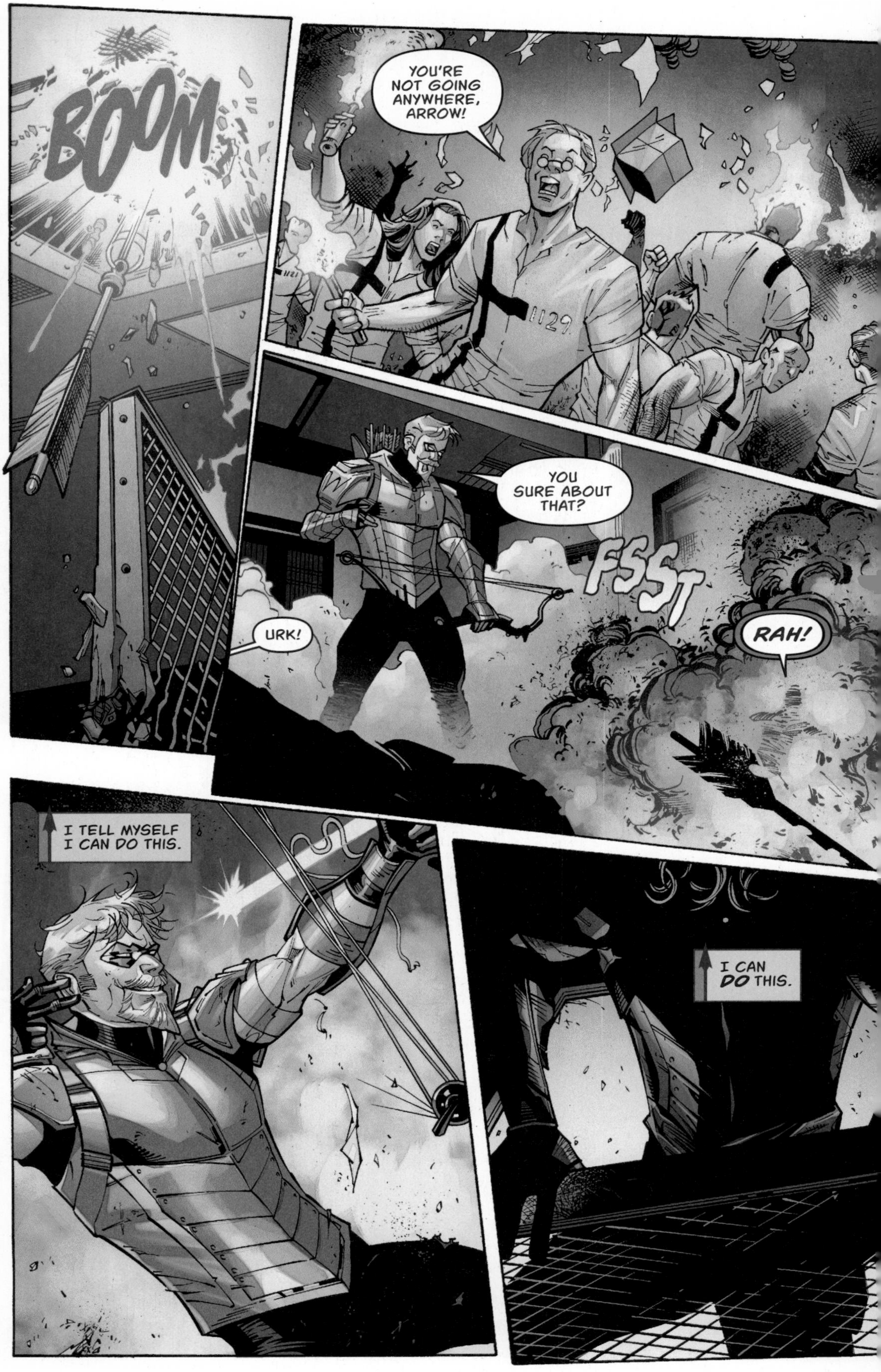
BOOM
YOU'RE NOT GOING ANYWHERE, ARROW!
1129
YOU SURE ABOUT THAT?
FSST
URK!
RAH!
I TELL MYSELF I CAN DO THIS.
I CAN *DO* THIS.

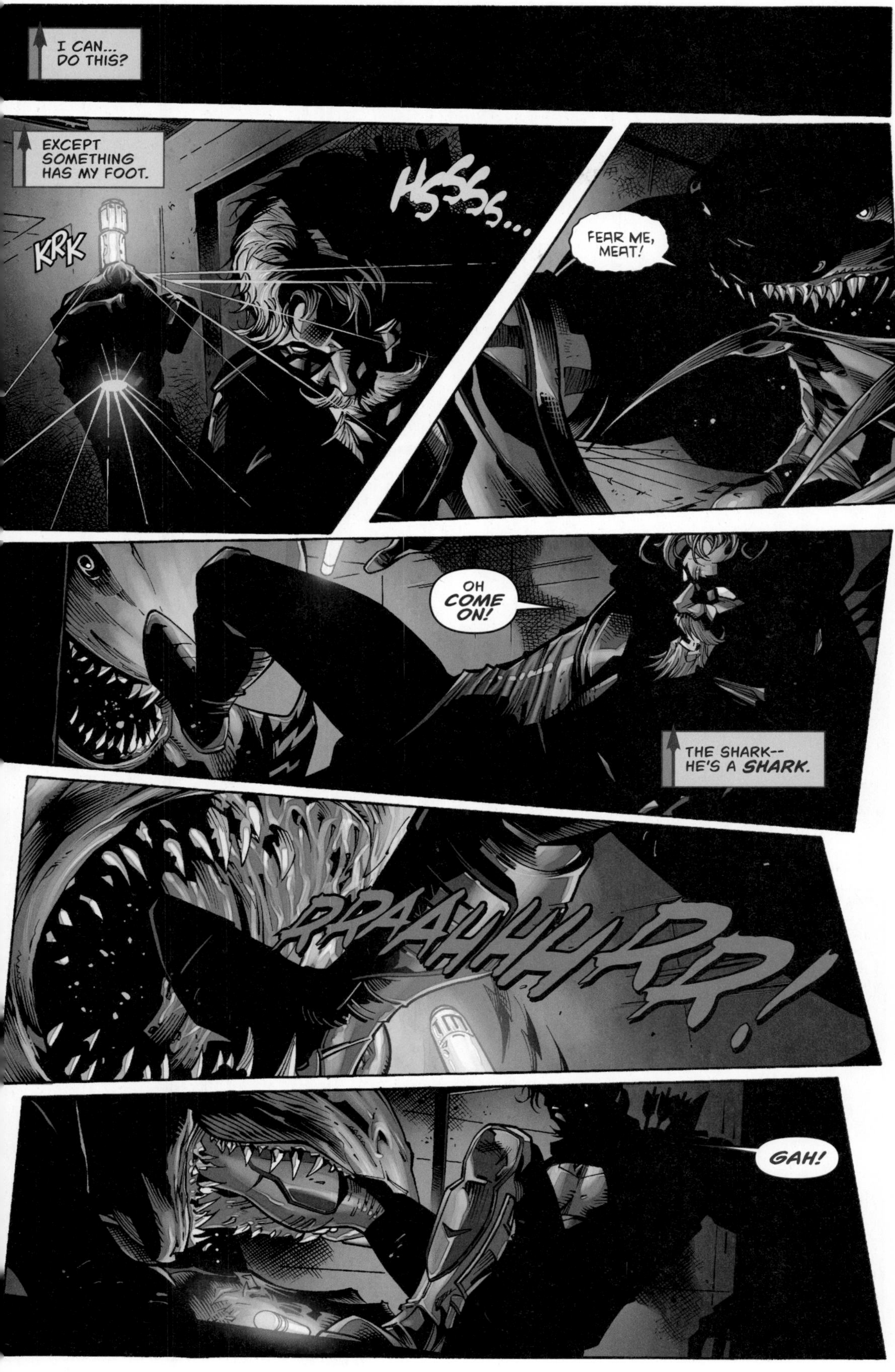
I CAN... DO THIS?
EXCEPT SOMETHING HAS MY FOOT.
KRK
HSSSS...
FEAR ME, MEAT!
OH COME ON!
THE SHARK-- HE'S A SHARK.
RRAAHHHRR!
GAH!

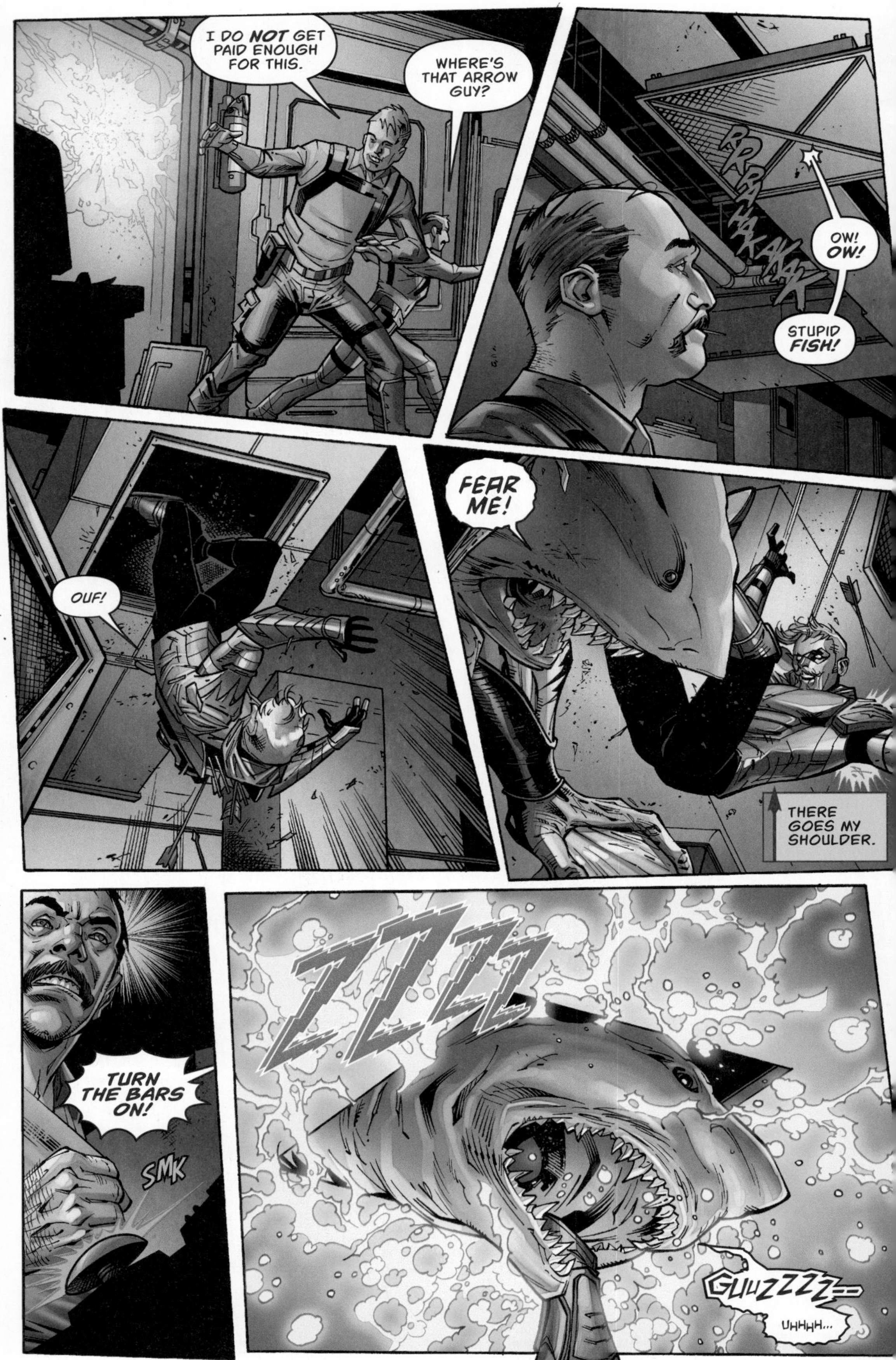
I DO NOT GET PAID ENOUGH FOR THIS.
WHERE'S THAT ARROW GUY?
PRRRAKAKAKAK
OW! OW!
STUPID FISH!
OUF!
FEAR ME!
THERE GOES MY SHOULDER.
TURN THE BARS ON!
SMK
ZZZZ
GUUZZZZ--
UHHHH...

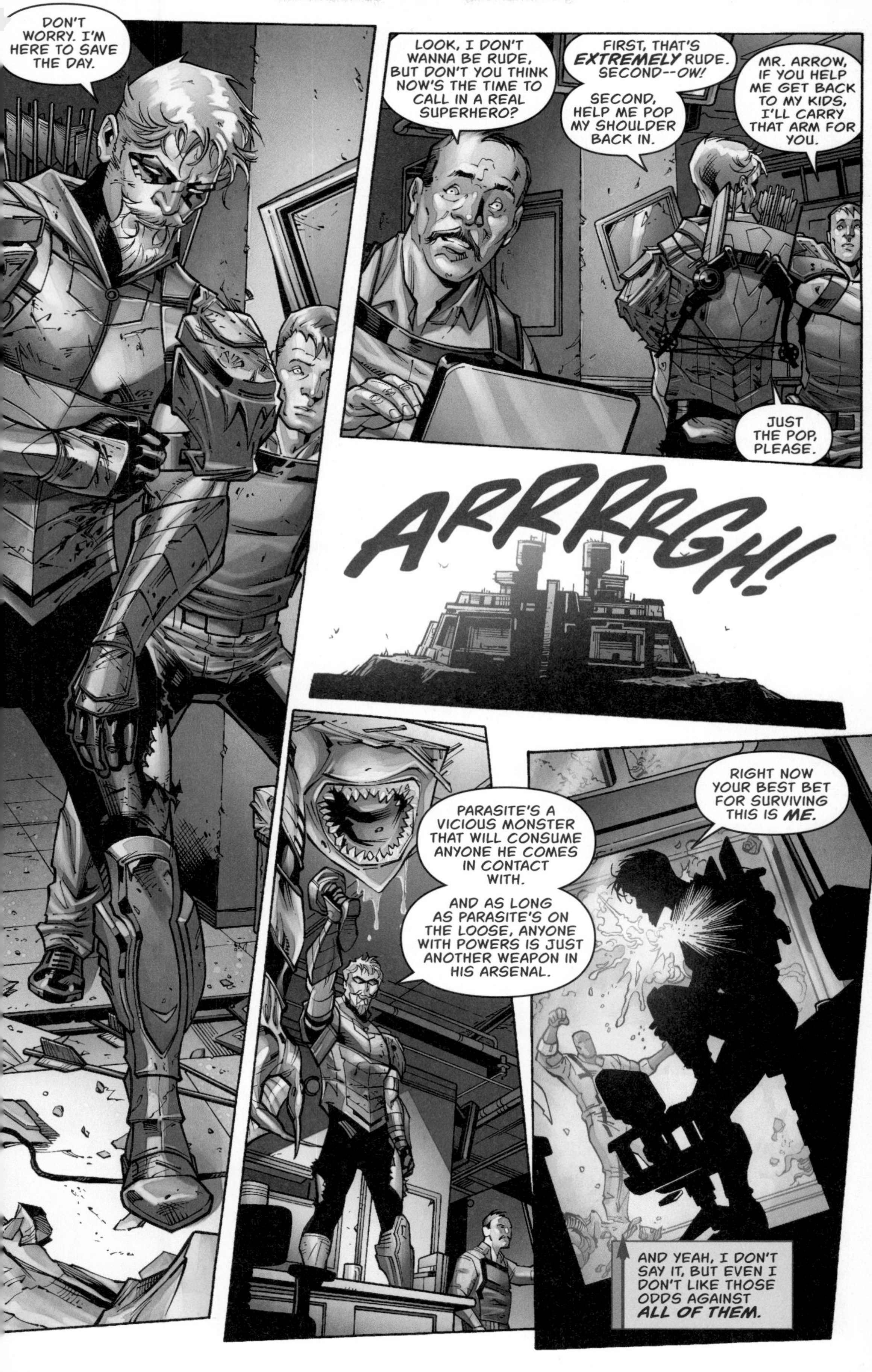
DON'T WORRY. I'M HERE TO SAVE THE DAY.
LOOK, I DON'T WANNA BE RUDE, BUT DON'T YOU THINK NOW'S THE TIME TO CALL IN A REAL SUPERHERO?
FIRST, THAT'S EXTREMELY RUDE. SECOND--OW!
SECOND, HELP ME POP MY SHOULDER BACK IN.
MR. ARROW, IF YOU HELP ME GET BACK TO MY KIDS, I'LL CARRY THAT ARM FOR YOU.
JUST THE POP, PLEASE.
ARRRRGH!
PARASITE'S A VICIOUS MONSTER THAT WILL CONSUME ANYONE HE COMES IN CONTACT WITH.
AND AS LONG AS PARASITE'S ON THE LOOSE, ANYONE WITH POWERS IS JUST ANOTHER WEAPON IN HIS ARSENAL.
RIGHT NOW YOUR BEST BET FOR SURVIVING THIS IS ME.
AND YEAH, I DON'T SAY IT, BUT EVEN I DON'T LIKE THOSE ODDS AGAINST ALL OF THEM.

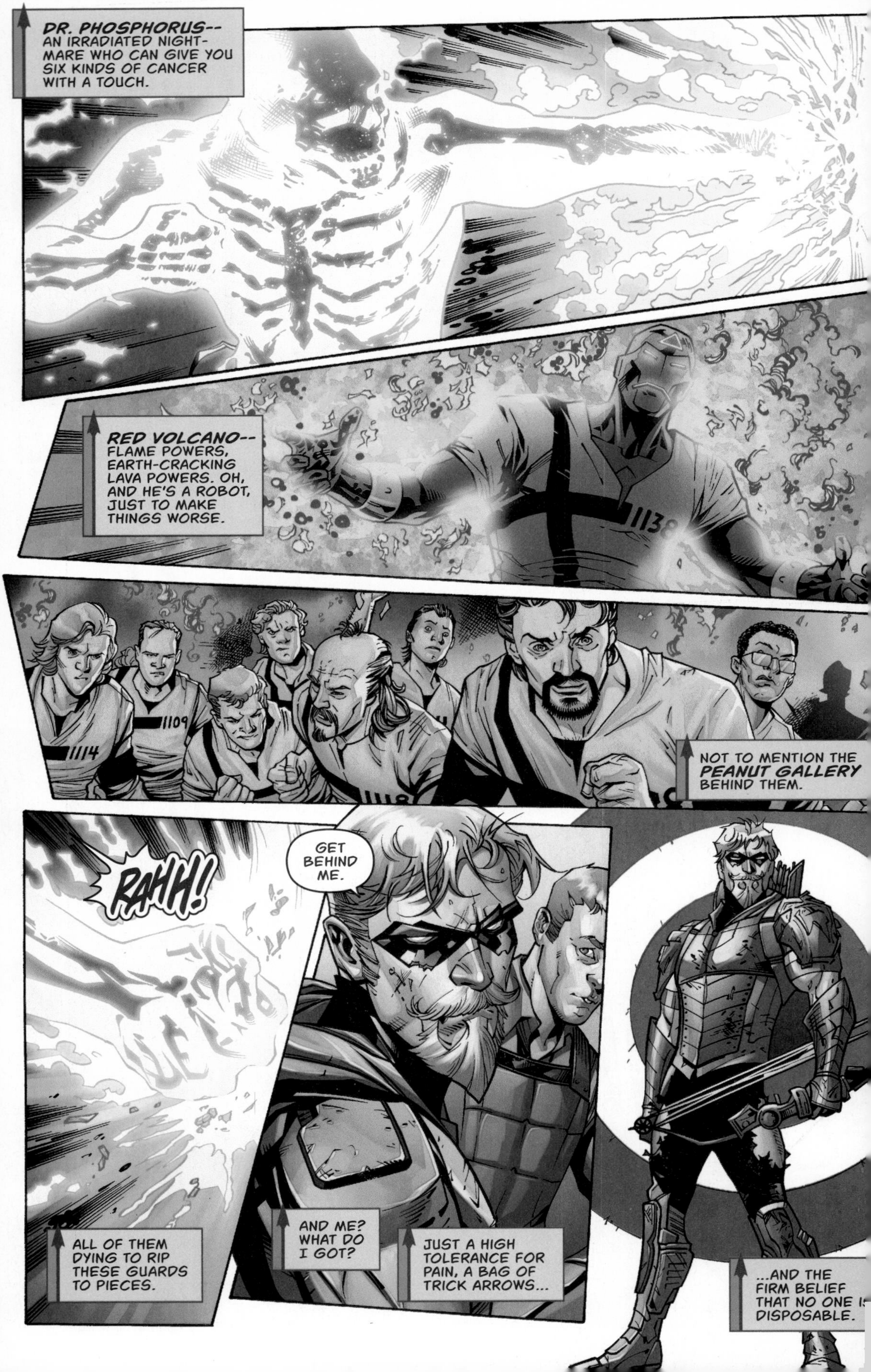
DR. PHOSPHORUS-- AN IRRADIATED NIGHTMARE WHO CAN GIVE YOU SIX KINDS OF CANCER WITH A TOUCH.
RED VOLCANO-- FLAME POWERS, EARTH-CRACKING LAVA POWERS. OH, AND HE'S A ROBOT, JUST TO MAKE THINGS WORSE.
1138
1114
1109
NOT TO MENTION THE PEANUT GALLERY BEHIND THEM.
RAHH!
GET BEHIND ME.
ALL OF THEM DYING TO RIP THESE GUARDS TO PIECES.
AND ME? WHAT DO I GOT?
JUST A HIGH TOLERANCE FOR PAIN, A BAG OF TRICK ARROWS...
...AND THE FIRM BELIEF THAT NO ONE IS DISPOSABLE.

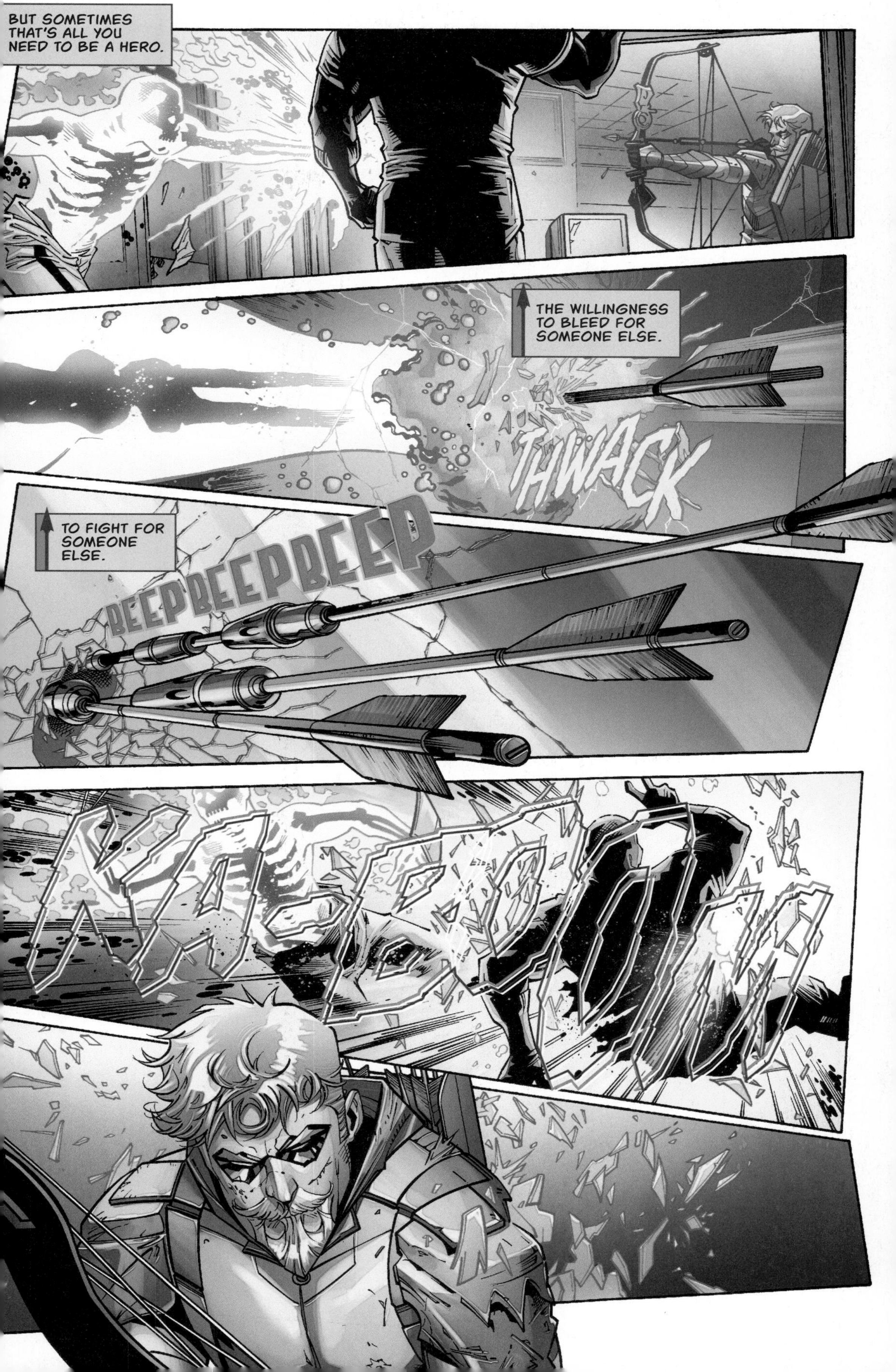
BUT SOMETIMES THAT'S ALL YOU NEED TO BE A HERO.
THE WILLINGNESS TO BLEED FOR SOMEONE ELSE.
THWACK
TO FIGHT FOR SOMEONE ELSE.
BEEPBEEPBEEP
KA-BOOM

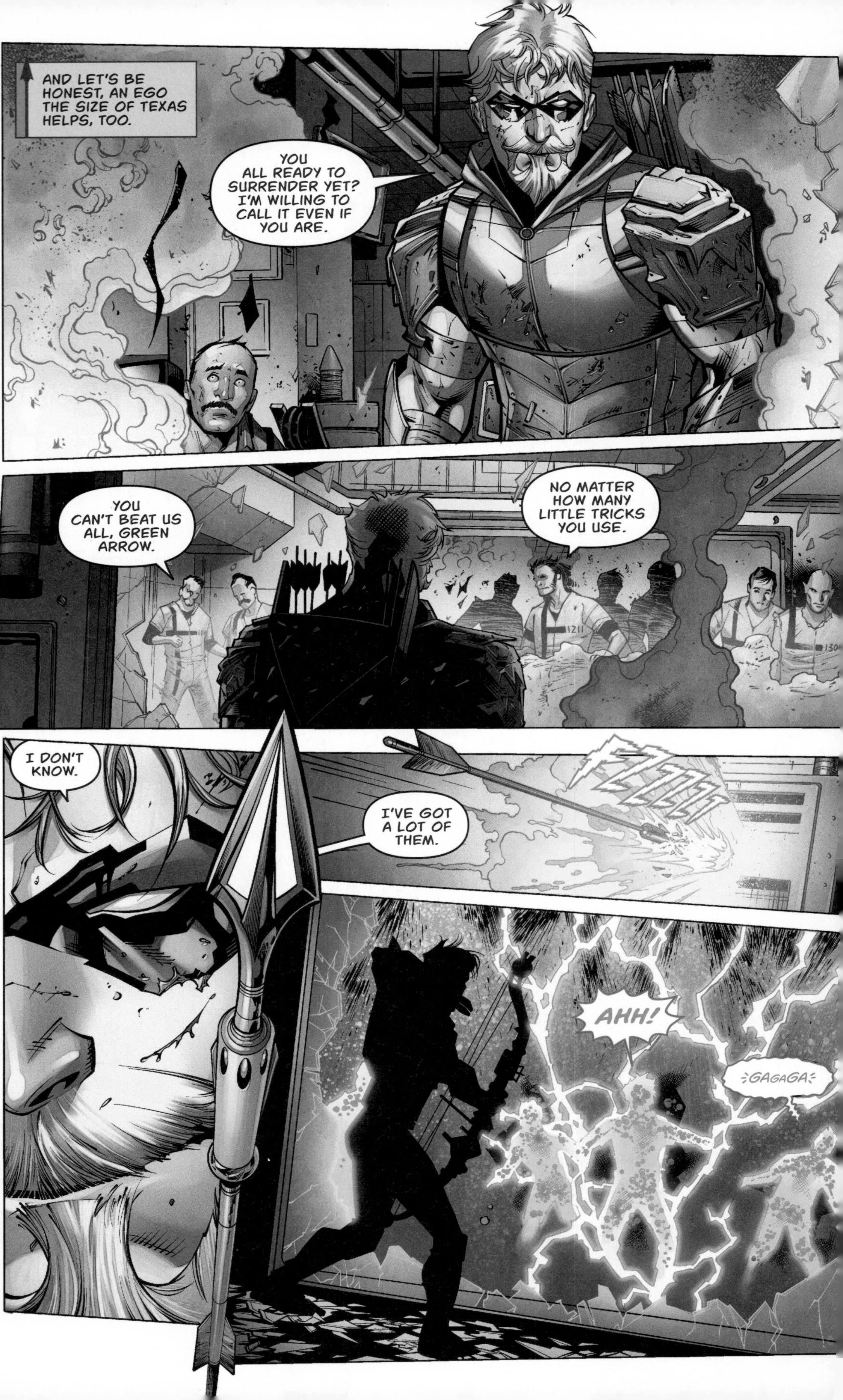
AND LET'S BE HONEST, AN EGO THE SIZE OF TEXAS HELPS, TOO.
YOU ALL READY TO SURRENDER YET? I'M WILLING TO CALL IT EVEN IF YOU ARE.
YOU CAN'T BEAT US ALL, GREEN ARROW.
NO MATTER HOW MANY LITTLE TRICKS YOU USE.
I DON'T KNOW.
I'VE GOT A LOT OF THEM.
AHH!
GAGAGA

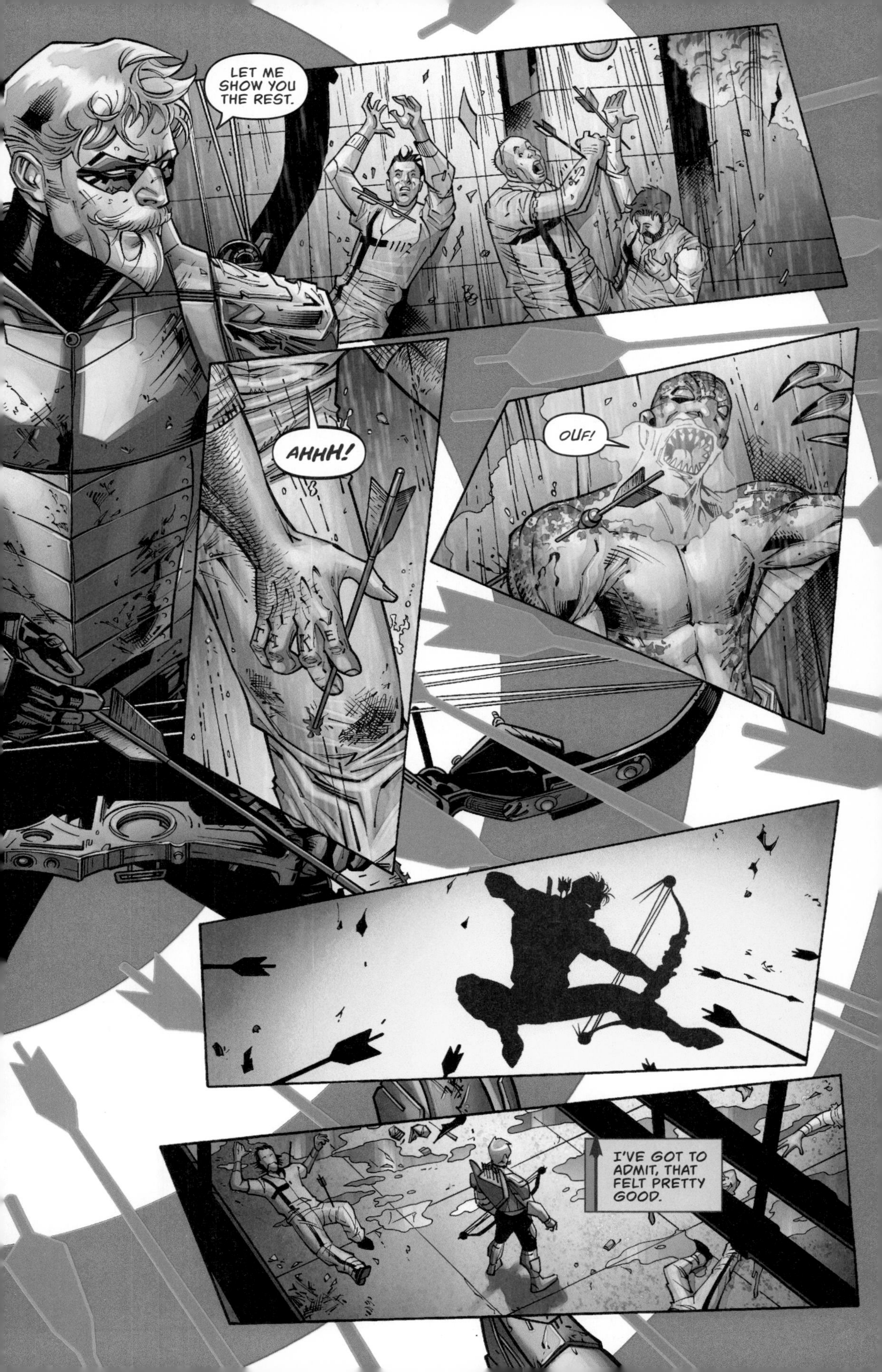

LET ME SHOW YOU THE REST.
AHHH!
OUF!
I'VE GOT TO ADMIT, THAT FELT PRETTY GOOD.

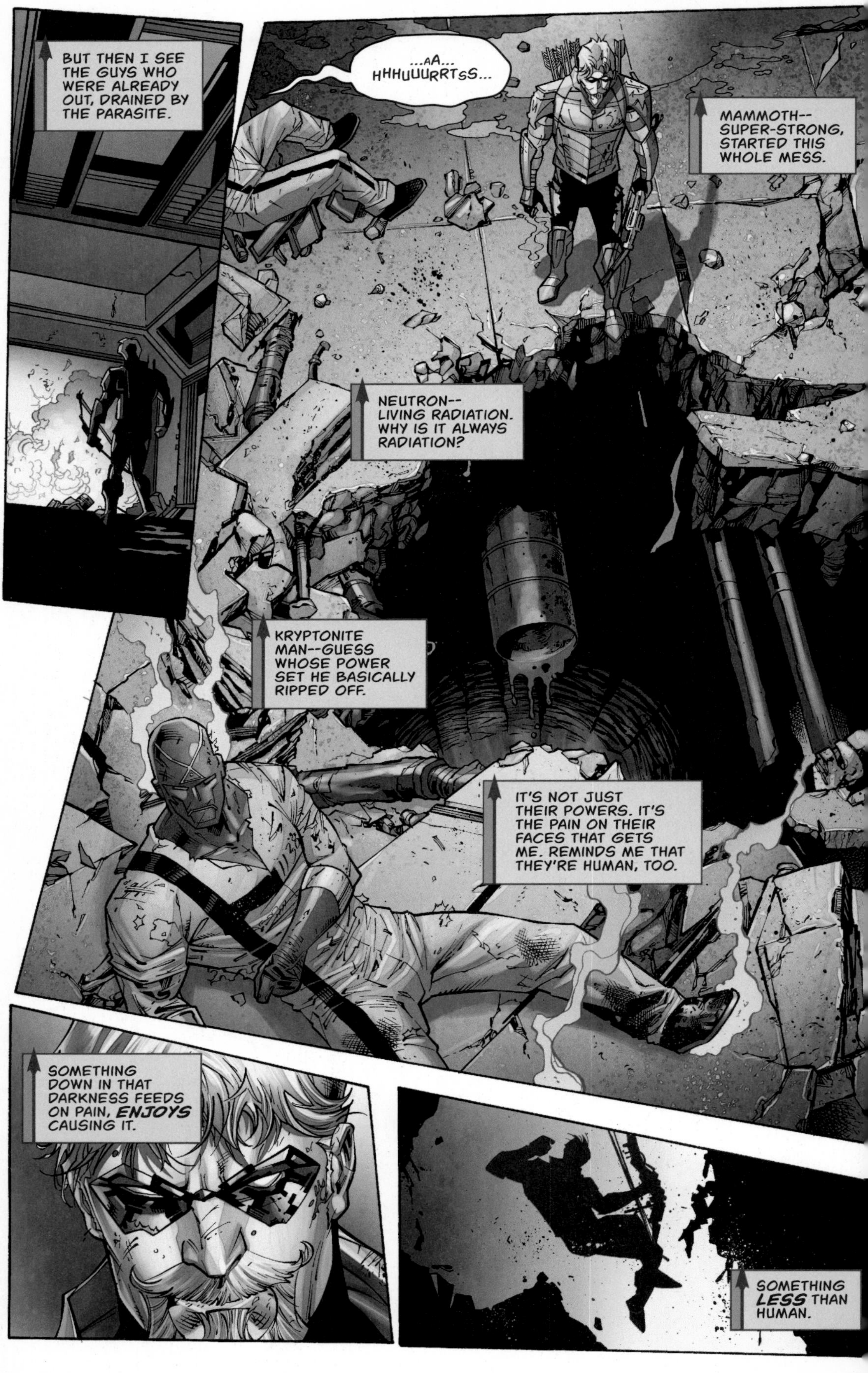

BUT THEN I SEE THE GUYS WHO WERE ALREADY OUT, DRAINED BY THE PARASITE.
...AA... HHHUUURRTSS...
MAMMOTH-- SUPER-STRONG, STARTED THIS WHOLE MESS.
NEUTRON-- LIVING RADIATION. WHY IS IT ALWAYS RADIATION?
KRYPTONITE MAN--GUESS WHOSE POWER SET HE BASICALLY RIPPED OFF.
IT'S NOT JUST THEIR POWERS. IT'S THE PAIN ON THEIR FACES THAT GETS ME. REMINDS ME THAT THEY'RE HUMAN, TOO.
SOMETHING DOWN IN THAT DARKNESS FEEDS ON PAIN, ENJOYS CAUSING IT.
SOMETHING LESS THAN HUMAN.

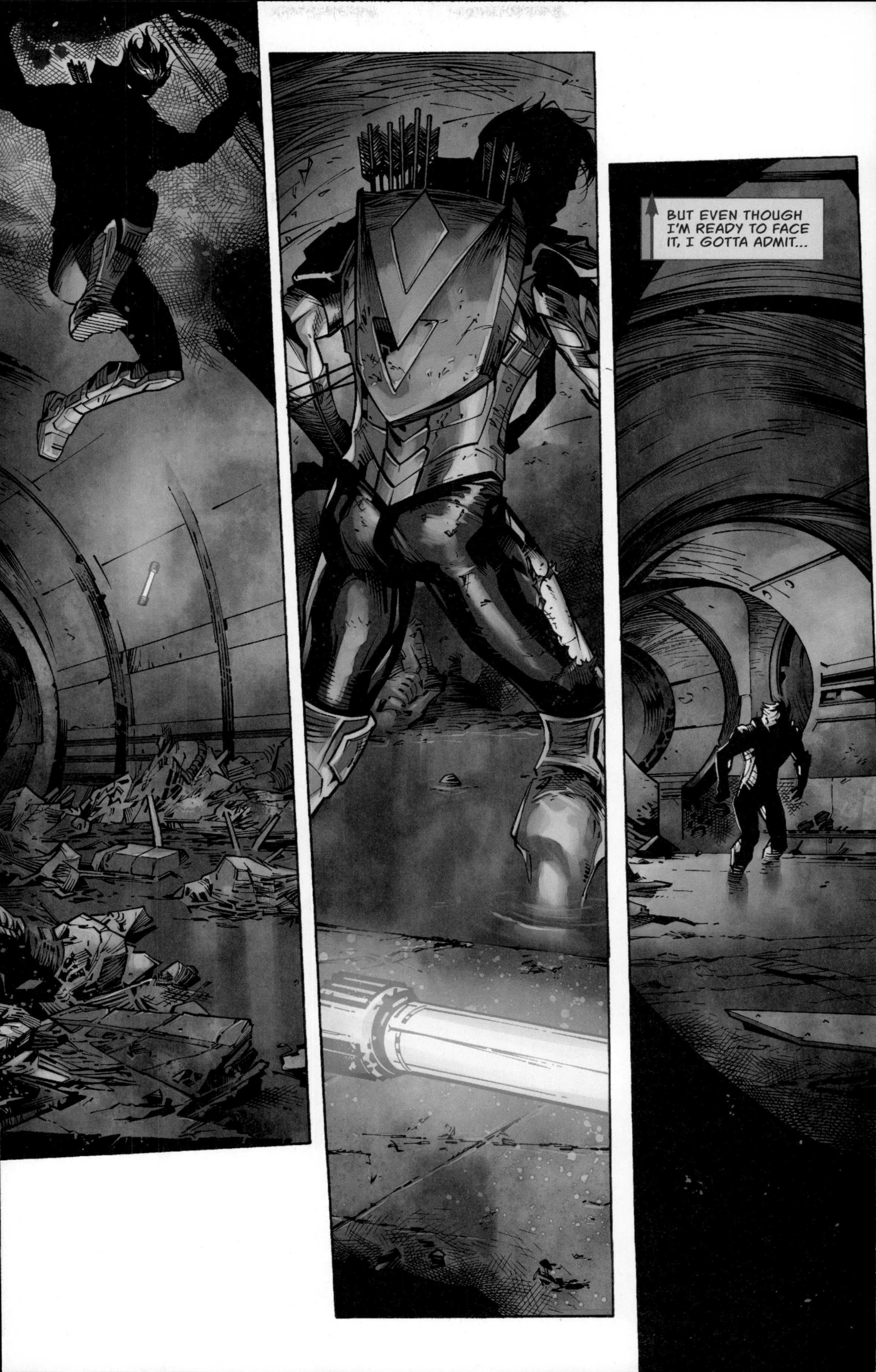
BUT EVEN THOUGH I'M READY TO FACE IT, I GOTTA ADMIT...

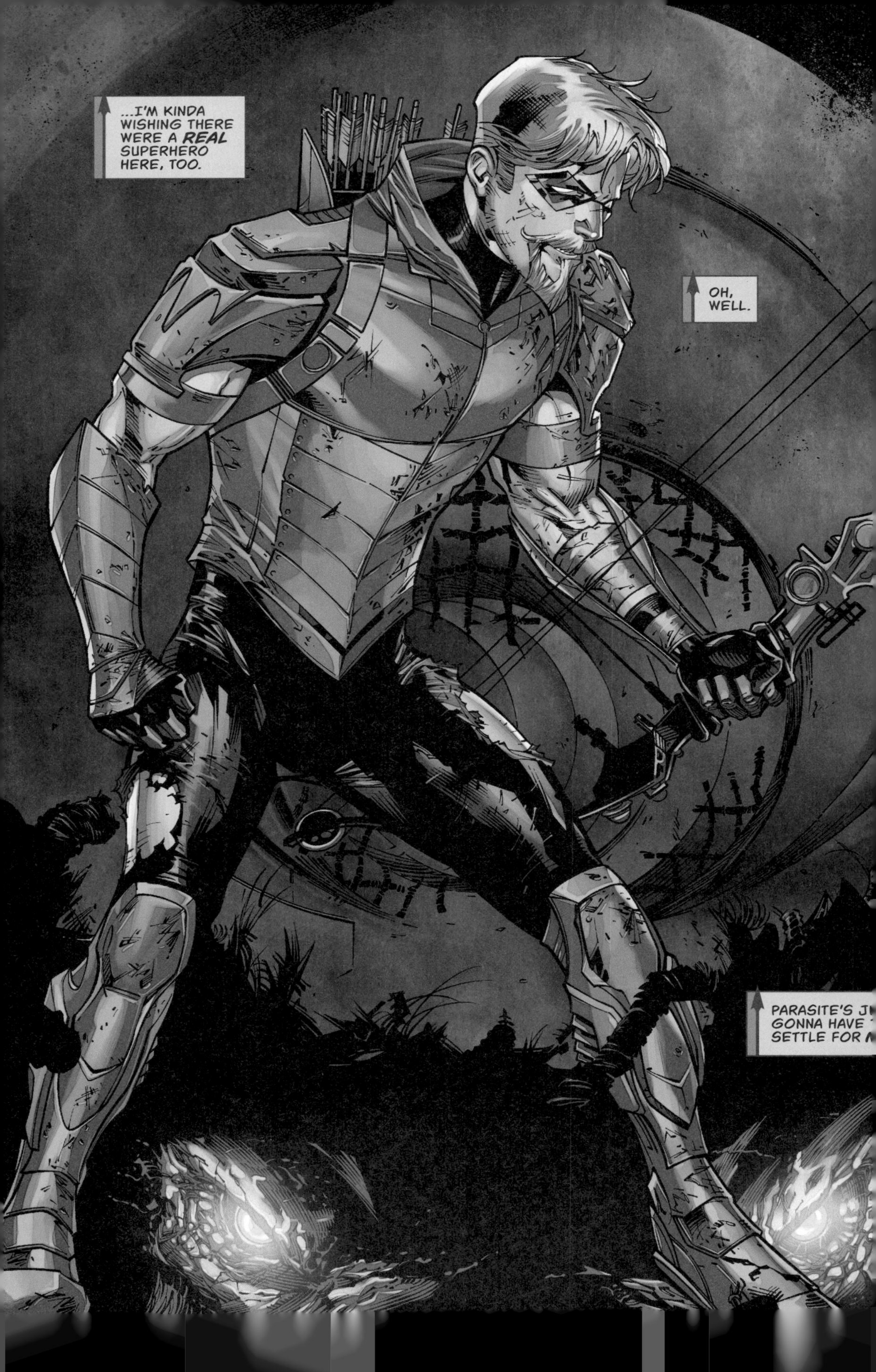
...I'M KINDA WISHING THERE WERE A REAL SUPERHERO HERE, TOO.
OH, WELL.
PARASITE'S J
GONNA HAVE
SETTLE FOR

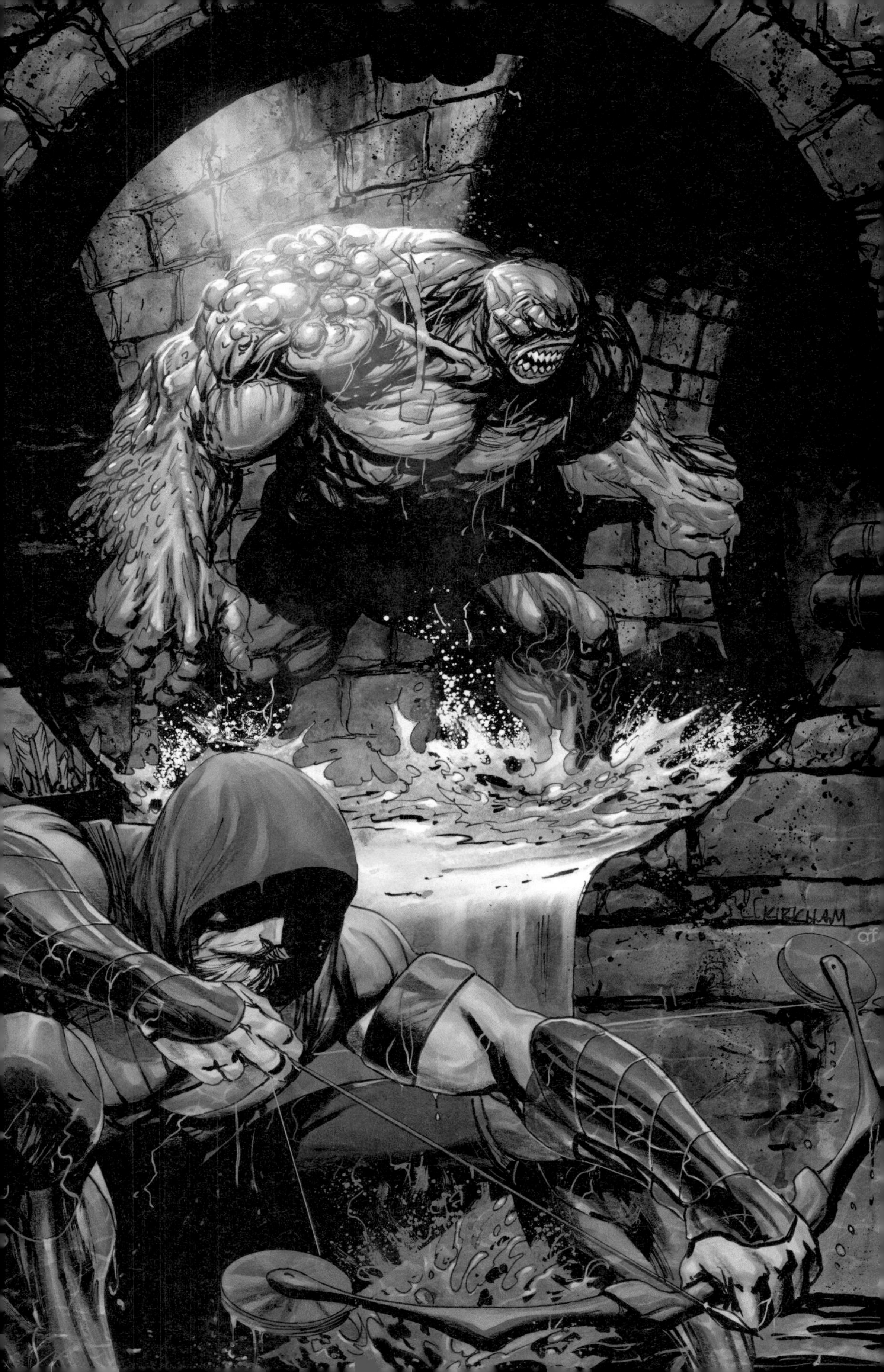
KIRKHAM
af

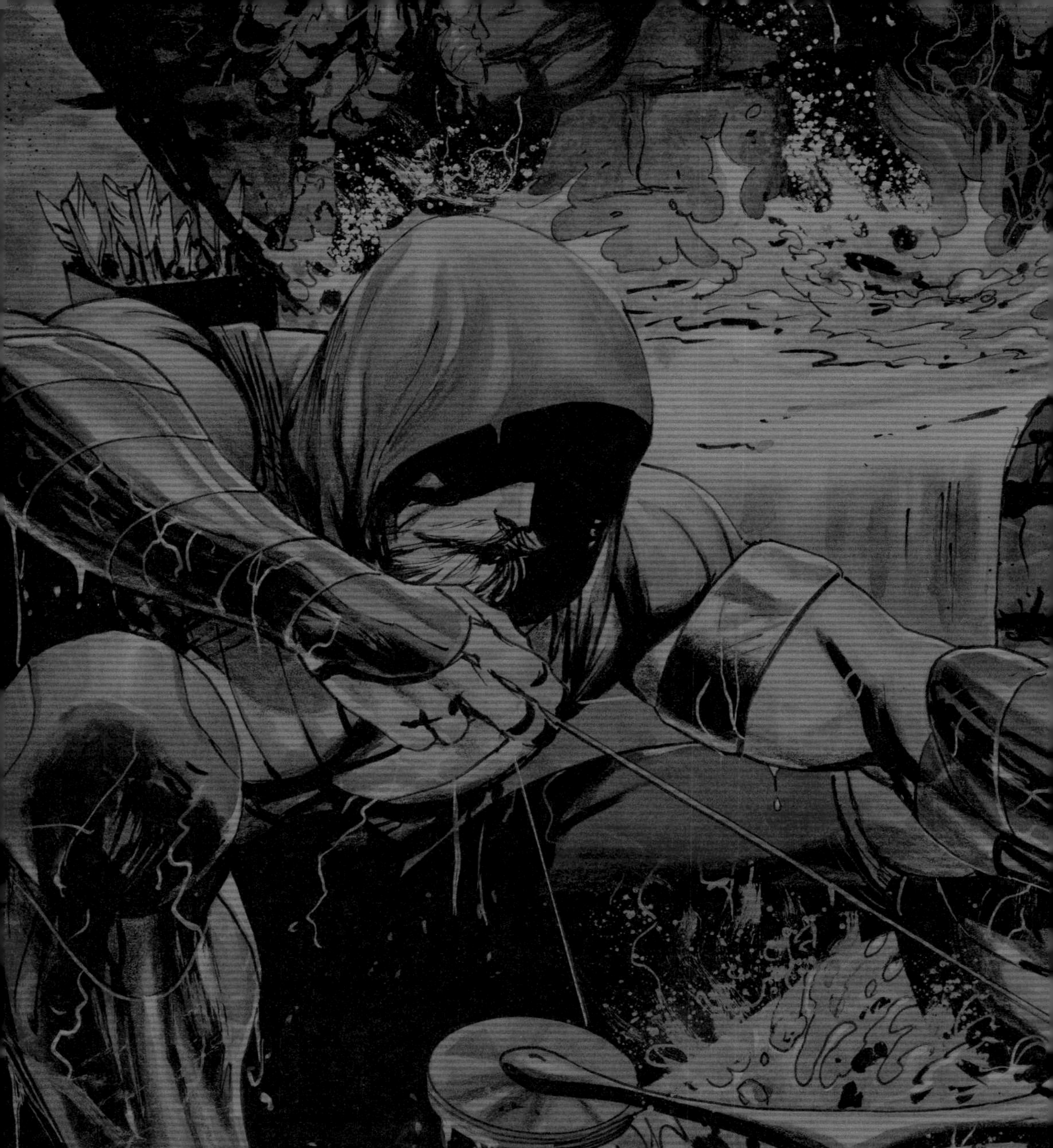

# GREEN ARROW
#42

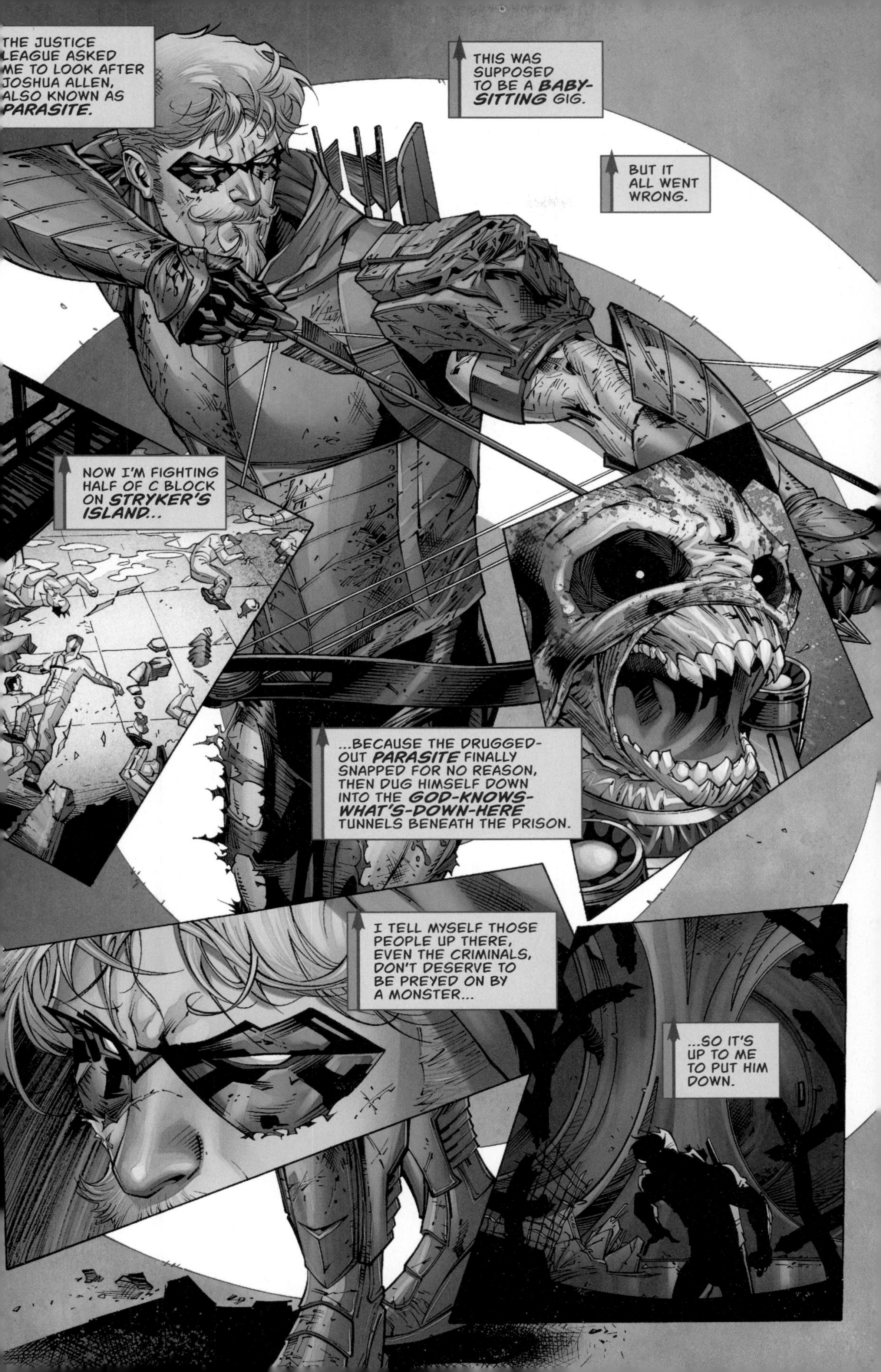
THE JUSTICE LEAGUE ASKED ME TO LOOK AFTER JOSHUA ALLEN, ALSO KNOWN AS PARASITE.
THIS WAS SUPPOSED TO BE A BABY-SITTING GIG.
BUT IT ALL WENT WRONG.
NOW I'M FIGHTING HALF OF C BLOCK ON STRYKER'S ISLAND...
...BECAUSE THE DRUGGED-OUT PARASITE FINALLY SNAPPED FOR NO REASON, THEN DUG HIMSELF DOWN INTO THE GOD-KNOWS-WHAT'S-DOWN-HERE TUNNELS BENEATH THE PRISON.
I TELL MYSELF THOSE PEOPLE UP THERE, EVEN THE CRIMINALS, DON'T DESERVE TO BE PREYED ON BY A MONSTER...
...SO IT'S UP TO ME TO PUT HIM DOWN.

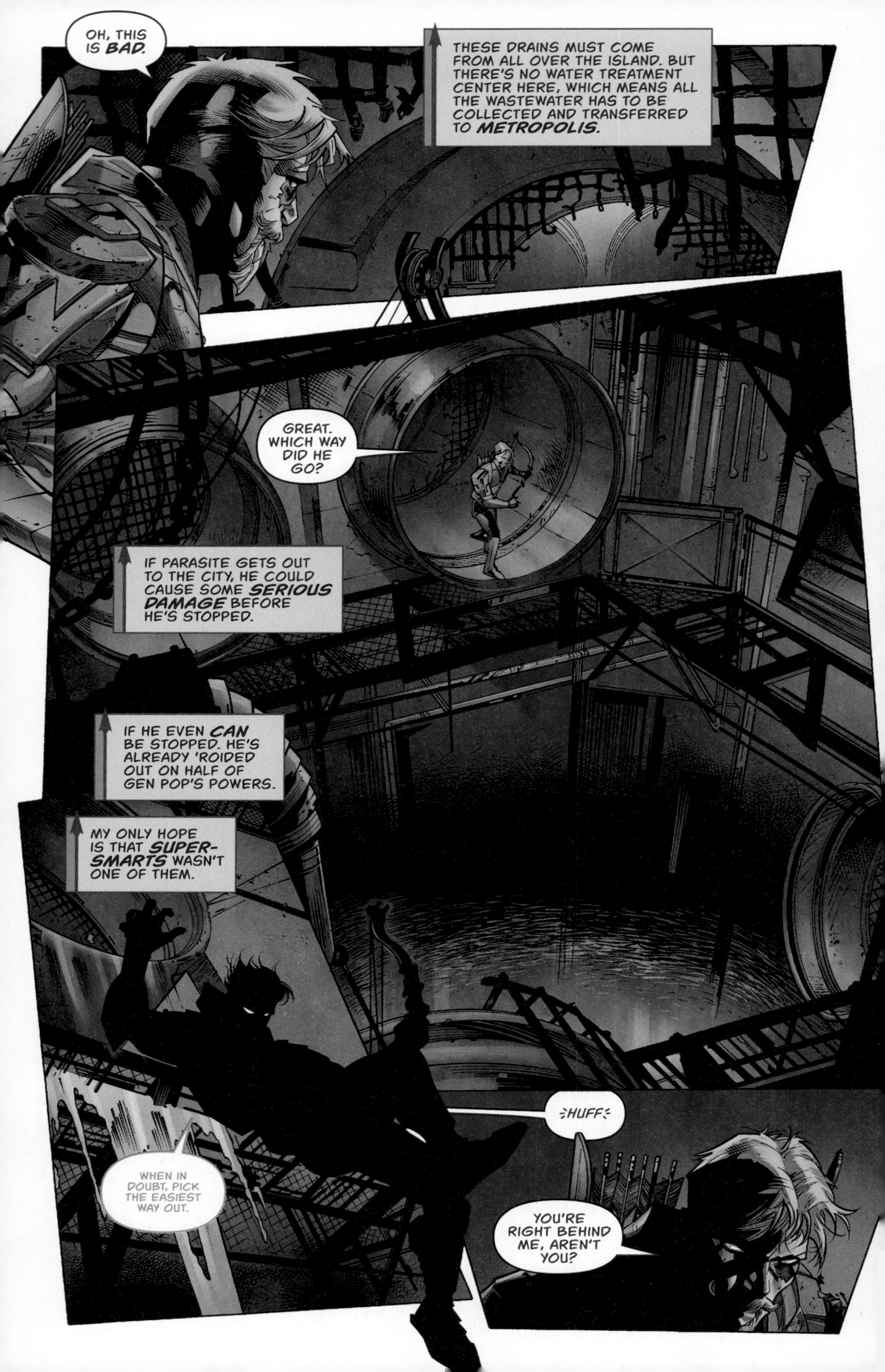
OH, THIS IS BAD.
THESE DRAINS MUST COME FROM ALL OVER THE ISLAND. BUT THERE'S NO WATER TREATMENT CENTER HERE, WHICH MEANS ALL THE WASTEWATER HAS TO BE COLLECTED AND TRANSFERRED TO METROPOLIS.
GREAT. WHICH WAY DID HE GO?
IF PARASITE GETS OUT TO THE CITY, HE COULD CAUSE SOME SERIOUS DAMAGE BEFORE HE'S STOPPED.
IF HE EVEN CAN BE STOPPED. HE'S ALREADY 'ROIDED OUT ON HALF OF GEN POP'S POWERS.
MY ONLY HOPE IS THAT SUPER-SMARTS WASN'T ONE OF THEM.
HUFF
WHEN IN DOUBT, PICK THE EASIEST WAY OUT.
YOU'RE RIGHT BEHIND ME, AREN'T YOU?

AND THEY SAY YOU'RE JUST A PRETTY BLOND.
BETTER THAN
FINALE
AIRGHREAD SCOTT Writer
ATTHEW CLARK Pencils
EAN PARSONS Inks JASON WRIGHT Colors
ERON BENNETT Letters
LER KIRKHAM & ARIF PRIANTO Cover
AVE WIELGOSZ Asst. Editor
LEX ANTONE Editor
AMIE S. RICH Group Editor

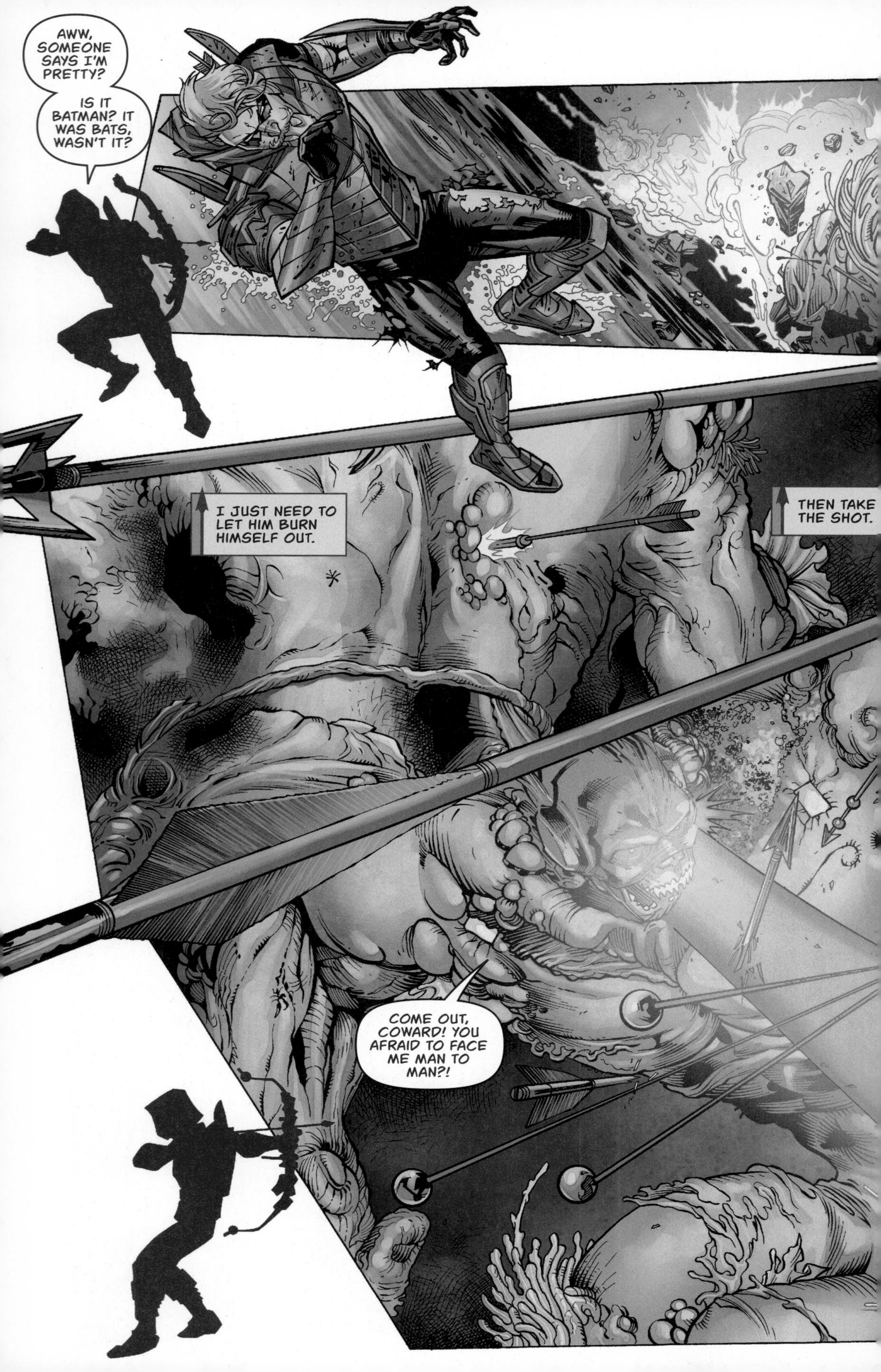
AWW, SOMEONE SAYS I'M PRETTY?
IS IT BATMAN? IT WAS BATS, WASN'T IT?
I JUST NEED TO LET HIM BURN HIMSELF OUT.
THEN TAKE THE SHOT.
COME OUT, COWARD! YOU AFRAID TO FACE ME MAN TO MAN?!

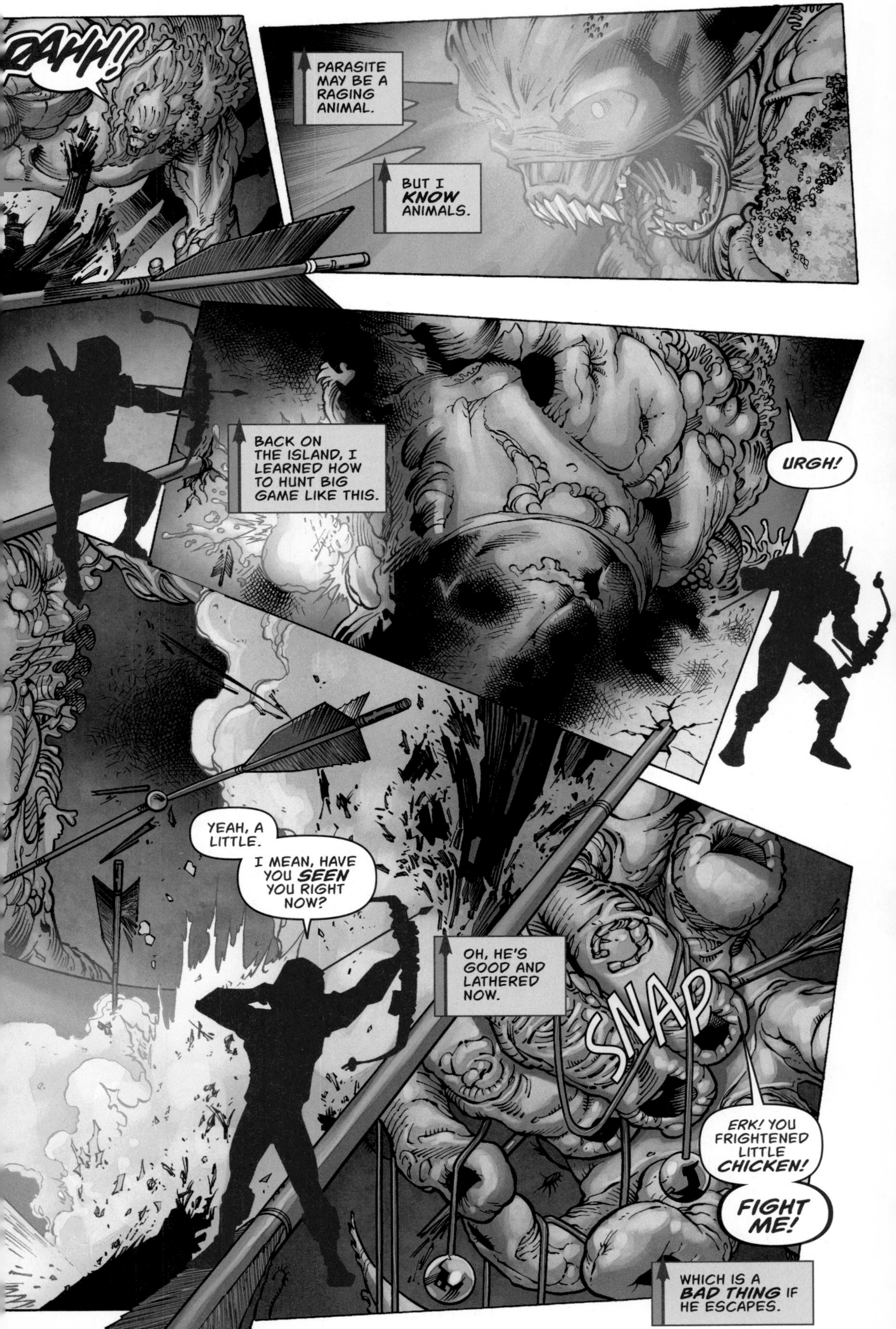

AAHH!
PARASITE MAY BE A RAGING ANIMAL.
BUT I KNOW ANIMALS.
BACK ON THE ISLAND, I LEARNED HOW TO HUNT BIG GAME LIKE THIS.
URGH!
YEAH, A LITTLE.
I MEAN, HAVE YOU SEEN YOU RIGHT NOW?
OH, HE'S GOOD AND LATHERED NOW.
SNAP
ERK! YOU FRIGHTENED LITTLE CHICKEN!
FIGHT ME!
WHICH IS A BAD THING IF HE ESCAPES.

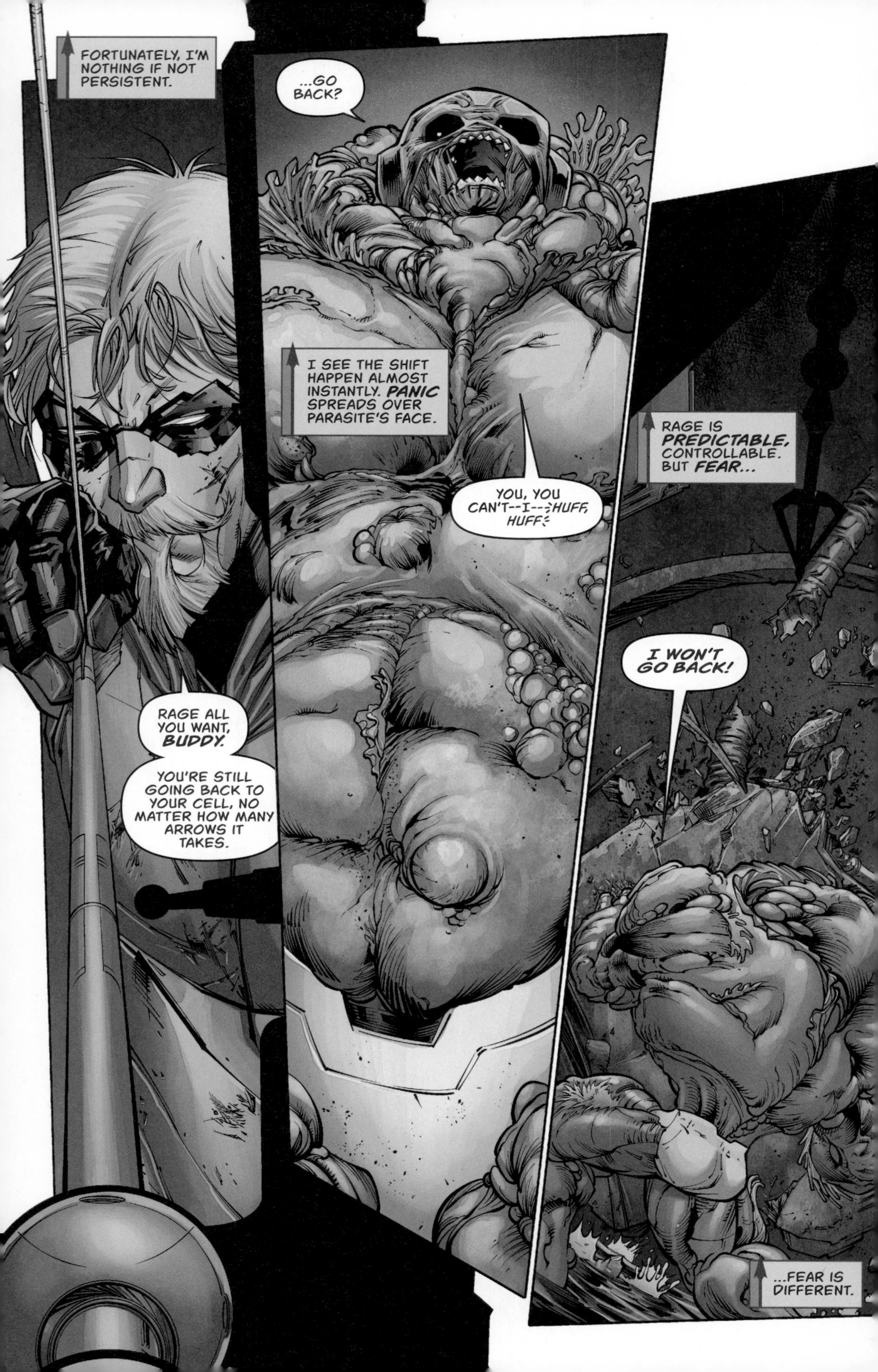
FORTUNATELY, I'M NOTHING IF NOT PERSISTENT.
...GO BACK?
I SEE THE SHIFT HAPPEN ALMOST INSTANTLY. PANIC SPREADS OVER PARASITE'S FACE.
YOU, YOU CAN'T--I--HUFF, HUFF
RAGE IS PREDICTABLE, CONTROLLABLE. BUT FEAR...
I WON'T GO BACK!
RAGE ALL YOU WANT, BUDDY.
YOU'RE STILL GOING BACK TO YOUR CELL, NO MATTER HOW MANY ARROWS IT TAKES.
...FEAR IS DIFFERENT.

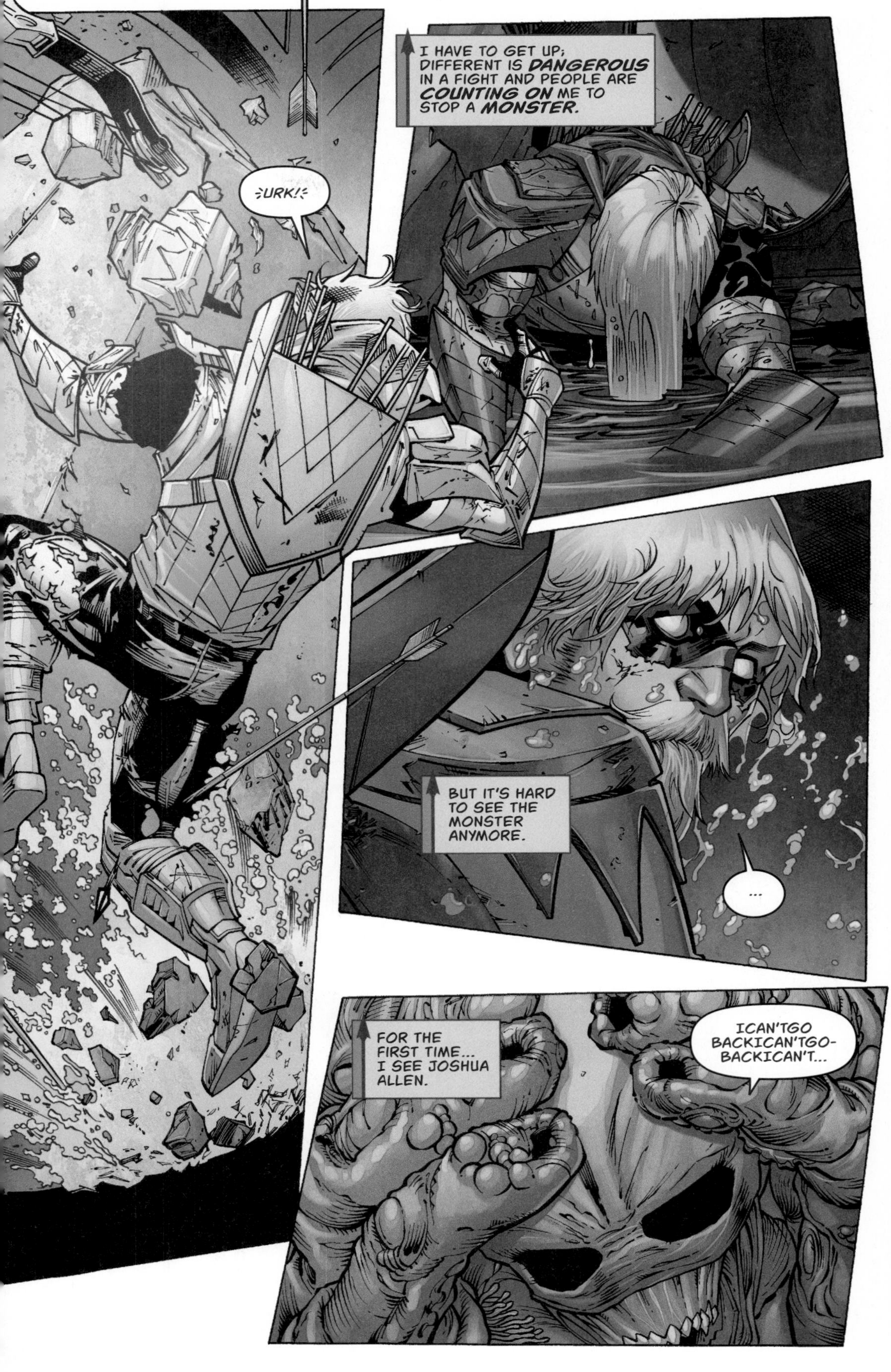
I HAVE TO GET UP; DIFFERENT IS DANGEROUS IN A FIGHT AND PEOPLE ARE COUNTING ON ME TO STOP A MONSTER.
URK!
BUT IT'S HARD TO SEE THE MONSTER ANYMORE.
...
FOR THE FIRST TIME... I SEE JOSHUA ALLEN.
ICAN'TGO BACKICAN'TGO-BACKICAN'T...

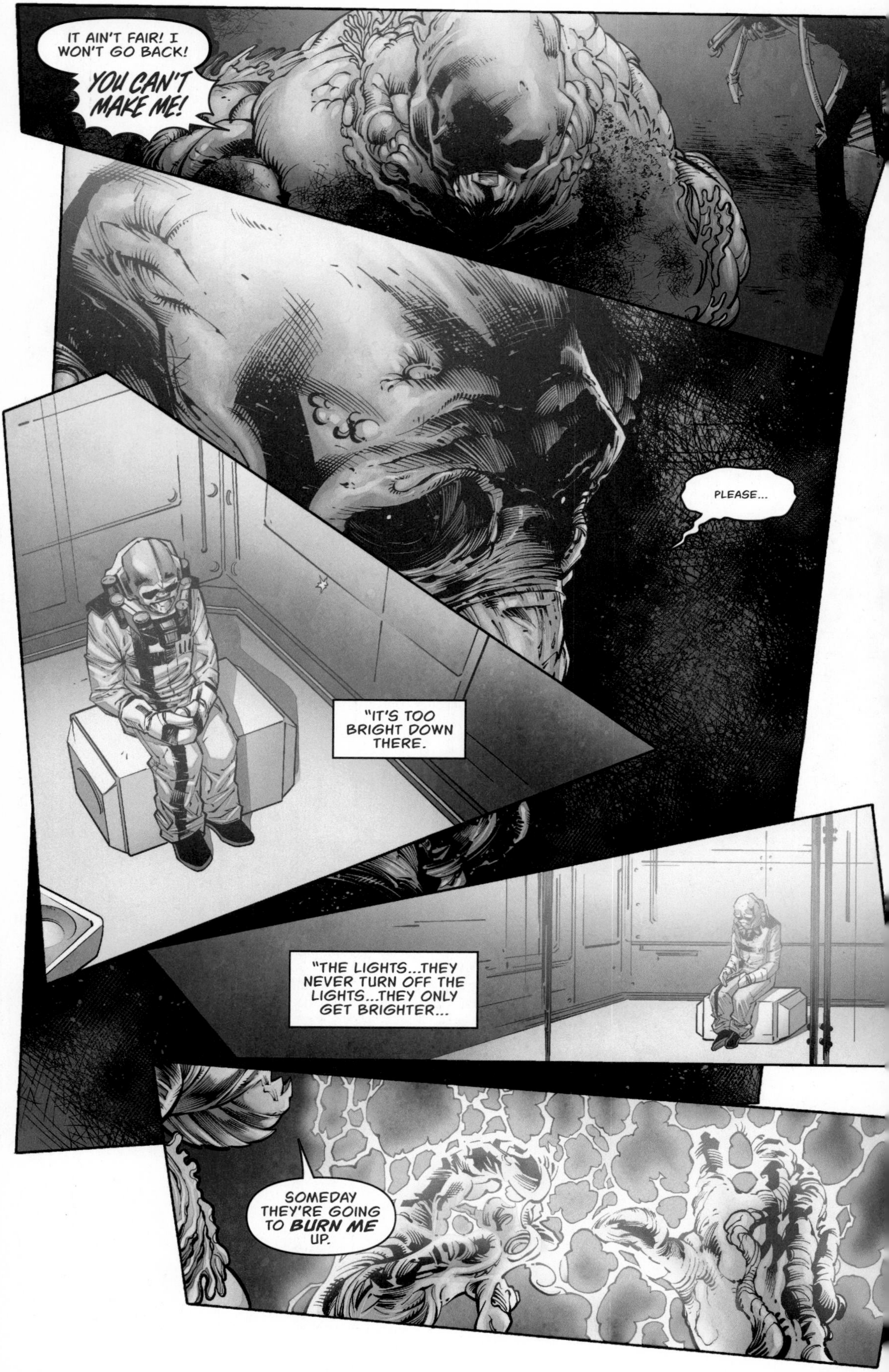

IT AIN'T FAIR! I WON'T GO BACK!
YOU CAN'T MAKE ME!
PLEASE...
"IT'S TOO BRIGHT DOWN THERE.
"THE LIGHTS...THEY NEVER TURN OFF THE LIGHTS...THEY ONLY GET BRIGHTER...
SOMEDAY THEY'RE GOING TO **BURN ME** UP.

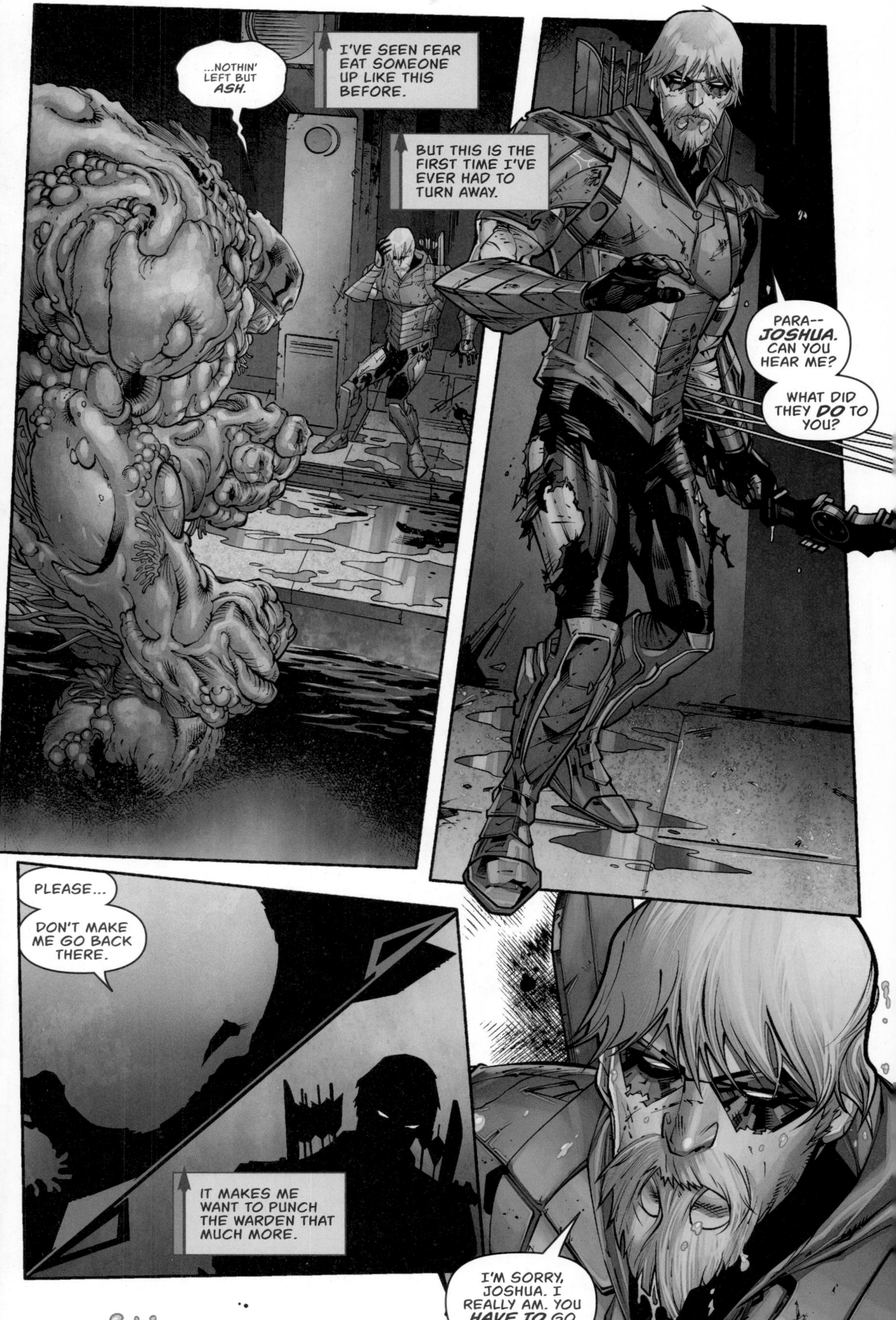
...NOTHIN' LEFT BUT ASH.
I'VE SEEN FEAR EAT SOMEONE UP LIKE THIS BEFORE.
BUT THIS IS THE FIRST TIME I'VE EVER HAD TO TURN AWAY.
PARA-- JOSHUA. CAN YOU HEAR ME?
WHAT DID THEY DO TO YOU?
PLEASE...
DON'T MAKE ME GO BACK THERE.
IT MAKES ME WANT TO PUNCH THE WARDEN THAT MUCH MORE.
I'M SORRY, JOSHUA. I REALLY AM. YOU HAVE TO GO BACK.

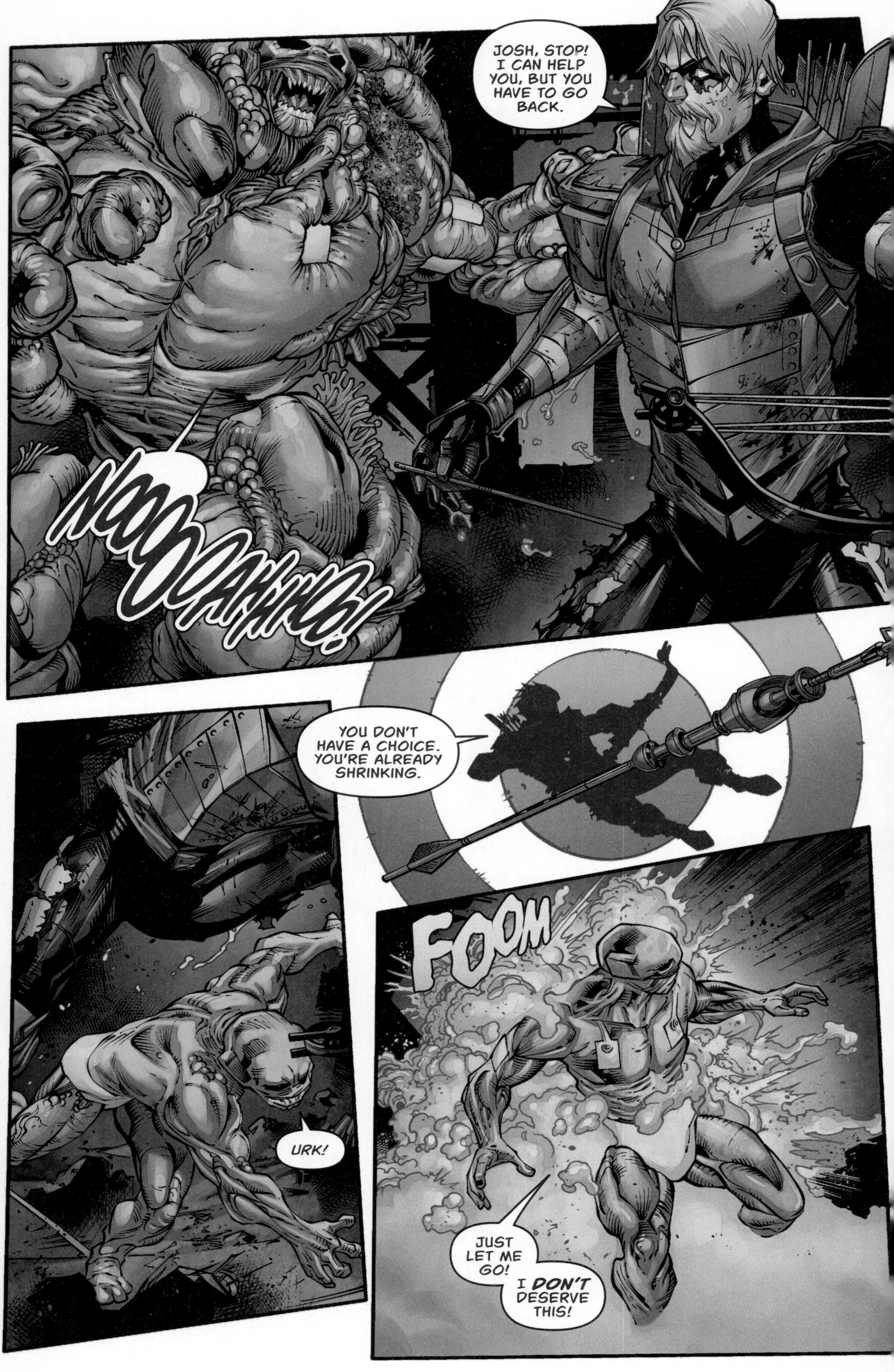
JOSH, STOP! I CAN HELP YOU, BUT YOU HAVE TO GO BACK.
NOOOOAHHHO!
YOU DON'T HAVE A CHOICE. YOU'RE ALREADY SHRINKING.
URK!
FOOM
JUST LET ME GO!
I DON'T DESERVE THIS!

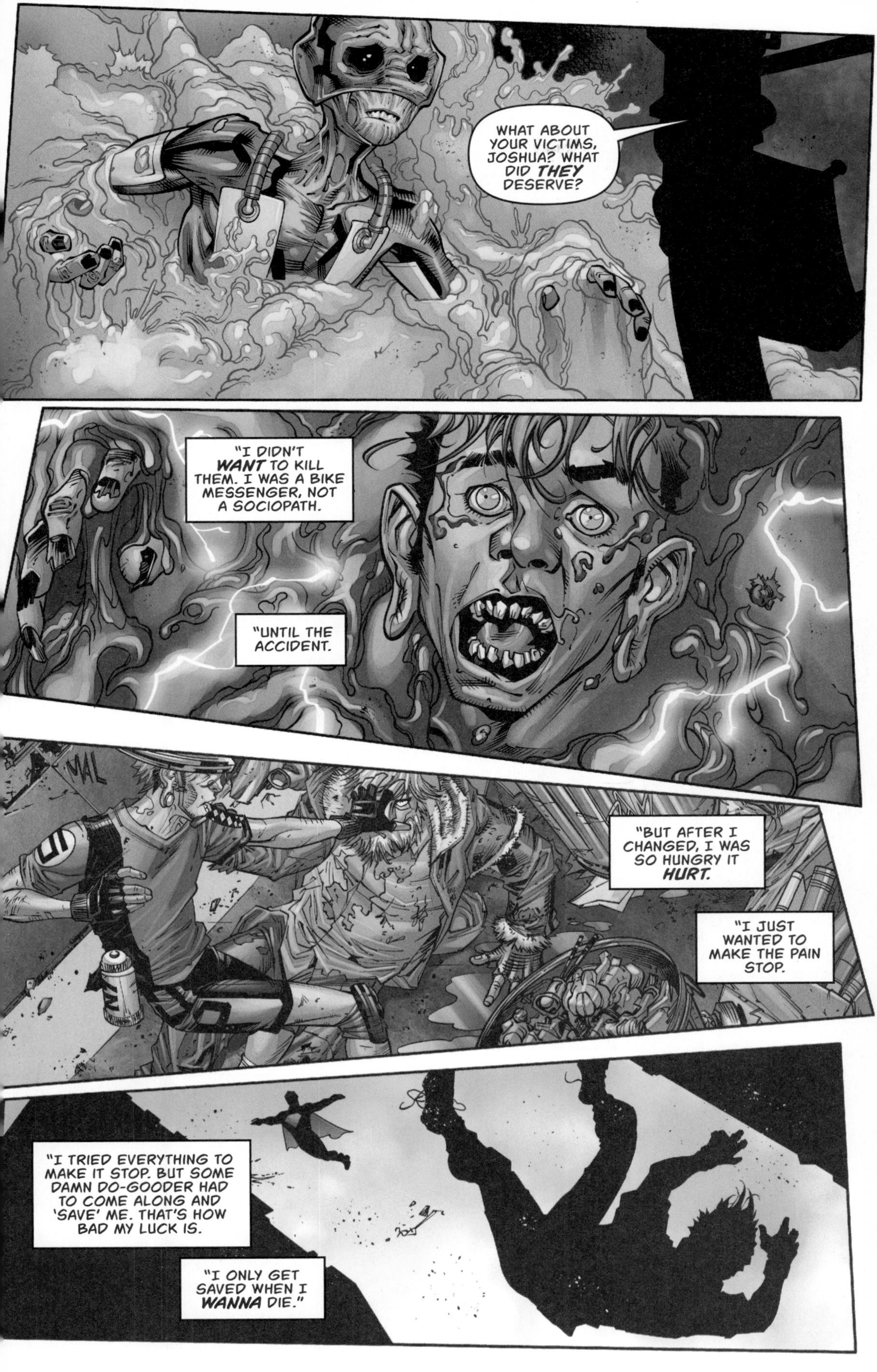

WHAT ABOUT YOUR VICTIMS, JOSHUA? WHAT DID *THEY* DESERVE?
"I DIDN'T *WANT* TO KILL THEM. I WAS A BIKE MESSENGER, NOT A SOCIOPATH.
"UNTIL THE ACCIDENT.
"BUT AFTER I CHANGED, I WAS SO HUNGRY IT *HURT.*
"I JUST WANTED TO MAKE THE PAIN STOP.
"I TRIED EVERYTHING TO MAKE IT STOP. BUT SOME DAMN DO-GOODER HAD TO COME ALONG AND 'SAVE' ME. THAT'S HOW BAD MY LUCK IS.
"I ONLY GET SAVED WHEN I *WANNA* DIE."

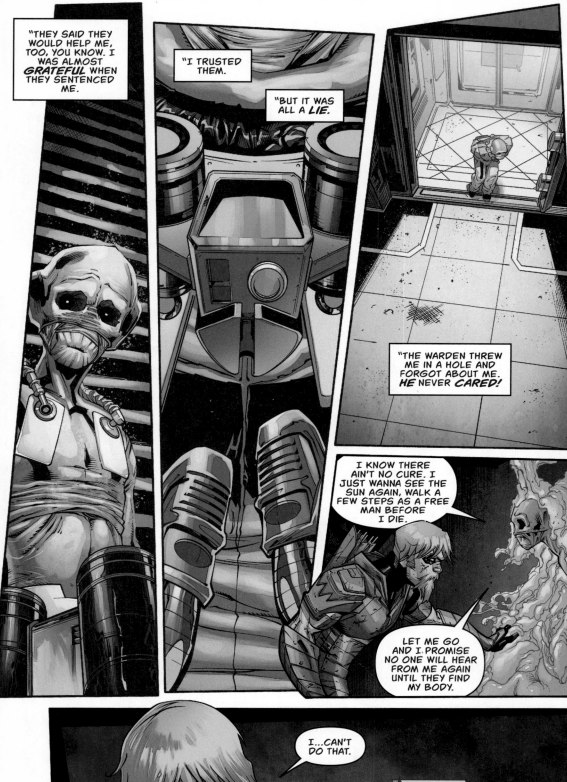

"THEY SAID THEY WOULD HELP ME, TOO, YOU KNOW. I WAS ALMOST *GRATEFUL* WHEN THEY SENTENCED ME.

"I TRUSTED THEM.

"BUT IT WAS ALL A *LIE.*

"THE WARDEN THREW ME IN A HOLE AND FORGOT ABOUT ME. *HE* NEVER *CARED!*

I KNOW THERE AIN'T NO CURE. I JUST WANNA SEE THE SUN AGAIN, WALK A FEW STEPS AS A FREE MAN BEFORE I DIE.

LET ME GO AND I PROMISE NO ONE WILL HEAR FROM ME AGAIN UNTIL THEY FIND MY BODY.

I...CAN'T DO THAT.

BUT I WANT TO.

GOD HELP ME... I *WANT* TO.

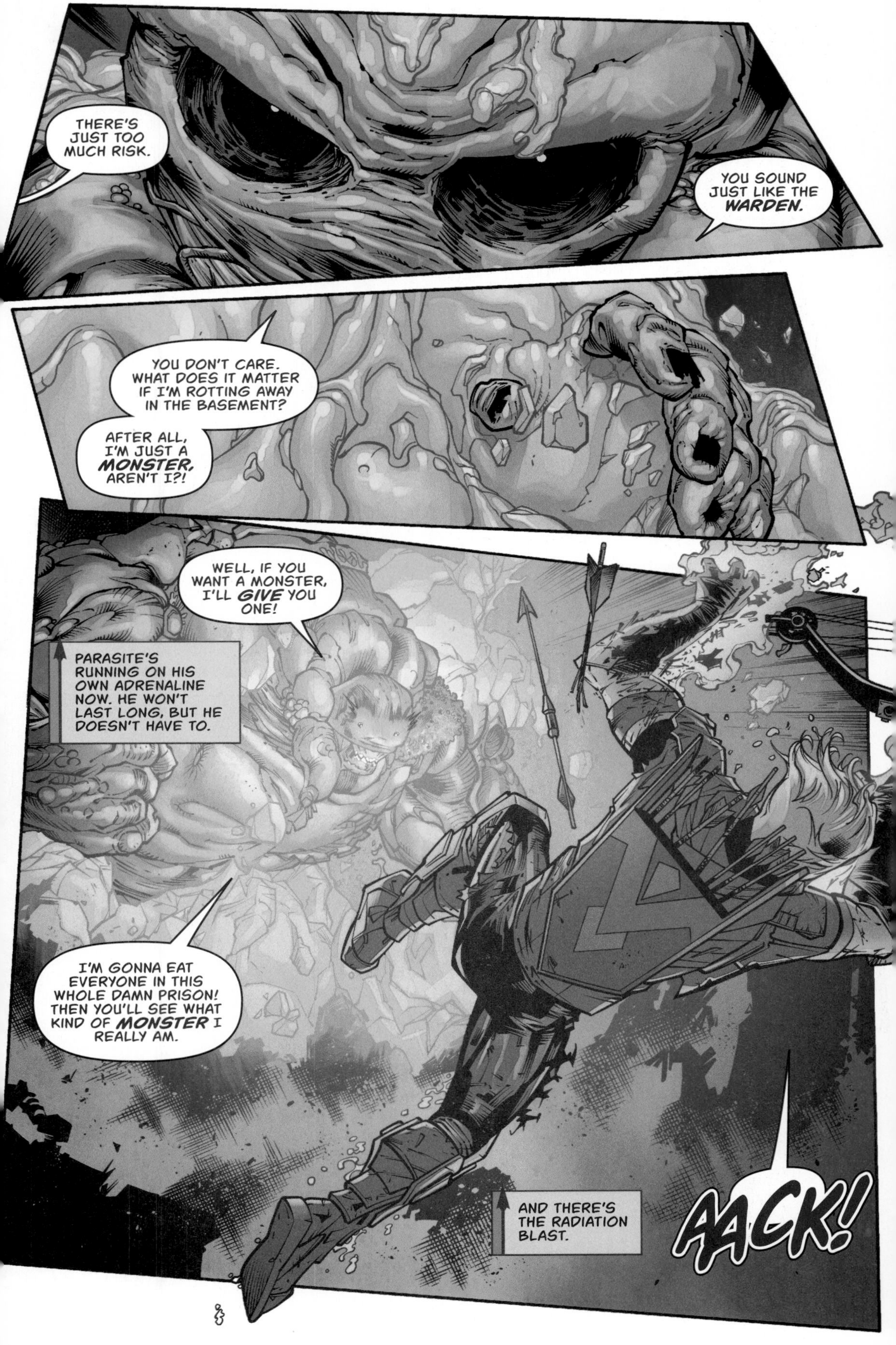

THERE'S JUST TOO MUCH RISK.
YOU SOUND JUST LIKE THE WARDEN.
YOU DON'T CARE. WHAT DOES IT MATTER IF I'M ROTTING AWAY IN THE BASEMENT?
AFTER ALL, I'M JUST A MONSTER, AREN'T I?!
WELL, IF YOU WANT A MONSTER, I'LL GIVE YOU ONE!
PARASITE'S RUNNING ON HIS OWN ADRENALINE NOW. HE WON'T LAST LONG, BUT HE DOESN'T HAVE TO.
I'M GONNA EAT EVERYONE IN THIS WHOLE DAMN PRISON! THEN YOU'LL SEE WHAT KIND OF MONSTER I REALLY AM.
AND THERE'S THE RADIATION BLAST.
AACK!

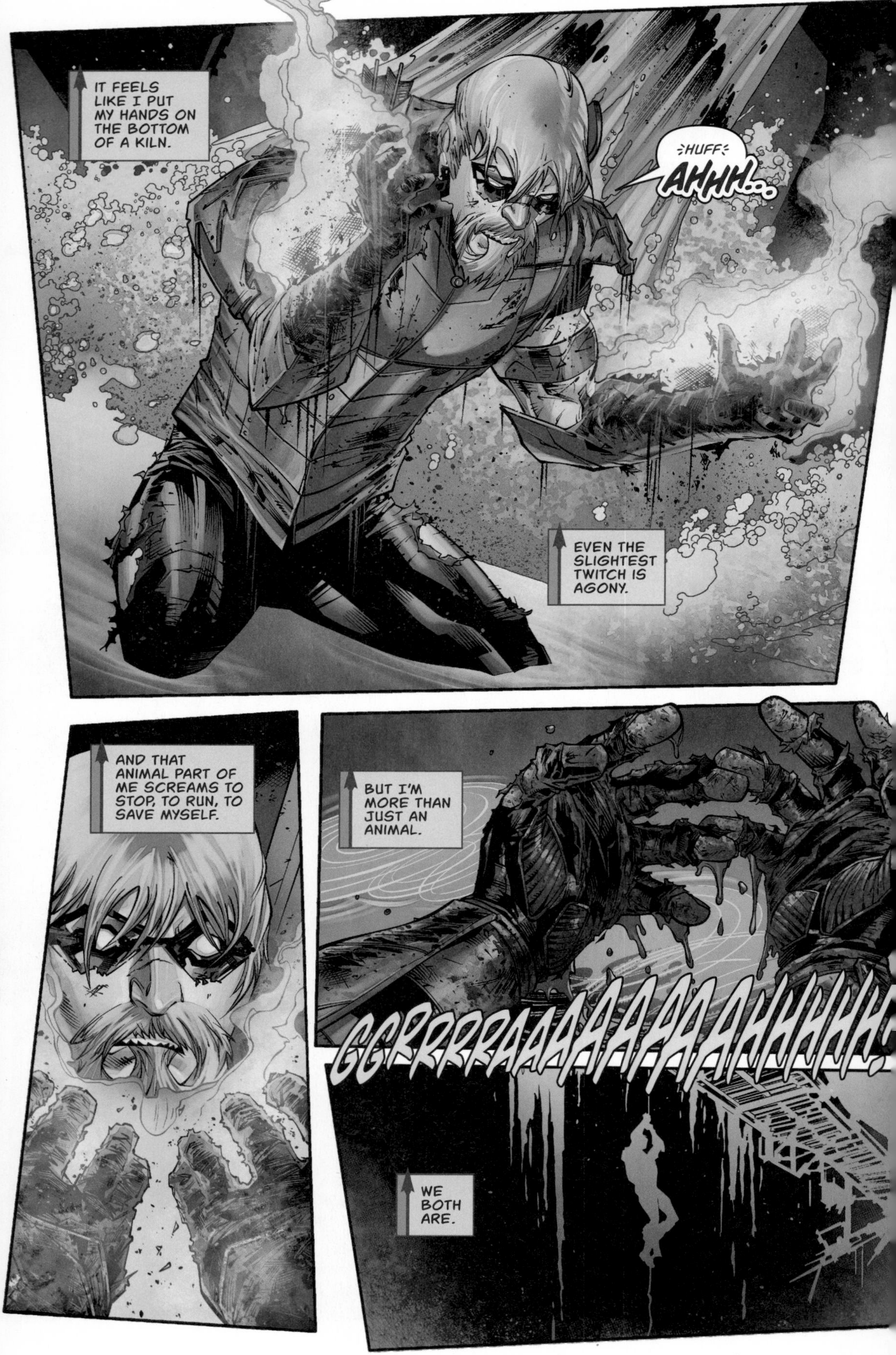
IT FEELS LIKE I PUT MY HANDS ON THE BOTTOM OF A KILN.
HUFF AHHH...
EVEN THE SLIGHTEST TWITCH IS AGONY.
AND THAT ANIMAL PART OF ME SCREAMS TO STOP, TO RUN, TO SAVE MYSELF.
BUT I'M MORE THAN JUST AN ANIMAL.
GGRRRRAAAAAAAAAAAAHHHHH
WE BOTH ARE.

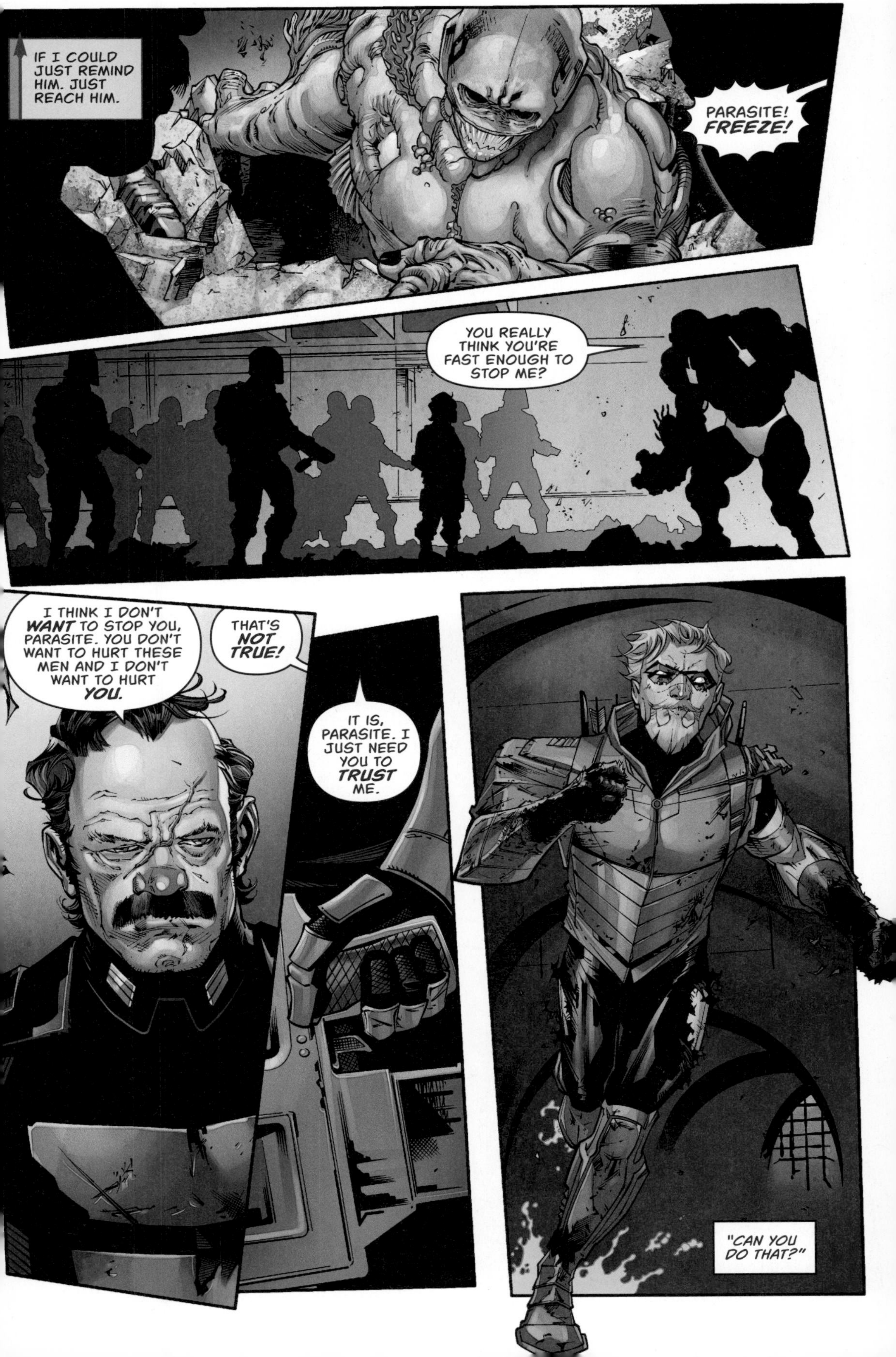
IF I COULD JUST REMIND HIM. JUST REACH HIM.
PARASITE! FREEZE!
YOU REALLY THINK YOU'RE FAST ENOUGH TO STOP ME?
I THINK I DON'T WANT TO STOP YOU, PARASITE. YOU DON'T WANT TO HURT THESE MEN AND I DON'T WANT TO HURT YOU.
THAT'S NOT TRUE!
IT IS, PARASITE. I JUST NEED YOU TO TRUST ME.
"CAN YOU DO THAT?"

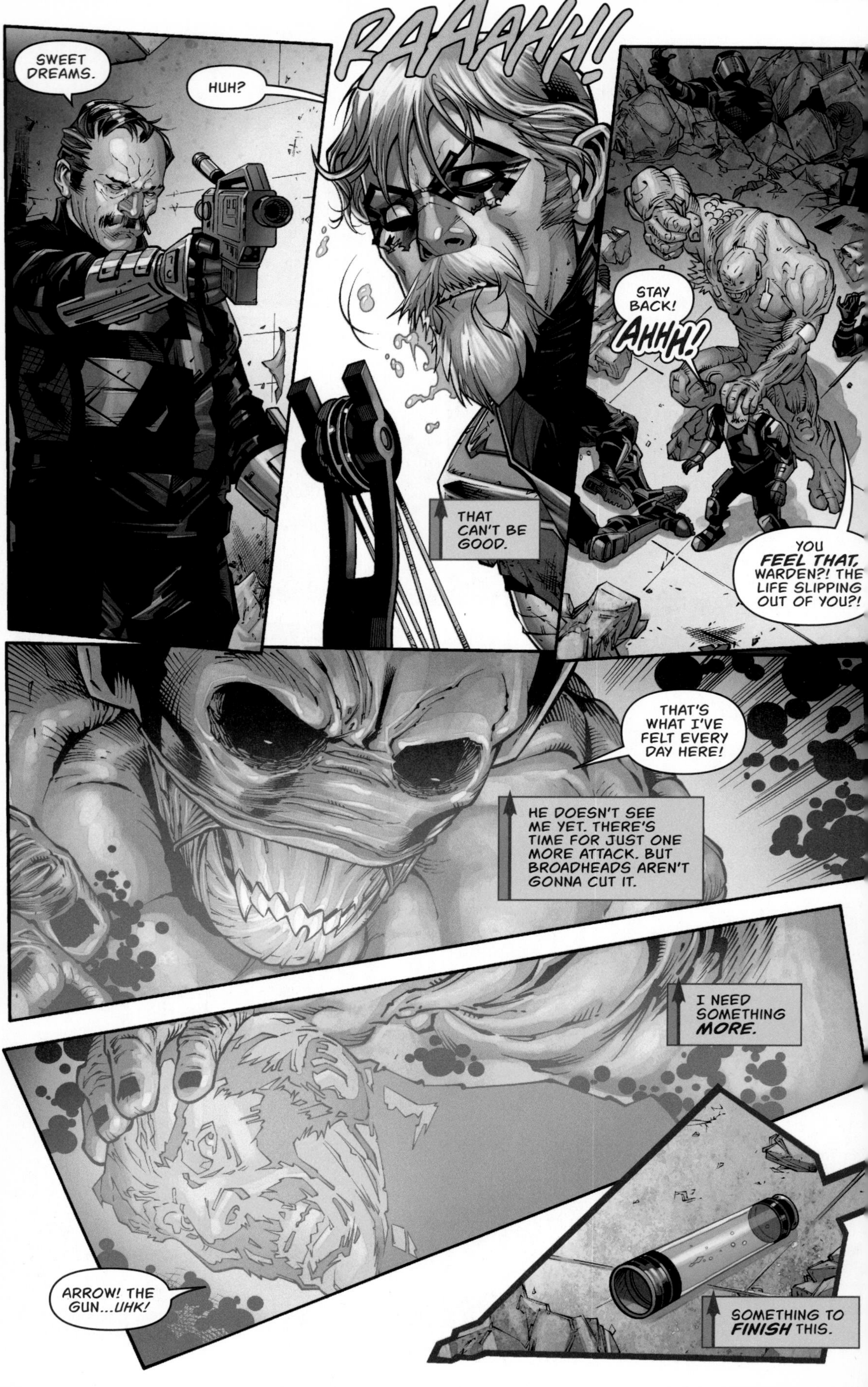
SWEET DREAMS.
HUH?
RAAAHH!
THAT CAN'T BE GOOD.
STAY BACK!
AHHH!
YOU FEEL THAT, WARDEN?! THE LIFE SLIPPING OUT OF YOU?!
THAT'S WHAT I'VE FELT EVERY DAY HERE!
HE DOESN'T SEE ME YET. THERE'S TIME FOR JUST ONE MORE ATTACK. BUT BROADHEADS AREN'T GONNA CUT IT.
I NEED SOMETHING MORE.
ARROW! THE GUN...UHK!
SOMETHING TO FINISH THIS.

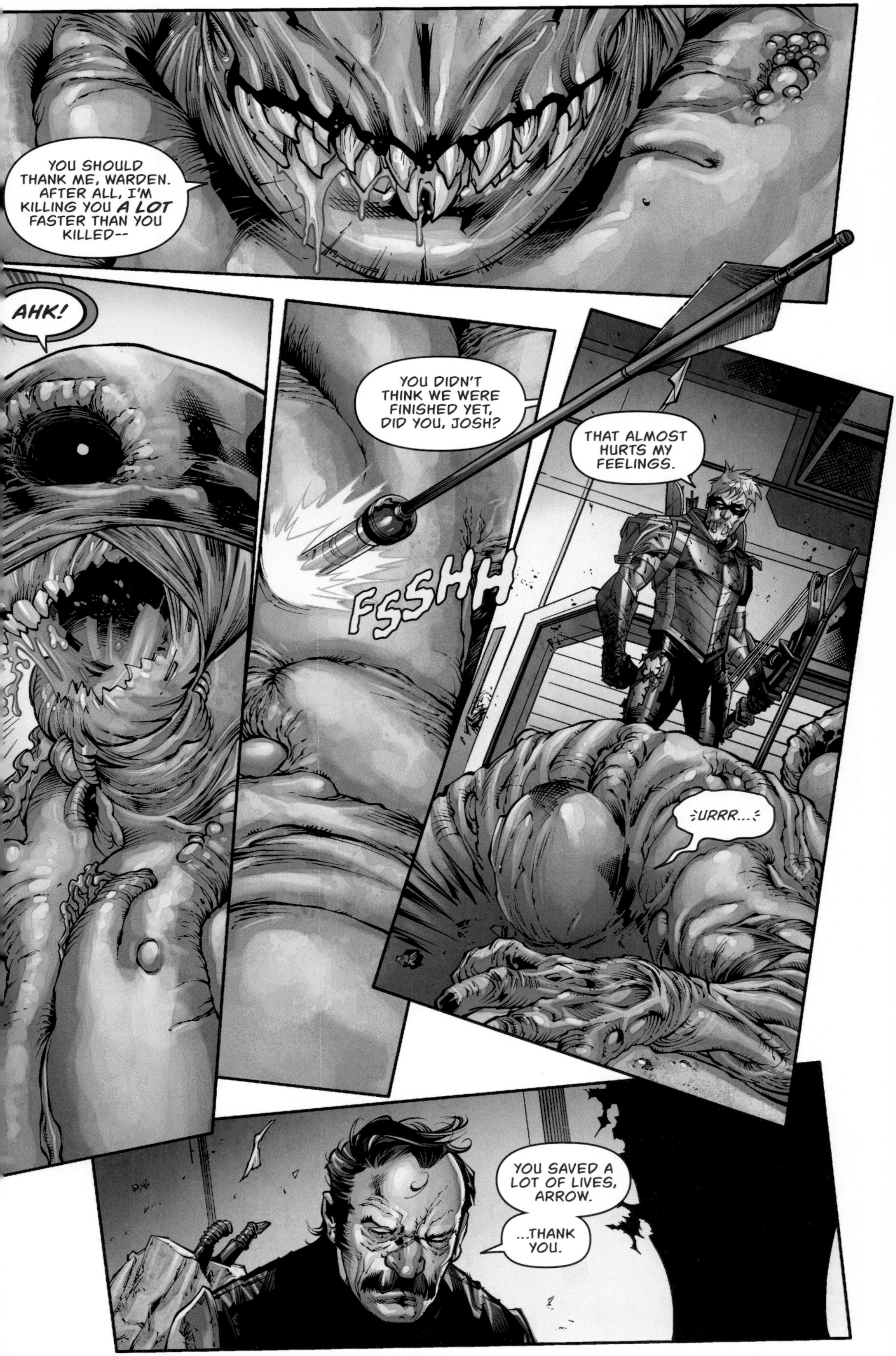
YOU SHOULD THANK ME, WARDEN. AFTER ALL, I'M KILLING YOU A LOT FASTER THAN YOU KILLED--
AHK!
YOU DIDN'T THINK WE WERE FINISHED YET, DID YOU, JOSH?
FSSHH
THAT ALMOST HURTS MY FEELINGS.
URRR...
YOU SAVED A LOT OF LIVES, ARROW.
...THANK YOU.

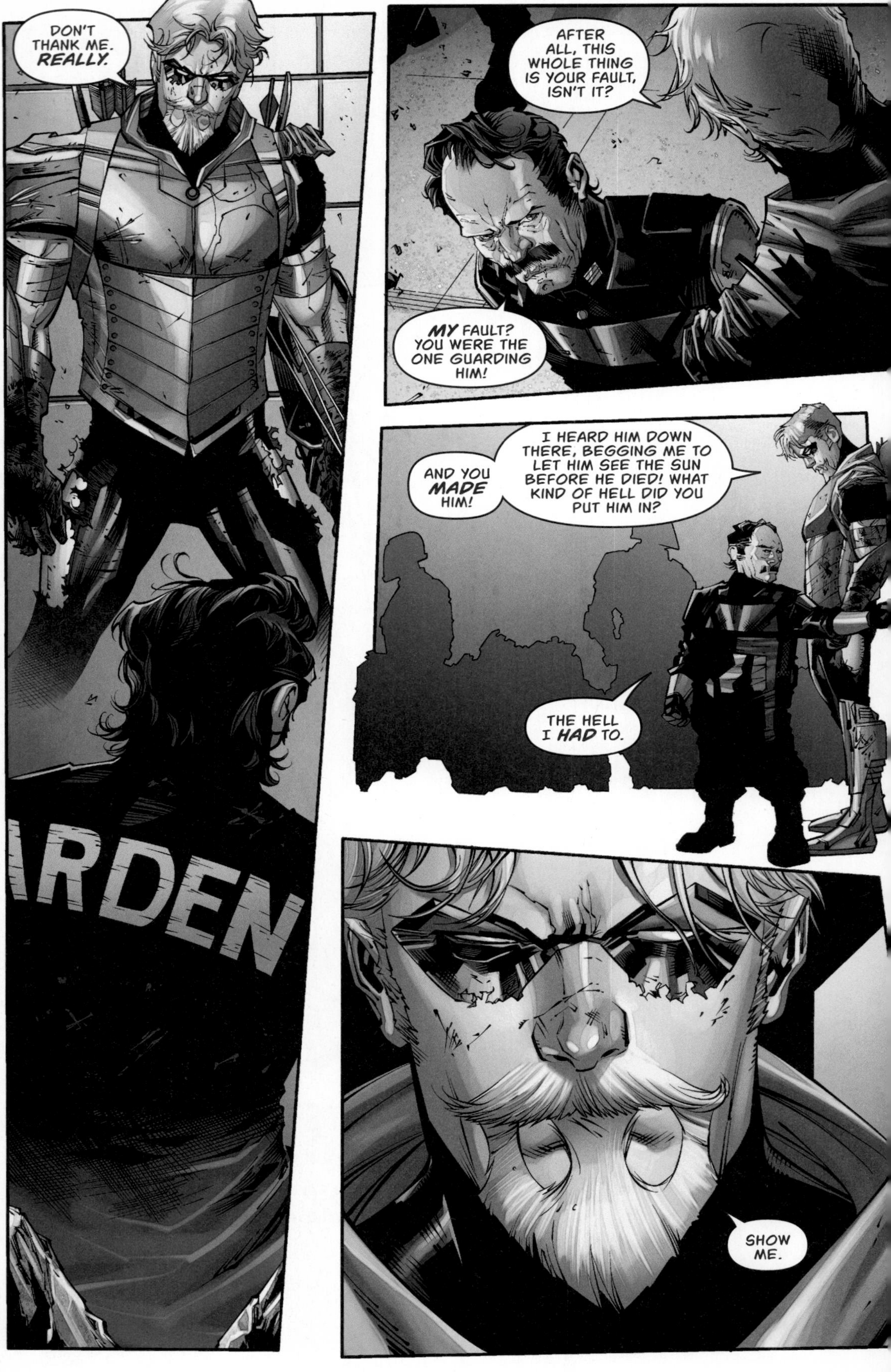
DON'T THANK ME. REALLY.
ARDEN
AFTER ALL, THIS WHOLE THING IS YOUR FAULT, ISN'T IT?
MY FAULT? YOU WERE THE ONE GUARDING HIM!
I HEARD HIM DOWN THERE, BEGGING ME TO LET HIM SEE THE SUN BEFORE HE DIED! WHAT KIND OF HELL DID YOU PUT HIM IN?
AND YOU MADE HIM!
THE HELL I HAD TO.
SHOW ME.

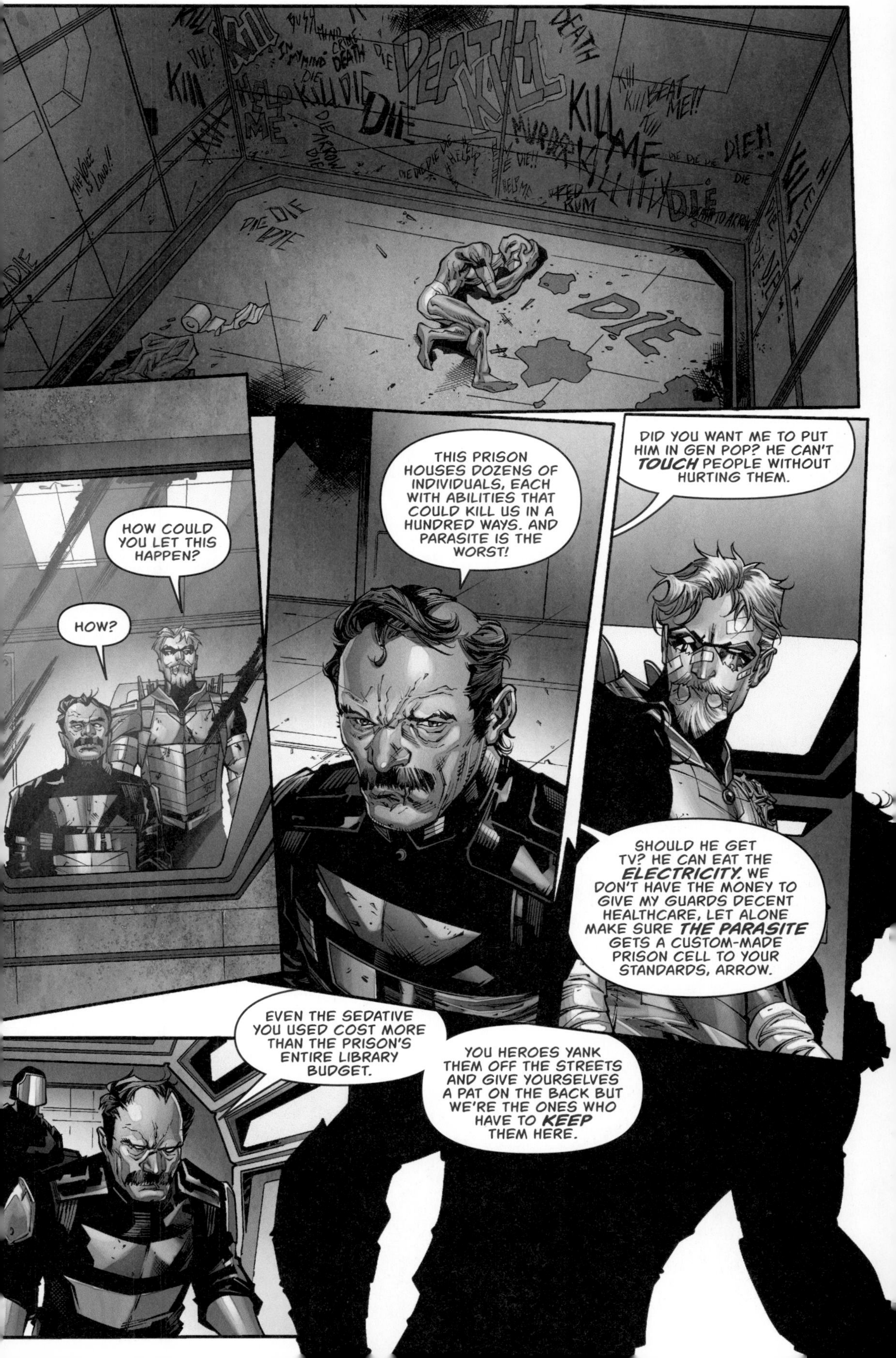
HOW COULD YOU LET THIS HAPPEN?
HOW?
THIS PRISON HOUSES DOZENS OF INDIVIDUALS, EACH WITH ABILITIES THAT COULD KILL US IN A HUNDRED WAYS. AND PARASITE IS THE WORST!
DID YOU WANT ME TO PUT HIM IN GEN POP? HE CAN'T TOUCH PEOPLE WITHOUT HURTING THEM.
SHOULD HE GET TV? HE CAN EAT THE ELECTRICITY. WE DON'T HAVE THE MONEY TO GIVE MY GUARDS DECENT HEALTHCARE, LET ALONE MAKE SURE THE PARASITE GETS A CUSTOM-MADE PRISON CELL TO YOUR STANDARDS, ARROW.
EVEN THE SEDATIVE YOU USED COST MORE THAN THE PRISON'S ENTIRE LIBRARY BUDGET.
YOU HEROES YANK THEM OFF THE STREETS AND GIVE YOURSELVES A PAT ON THE BACK BUT WE'RE THE ONES WHO HAVE TO KEEP THEM HERE.

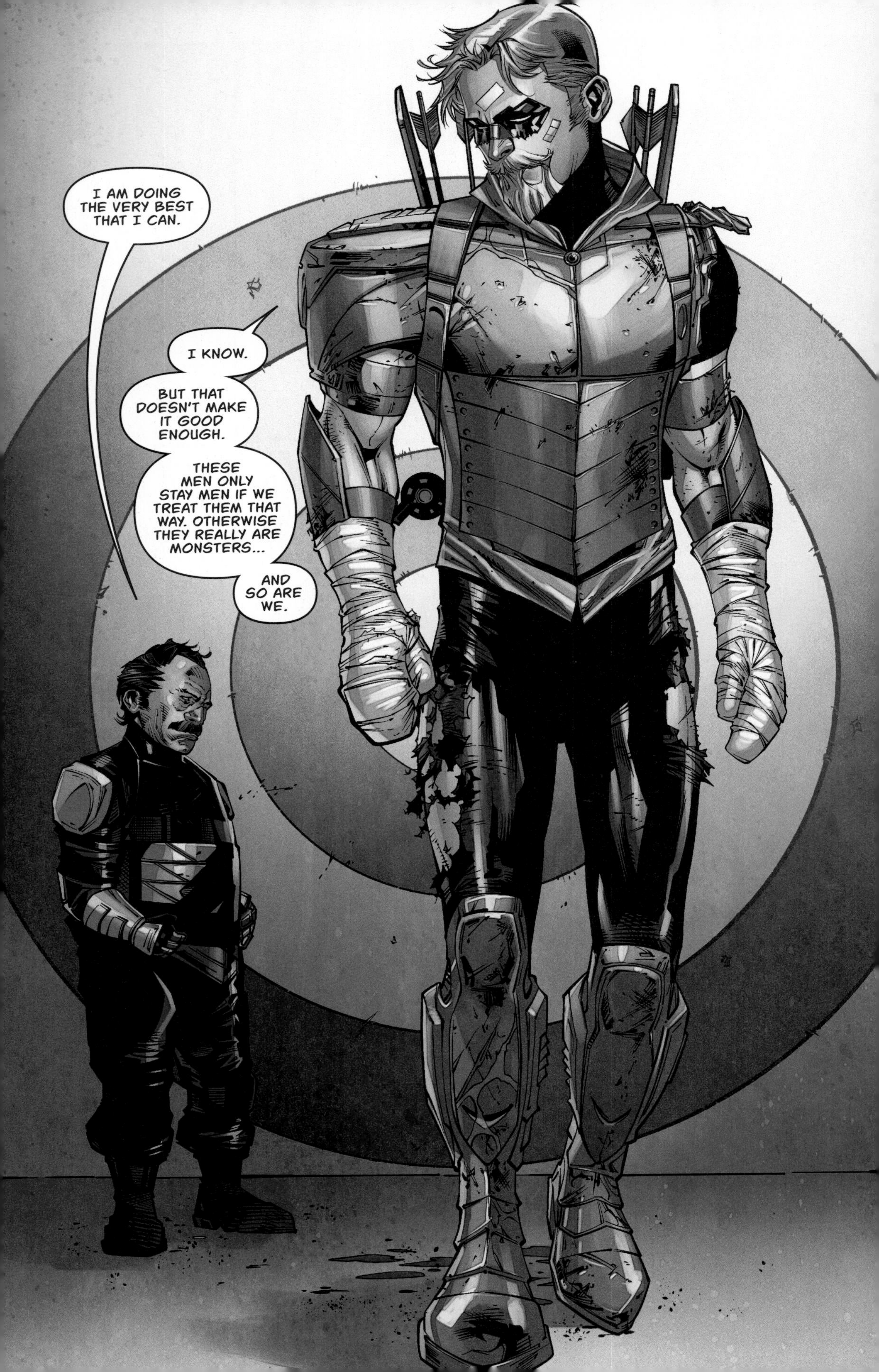
I AM DOING THE VERY BEST THAT I CAN.
I KNOW.
BUT THAT DOESN'T MAKE IT GOOD ENOUGH.
THESE MEN ONLY STAY MEN IF WE TREAT THEM THAT WAY. OTHERWISE THEY REALLY ARE MONSTERS...
AND SO ARE WE.

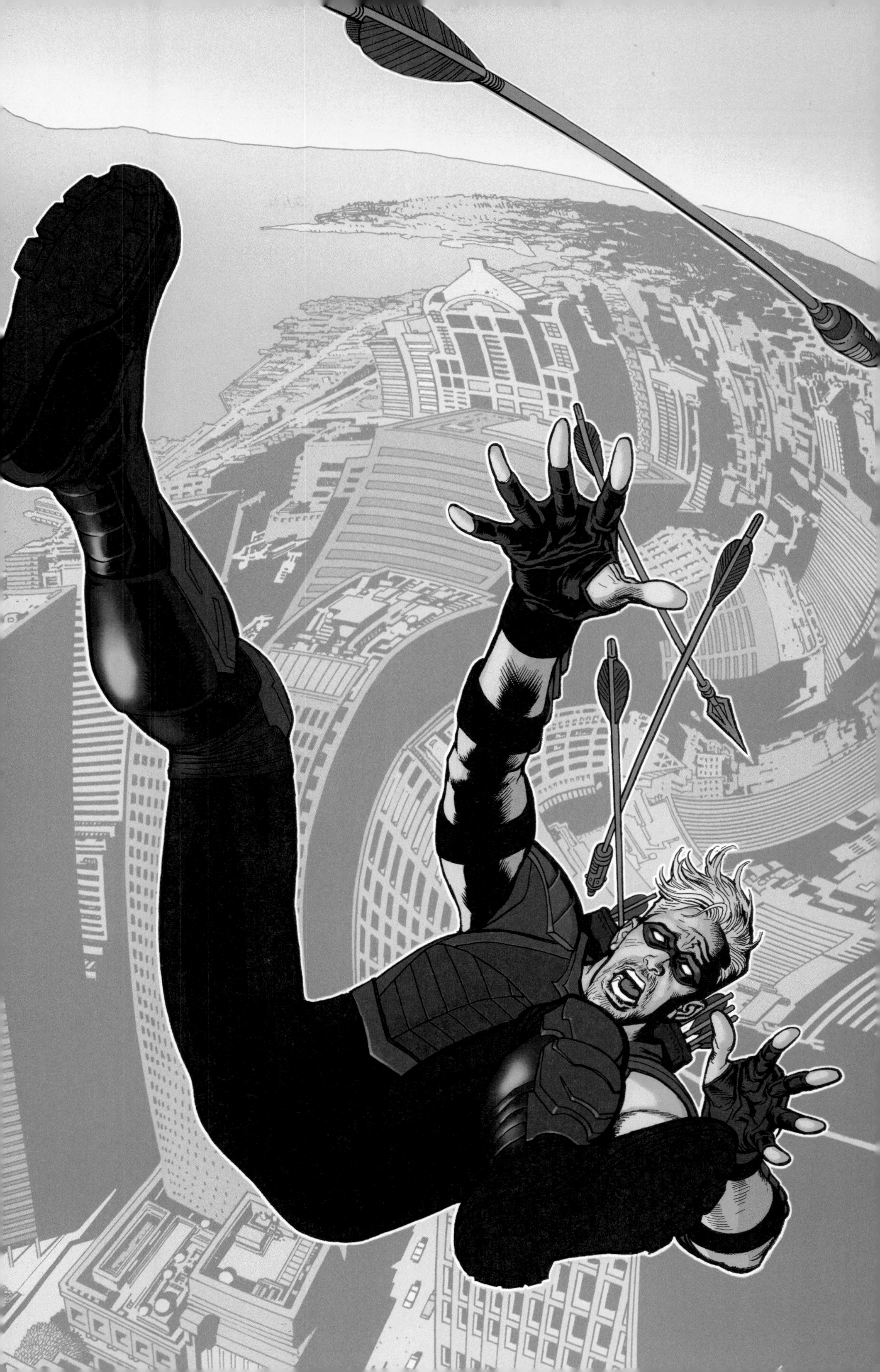

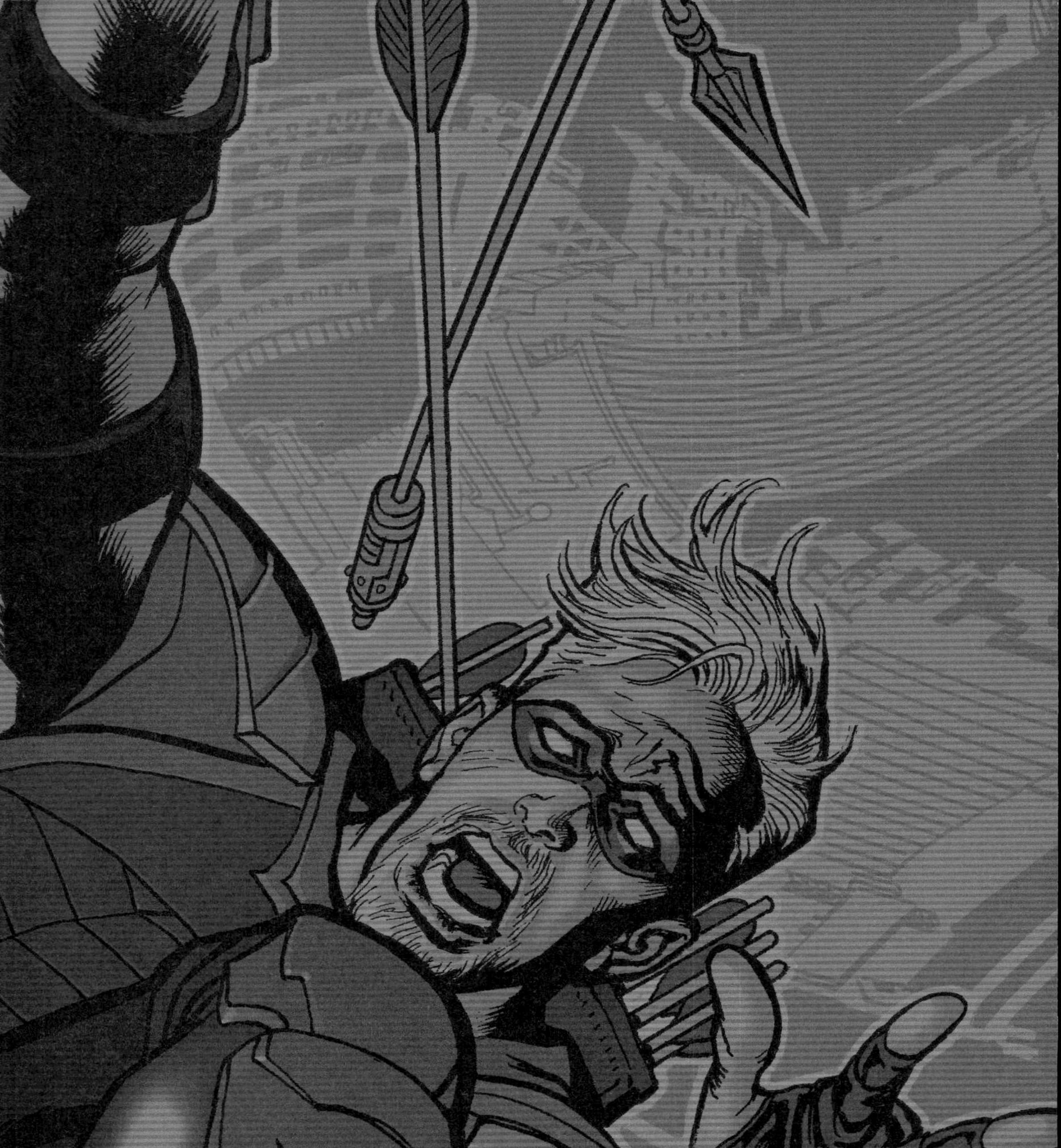

# GREEN ARROW

#48

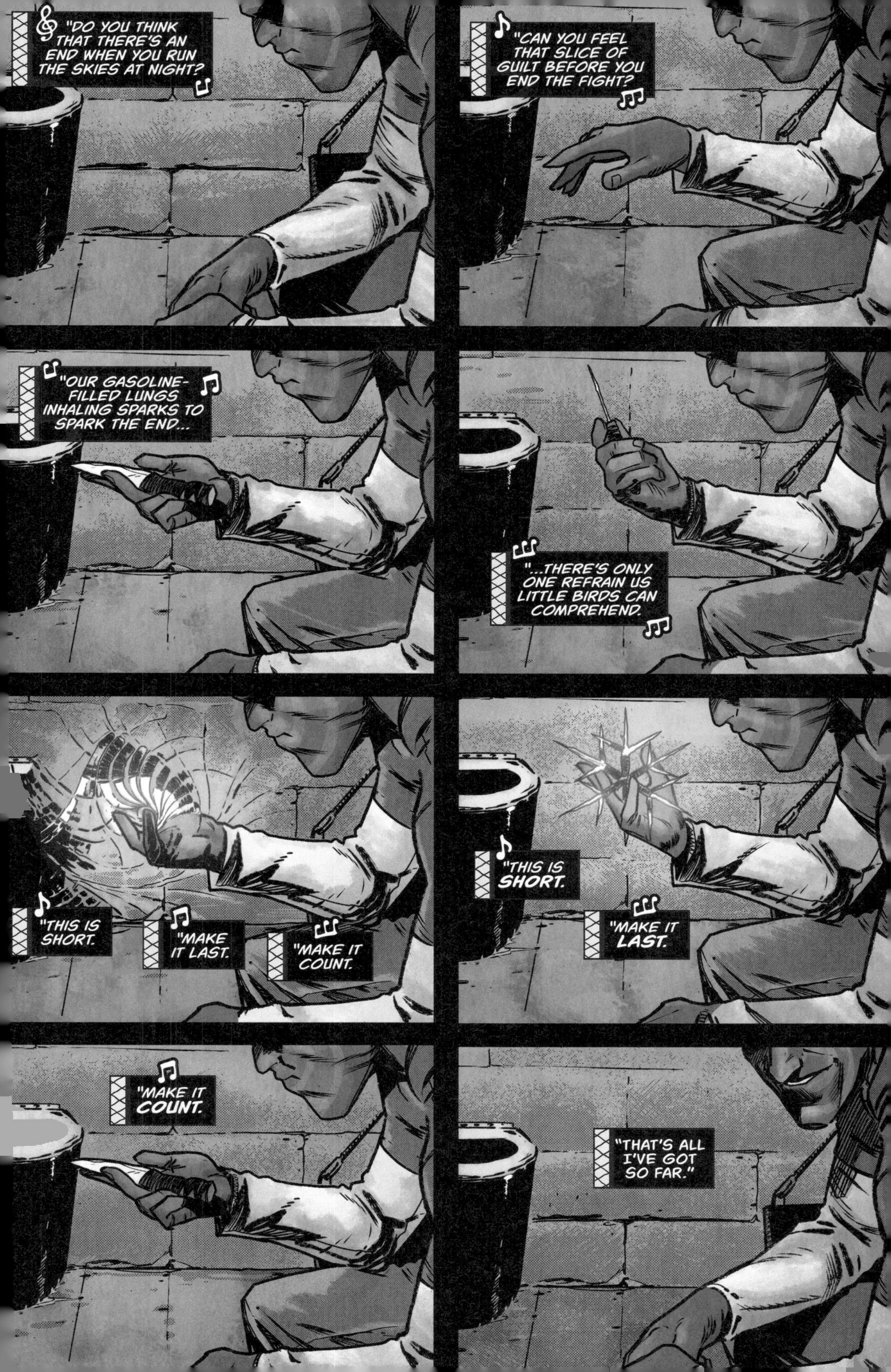
"DO YOU THINK THAT THERE'S AN END WHEN YOU RUN THE SKIES AT NIGHT?
"CAN YOU FEEL THAT SLICE OF GUILT BEFORE YOU END THE FIGHT?
"OUR GASOLINE-FILLED LUNGS INHALING SPARKS TO SPARK THE END...
"...THERE'S ONLY ONE REFRAIN US LITTLE BIRDS CAN COMPREHEND.
"THIS IS SHORT.
"MAKE IT LAST.
"MAKE IT COUNT.
"THIS IS SHORT.
"MAKE IT LAST.
"MAKE IT COUNT.
"THAT'S ALL I'VE GOT SO FAR."

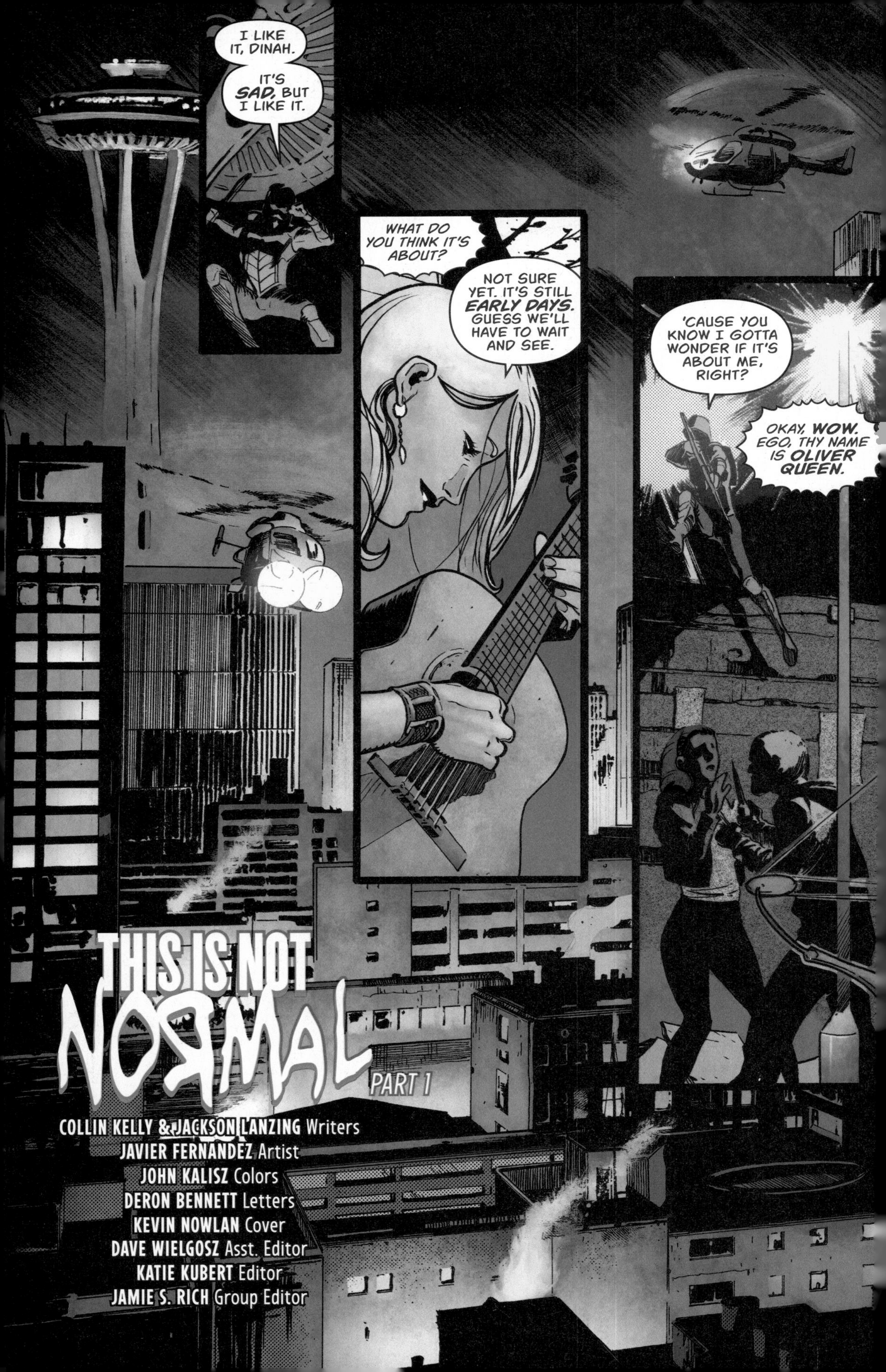
I LIKE IT, DINAH.
IT'S SAD, BUT I LIKE IT.
WHAT DO YOU THINK IT'S ABOUT?
NOT SURE YET. IT'S STILL EARLY DAYS. GUESS WE'LL HAVE TO WAIT AND SEE.
'CAUSE YOU KNOW I GOTTA WONDER IF IT'S ABOUT ME, RIGHT?
OKAY, WOW. EGO, THY NAME IS OLIVER QUEEN.
THIS IS NOT NORMAL
PART 1
COLLIN KELLY & JACKSON LANZING Writers
JAVIER FERNANDEZ Artist
JOHN KALISZ Colors
DERON BENNETT Letters
KEVIN NOWLAN Cover
DAVE WIELGOSZ Asst. Editor
KATIE KUBERT Editor
JAMIE S. RICH Group Editor

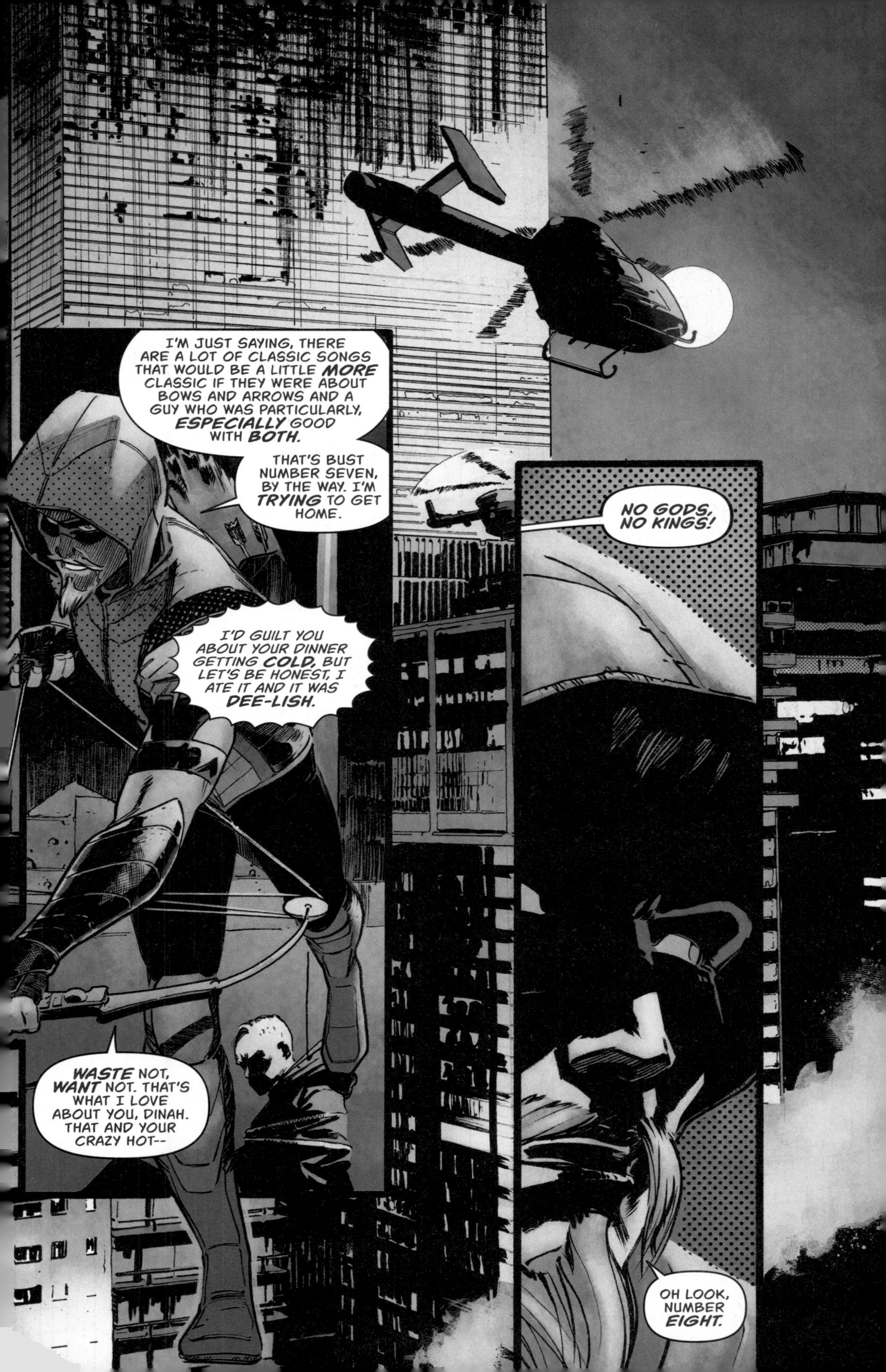
I'M JUST SAYING, THERE ARE A LOT OF CLASSIC SONGS THAT WOULD BE A LITTLE MORE CLASSIC IF THEY WERE ABOUT BOWS AND ARROWS AND A GUY WHO WAS PARTICULARLY, ESPECIALLY GOOD WITH BOTH.
THAT'S BUST NUMBER SEVEN, BY THE WAY. I'M TRYING TO GET HOME.
I'D GUILT YOU ABOUT YOUR DINNER GETTING COLD, BUT LET'S BE HONEST, I ATE IT AND IT WAS DEE-LISH.
WASTE NOT, WANT NOT. THAT'S WHAT I LOVE ABOUT YOU, DINAH. THAT AND YOUR CRAZY HOT--
NO GODS, NO KINGS!
OH LOOK, NUMBER EIGHT.

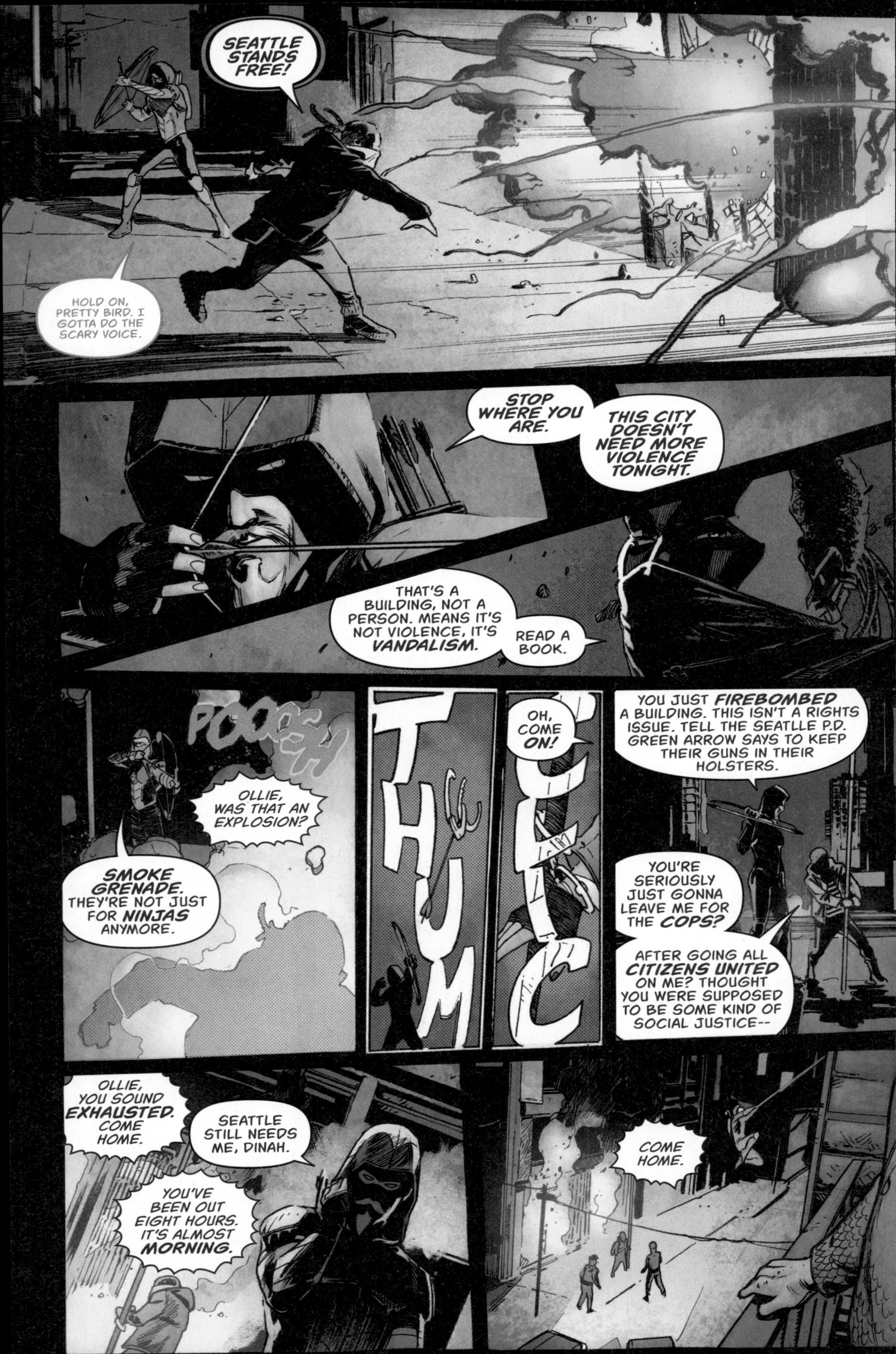
SEATTLE STANDS FREE!
HOLD ON, PRETTY BIRD. I GOTTA DO THE SCARY VOICE.
STOP WHERE YOU ARE.
THIS CITY DOESN'T NEED MORE VIOLENCE TONIGHT.
THAT'S A BUILDING, NOT A PERSON. MEANS IT'S NOT VIOLENCE, IT'S VANDALISM.
READ A BOOK.
POOOSH
OLLIE, WAS THAT AN EXPLOSION?
SMOKE GRENADE. THEY'RE NOT JUST FOR NINJAS ANYMORE.
THUM
OH, COME ON!
CLIC
YOU JUST FIREBOMBED A BUILDING. THIS ISN'T A RIGHTS ISSUE. TELL THE SEATTLE P.D. GREEN ARROW SAYS TO KEEP THEIR GUNS IN THEIR HOLSTERS.
YOU'RE SERIOUSLY JUST GONNA LEAVE ME FOR THE COPS?
AFTER GOING ALL CITIZENS UNITED ON ME? THOUGHT YOU WERE SUPPOSED TO BE SOME KIND OF SOCIAL JUSTICE--
OLLIE, YOU SOUND EXHAUSTED. COME HOME.
SEATTLE STILL NEEDS ME, DINAH.
YOU'VE BEEN OUT EIGHT HOURS. IT'S ALMOST MORNING.
COME HOME.

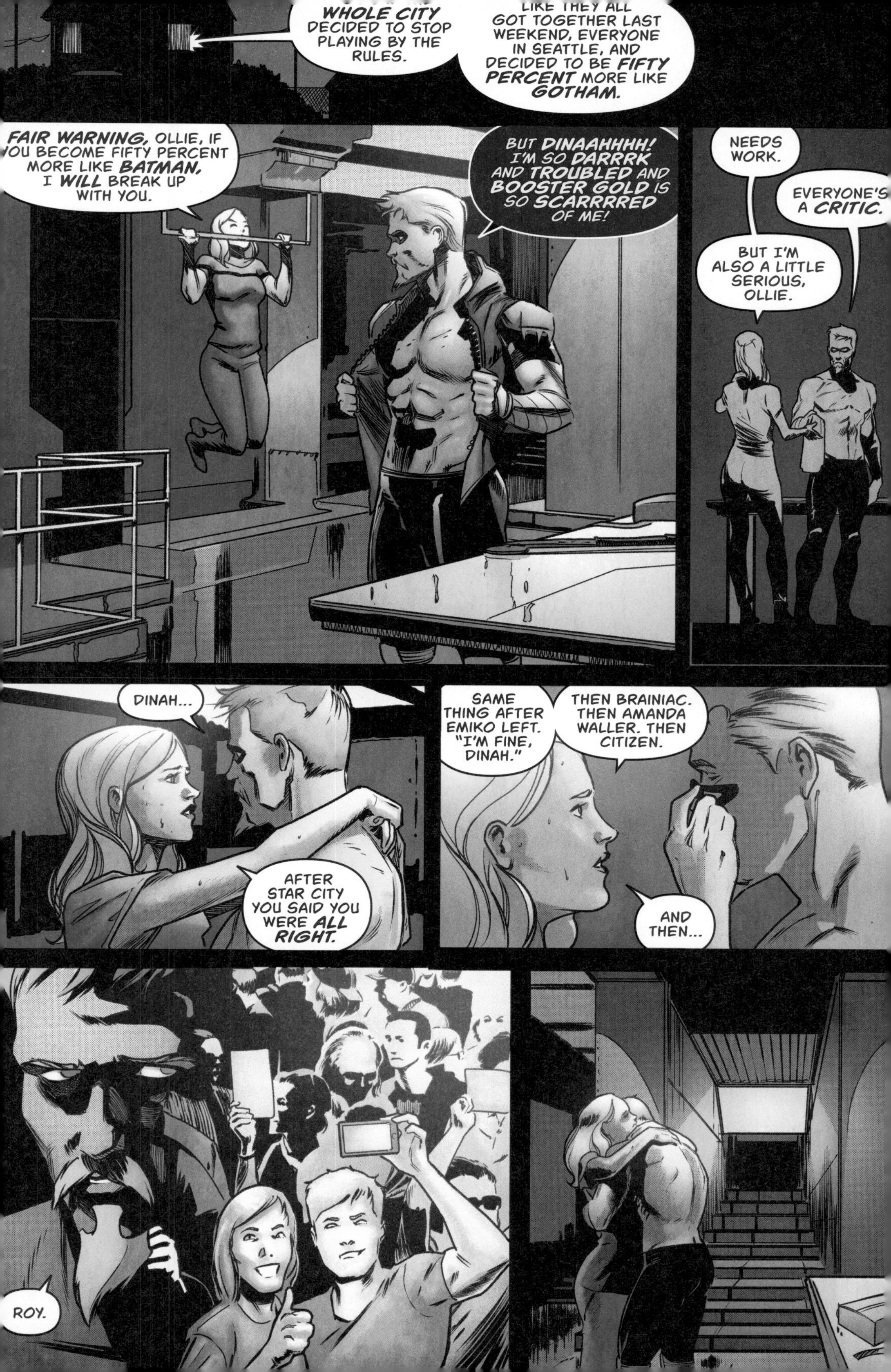

WHOLE CITY DECIDED TO STOP PLAYING BY THE RULES.
LIKE THEY ALL GOT TOGETHER LAST WEEKEND, EVERYONE IN SEATTLE, AND DECIDED TO BE FIFTY PERCENT MORE LIKE GOTHAM.
FAIR WARNING, OLLIE, IF YOU BECOME FIFTY PERCENT MORE LIKE BATMAN, I WILL BREAK UP WITH YOU.
BUT DINAAHHHH! I'M SO DARRRK AND TROUBLED AND BOOSTER GOLD IS SO SCARRRRED OF ME!
NEEDS WORK.
EVERYONE'S A CRITIC.
BUT I'M ALSO A LITTLE SERIOUS, OLLIE.
DINAH...
AFTER STAR CITY YOU SAID YOU WERE ALL RIGHT.
SAME THING AFTER EMIKO LEFT. "I'M FINE, DINAH."
THEN BRAINIAC. THEN AMANDA WALLER. THEN CITIZEN.
AND THEN...
ROY.

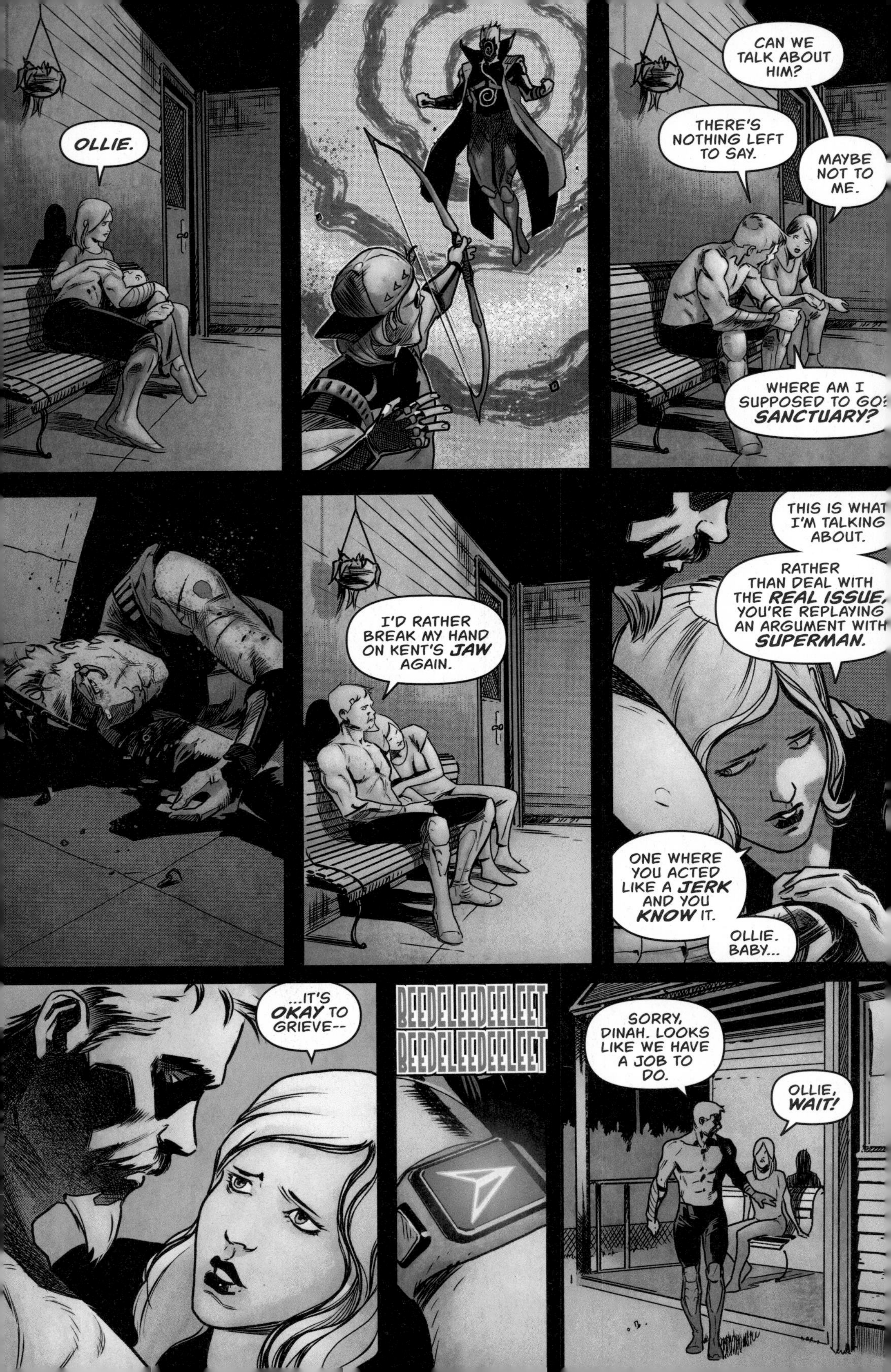
OLLIE.
CAN WE TALK ABOUT HIM?
THERE'S NOTHING LEFT TO SAY.
MAYBE NOT TO ME.
WHERE AM I SUPPOSED TO GO: SANCTUARY?
I'D RATHER BREAK MY HAND ON KENT'S JAW AGAIN.
THIS IS WHAT I'M TALKING ABOUT.
RATHER THAN DEAL WITH THE REAL ISSUE, YOU'RE REPLAYING AN ARGUMENT WITH SUPERMAN.
ONE WHERE YOU ACTED LIKE A JERK AND YOU KNOW IT.
OLLIE. BABY...
...IT'S OKAY TO GRIEVE--
BEEDELEEDEELEET
BEEDELEEDEELEET
SORRY, DINAH. LOOKS LIKE WE HAVE A JOB TO DO.
OLLIE, WAIT!

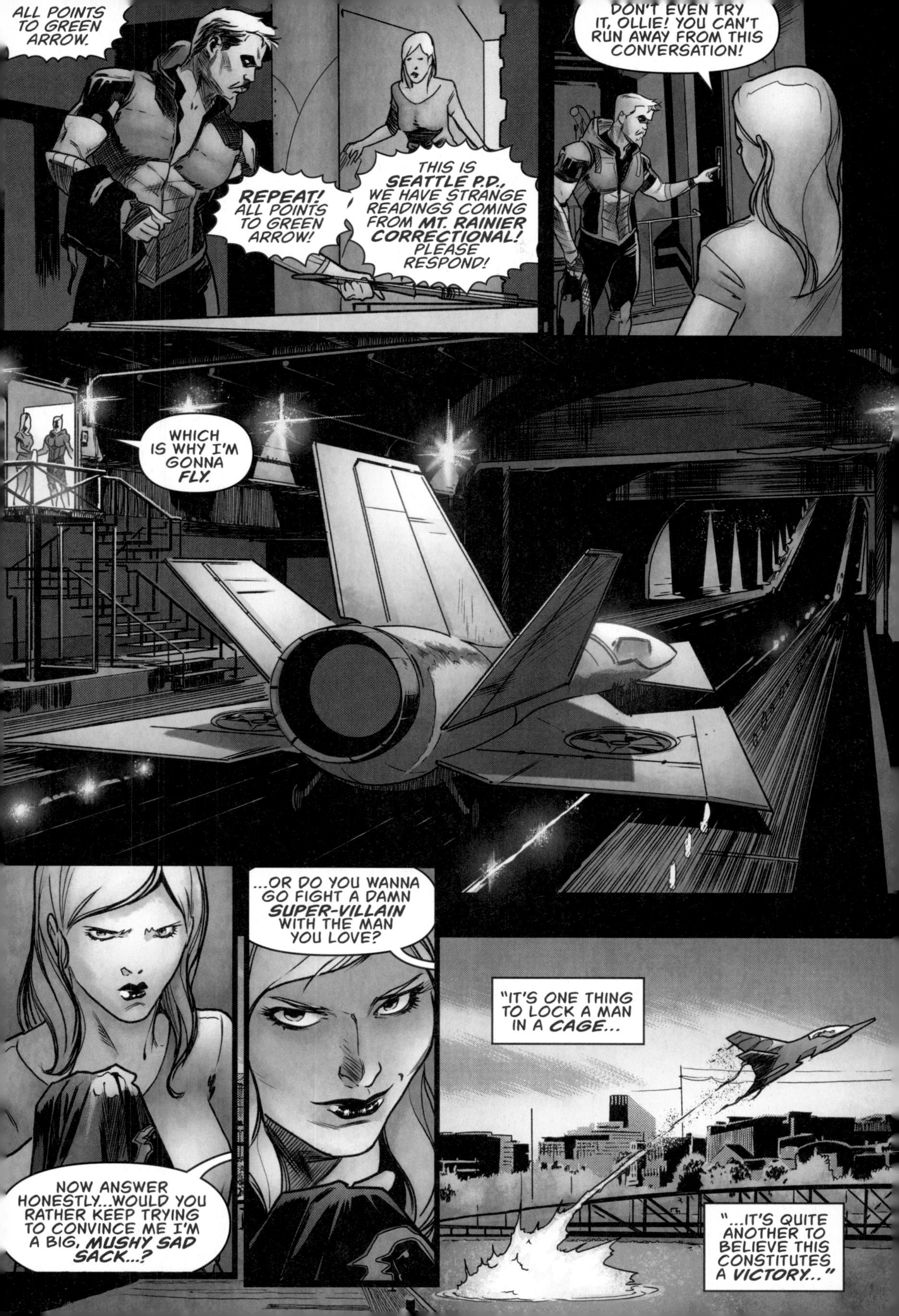
ALL POINTS TO GREEN ARROW.
REPEAT! ALL POINTS TO GREEN ARROW!
THIS IS SEATTLE P.D., WE HAVE STRANGE READINGS COMING FROM MT. RAINIER CORRECTIONAL! PLEASE RESPOND!
DON'T EVEN TRY IT, OLLIE! YOU CAN'T RUN AWAY FROM THIS CONVERSATION!
WHICH IS WHY I'M GONNA FLY.
NOW ANSWER HONESTLY...WOULD YOU RATHER KEEP TRYING TO CONVINCE ME I'M A BIG, MUSHY SAD SACK...?
...OR DO YOU WANNA GO FIGHT A DAMN SUPER-VILLAIN WITH THE MAN YOU LOVE?
"IT'S ONE THING TO LOCK A MAN IN A CAGE...
"...IT'S QUITE ANOTHER TO BELIEVE THIS CONSTITUTES A VICTORY..."

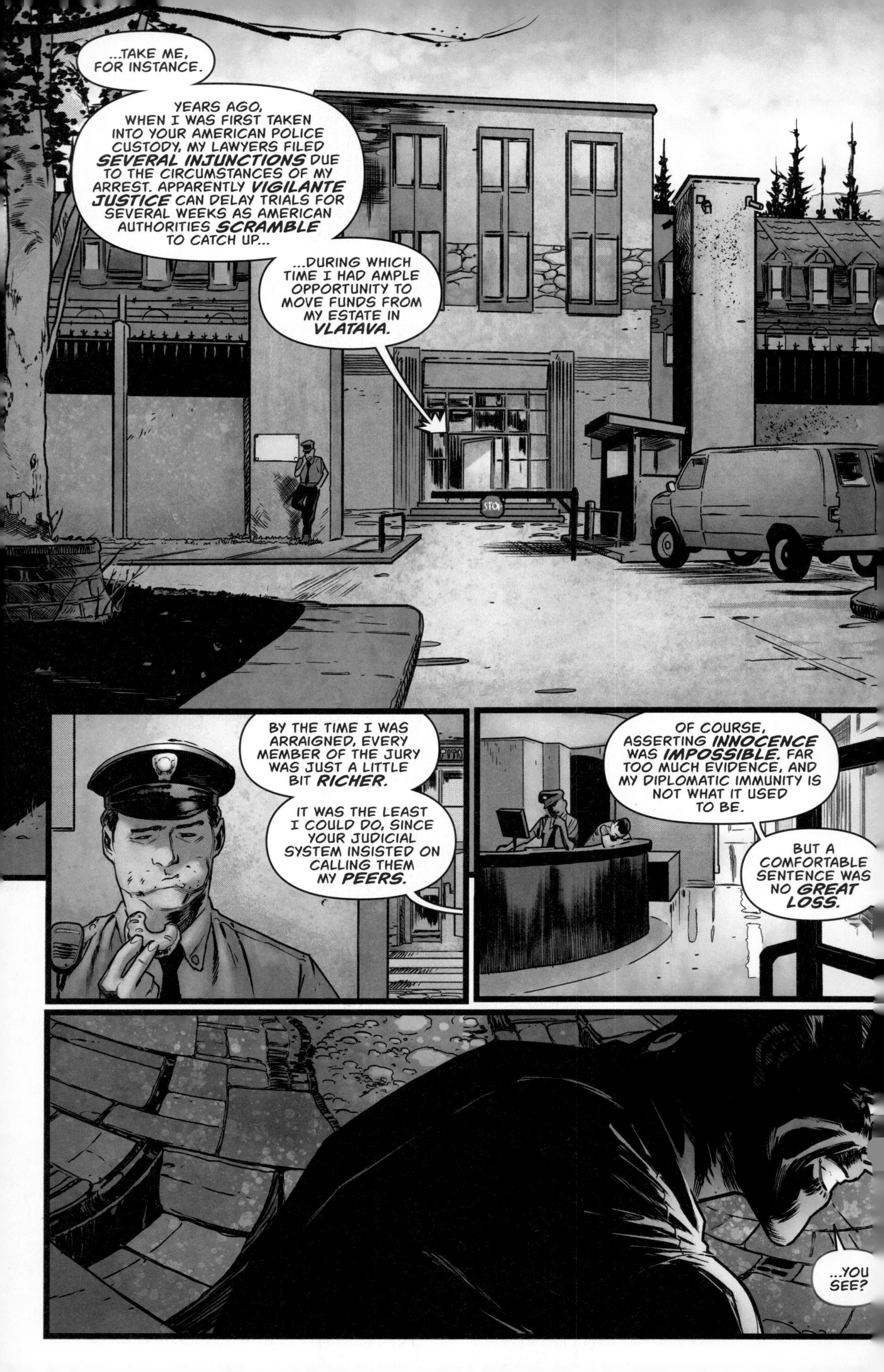
...TAKE ME, FOR INSTANCE.
YEARS AGO, WHEN I WAS FIRST TAKEN INTO YOUR AMERICAN POLICE CUSTODY, MY LAWYERS FILED SEVERAL INJUNCTIONS DUE TO THE CIRCUMSTANCES OF MY ARREST. APPARENTLY VIGILANTE JUSTICE CAN DELAY TRIALS FOR SEVERAL WEEKS AS AMERICAN AUTHORITIES SCRAMBLE TO CATCH UP...
...DURING WHICH TIME I HAD AMPLE OPPORTUNITY TO MOVE FUNDS FROM MY ESTATE IN VLATAVA.
STOP
BY THE TIME I WAS ARRAIGNED, EVERY MEMBER OF THE JURY WAS JUST A LITTLE BIT RICHER.
IT WAS THE LEAST I COULD DO, SINCE YOUR JUDICIAL SYSTEM INSISTED ON CALLING THEM MY PEERS.
OF COURSE, ASSERTING INNOCENCE WAS IMPOSSIBLE. FAR TOO MUCH EVIDENCE, AND MY DIPLOMATIC IMMUNITY IS NOT WHAT IT USED TO BE.
BUT A COMFORTABLE SENTENCE WAS NO GREAT LOSS.
...YOU SEE?

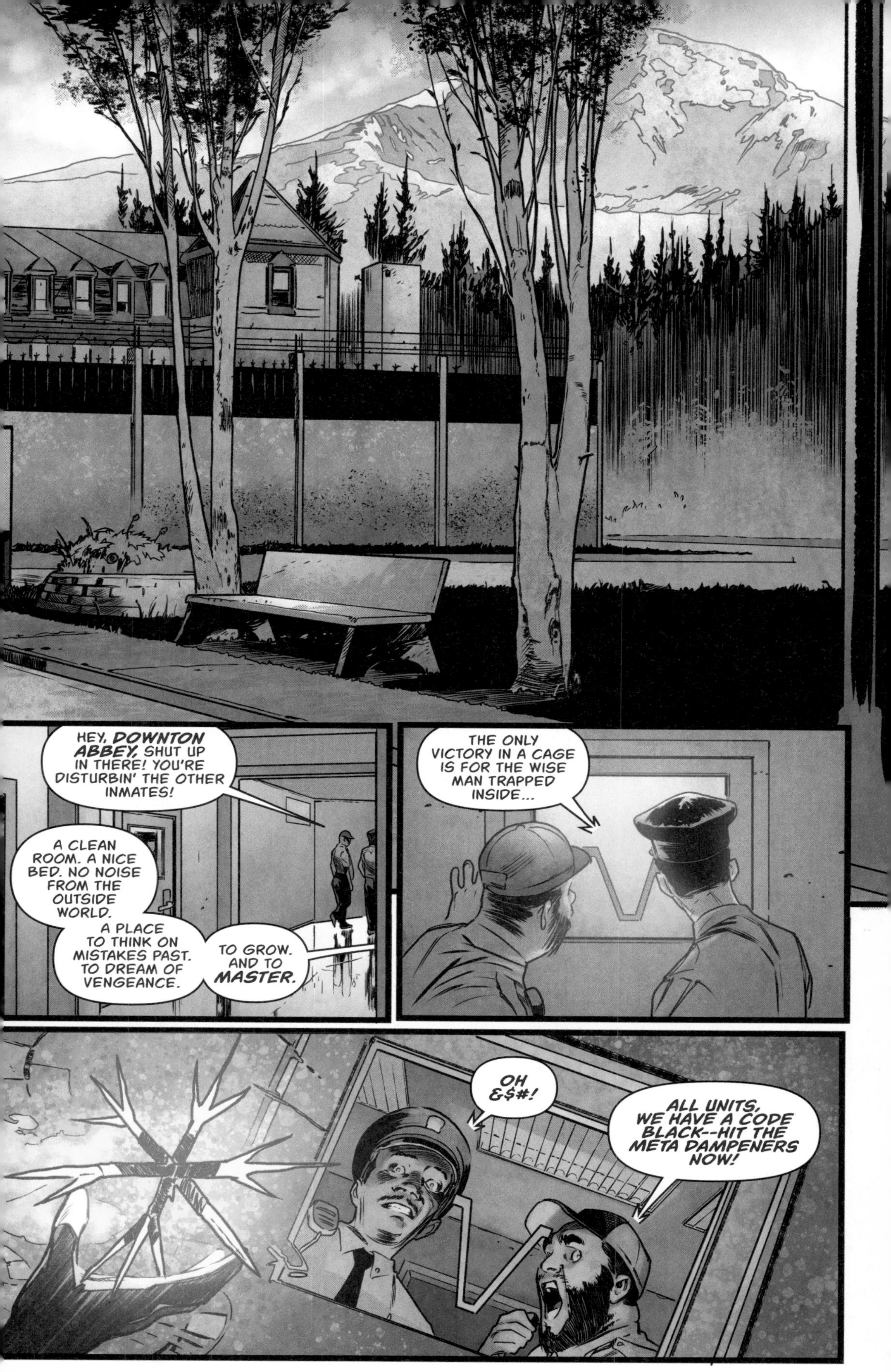
HEY, DOWNTON ABBEY, SHUT UP IN THERE! YOU'RE DISTURBIN' THE OTHER INMATES!
A CLEAN ROOM. A NICE BED. NO NOISE FROM THE OUTSIDE WORLD.
A PLACE TO THINK ON MISTAKES PAST. TO DREAM OF VENGEANCE.
TO GROW. AND TO MASTER.
THE ONLY VICTORY IN A CAGE IS FOR THE WISE MAN TRAPPED INSIDE...
OH &$#!
ALL UNITS, WE HAVE A CODE BLACK--HIT THE META DAMPENERS NOW!

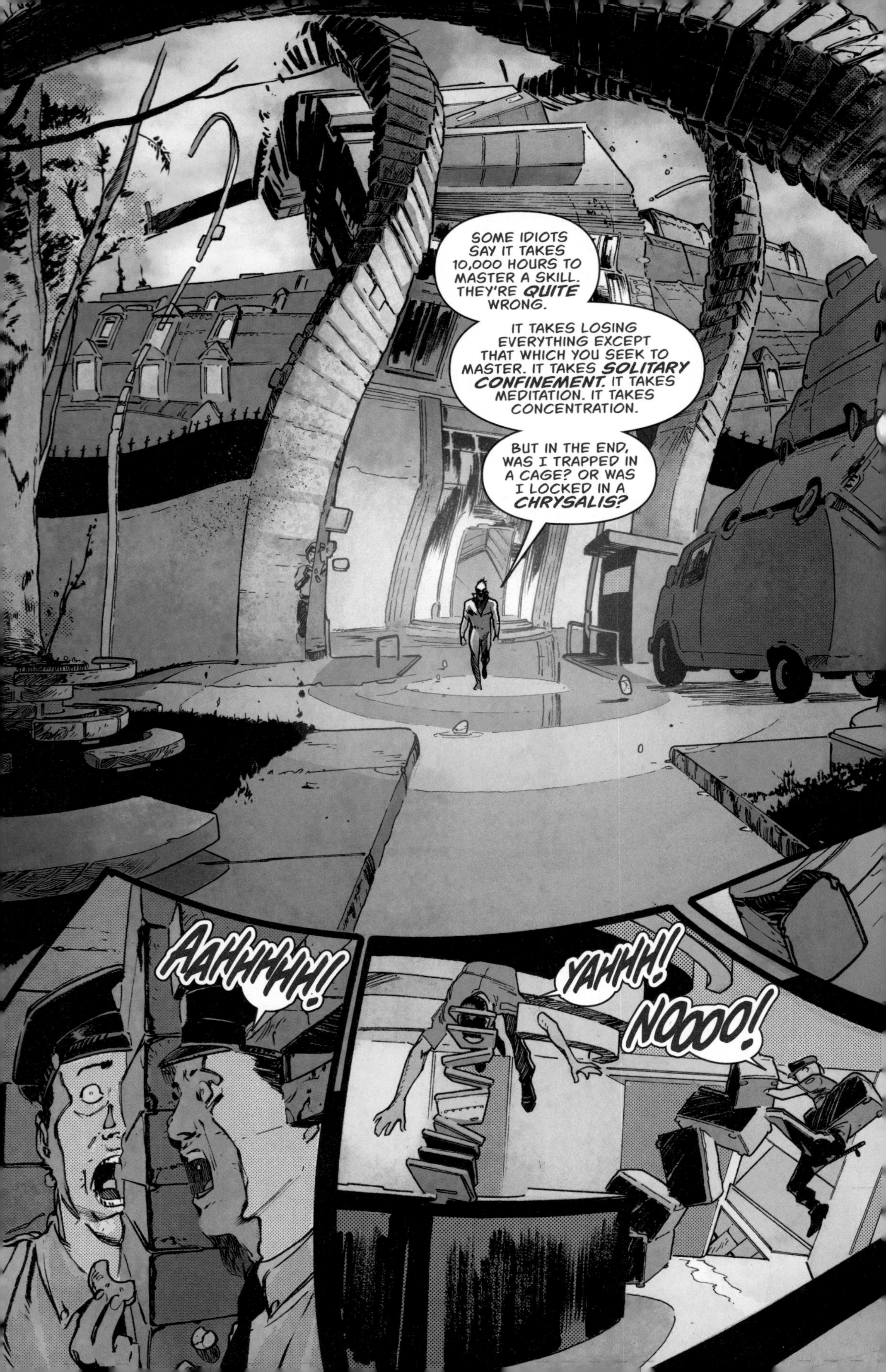
SOME IDIOTS SAY IT TAKES 10,000 HOURS TO MASTER A SKILL. THEY'RE QUITE WRONG.
IT TAKES LOSING EVERYTHING EXCEPT THAT WHICH YOU SEEK TO MASTER. IT TAKES SOLITARY CONFINEMENT. IT TAKES MEDITATION. IT TAKES CONCENTRATION.
BUT IN THE END, WAS I TRAPPED IN A CAGE? OR WAS I LOCKED IN A CHRYSALIS?
AAHHHHH!
YAHHH!
NOOOO!

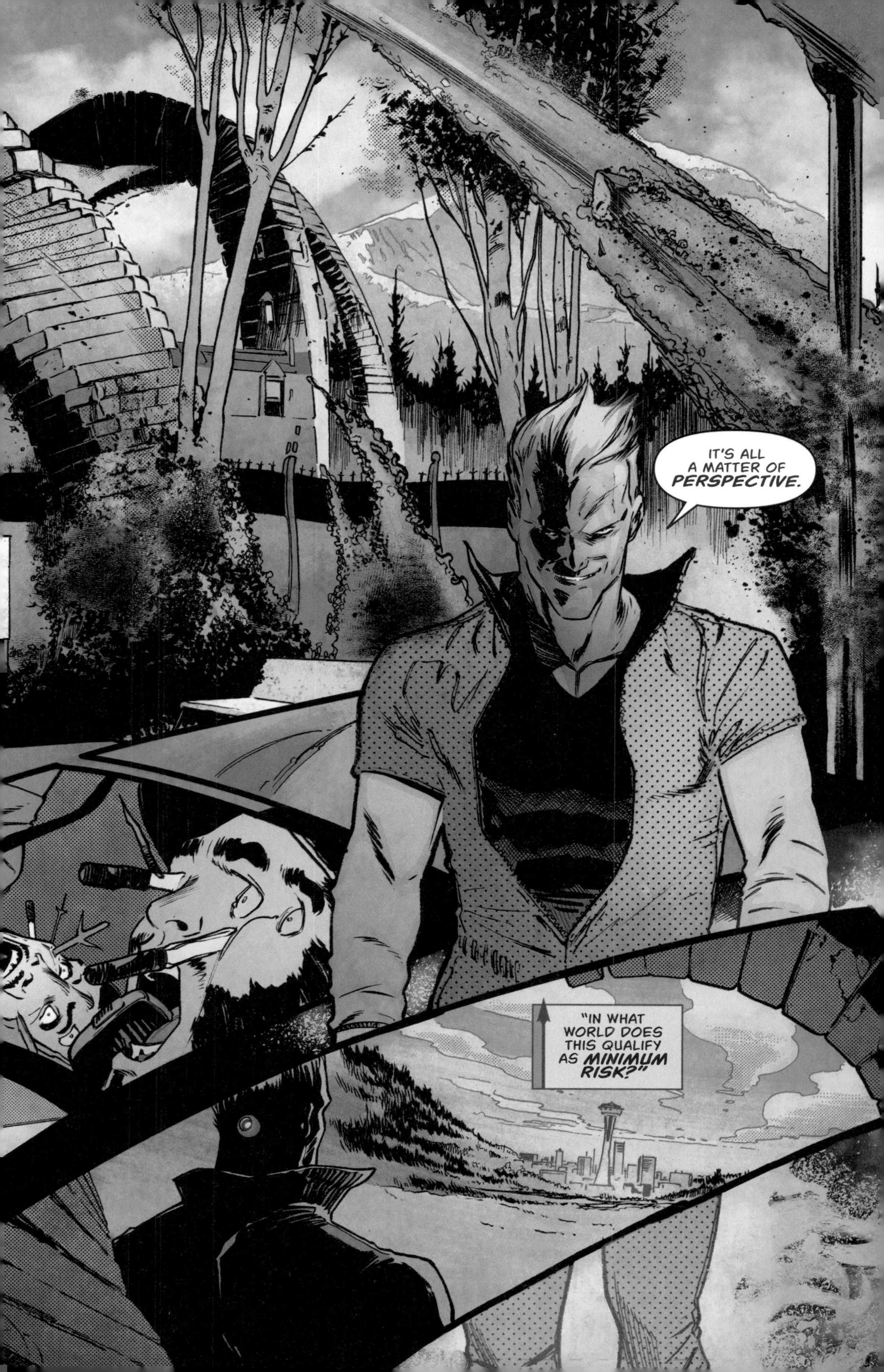
IT'S ALL A MATTER OF PERSPECTIVE.
"IN WHAT WORLD DOES THIS QUALIFY AS MINIMUM RISK?"

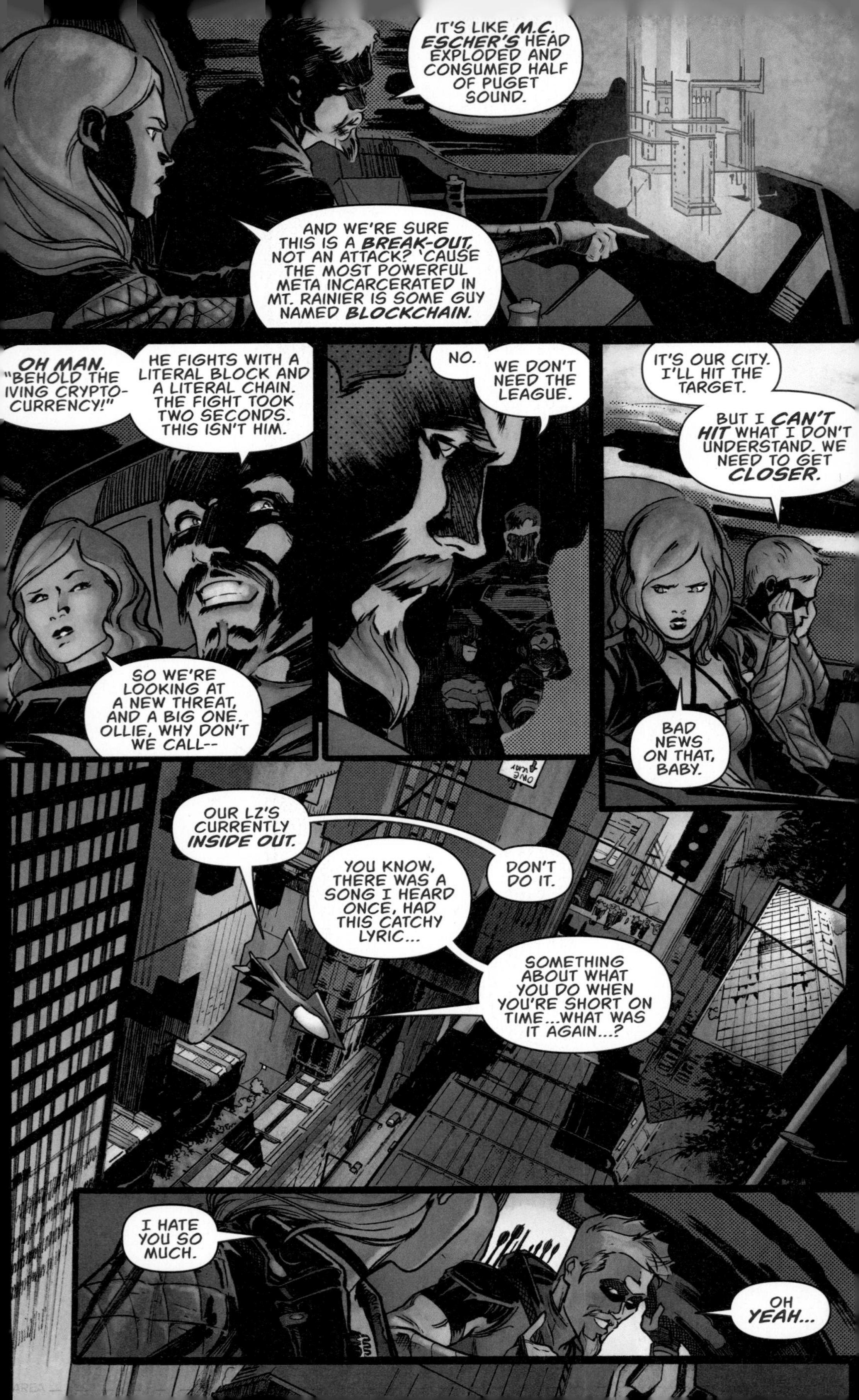

IT'S LIKE M.C. ESCHER'S HEAD EXPLODED AND CONSUMED HALF OF PUGET SOUND.
AND WE'RE SURE THIS IS A BREAK-OUT, NOT AN ATTACK? 'CAUSE THE MOST POWERFUL META INCARCERATED IN MT. RAINIER IS SOME GUY NAMED BLOCKCHAIN.
OH MAN. "BEHOLD THE LIVING CRYPTO-CURRENCY!"
HE FIGHTS WITH A LITERAL BLOCK AND A LITERAL CHAIN. THE FIGHT TOOK TWO SECONDS. THIS ISN'T HIM.
SO WE'RE LOOKING AT A NEW THREAT, AND A BIG ONE. OLLIE, WHY DON'T WE CALL--
NO.
WE DON'T NEED THE LEAGUE.
IT'S OUR CITY. I'LL HIT THE TARGET.
BUT I CAN'T HIT WHAT I DON'T UNDERSTAND. WE NEED TO GET CLOSER.
BAD NEWS ON THAT, BABY.
ONE WAY
OUR LZ'S CURRENTLY INSIDE OUT.
DON'T DO IT.
YOU KNOW, THERE WAS A SONG I HEARD ONCE, HAD THIS CATCHY LYRIC...
SOMETHING ABOUT WHAT YOU DO WHEN YOU'RE SHORT ON TIME...WHAT WAS IT AGAIN...?
I HATE YOU SO MUCH.
OH YEAH...

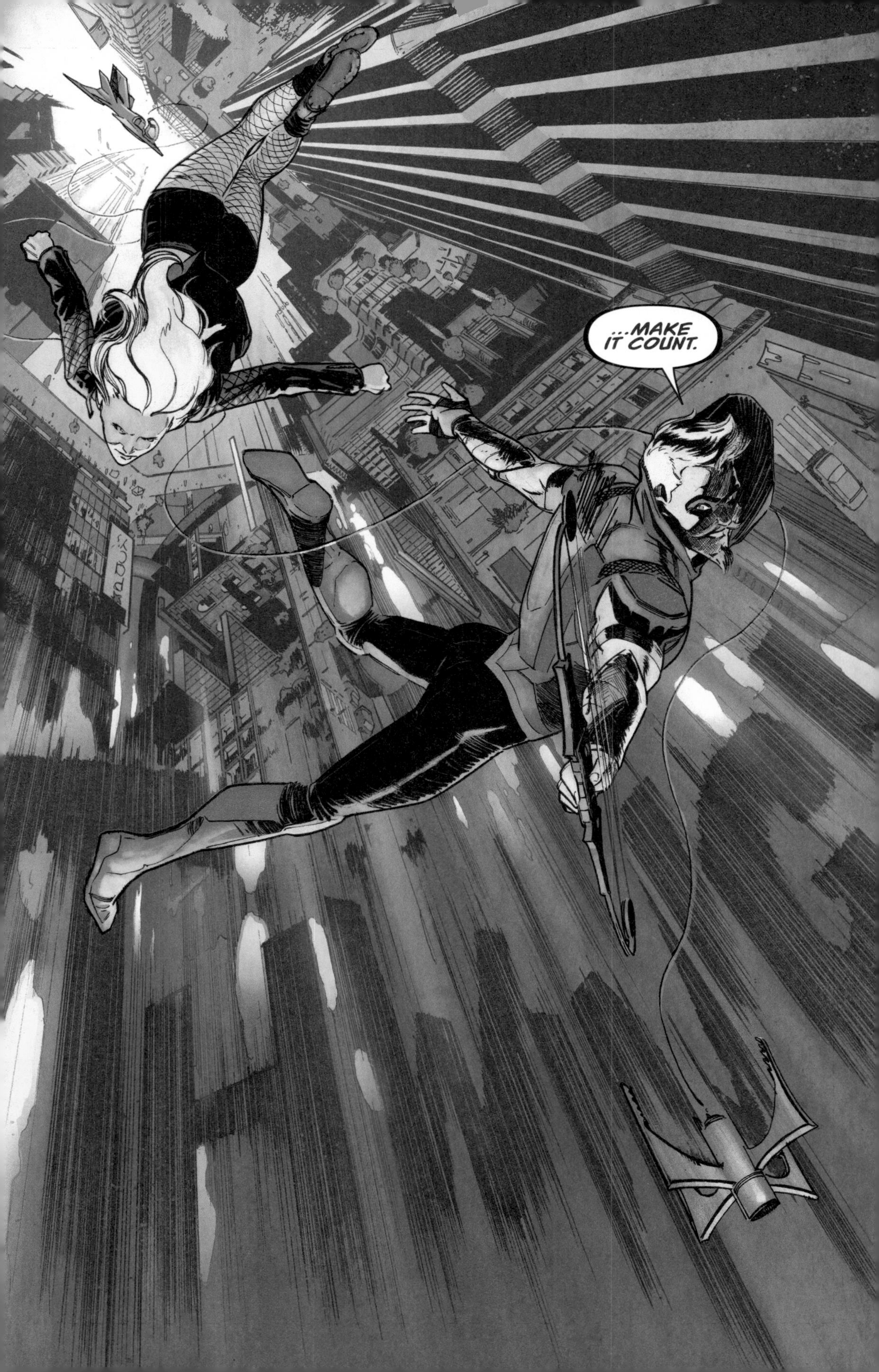
...MAKE IT COUNT.

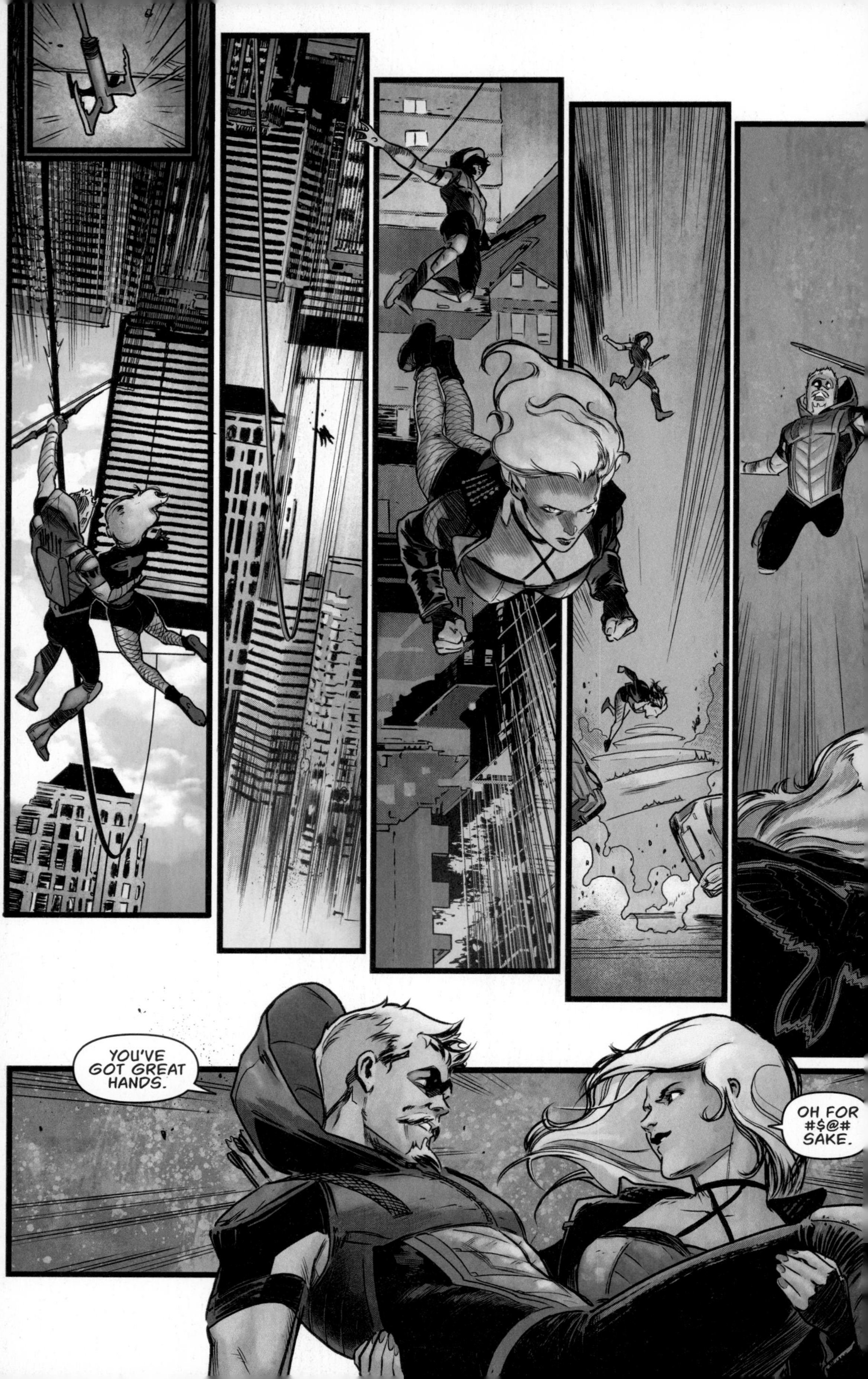
YOU'VE GOT GREAT HANDS.
OH FOR #$@# SAKE.

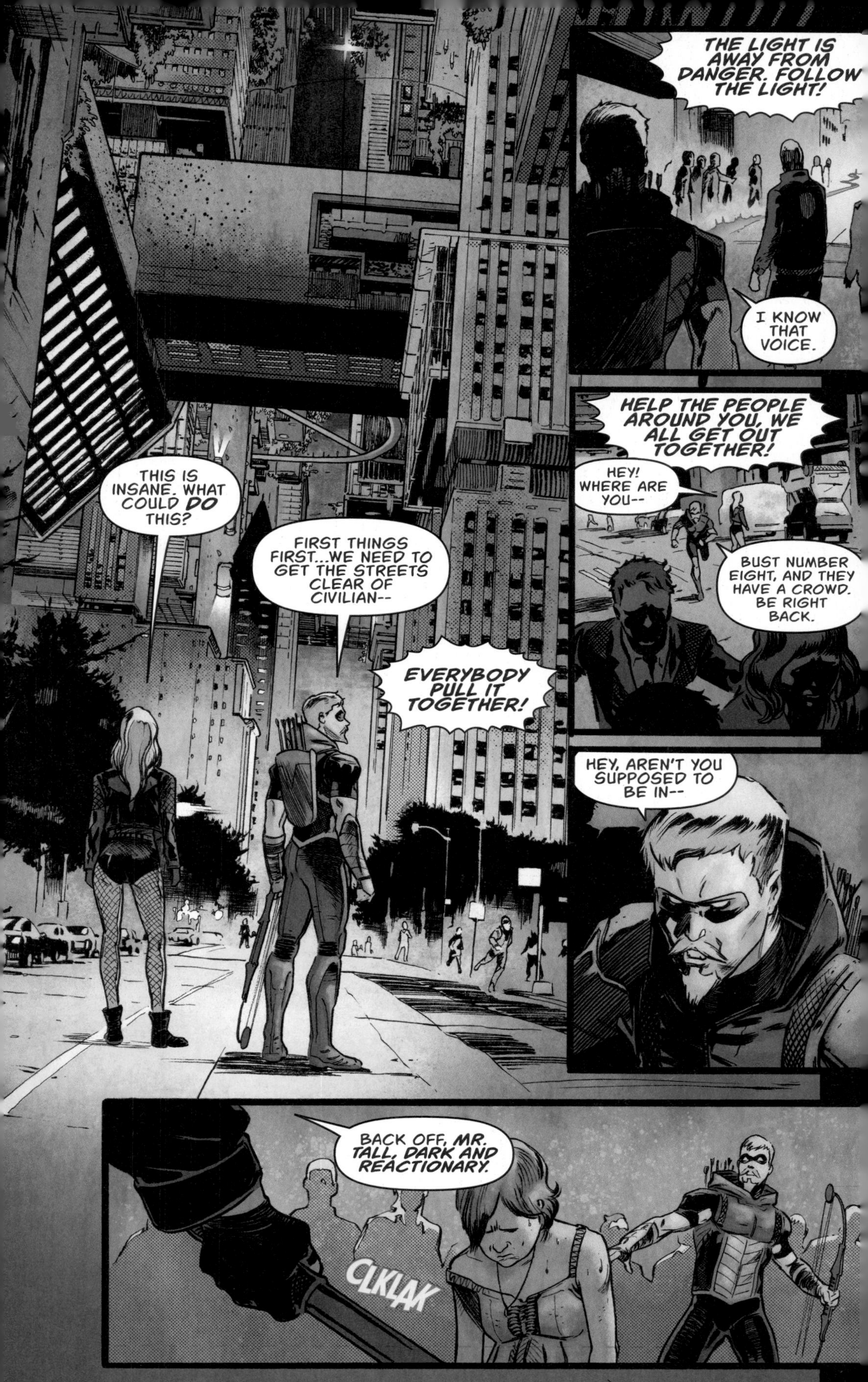
THIS IS INSANE. WHAT COULD DO THIS?
FIRST THINGS FIRST...WE NEED TO GET THE STREETS CLEAR OF CIVILIAN--
EVERYBODY PULL IT TOGETHER!
THE LIGHT IS AWAY FROM DANGER. FOLLOW THE LIGHT!
I KNOW THAT VOICE.
HELP THE PEOPLE AROUND YOU, WE ALL GET OUT TOGETHER!
HEY! WHERE ARE YOU--
BUST NUMBER EIGHT, AND THEY HAVE A CROWD. BE RIGHT BACK.
HEY, AREN'T YOU SUPPOSED TO BE IN--
BACK OFF, MR. TALL, DARK AND REACTIONARY.
CLKLAK

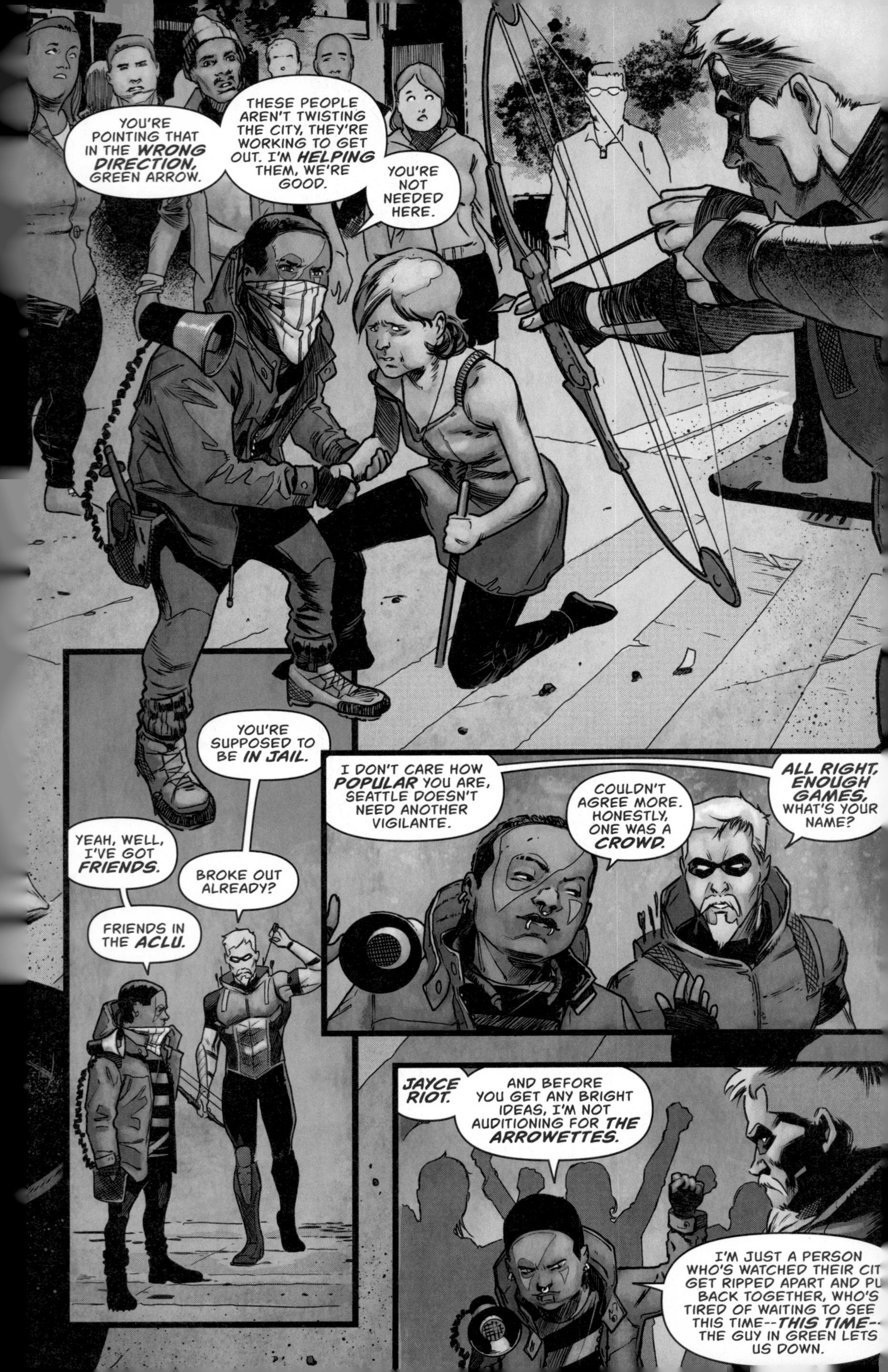
YOU'RE POINTING THAT IN THE WRONG DIRECTION, GREEN ARROW.
THESE PEOPLE AREN'T TWISTING THE CITY, THEY'RE WORKING TO GET OUT. I'M HELPING THEM, WE'RE GOOD.
YOU'RE NOT NEEDED HERE.
YOU'RE SUPPOSED TO BE IN JAIL.
YEAH, WELL, I'VE GOT FRIENDS.
BROKE OUT ALREADY?
FRIENDS IN THE ACLU.
I DON'T CARE HOW POPULAR YOU ARE, SEATTLE DOESN'T NEED ANOTHER VIGILANTE.
COULDN'T AGREE MORE. HONESTLY, ONE WAS A CROWD.
ALL RIGHT, ENOUGH GAMES. WHAT'S YOUR NAME?
JAYCE RIOT.
AND BEFORE YOU GET ANY BRIGHT IDEAS, I'M NOT AUDITIONING FOR THE ARROWETTES.
I'M JUST A PERSON WHO'S WATCHED THEIR CIT GET RIPPED APART AND PU BACK TOGETHER, WHO'S TIRED OF WAITING TO SEE THIS TIME--THIS TIME-- THE GUY IN GREEN LETS US DOWN.

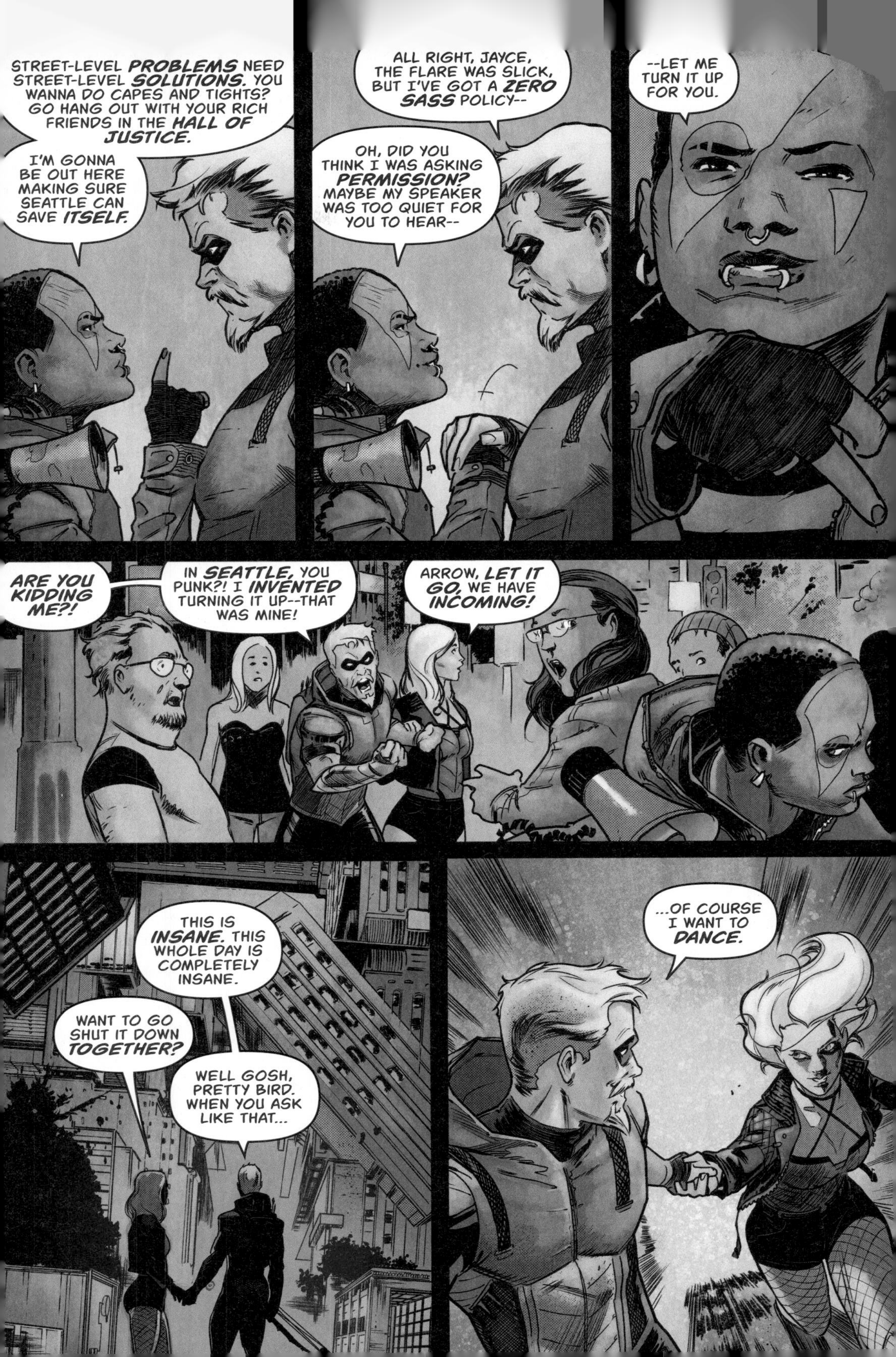
STREET-LEVEL PROBLEMS NEED STREET-LEVEL SOLUTIONS. YOU WANNA DO CAPES AND TIGHTS? GO HANG OUT WITH YOUR RICH FRIENDS IN THE HALL OF JUSTICE.
I'M GONNA BE OUT HERE MAKING SURE SEATTLE CAN SAVE ITSELF.
ALL RIGHT, JAYCE, THE FLARE WAS SLICK, BUT I'VE GOT A ZERO SASS POLICY--
OH, DID YOU THINK I WAS ASKING PERMISSION? MAYBE MY SPEAKER WAS TOO QUIET FOR YOU TO HEAR--
--LET ME TURN IT UP FOR YOU.
ARE YOU KIDDING ME?!
IN SEATTLE, YOU PUNK?! I INVENTED TURNING IT UP--THAT WAS MINE!
ARROW, LET IT GO, WE HAVE INCOMING!
THIS IS INSANE. THIS WHOLE DAY IS COMPLETELY INSANE.
WANT TO GO SHUT IT DOWN TOGETHER?
WELL GOSH, PRETTY BIRD. WHEN YOU ASK LIKE THAT...
...OF COURSE I WANT TO DANCE.

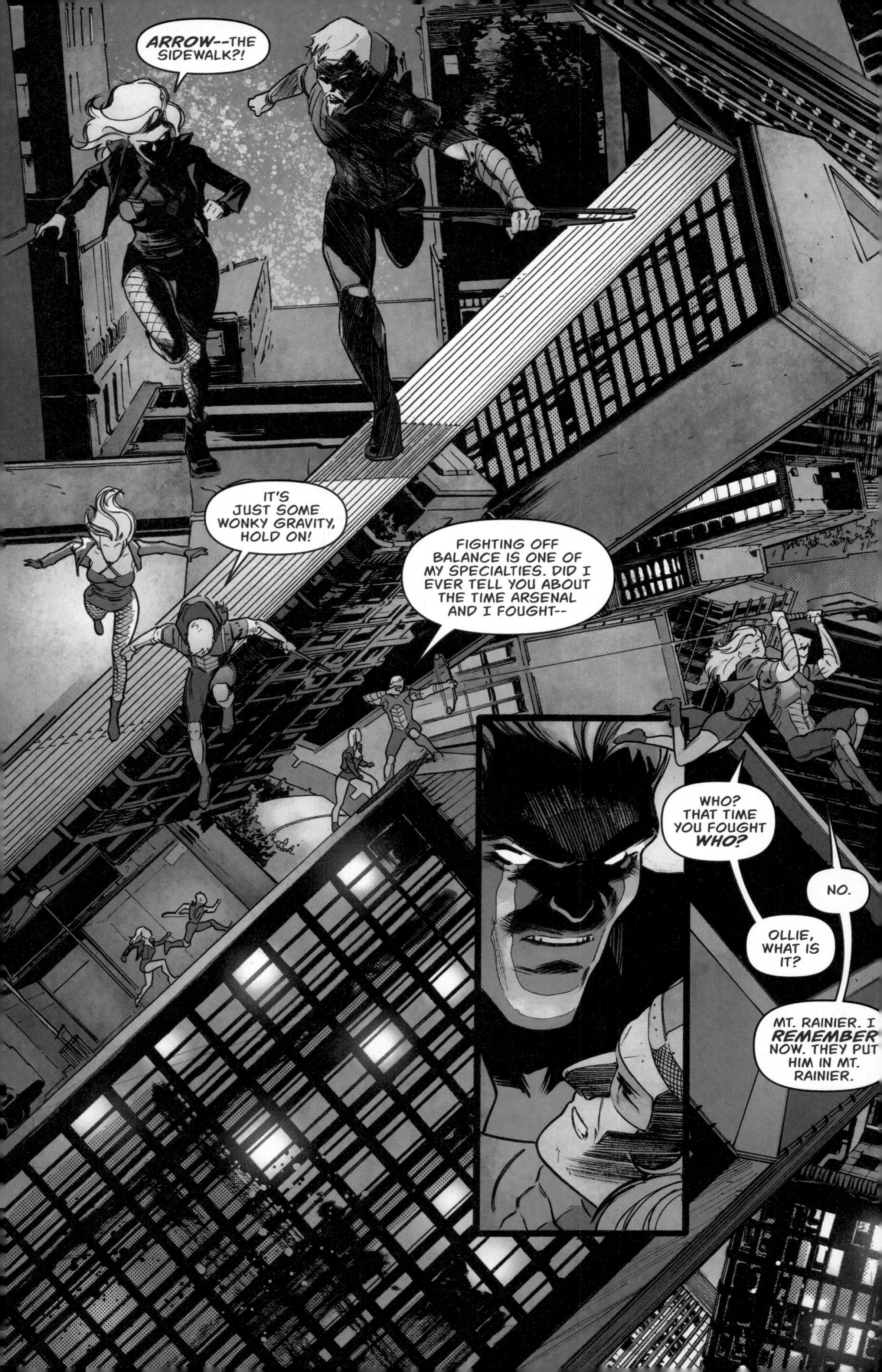
ARROW--THE SIDEWALK?!
IT'S JUST SOME WONKY GRAVITY, HOLD ON!
FIGHTING OFF BALANCE IS ONE OF MY SPECIALTIES. DID I EVER TELL YOU ABOUT THE TIME ARSENAL AND I FOUGHT--
WHO? THAT TIME YOU FOUGHT WHO?
NO.
OLLIE, WHAT IS IT?
MT. RAINIER. I REMEMBER NOW. THEY PUT HIM IN MT. RAINIER.

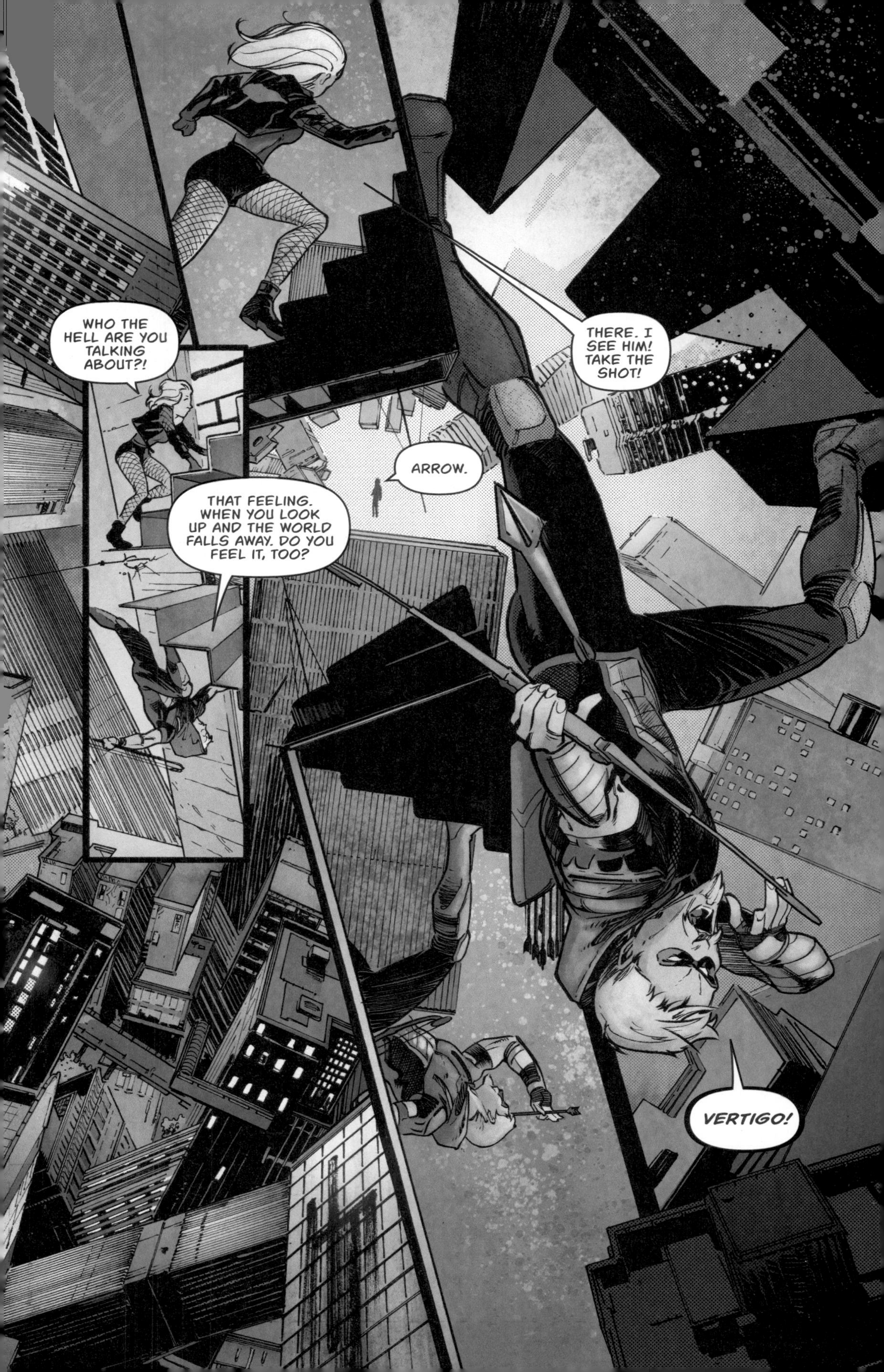
WHO THE HELL ARE YOU TALKING ABOUT?!
THERE. I SEE HIM! TAKE THE SHOT!
ARROW.
THAT FEELING. WHEN YOU LOOK UP AND THE WORLD FALLS AWAY. DO YOU FEEL IT, TOO?
VERTIGO!

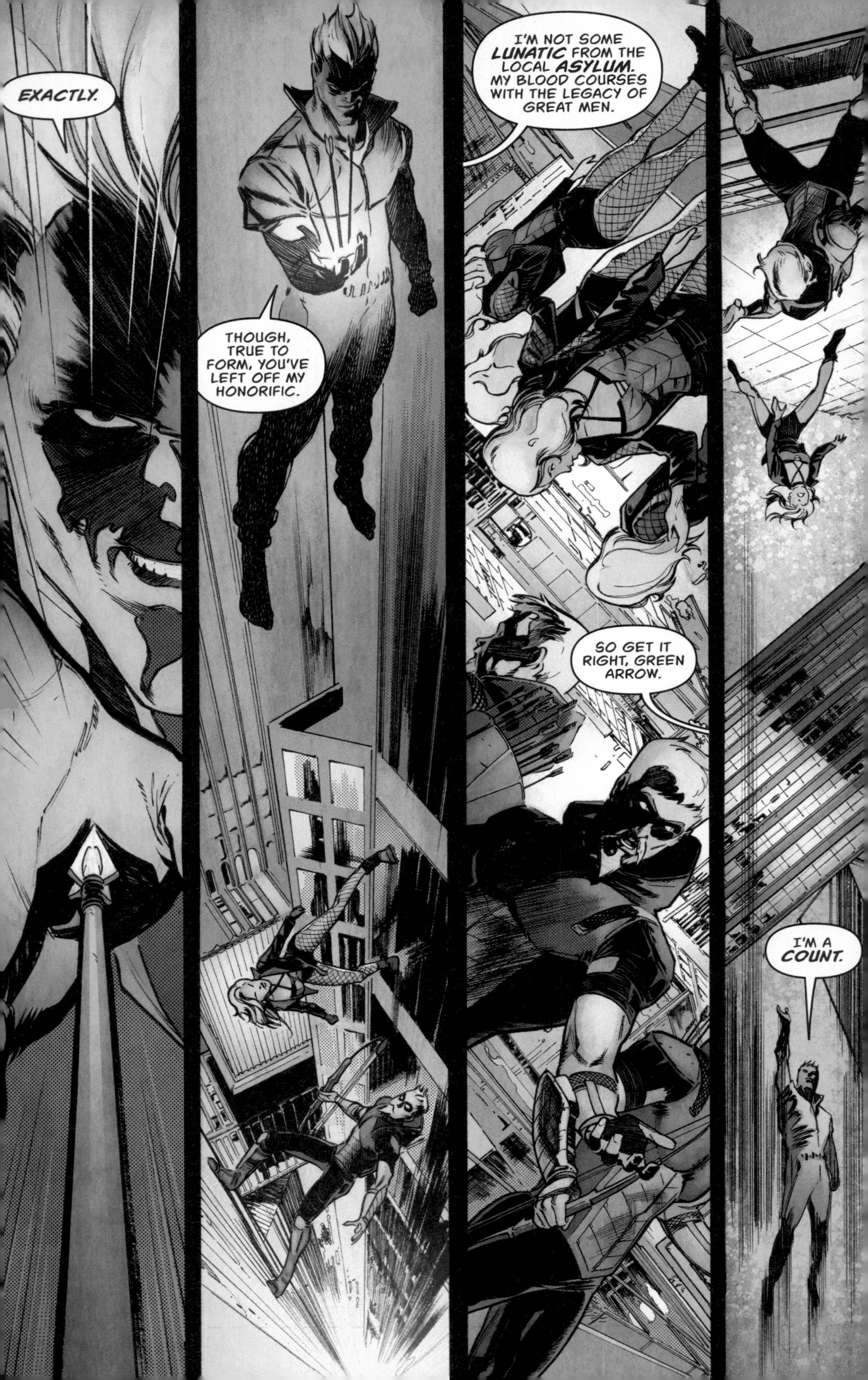
EXACTLY.
THOUGH, TRUE TO FORM, YOU'VE LEFT OFF MY HONORIFIC.
I'M NOT SOME LUNATIC FROM THE LOCAL ASYLUM. MY BLOOD COURSES WITH THE LEGACY OF GREAT MEN.
SO GET IT RIGHT, GREEN ARROW.
I'M A COUNT.

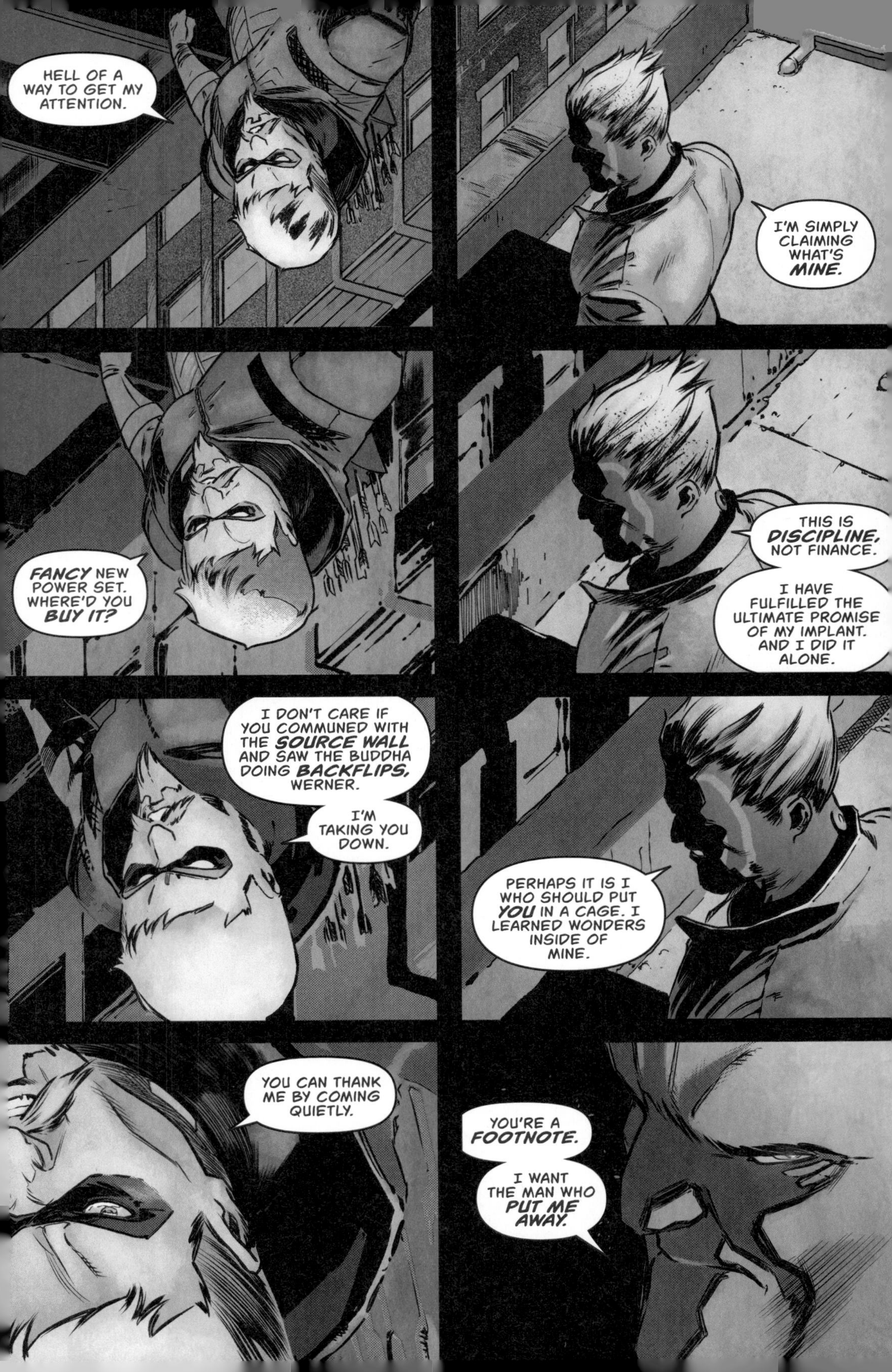
HELL OF A WAY TO GET MY ATTENTION.
I'M SIMPLY CLAIMING WHAT'S MINE.
FANCY NEW POWER SET. WHERE'D YOU BUY IT?
THIS IS DISCIPLINE, NOT FINANCE.
I HAVE FULFILLED THE ULTIMATE PROMISE OF MY IMPLANT. AND I DID IT ALONE.
I DON'T CARE IF YOU COMMUNED WITH THE SOURCE WALL AND SAW THE BUDDHA DOING BACKFLIPS, WERNER.
I'M TAKING YOU DOWN.
PERHAPS IT IS I WHO SHOULD PUT YOU IN A CAGE. I LEARNED WONDERS INSIDE OF MINE.
YOU CAN THANK ME BY COMING QUIETLY.
YOU'RE A FOOTNOTE.
I WANT THE MAN WHO PUT ME AWAY.

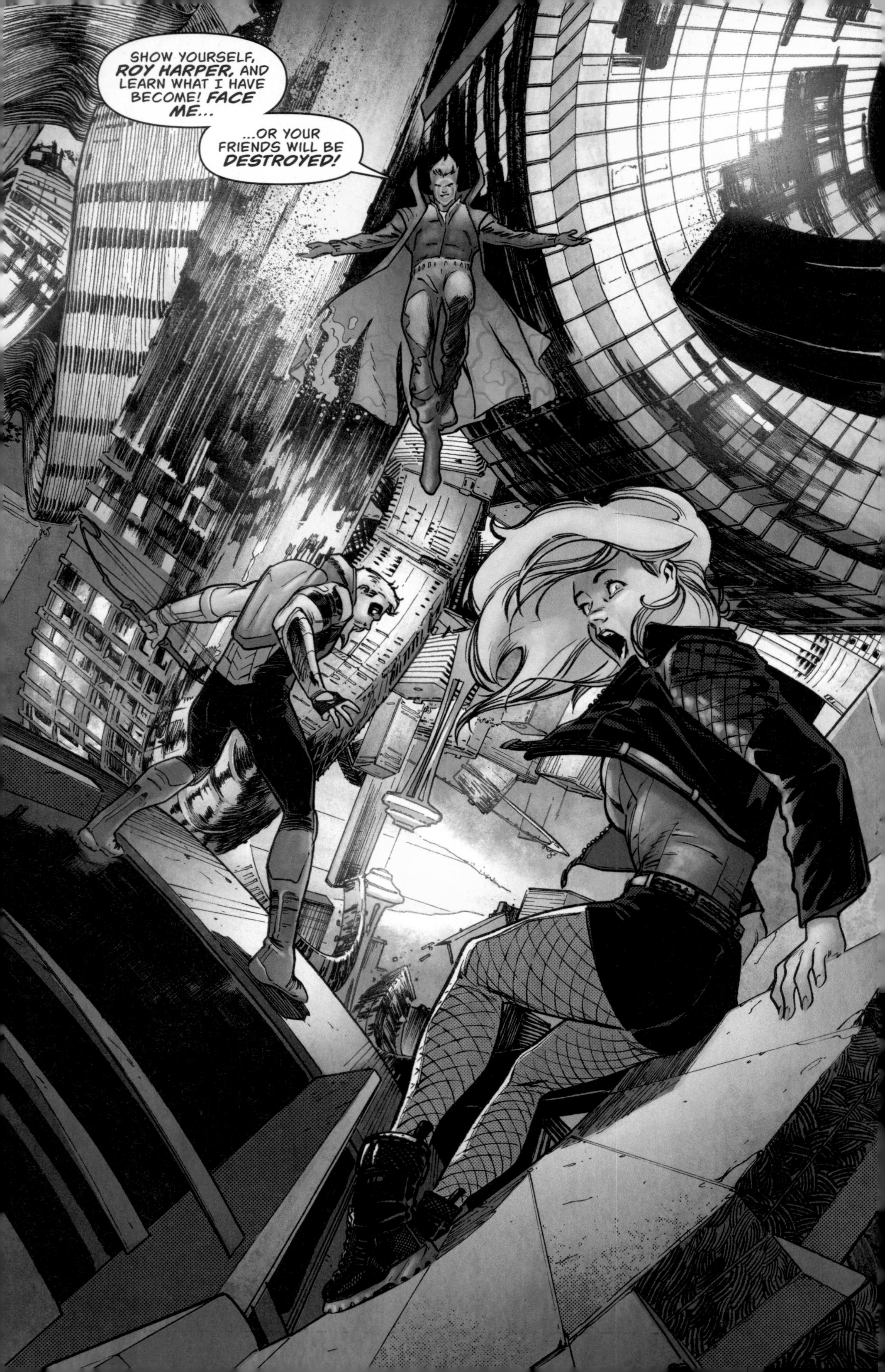
SHOW YOURSELF, ROY HARPER, AND LEARN WHAT I HAVE BECOME! FACE ME...
...OR YOUR FRIENDS WILL BE DESTROYED!

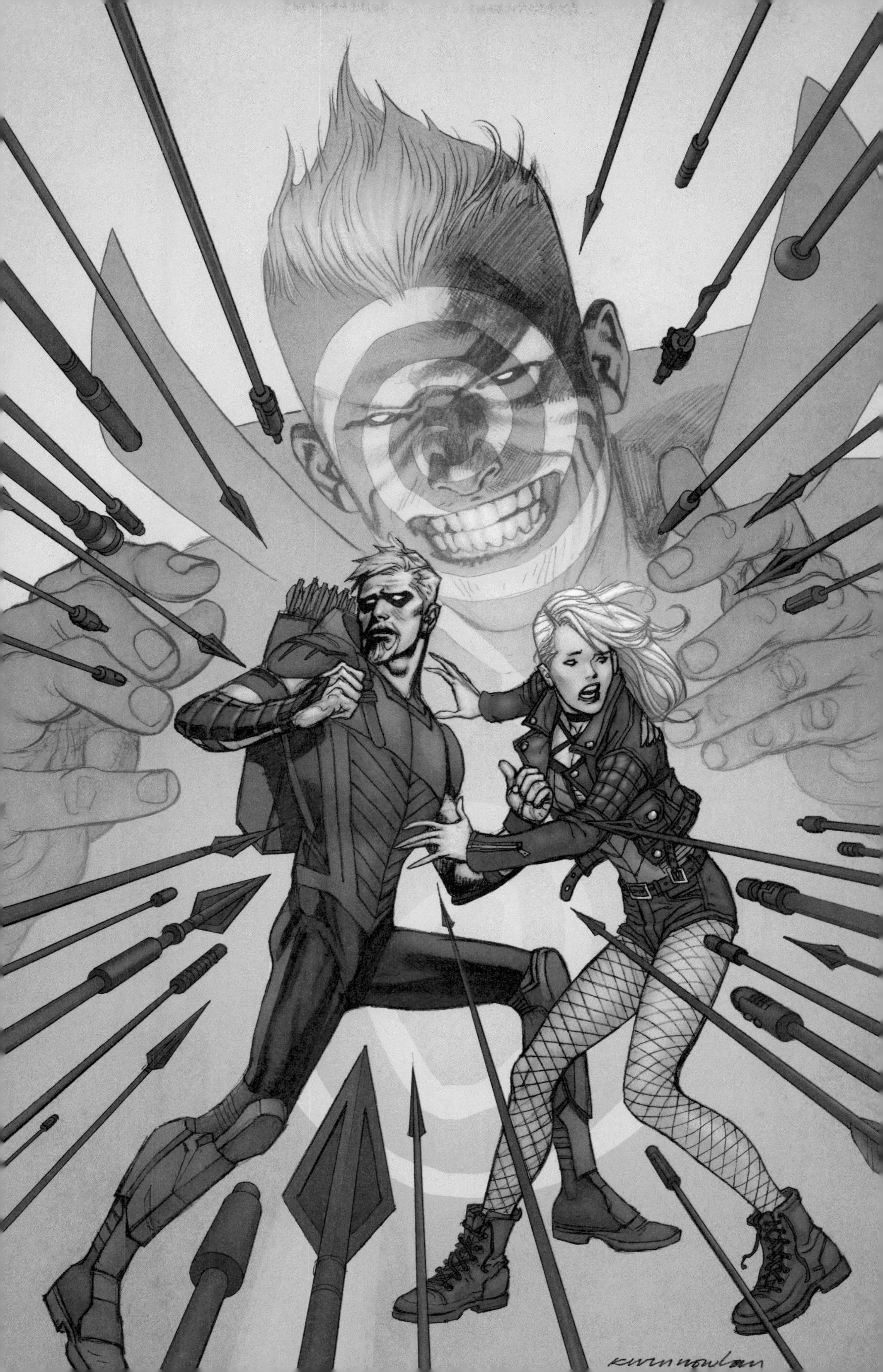
kevinnowlan

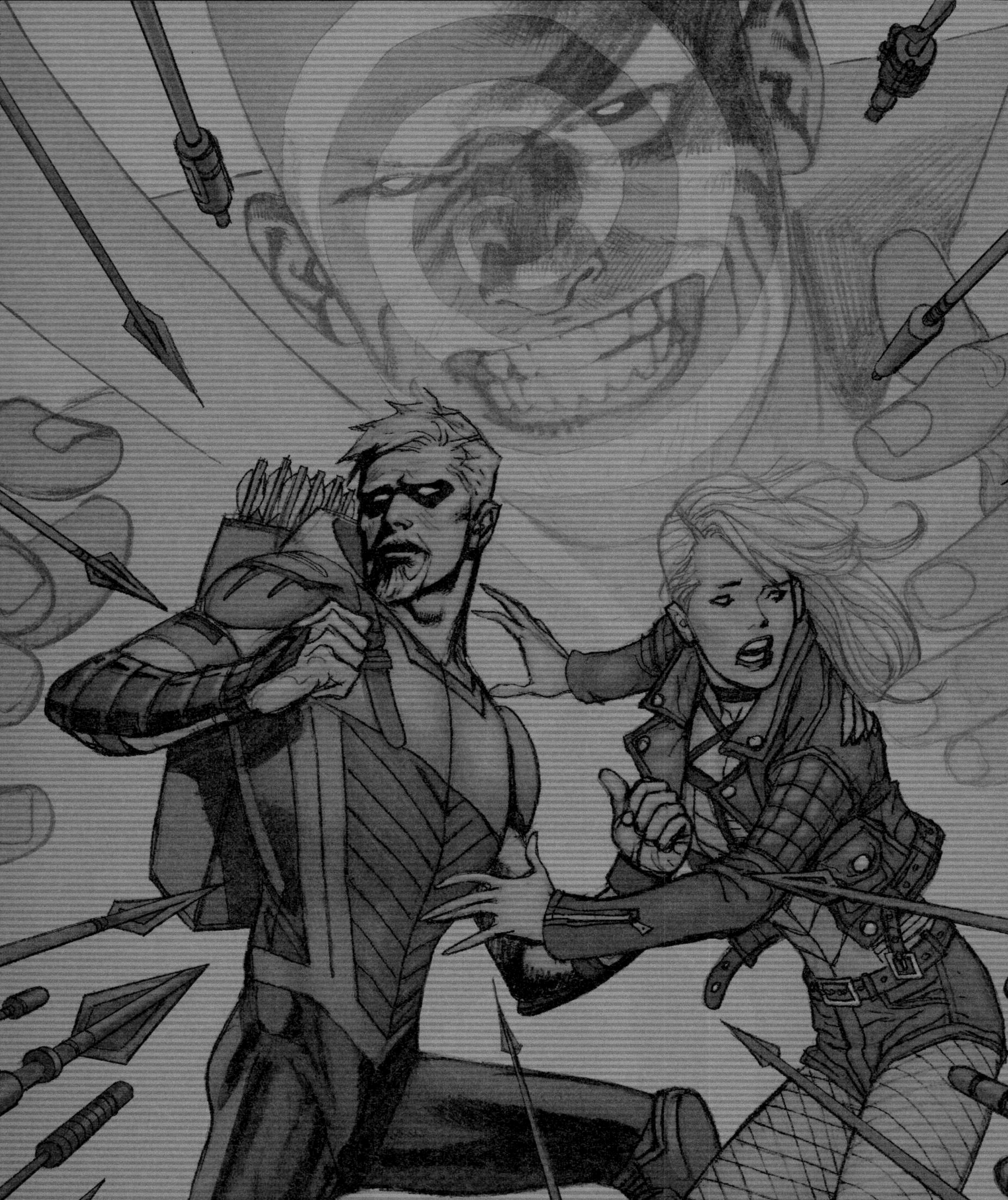

# GREEN ARROW
#49

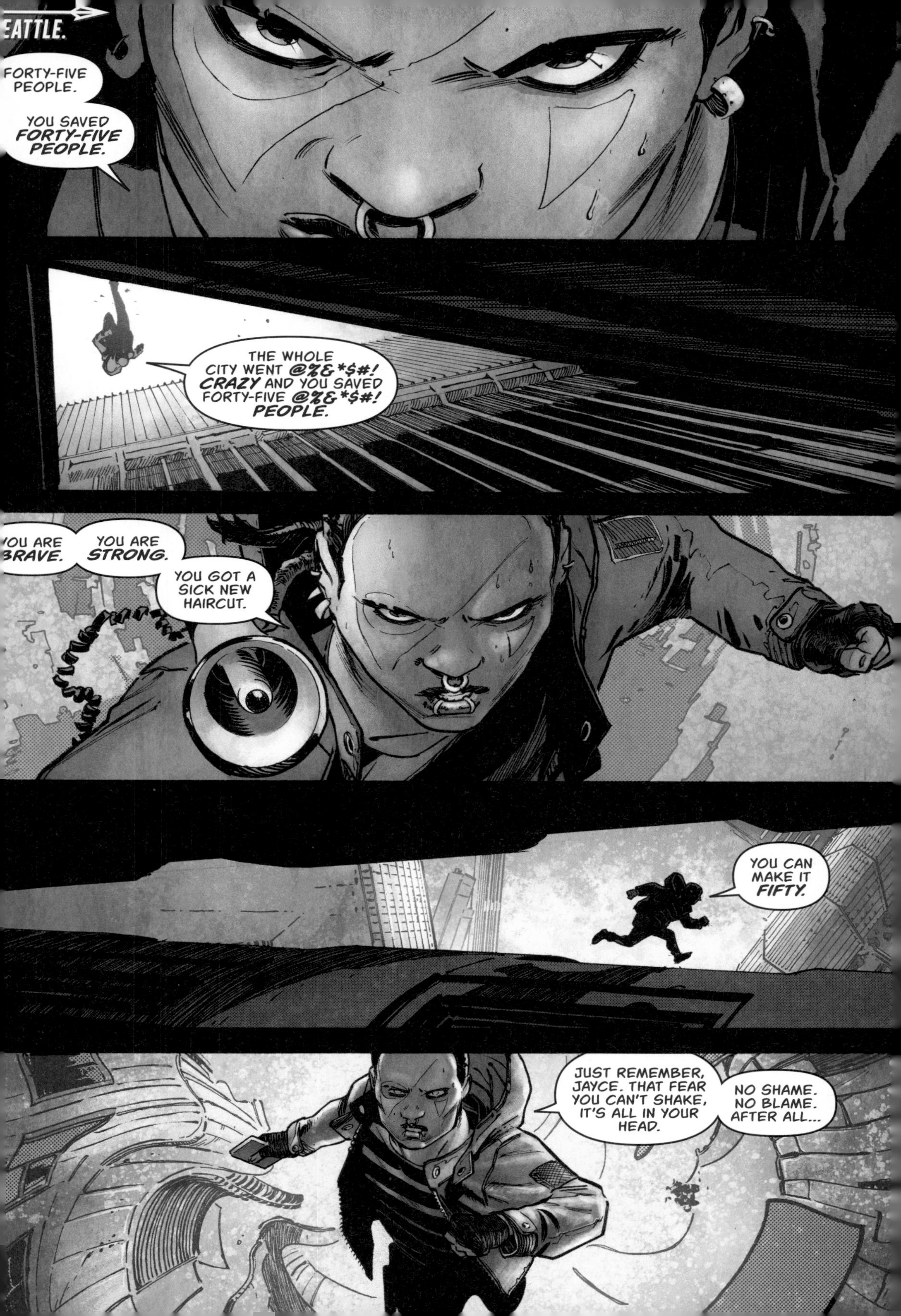
EATTLE.
FORTY-FIVE PEOPLE.
YOU SAVED FORTY-FIVE PEOPLE.
THE WHOLE CITY WENT @%&*$#! CRAZY AND YOU SAVED FORTY-FIVE @%&*$#! PEOPLE.
YOU ARE BRAVE.
YOU ARE STRONG.
YOU GOT A SICK NEW HAIRCUT.
YOU CAN MAKE IT FIFTY.
JUST REMEMBER, JAYCE. THAT FEAR YOU CAN'T SHAKE, IT'S ALL IN YOUR HEAD.
NO SHAME. NO BLAME. AFTER ALL...

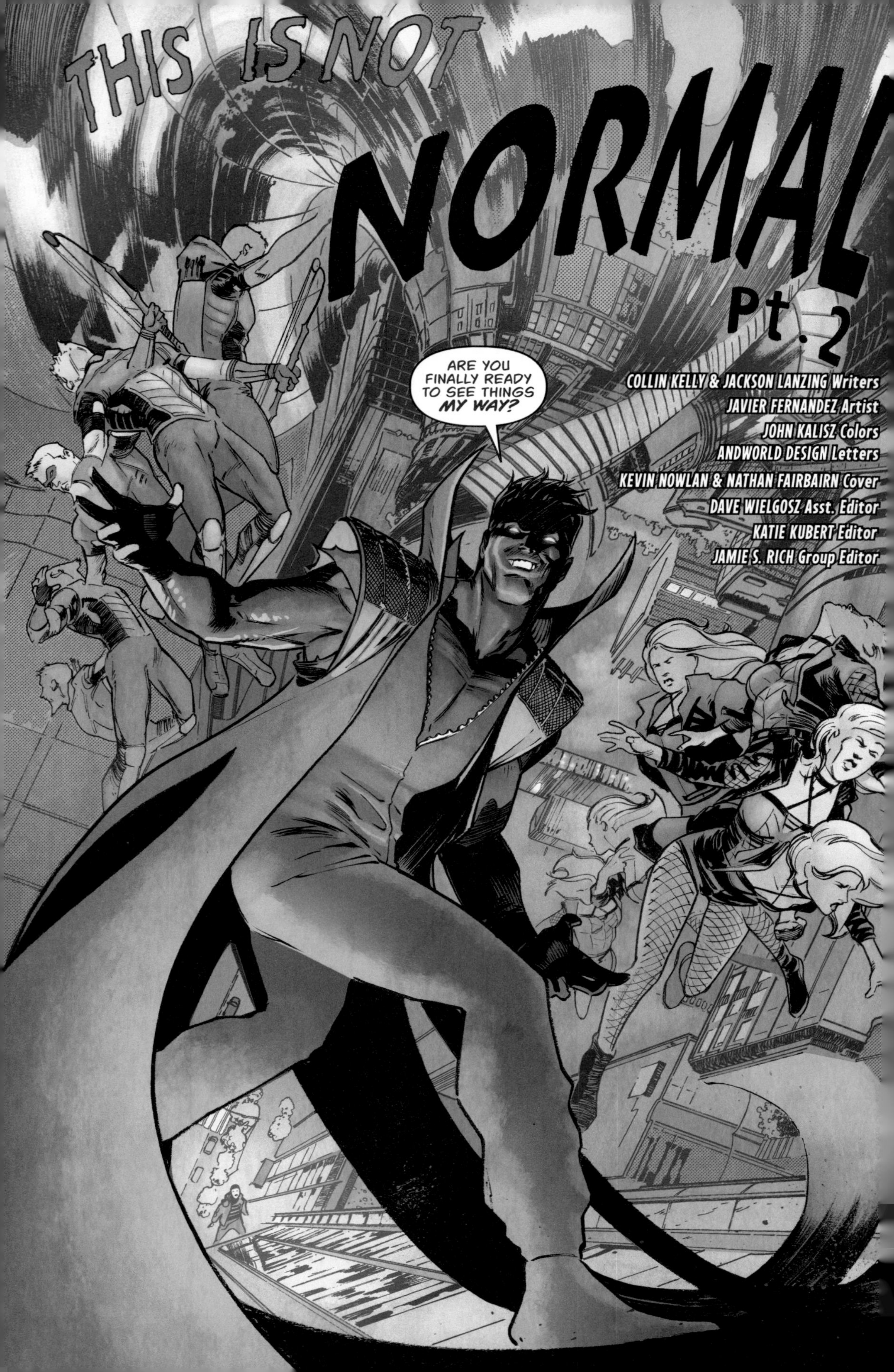
THIS IS NOT NORMAL Pt. 2
ARE YOU FINALLY READY TO SEE THINGS MY WAY?
COLLIN KELLY & JACKSON LANZING Writers
JAVIER FERNANDEZ Artist
JOHN KALISZ Colors
ANDWORLD DESIGN Letters
KEVIN NOWLAN & NATHAN FAIRBAIRN Cover
DAVE WIELGOSZ Asst. Editor
KATIE KUBERT Editor
JAMIE S. RICH Group Editor

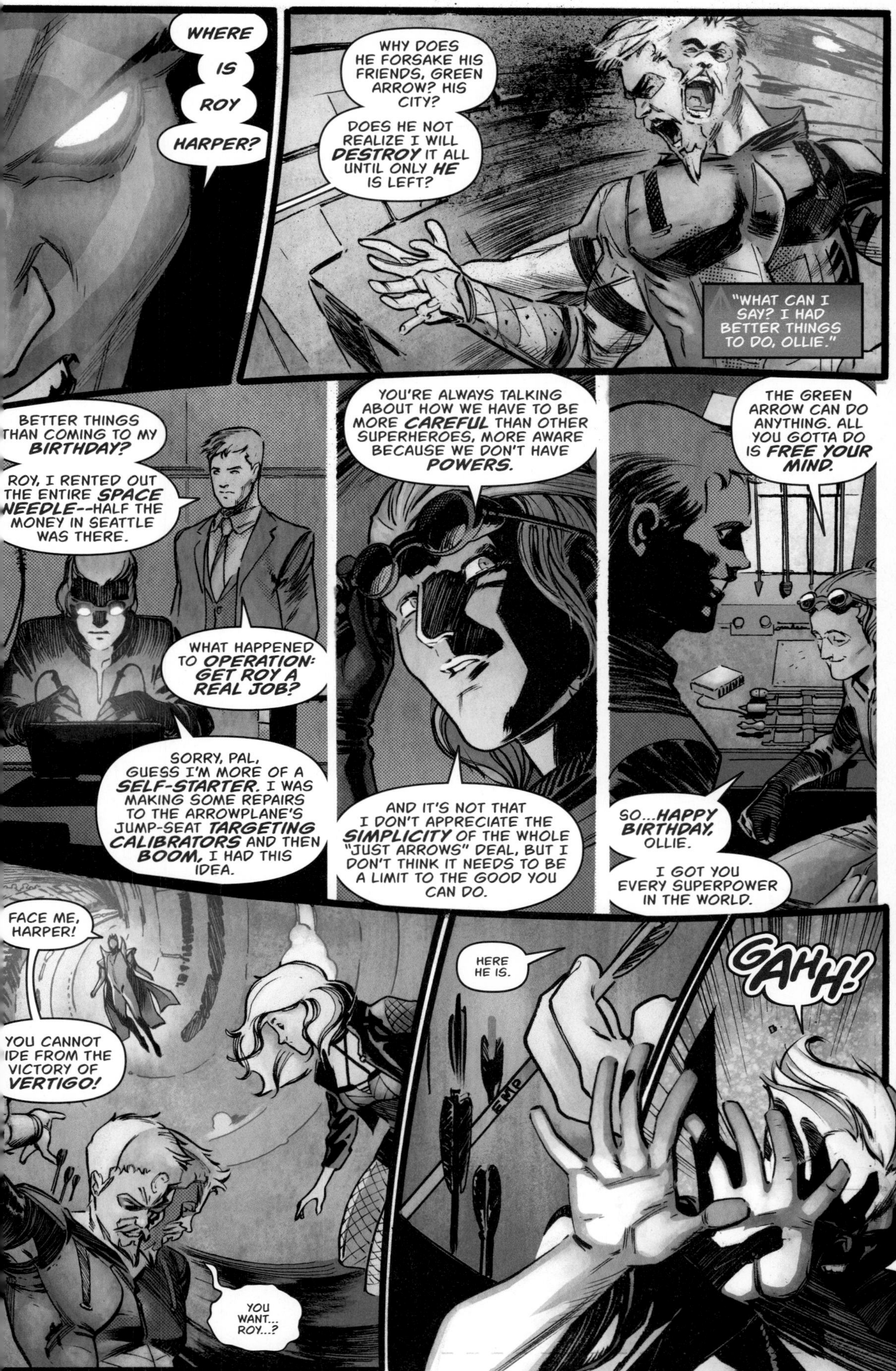
WHERE IS ROY HARPER?
WHY DOES HE FORSAKE HIS FRIENDS, GREEN ARROW? HIS CITY?
DOES HE NOT REALIZE I WILL DESTROY IT ALL UNTIL ONLY HE IS LEFT?
"WHAT CAN I SAY? I HAD BETTER THINGS TO DO, OLLIE."
BETTER THINGS THAN COMING TO MY BIRTHDAY?
ROY, I RENTED OUT THE ENTIRE SPACE NEEDLE--HALF THE MONEY IN SEATTLE WAS THERE.
WHAT HAPPENED TO OPERATION: GET ROY A REAL JOB?
SORRY, PAL, GUESS I'M MORE OF A SELF-STARTER. I WAS MAKING SOME REPAIRS TO THE ARROWPLANE'S JUMP-SEAT TARGETING CALIBRATORS AND THEN BOOM, I HAD THIS IDEA.
YOU'RE ALWAYS TALKING ABOUT HOW WE HAVE TO BE MORE CAREFUL THAN OTHER SUPERHEROES, MORE AWARE BECAUSE WE DON'T HAVE POWERS.
AND IT'S NOT THAT I DON'T APPRECIATE THE SIMPLICITY OF THE WHOLE "JUST ARROWS" DEAL, BUT I DON'T THINK IT NEEDS TO BE A LIMIT TO THE GOOD YOU CAN DO.
THE GREEN ARROW CAN DO ANYTHING. ALL YOU GOTTA DO IS FREE YOUR MIND.
SO...HAPPY BIRTHDAY, OLLIE.
I GOT YOU EVERY SUPERPOWER IN THE WORLD.
FACE ME, HARPER!
YOU CANNOT IDE FROM THE VICTORY OF VERTIGO!
YOU WANT... ROY...?
HERE HE IS.
EMP
GAHH!

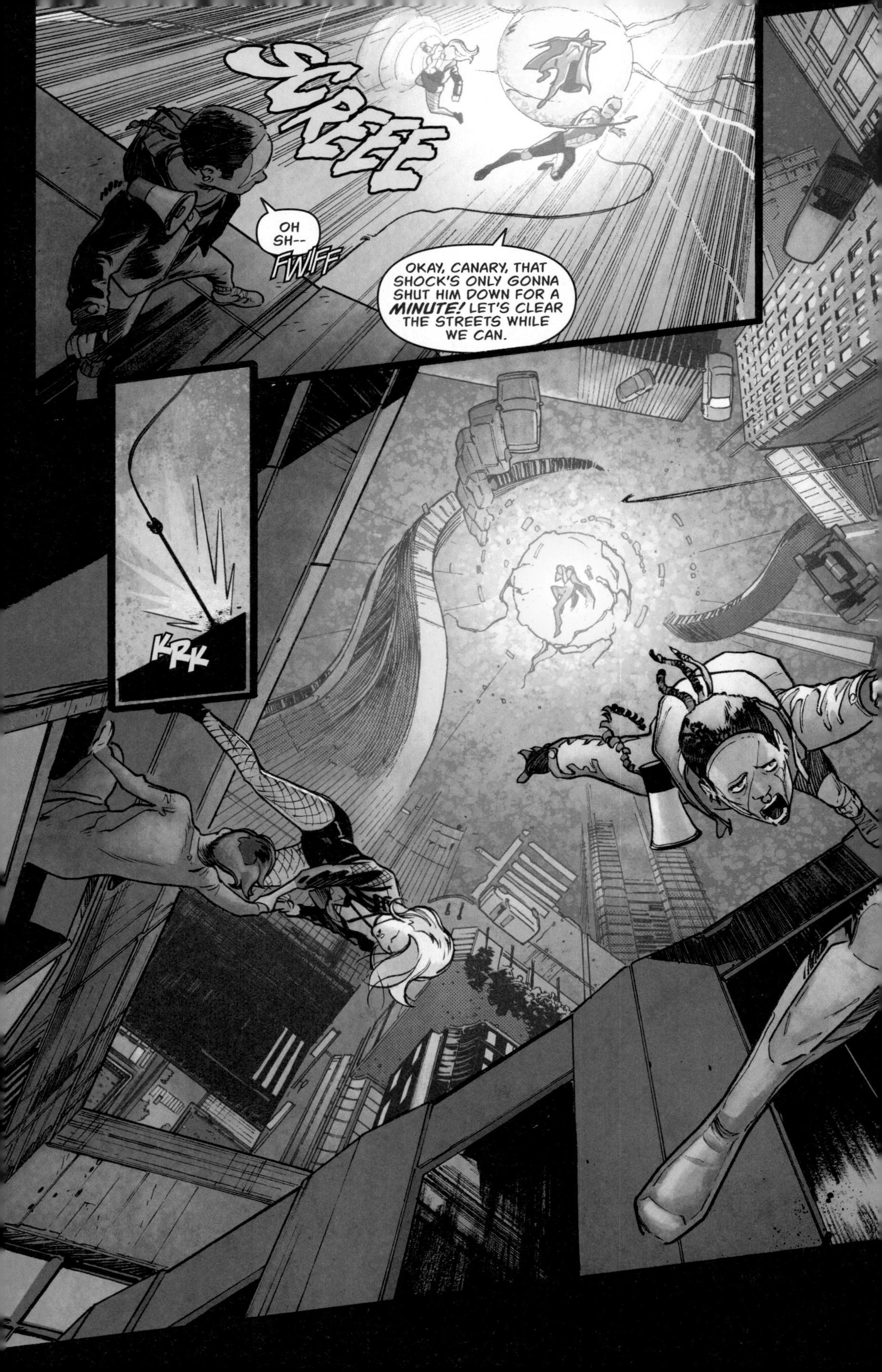
SCREEE
OH SH--
FWIFF
OKAY, CANARY, THAT SHOCK'S ONLY GONNA SHUT HIM DOWN FOR A *MINUTE!* LET'S CLEAR THE STREETS WHILE WE CAN.
KRK

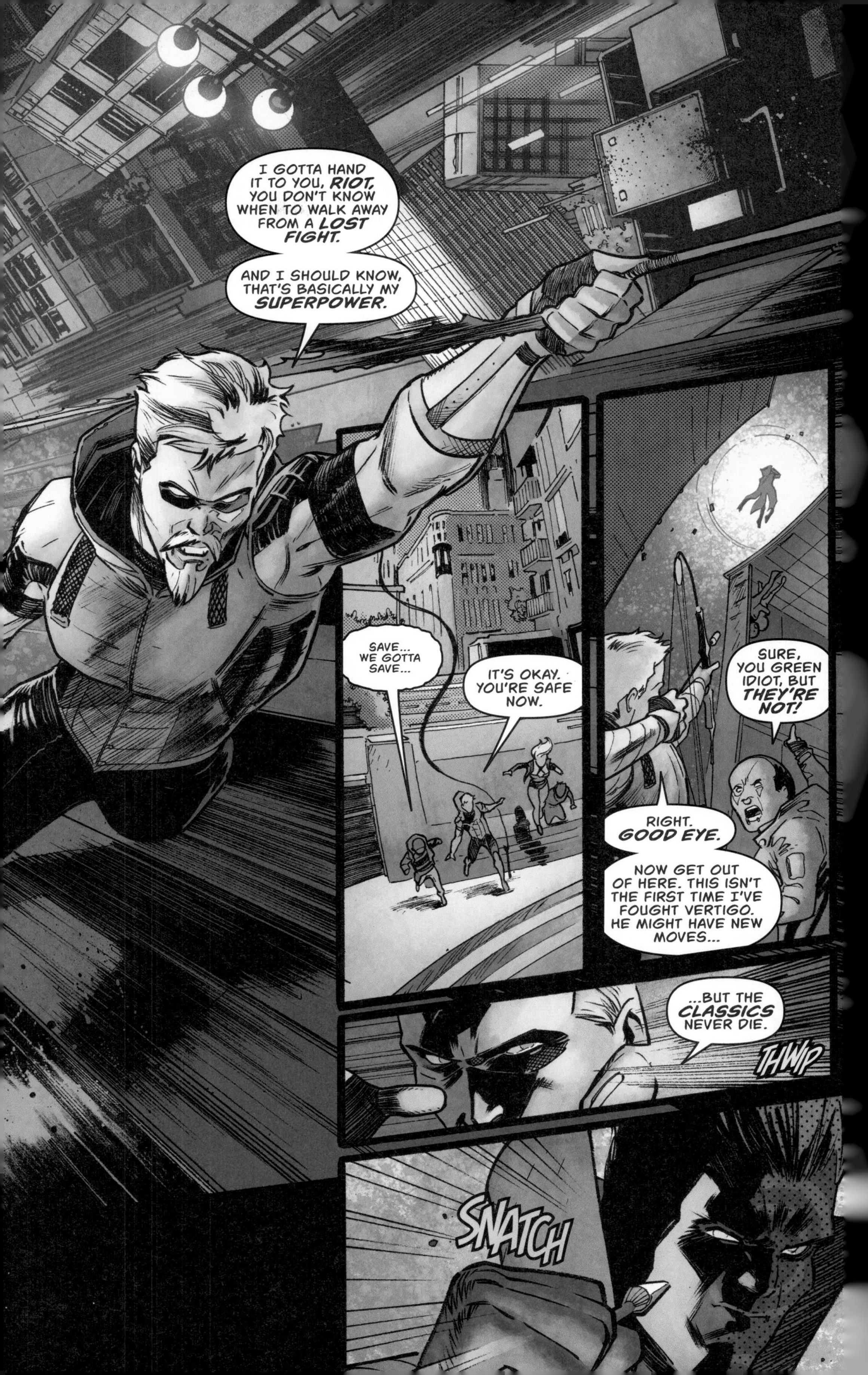
I GOTTA HAND IT TO YOU, RIOT, YOU DON'T KNOW WHEN TO WALK AWAY FROM A LOST FIGHT.
AND I SHOULD KNOW, THAT'S BASICALLY MY SUPERPOWER.
SAVE... WE GOTTA SAVE...
IT'S OKAY. YOU'RE SAFE NOW.
SURE, YOU GREEN IDIOT, BUT THEY'RE NOT!
RIGHT. GOOD EYE.
NOW GET OUT OF HERE. THIS ISN'T THE FIRST TIME I'VE FOUGHT VERTIGO. HE MIGHT HAVE NEW MOVES...
...BUT THE CLASSICS NEVER DIE.
THWIP
SNATCH

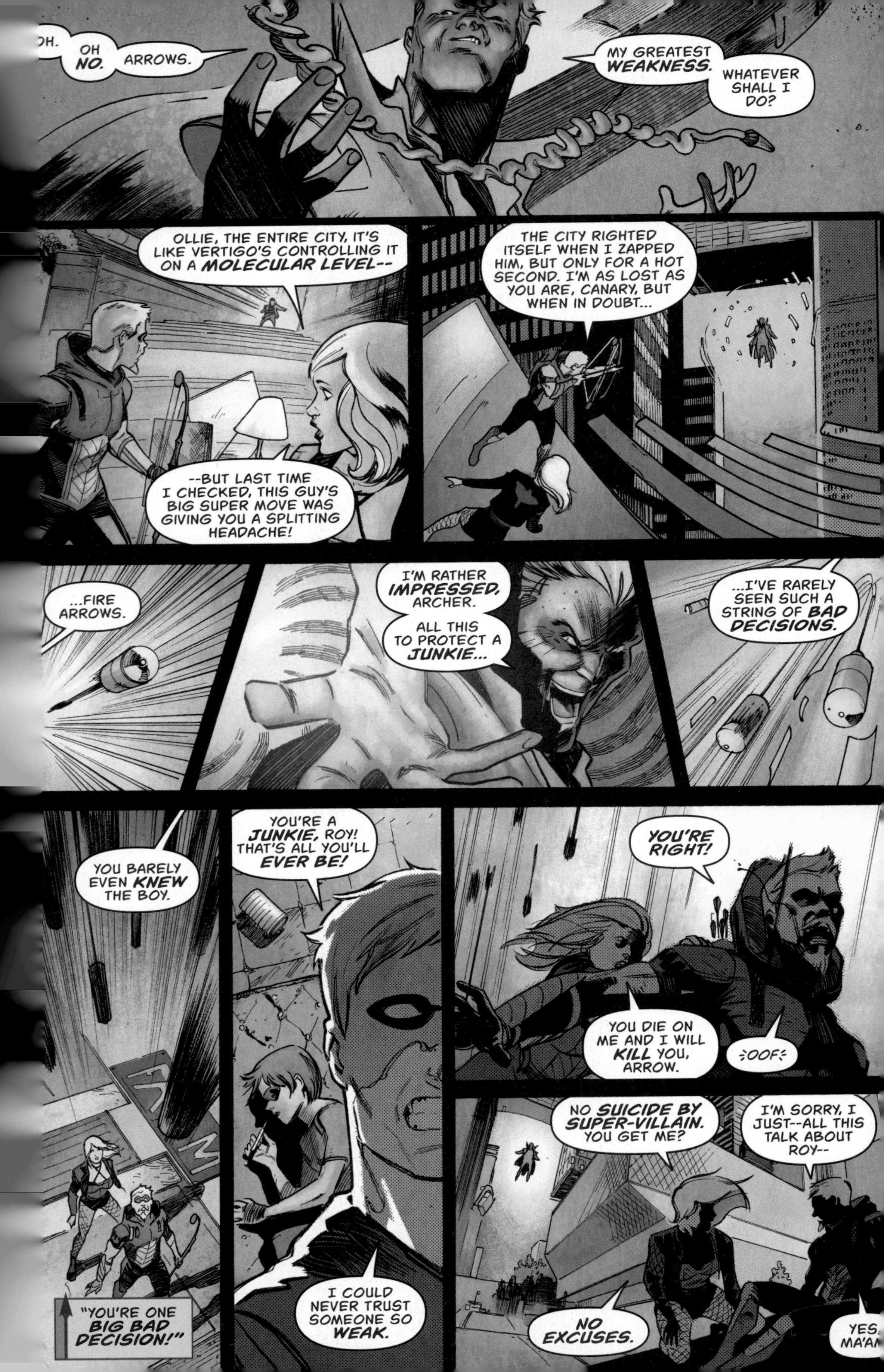
OH. OH NO. ARROWS.
MY GREATEST WEAKNESS.
WHATEVER SHALL I DO?
OLLIE, THE ENTIRE CITY, IT'S LIKE VERTIGO'S CONTROLLING IT ON A MOLECULAR LEVEL--
--BUT LAST TIME I CHECKED, THIS GUY'S BIG SUPER MOVE WAS GIVING YOU A SPLITTING HEADACHE!
THE CITY RIGHTED ITSELF WHEN I ZAPPED HIM, BUT ONLY FOR A HOT SECOND. I'M AS LOST AS YOU ARE, CANARY, BUT WHEN IN DOUBT...
...FIRE ARROWS.
I'M RATHER IMPRESSED, ARCHER.
ALL THIS TO PROTECT A JUNKIE...
...I'VE RARELY SEEN SUCH A STRING OF BAD DECISIONS.
YOU BARELY EVEN KNEW THE BOY.
"YOU'RE ONE BIG BAD DECISION!"
YOU'RE A JUNKIE, ROY! THAT'S ALL YOU'LL EVER BE!
I COULD NEVER TRUST SOMEONE SO WEAK.
YOU'RE RIGHT!
YOU DIE ON ME AND I WILL KILL YOU, ARROW.
OOF
NO SUICIDE BY SUPER-VILLAIN. YOU GET ME?
I'M SORRY, I JUST--ALL THIS TALK ABOUT ROY--
NO EXCUSES.
YES, MA'AM

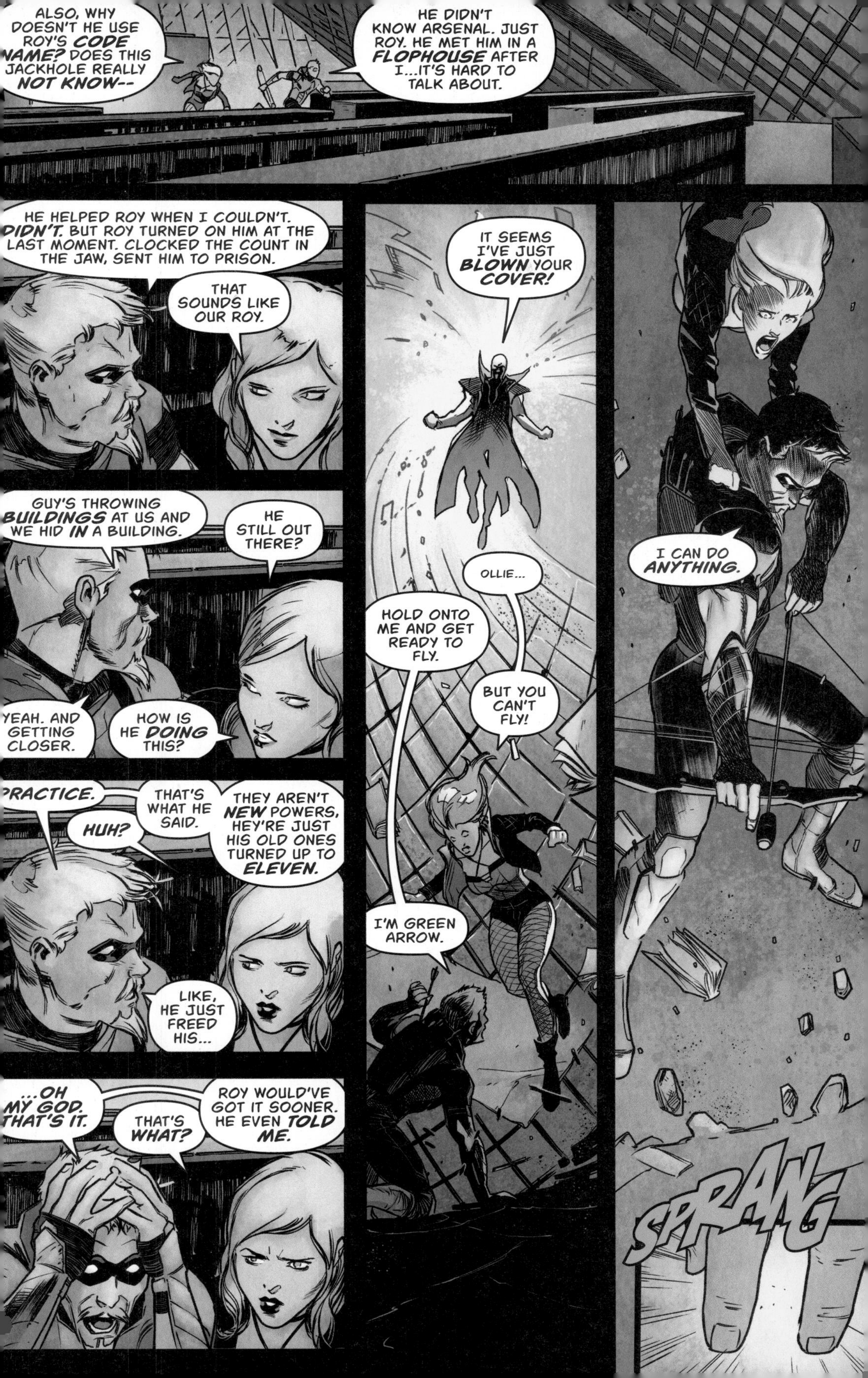
ALSO, WHY DOESN'T HE USE ROY'S CODE NAME? DOES THIS JACKHOLE REALLY NOT KNOW--
HE DIDN'T KNOW ARSENAL. JUST ROY. HE MET HIM IN A FLOPHOUSE AFTER I...IT'S HARD TO TALK ABOUT.
HE HELPED ROY WHEN I COULDN'T. DIDN'T. BUT ROY TURNED ON HIM AT THE LAST MOMENT. CLOCKED THE COUNT IN THE JAW, SENT HIM TO PRISON.
THAT SOUNDS LIKE OUR ROY.
GUY'S THROWING BUILDINGS AT US AND WE HID IN A BUILDING.
HE STILL OUT THERE?
YEAH. AND GETTING CLOSER.
HOW IS HE DOING THIS?
PRACTICE.
HUH?
THAT'S WHAT HE SAID.
THEY AREN'T NEW POWERS, HEY'RE JUST HIS OLD ONES TURNED UP TO ELEVEN.
LIKE, HE JUST FREED HIS...
...OH MY GOD. THAT'S IT.
THAT'S WHAT?
ROY WOULD'VE GOT IT SOONER. HE EVEN TOLD ME.
IT SEEMS I'VE JUST BLOWN YOUR COVER!
OLLIE...
HOLD ONTO ME AND GET READY TO FLY.
BUT YOU CAN'T FLY!
I'M GREEN ARROW.
I CAN DO ANYTHING.
SPRANG

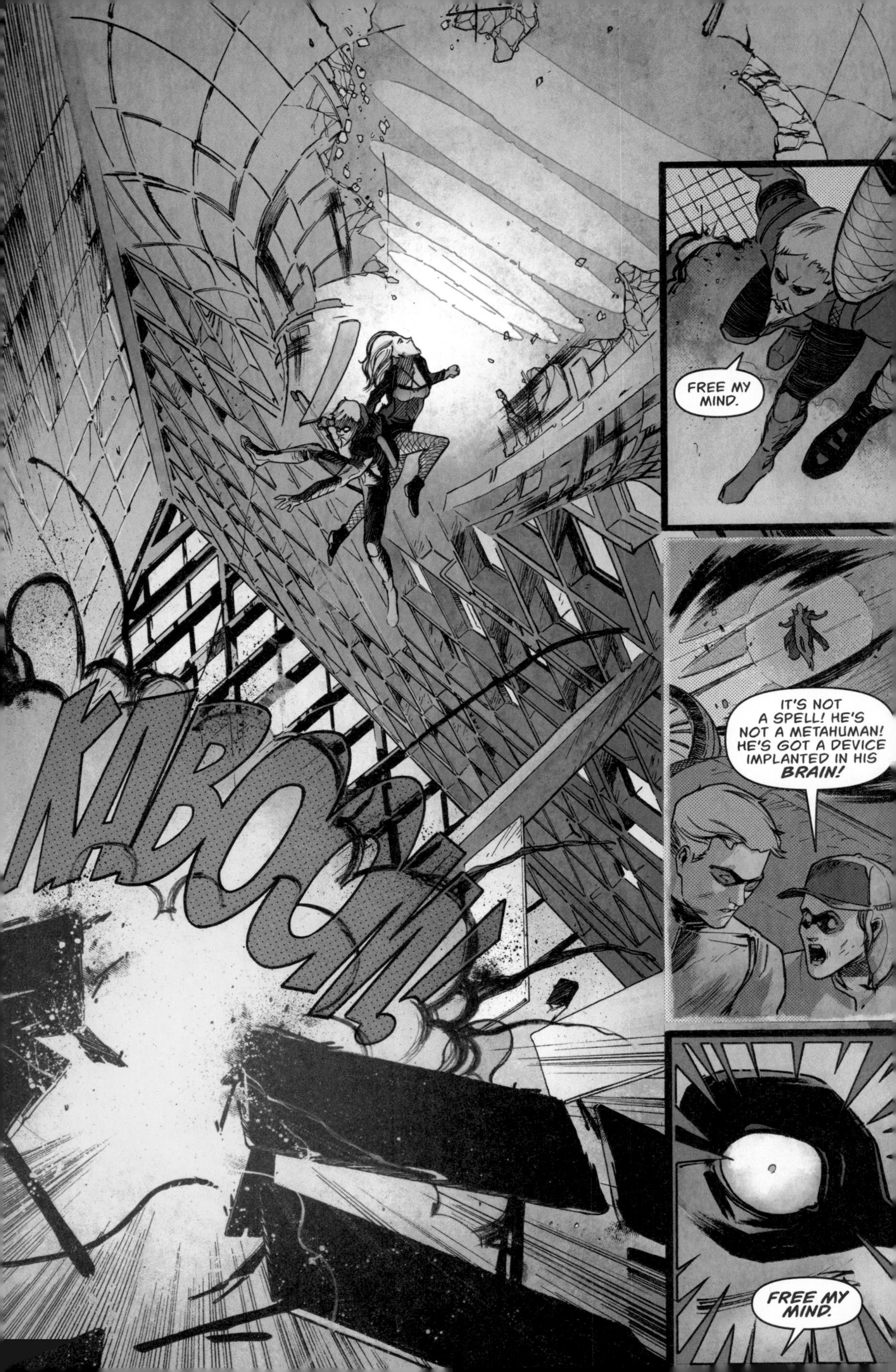
FREE MY MIND.
KABOOM!
IT'S NOT A SPELL! HE'S NOT A METAHUMAN! HE'S GOT A DEVICE IMPLANTED IN HIS BRAIN!
FREE MY MIND.

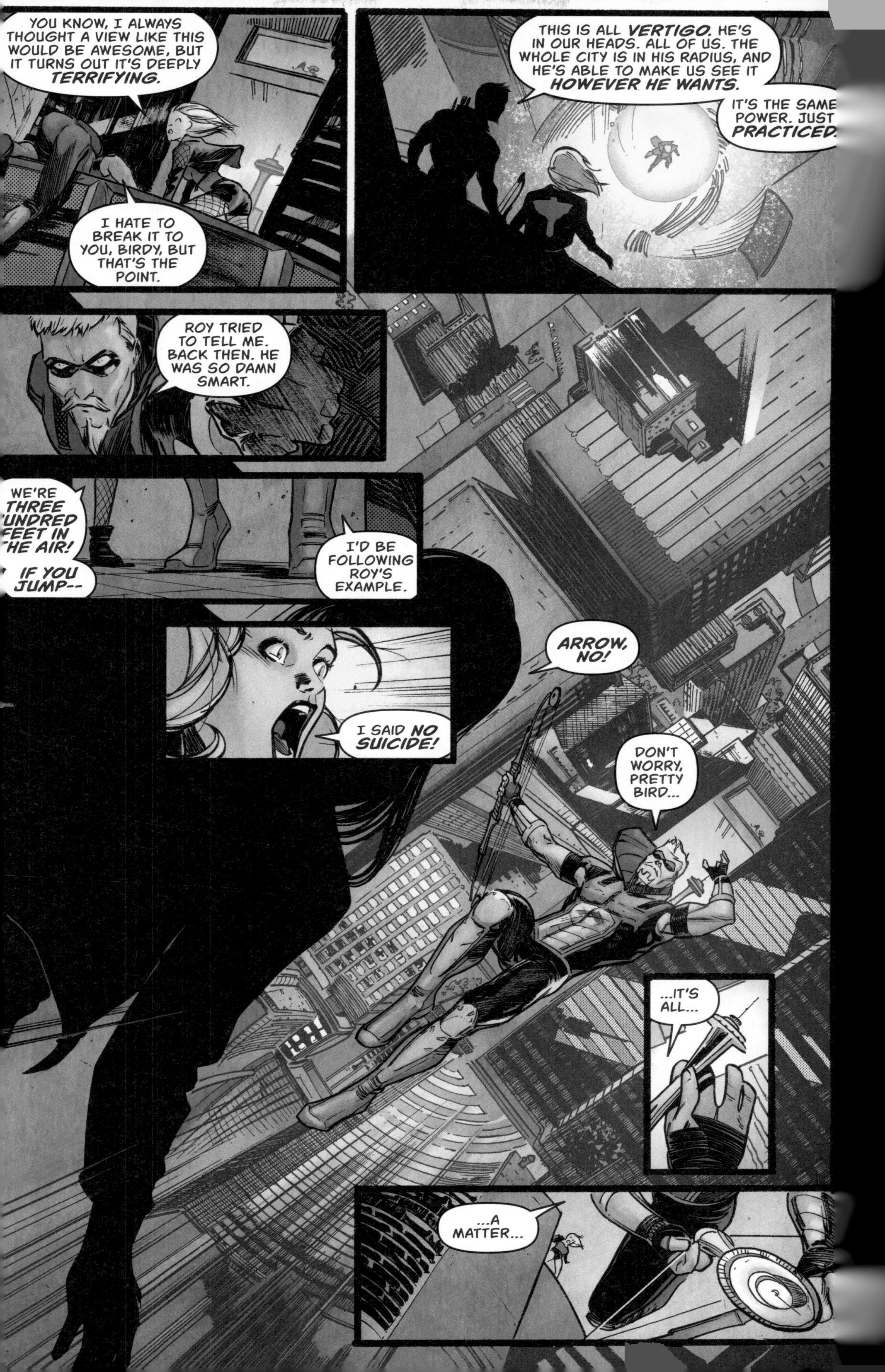
YOU KNOW, I ALWAYS THOUGHT A VIEW LIKE THIS WOULD BE AWESOME, BUT IT TURNS OUT IT'S DEEPLY TERRIFYING.
I HATE TO BREAK IT TO YOU, BIRDY, BUT THAT'S THE POINT.
THIS IS ALL VERTIGO. HE'S IN OUR HEADS. ALL OF US. THE WHOLE CITY IS IN HIS RADIUS, AND HE'S ABLE TO MAKE US SEE IT HOWEVER HE WANTS.
IT'S THE SAME POWER. JUST PRACTICED.
ROY TRIED TO TELL ME. BACK THEN. HE WAS SO DAMN SMART.
WE'RE THREE UNDRED FEET IN HE AIR!
IF YOU JUMP--
I'D BE FOLLOWING ROY'S EXAMPLE.
ARROW, NO!
I SAID NO SUICIDE!
DON'T WORRY, PRETTY BIRD...
...IT'S ALL...
...A MATTER...

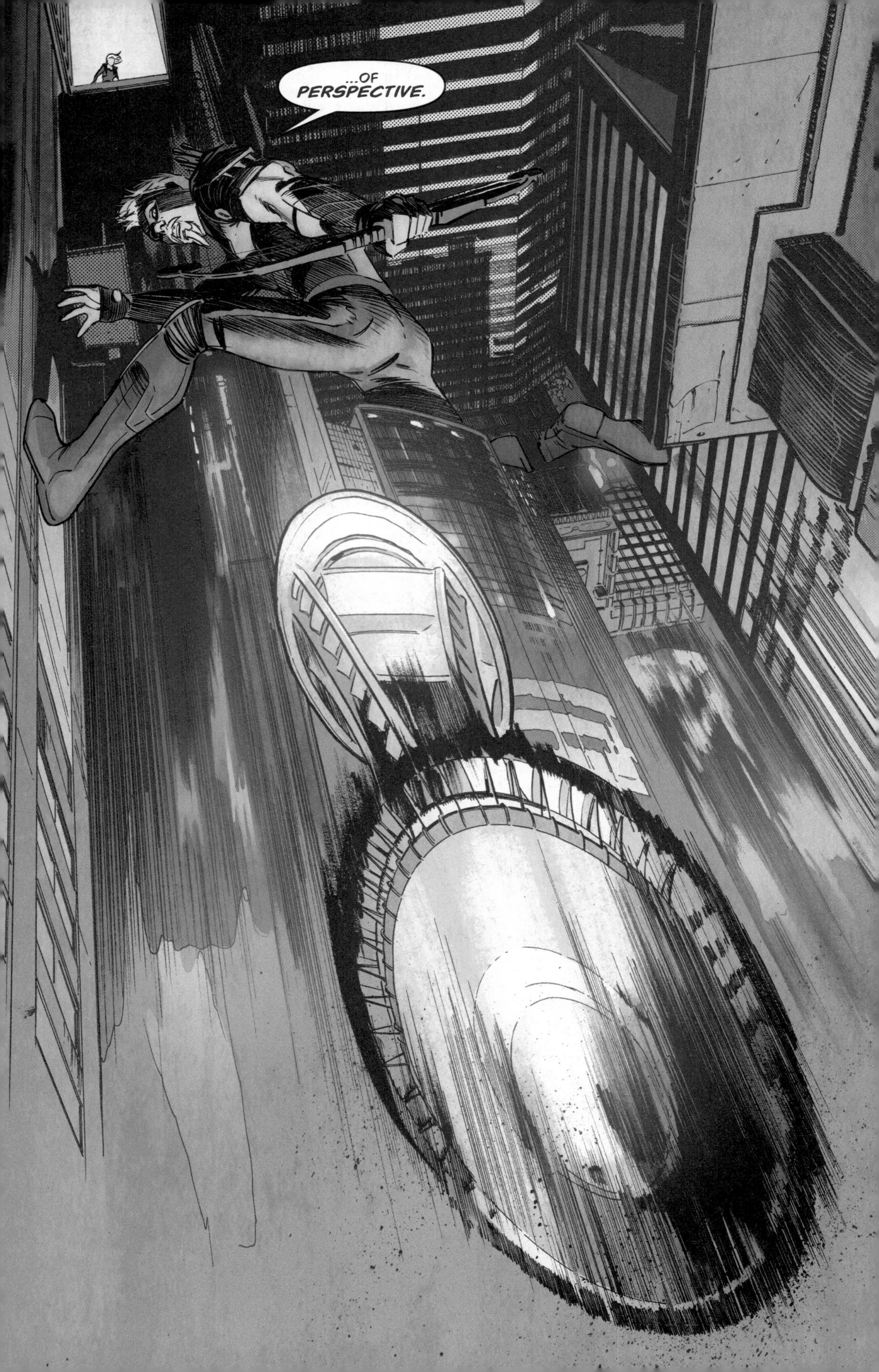
...OF PERSPECTIVE.

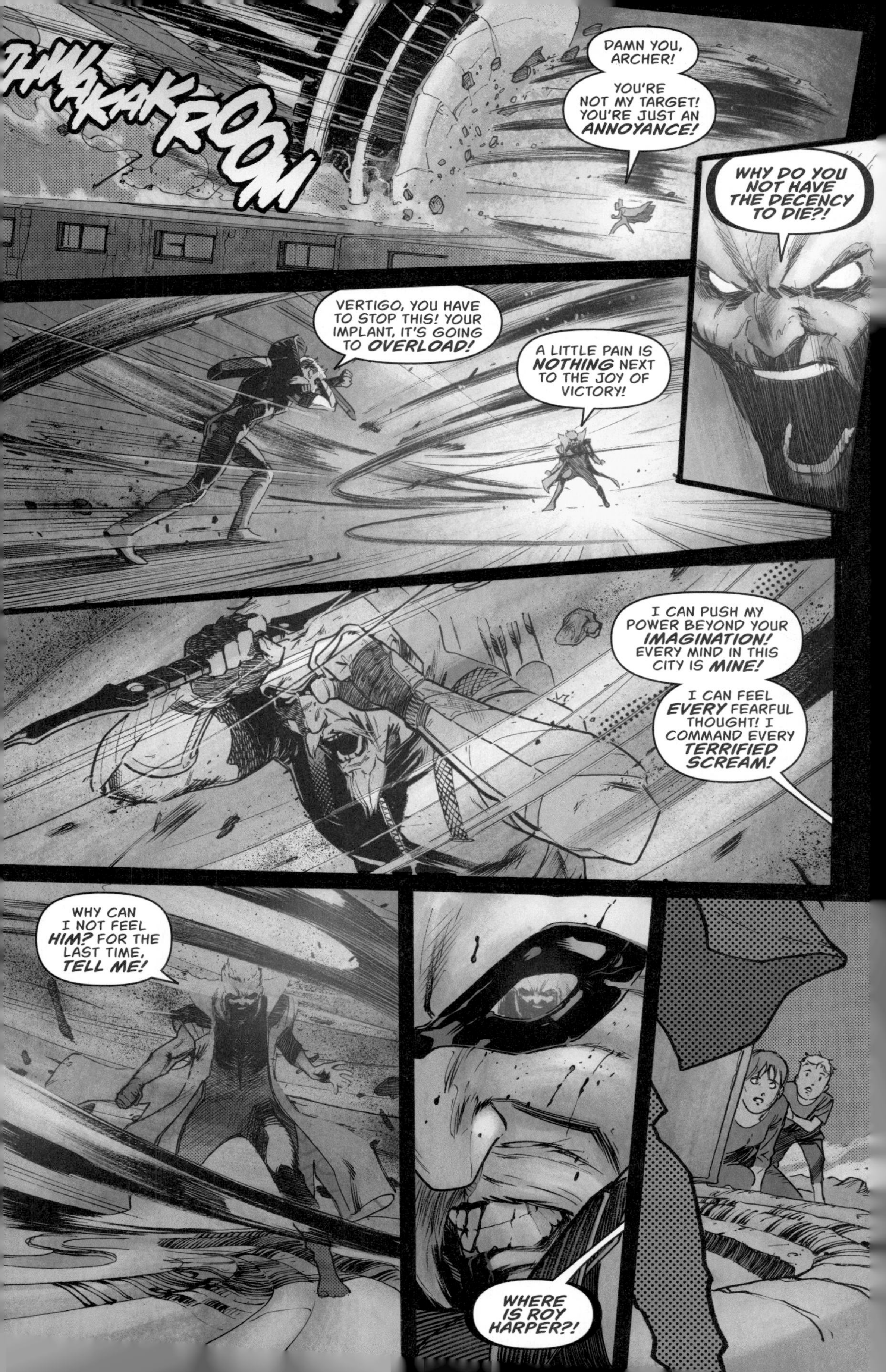

THWAKAKAKROOOM
DAMN YOU, ARCHER!
YOU'RE NOT MY TARGET! YOU'RE JUST AN ANNOYANCE!
WHY DO YOU NOT HAVE THE DECENCY TO DIE?!
VERTIGO, YOU HAVE TO STOP THIS! YOUR IMPLANT, IT'S GOING TO OVERLOAD!
A LITTLE PAIN IS NOTHING NEXT TO THE JOY OF VICTORY!
I CAN PUSH MY POWER BEYOND YOUR IMAGINATION! EVERY MIND IN THIS CITY IS MINE!
I CAN FEEL EVERY FEARFUL THOUGHT! I COMMAND EVERY TERRIFIED SCREAM!
WHY CAN I NOT FEEL HIM? FOR THE LAST TIME, TELL ME!
WHERE IS ROY HARPER?!

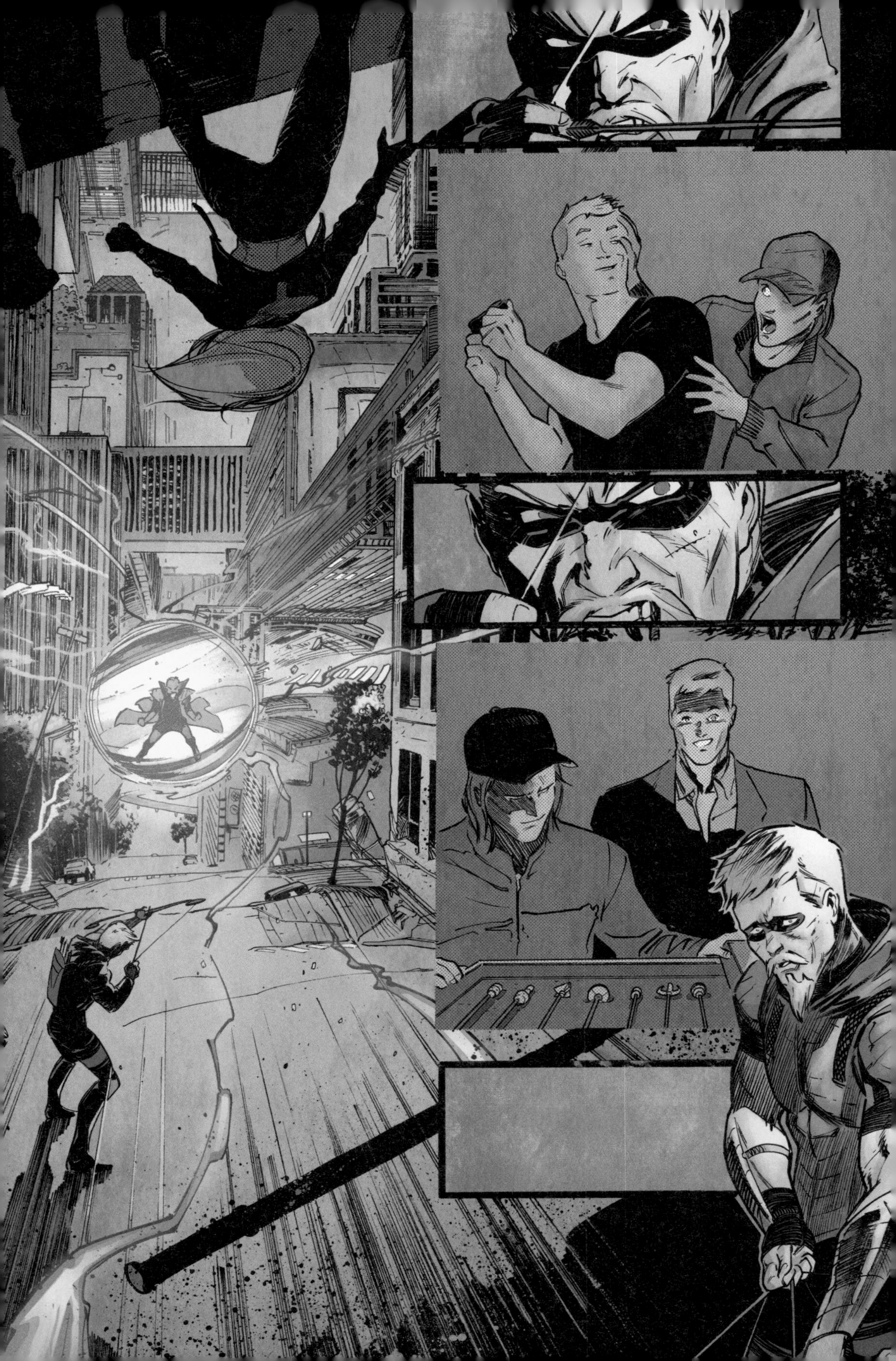

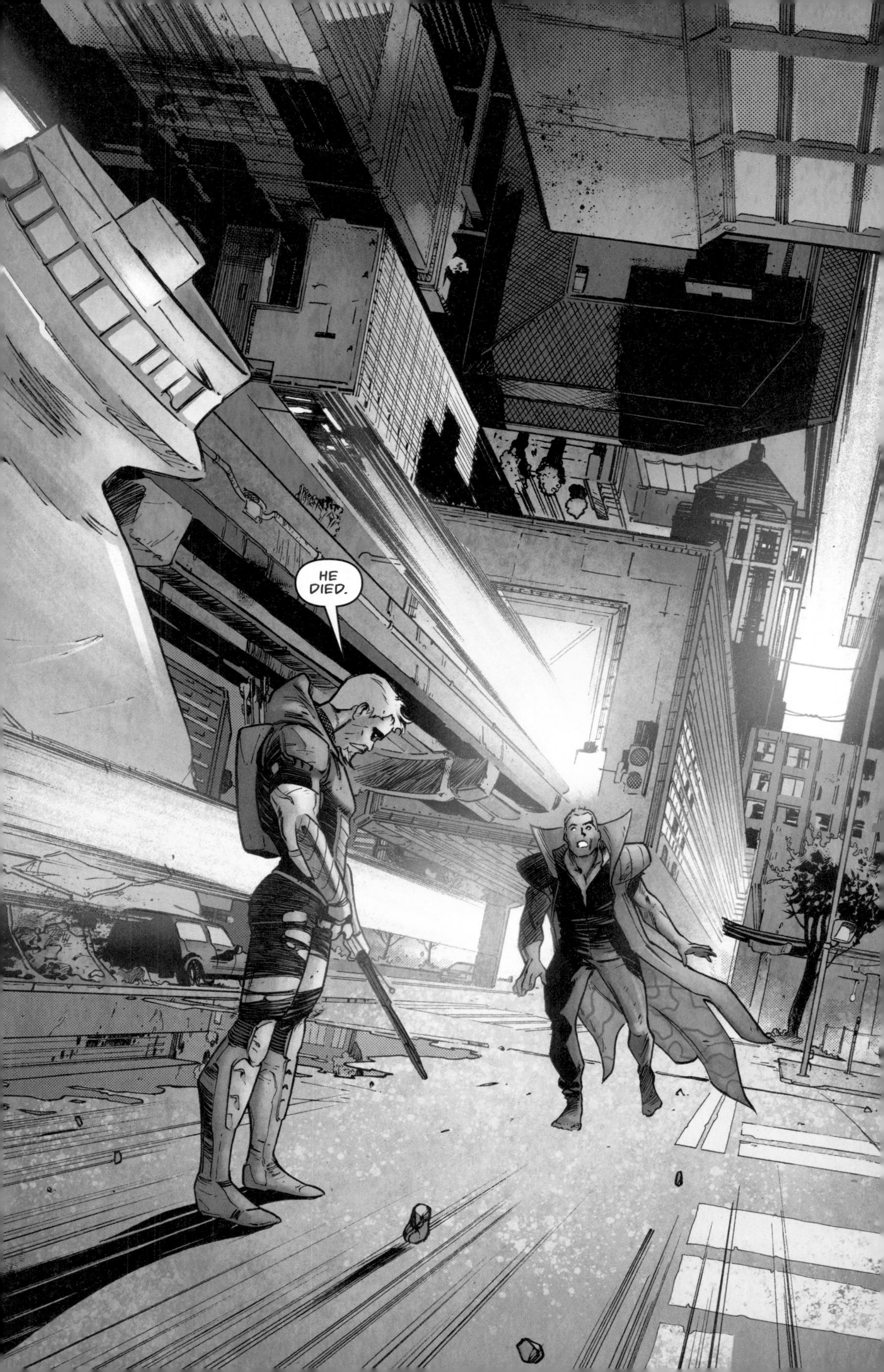
HE DIED.

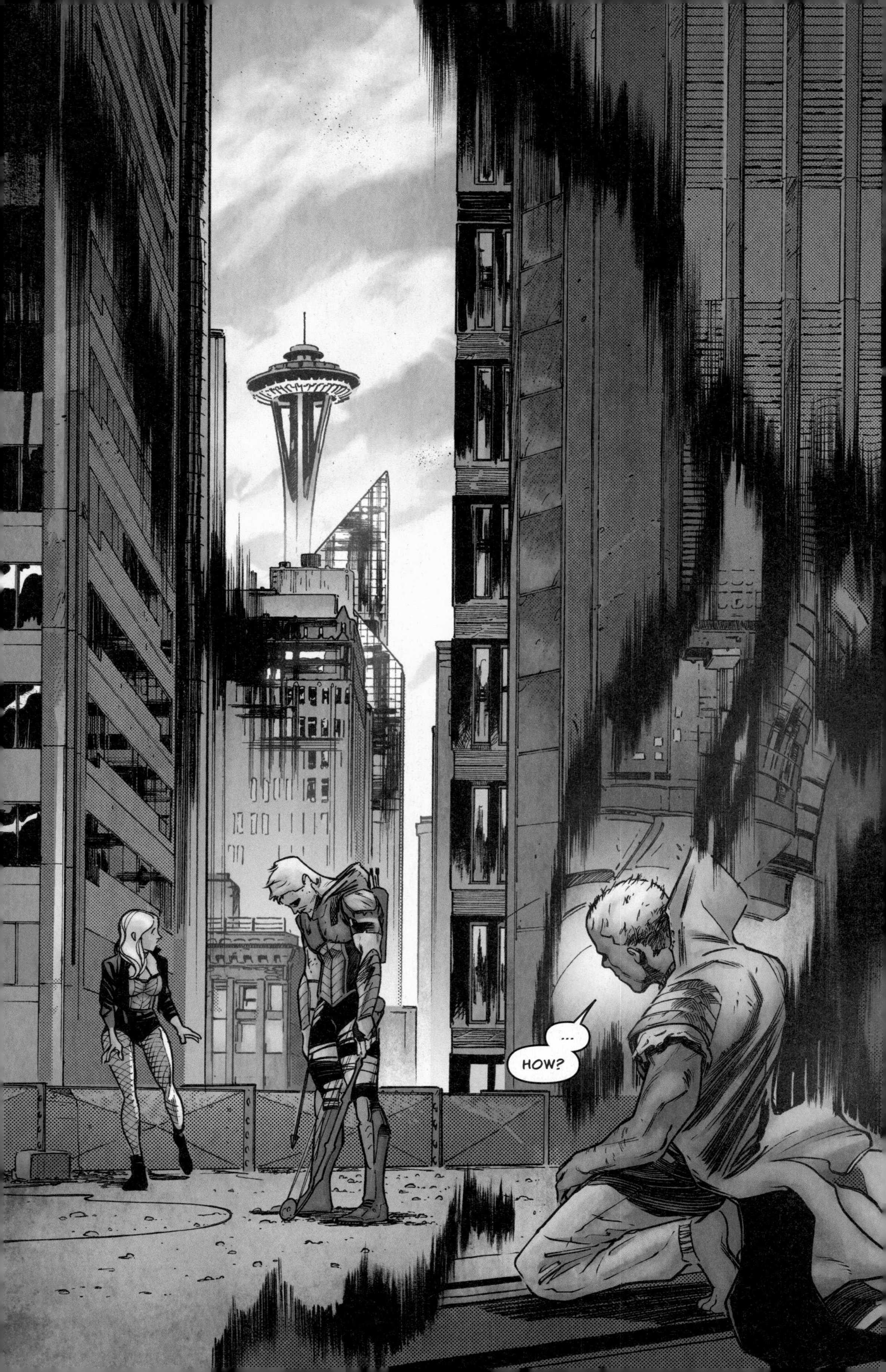
...
HOW?

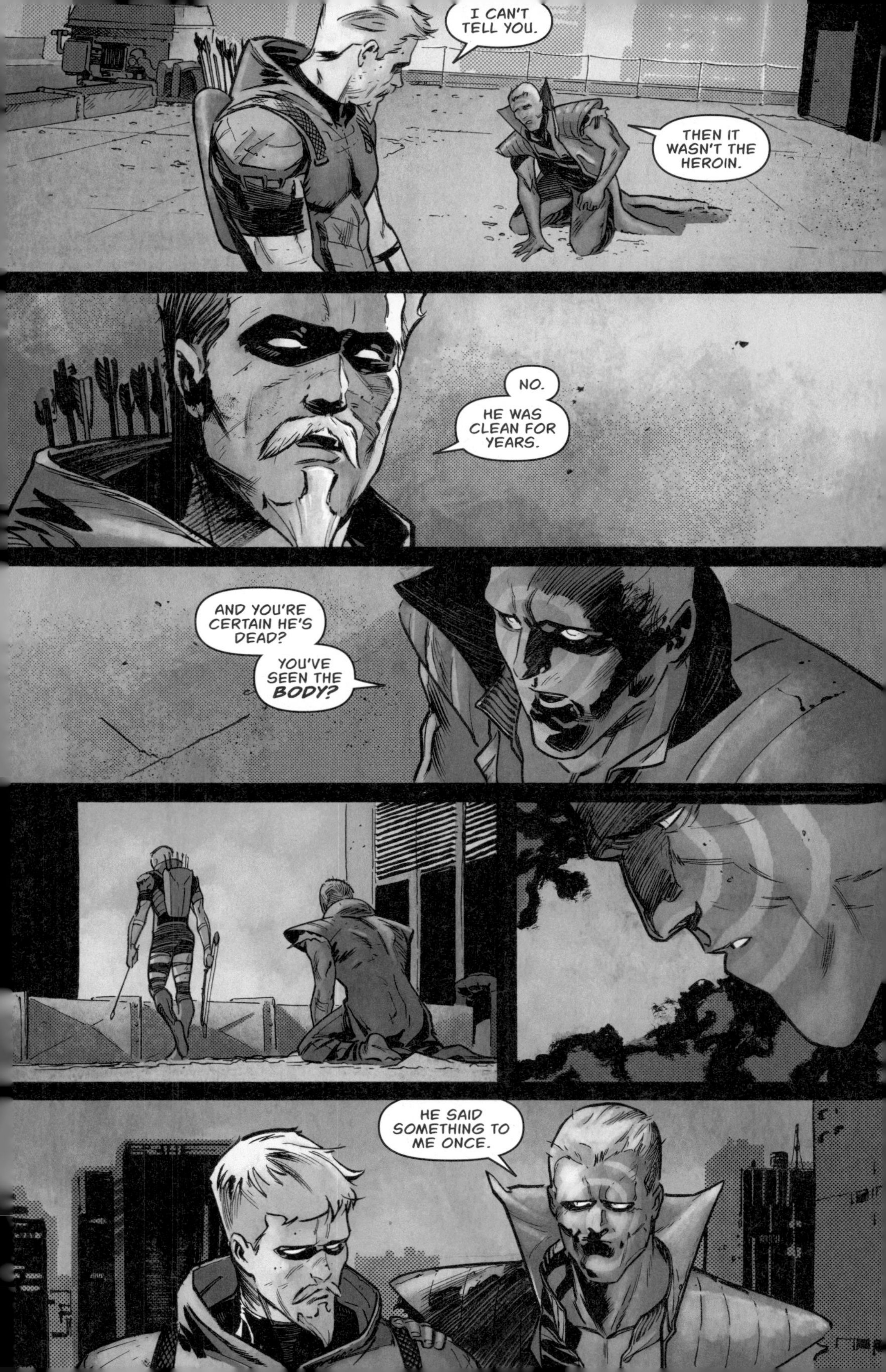
I CAN'T TELL YOU.
THEN IT WASN'T THE HEROIN.
NO.
HE WAS CLEAN FOR YEARS.
AND YOU'RE CERTAIN HE'S DEAD?
YOU'VE SEEN THE *BODY?*
HE SAID SOMETHING TO ME ONCE.

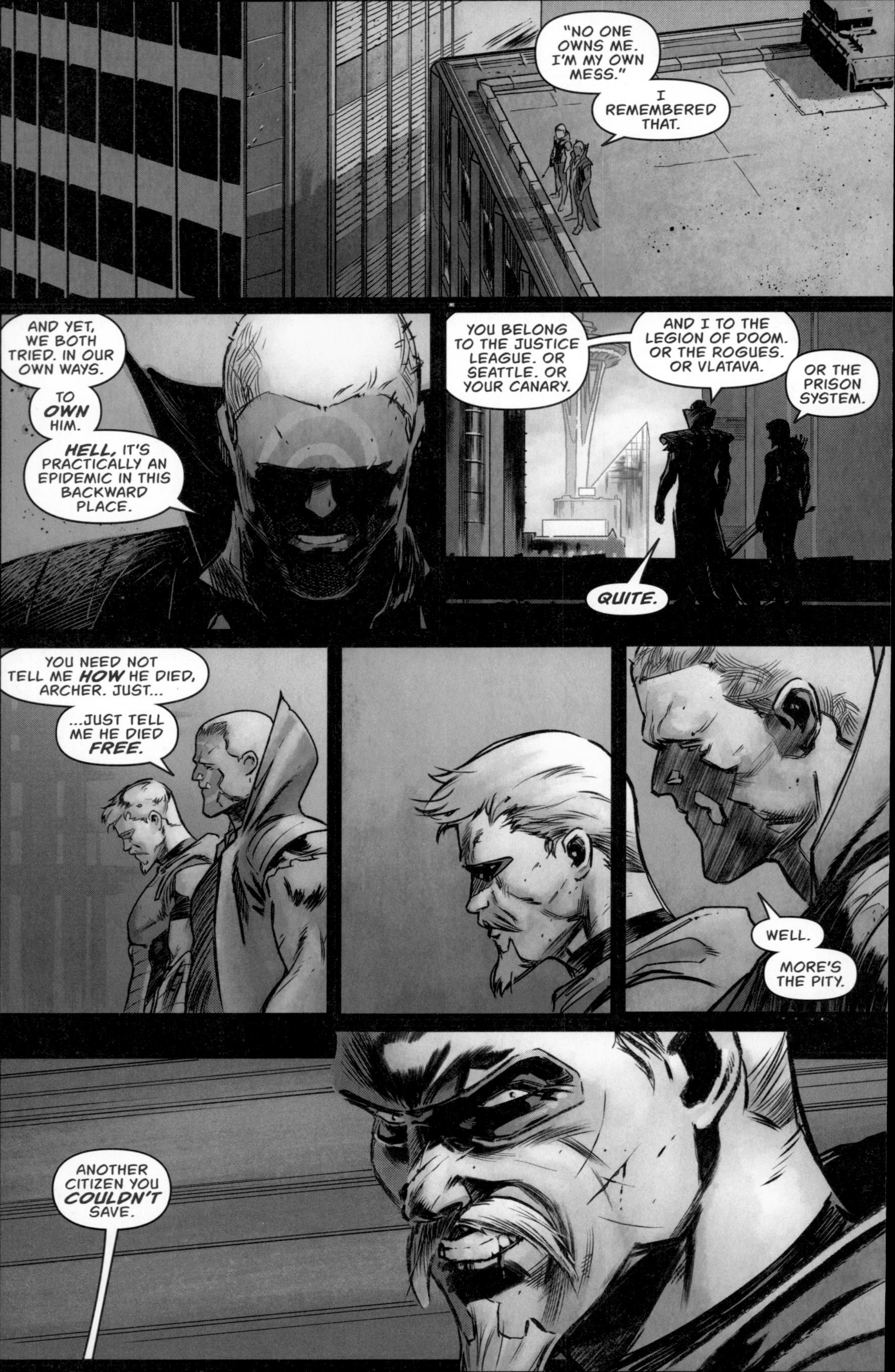
"NO ONE OWNS ME. I'M MY OWN MESS."
I REMEMBERED THAT.
AND YET, WE BOTH TRIED. IN OUR OWN WAYS.
TO OWN HIM.
HELL, IT'S PRACTICALLY AN EPIDEMIC IN THIS BACKWARD PLACE.
YOU BELONG TO THE JUSTICE LEAGUE. OR SEATTLE. OR YOUR CANARY.
AND I TO THE LEGION OF DOOM. OR THE ROGUES. OR VLATAVA.
OR THE PRISON SYSTEM.
QUITE.
YOU NEED NOT TELL ME HOW HE DIED, ARCHER. JUST...
...JUST TELL ME HE DIED FREE.
WELL.
MORE'S THE PITY.
ANOTHER CITIZEN YOU COULDN'T SAVE.

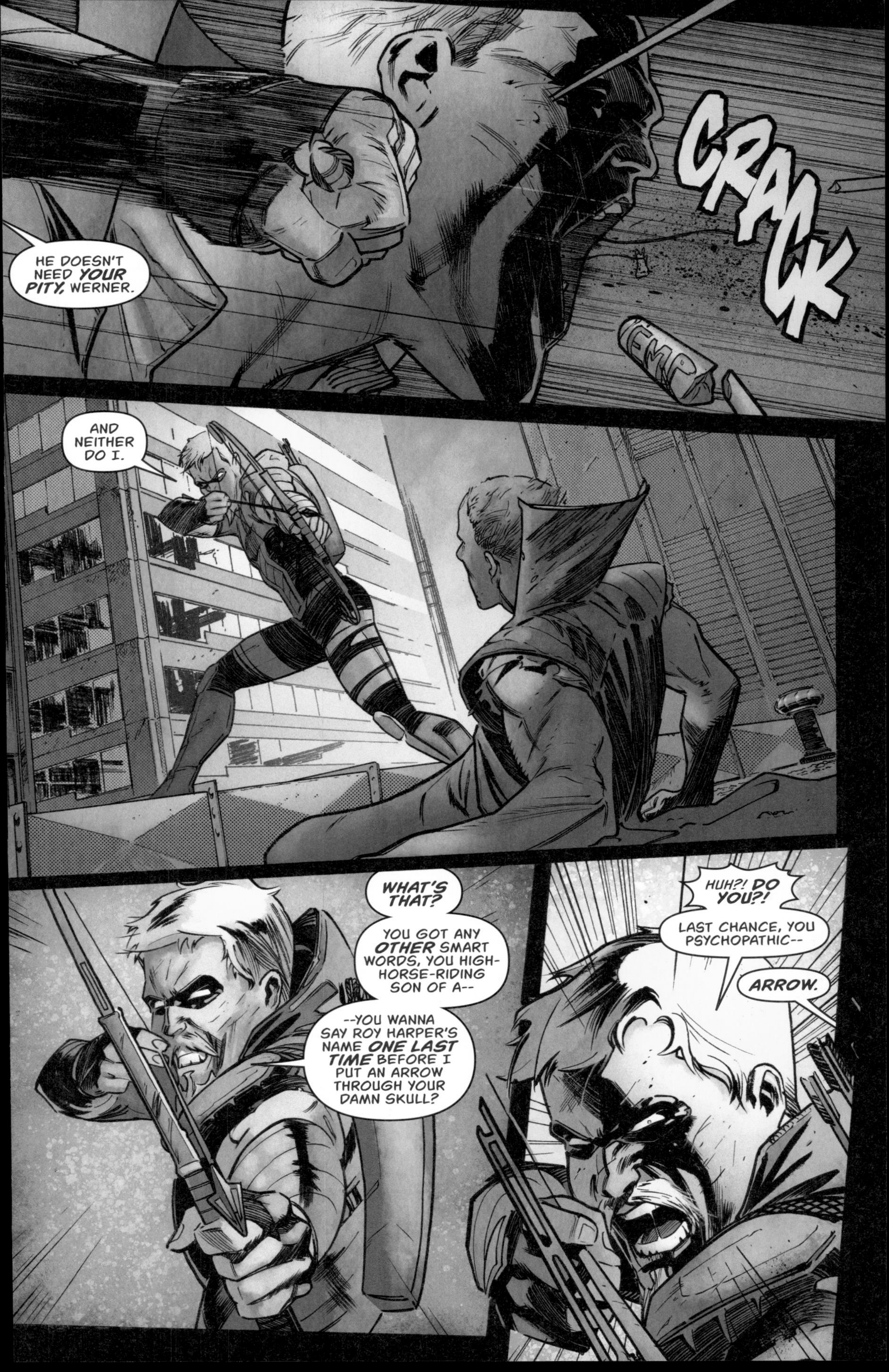
HE DOESN'T NEED YOUR PITY, WERNER.
CRACK
EMP
AND NEITHER DO I.
WHAT'S THAT?
YOU GOT ANY OTHER SMART WORDS, YOU HIGH-HORSE-RIDING SON OF A--
--YOU WANNA SAY ROY HARPER'S NAME ONE LAST TIME BEFORE I PUT AN ARROW THROUGH YOUR DAMN SKULL?
HUH?! DO YOU?!
LAST CHANCE, YOU PSYCHOPATHIC--
ARROW.

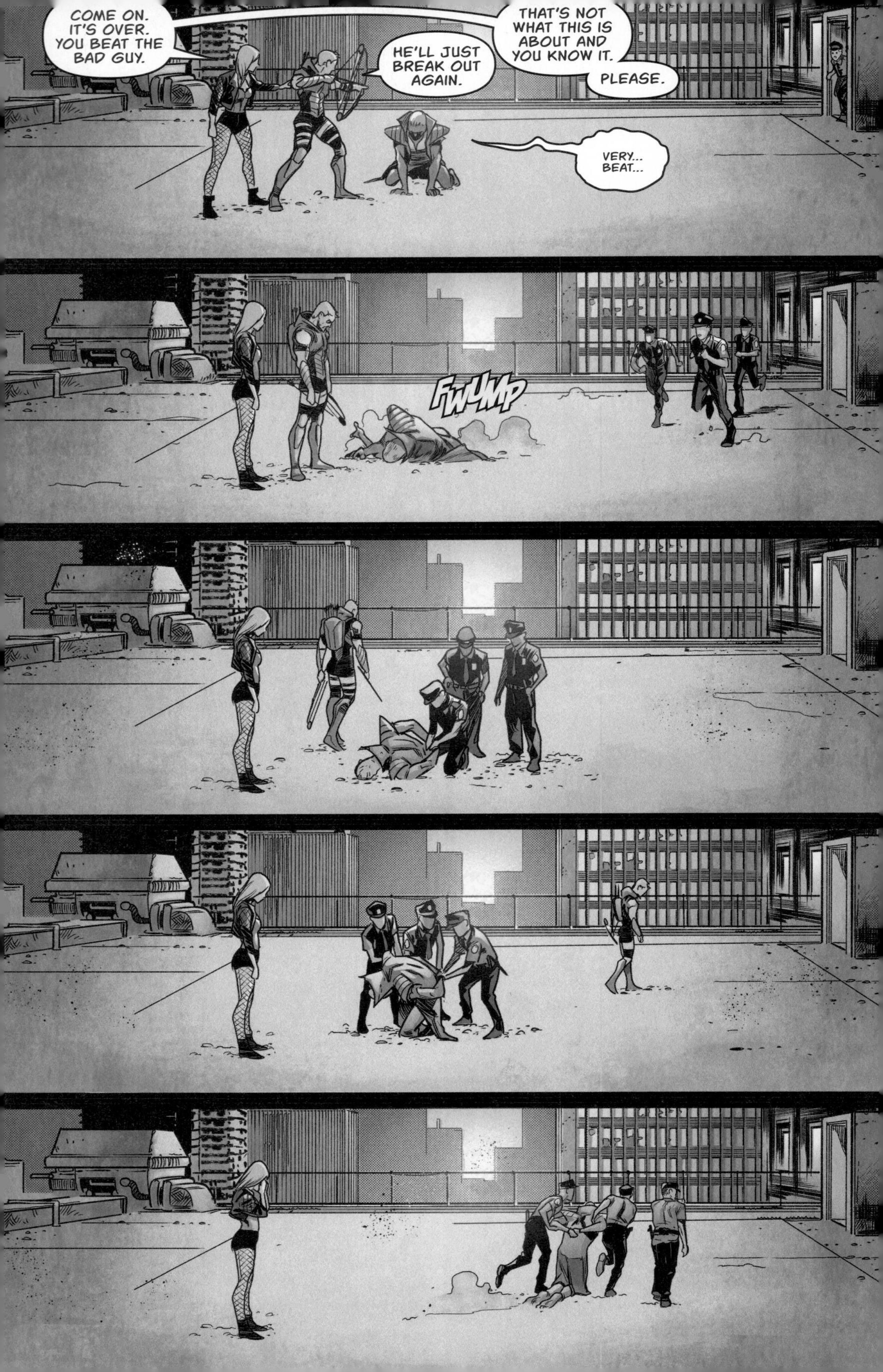

COME ON. IT'S OVER. YOU BEAT THE BAD GUY.
HE'LL JUST BREAK OUT AGAIN.
THAT'S NOT WHAT THIS IS ABOUT AND YOU KNOW IT.
PLEASE.
VERY... BEAT...
FWUMP

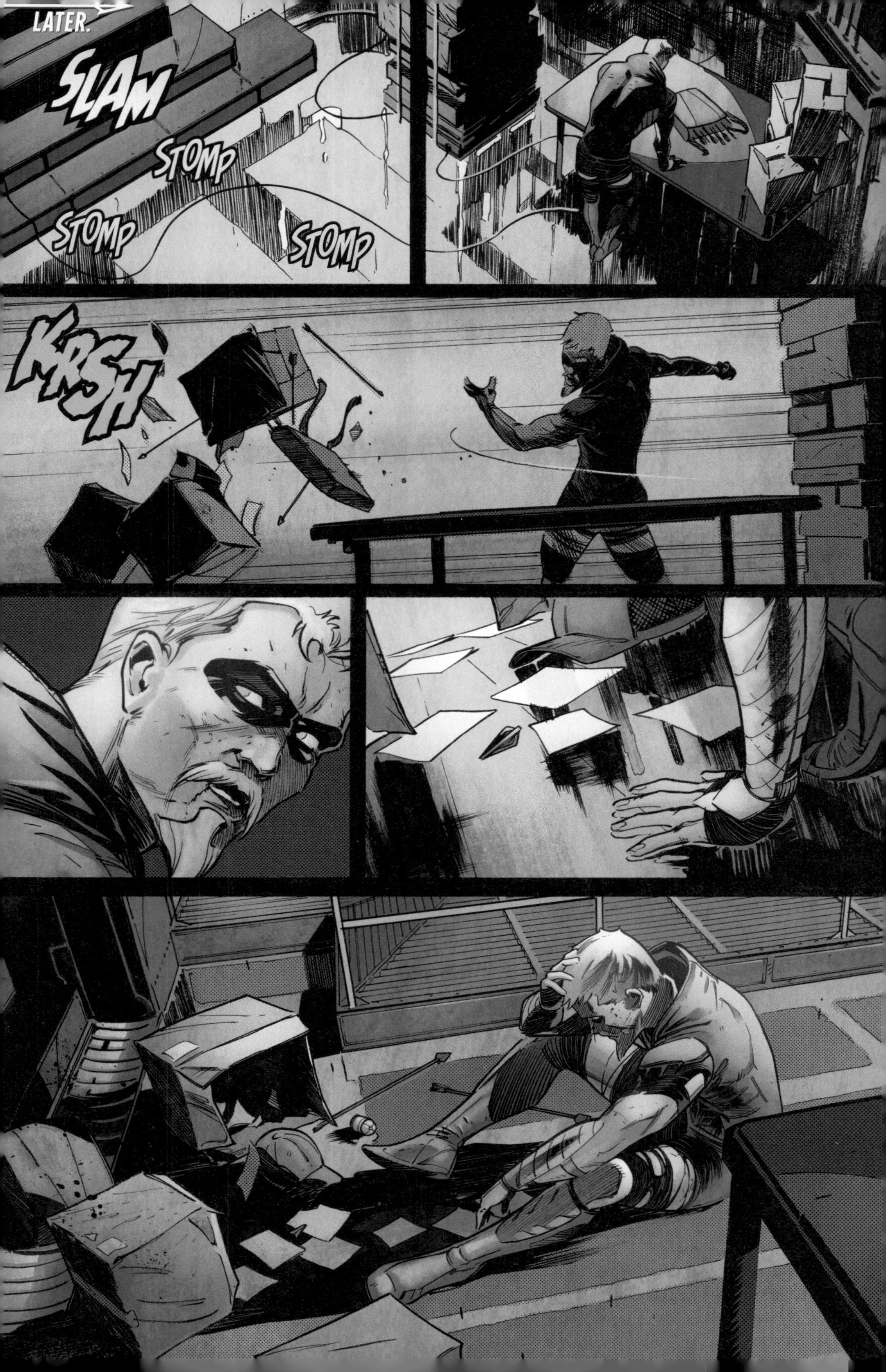
LATER.
SLAM
STOMP
STOMP
STOMP
KRSH

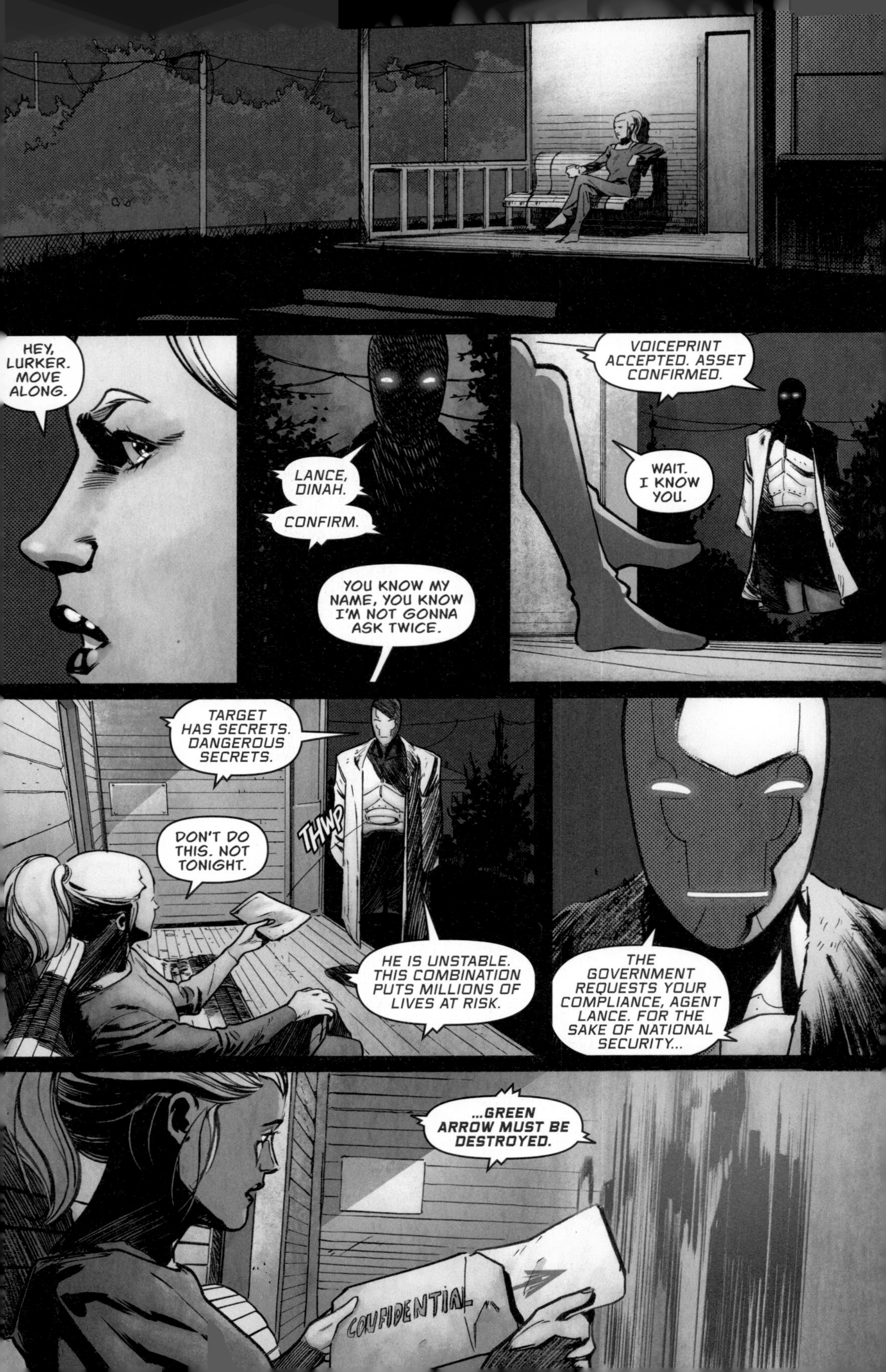
HEY, LURKER. MOVE ALONG.
LANCE, DINAH.
CONFIRM.
YOU KNOW MY NAME, YOU KNOW I'M NOT GONNA ASK TWICE.
VOICEPRINT ACCEPTED. ASSET CONFIRMED.
WAIT. I KNOW YOU.
TARGET HAS SECRETS. DANGEROUS SECRETS.
THWP
DON'T DO THIS. NOT TONIGHT.
HE IS UNSTABLE. THIS COMBINATION PUTS MILLIONS OF LIVES AT RISK.
THE GOVERNMENT REQUESTS YOUR COMPLIANCE, AGENT LANCE. FOR THE SAKE OF NATIONAL SECURITY...
...GREEN ARROW MUST BE DESTROYED.
CONFIDENTIAL

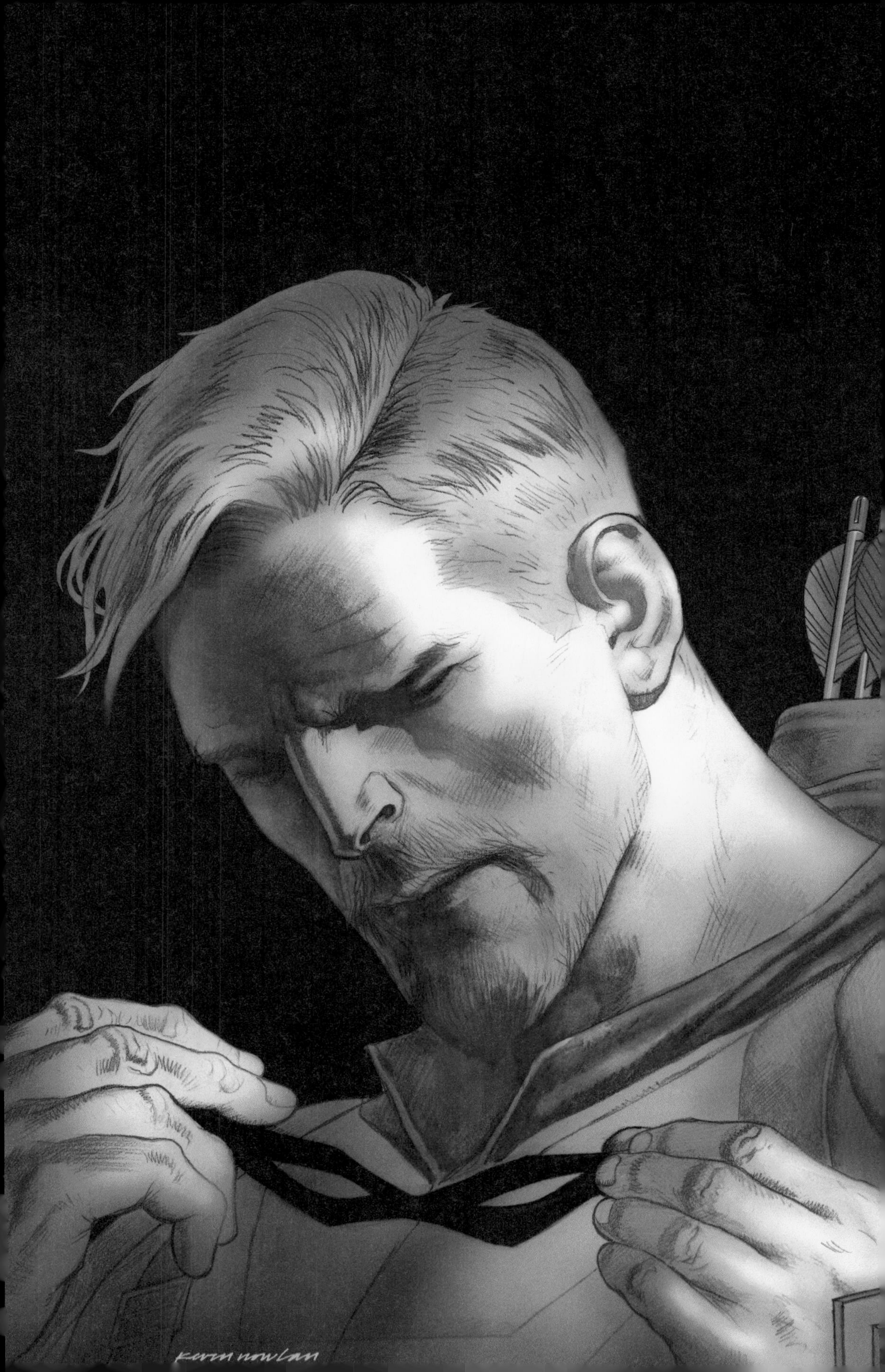
kevin nowlan

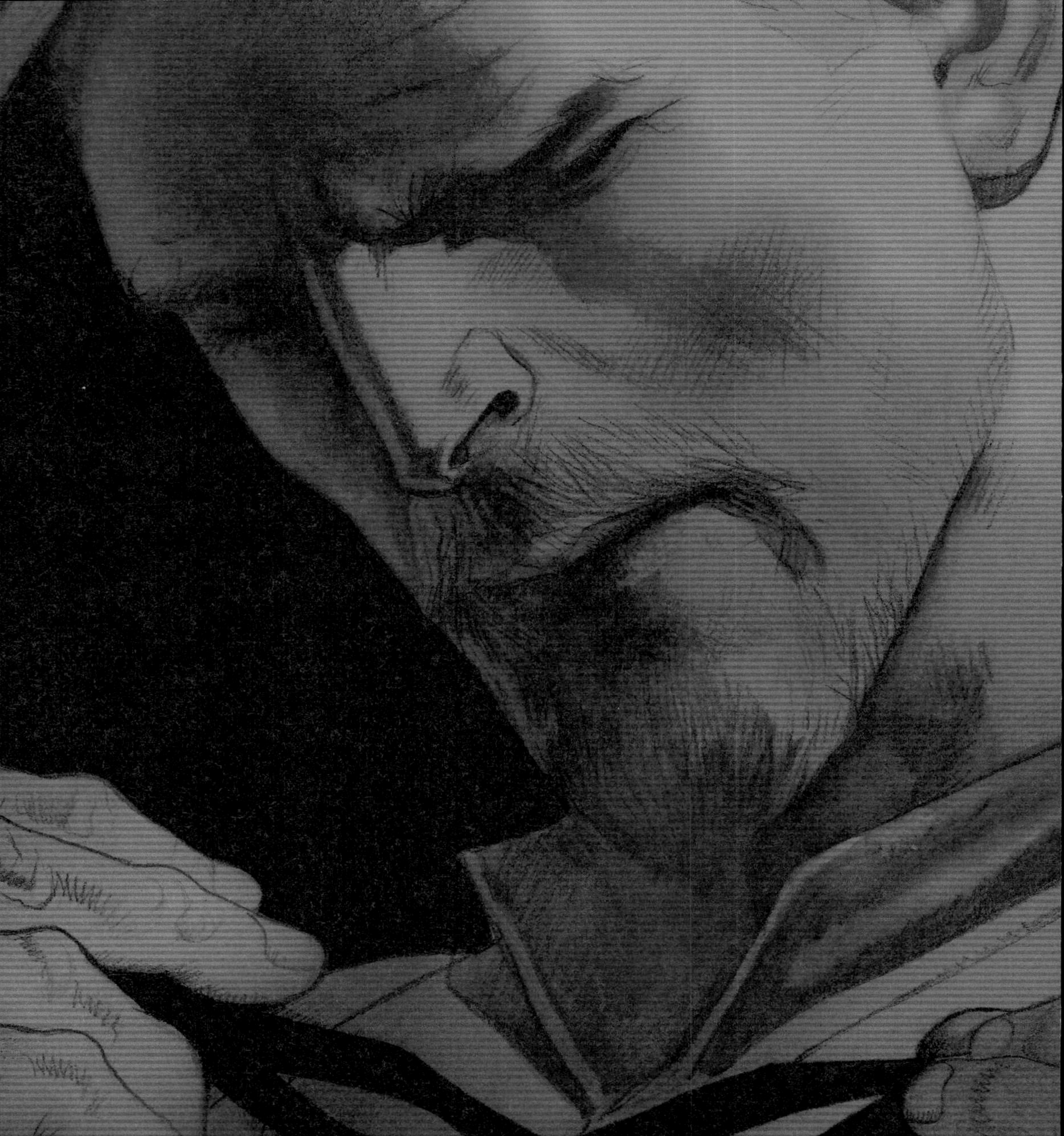

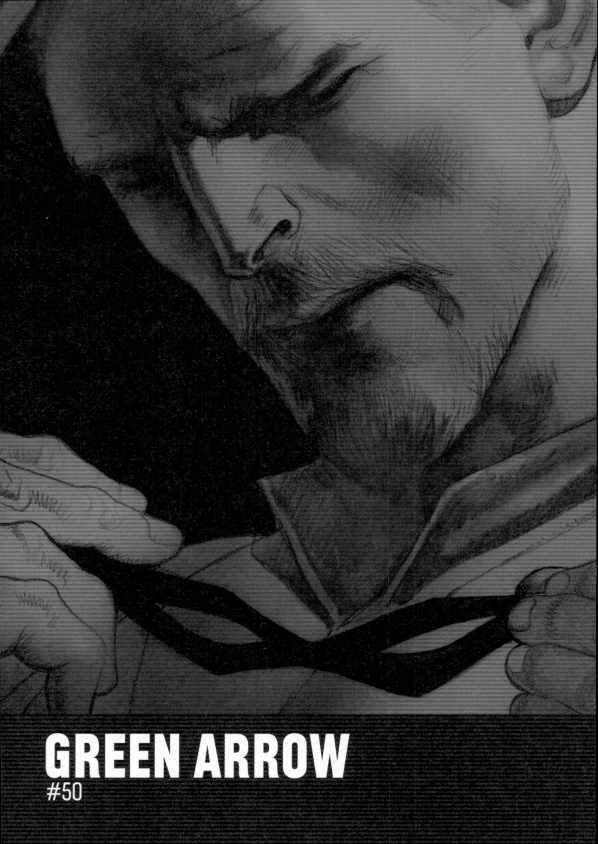

# GREEN ARROW

#50

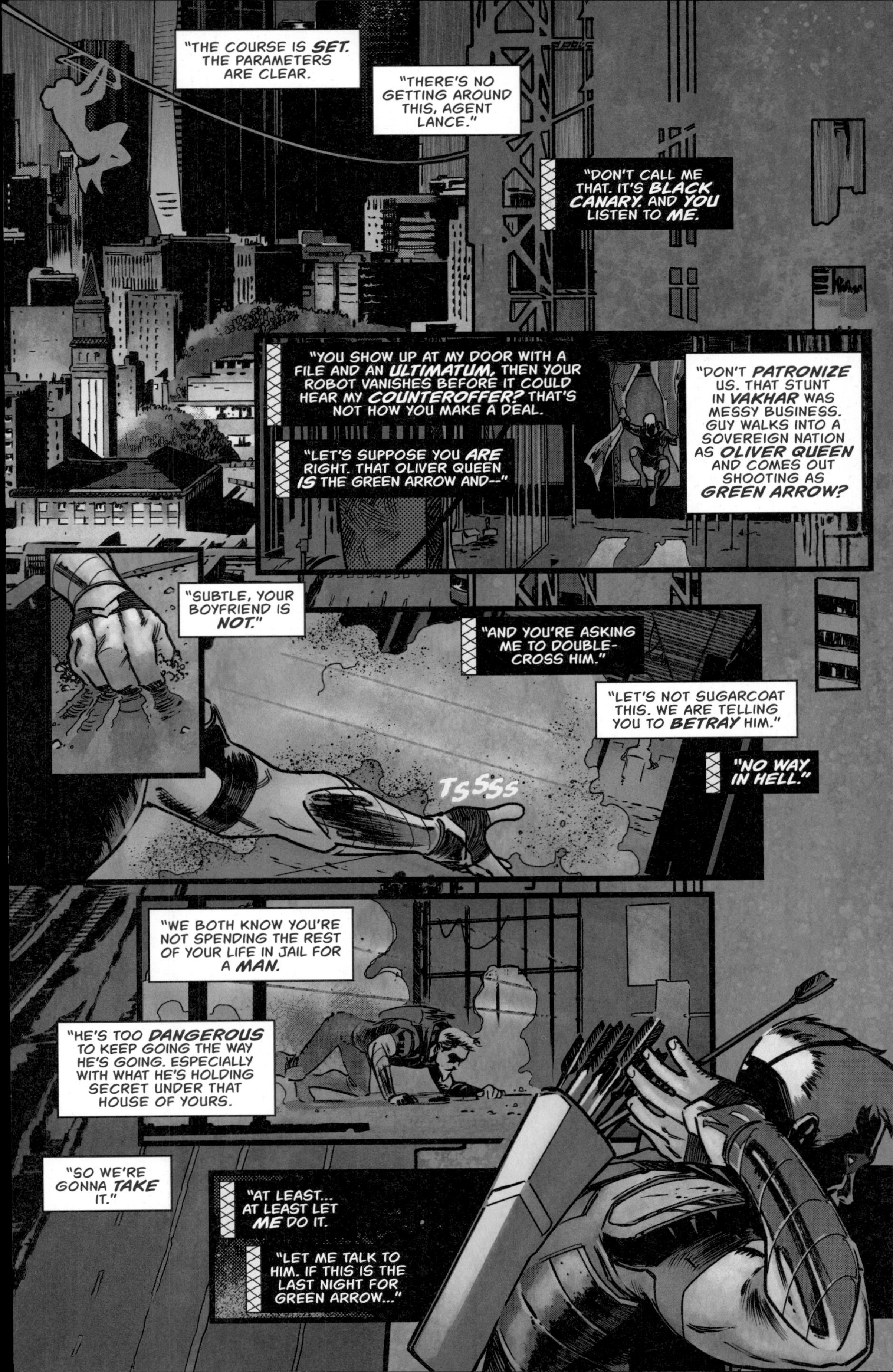
"THE COURSE IS SET. THE PARAMETERS ARE CLEAR.
"THERE'S NO GETTING AROUND THIS, AGENT LANCE."
"DON'T CALL ME THAT. IT'S BLACK CANARY. AND YOU LISTEN TO ME.
"YOU SHOW UP AT MY DOOR WITH A FILE AND AN ULTIMATUM, THEN YOUR ROBOT VANISHES BEFORE IT COULD HEAR MY COUNTEROFFER? THAT'S NOT HOW YOU MAKE A DEAL.
"LET'S SUPPOSE YOU ARE RIGHT. THAT OLIVER QUEEN IS THE GREEN ARROW AND--"
"DON'T PATRONIZE US. THAT STUNT IN VAKHAR WAS MESSY BUSINESS. GUY WALKS INTO A SOVEREIGN NATION AS OLIVER QUEEN AND COMES OUT SHOOTING AS GREEN ARROW?
"SUBTLE, YOUR BOYFRIEND IS NOT."
"AND YOU'RE ASKING ME TO DOUBLE-CROSS HIM."
"LET'S NOT SUGARCOAT THIS. WE ARE TELLING YOU TO BETRAY HIM."
"NO WAY IN HELL."
TSSSS
"WE BOTH KNOW YOU'RE NOT SPENDING THE REST OF YOUR LIFE IN JAIL FOR A MAN.
"HE'S TOO DANGEROUS TO KEEP GOING THE WAY HE'S GOING. ESPECIALLY WITH WHAT HE'S HOLDING SECRET UNDER THAT HOUSE OF YOURS.
"SO WE'RE GONNA TAKE IT."
"AT LEAST... AT LEAST LET ME DO IT.
"LET ME TALK TO HIM. IF THIS IS THE LAST NIGHT FOR GREEN ARROW..."

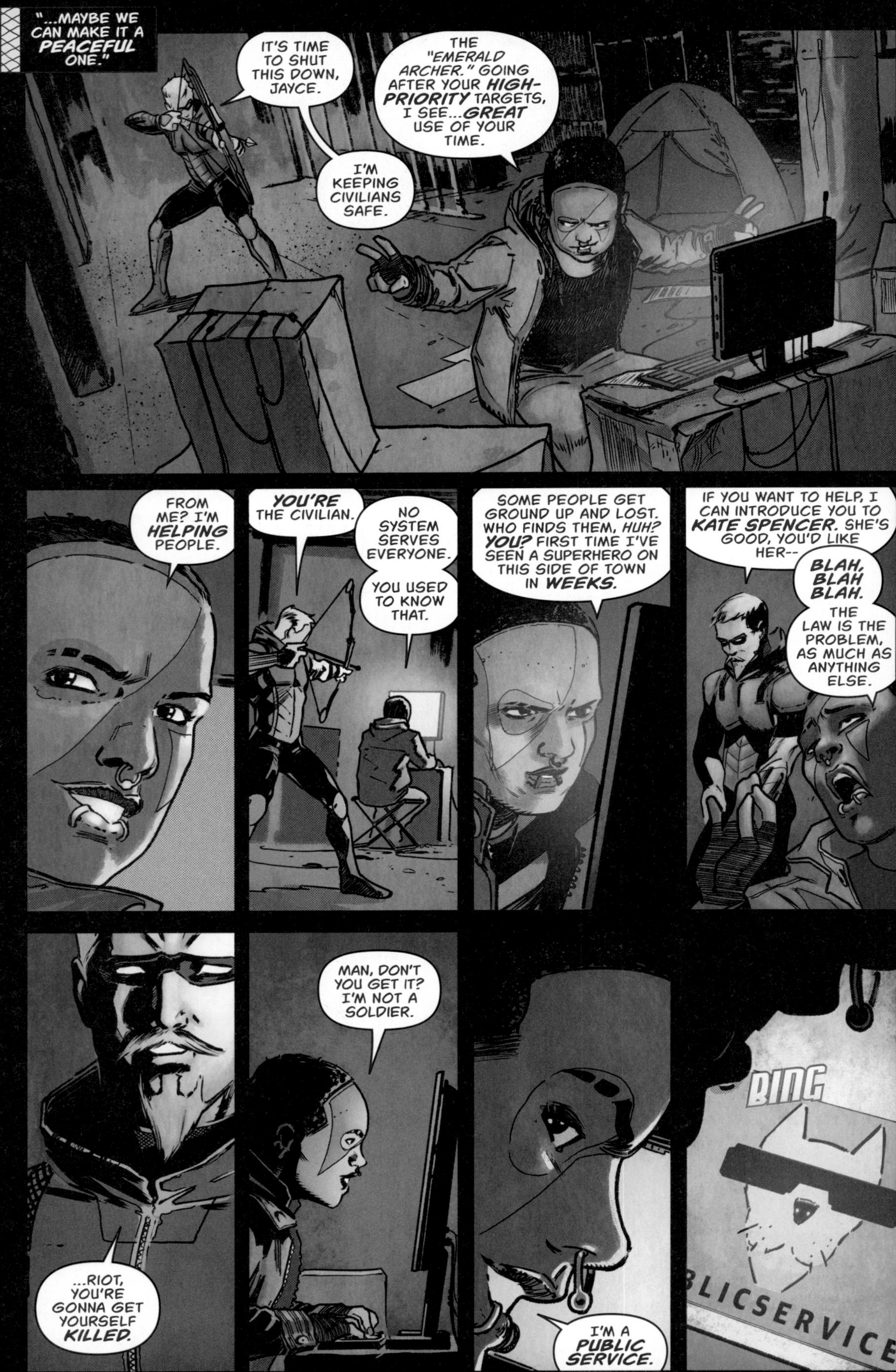
"...MAYBE WE CAN MAKE IT A PEACEFUL ONE."
IT'S TIME TO SHUT THIS DOWN, JAYCE.
THE "EMERALD ARCHER." GOING AFTER YOUR HIGH-PRIORITY TARGETS, I SEE...GREAT USE OF YOUR TIME.
I'M KEEPING CIVILIANS SAFE.
FROM ME? I'M HELPING PEOPLE.
YOU'RE THE CIVILIAN.
NO SYSTEM SERVES EVERYONE.
YOU USED TO KNOW THAT.
SOME PEOPLE GET GROUND UP AND LOST. WHO FINDS THEM, HUH? YOU? FIRST TIME I'VE SEEN A SUPERHERO ON THIS SIDE OF TOWN IN WEEKS.
IF YOU WANT TO HELP, I CAN INTRODUCE YOU TO KATE SPENCER. SHE'S GOOD, YOU'D LIKE HER--
BLAH, BLAH BLAH.
THE LAW IS THE PROBLEM, AS MUCH AS ANYTHING ELSE.
...RIOT, YOU'RE GONNA GET YOURSELF KILLED.
MAN, DON'T YOU GET IT? I'M NOT A SOLDIER.
I'M A PUBLIC SERVICE.
BING
BLICSERVICE

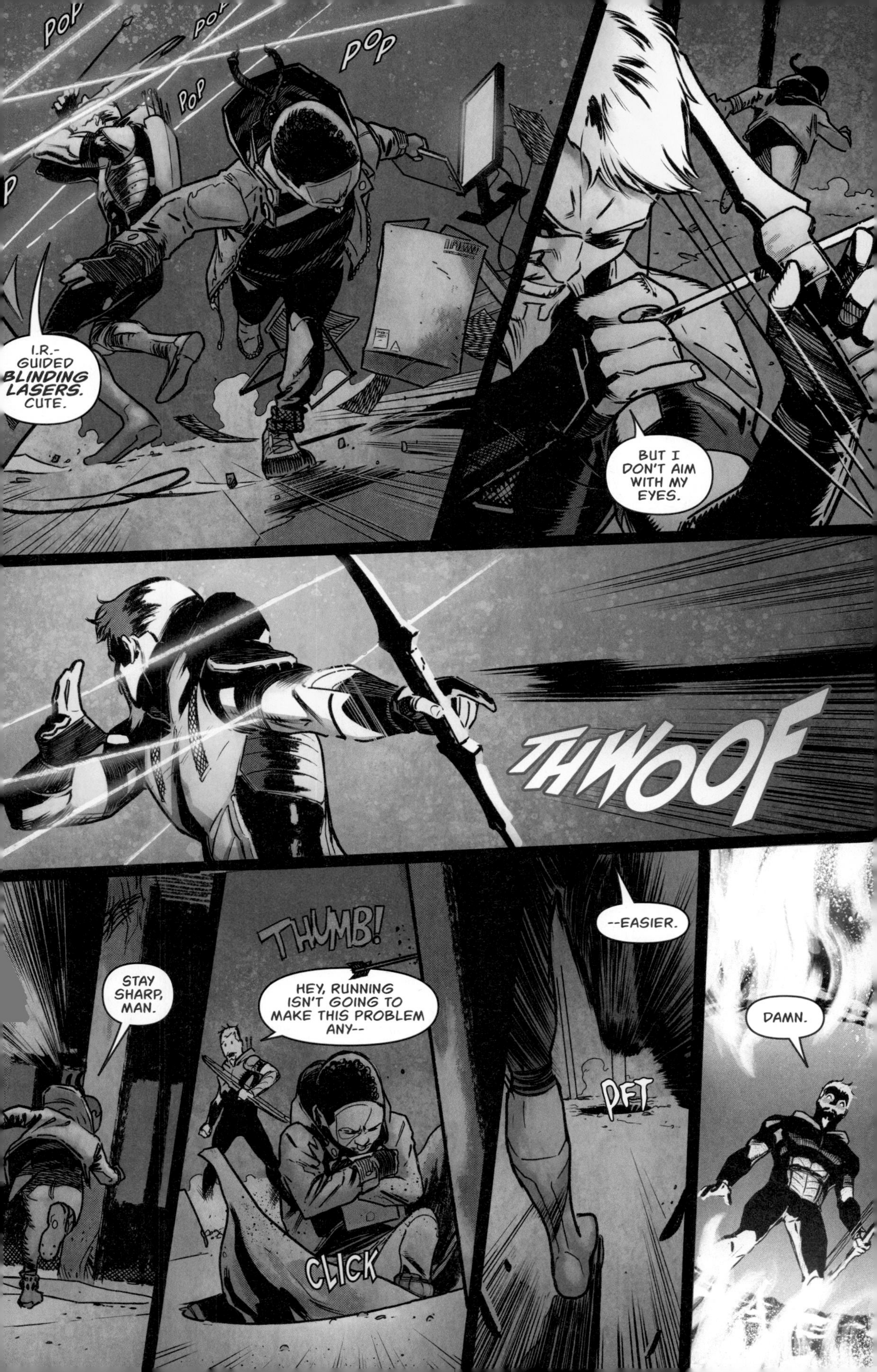
POP
POP
POP
POP
P
I.R.-GUIDED BLINDING LASERS. CUTE.
BUT I DON'T AIM WITH MY EYES.
THWOOF
STAY SHARP, MAN.
THUMB!
HEY, RUNNING ISN'T GOING TO MAKE THIS PROBLEM ANY--
CLICK
--EASIER.
PFT
DAMN.

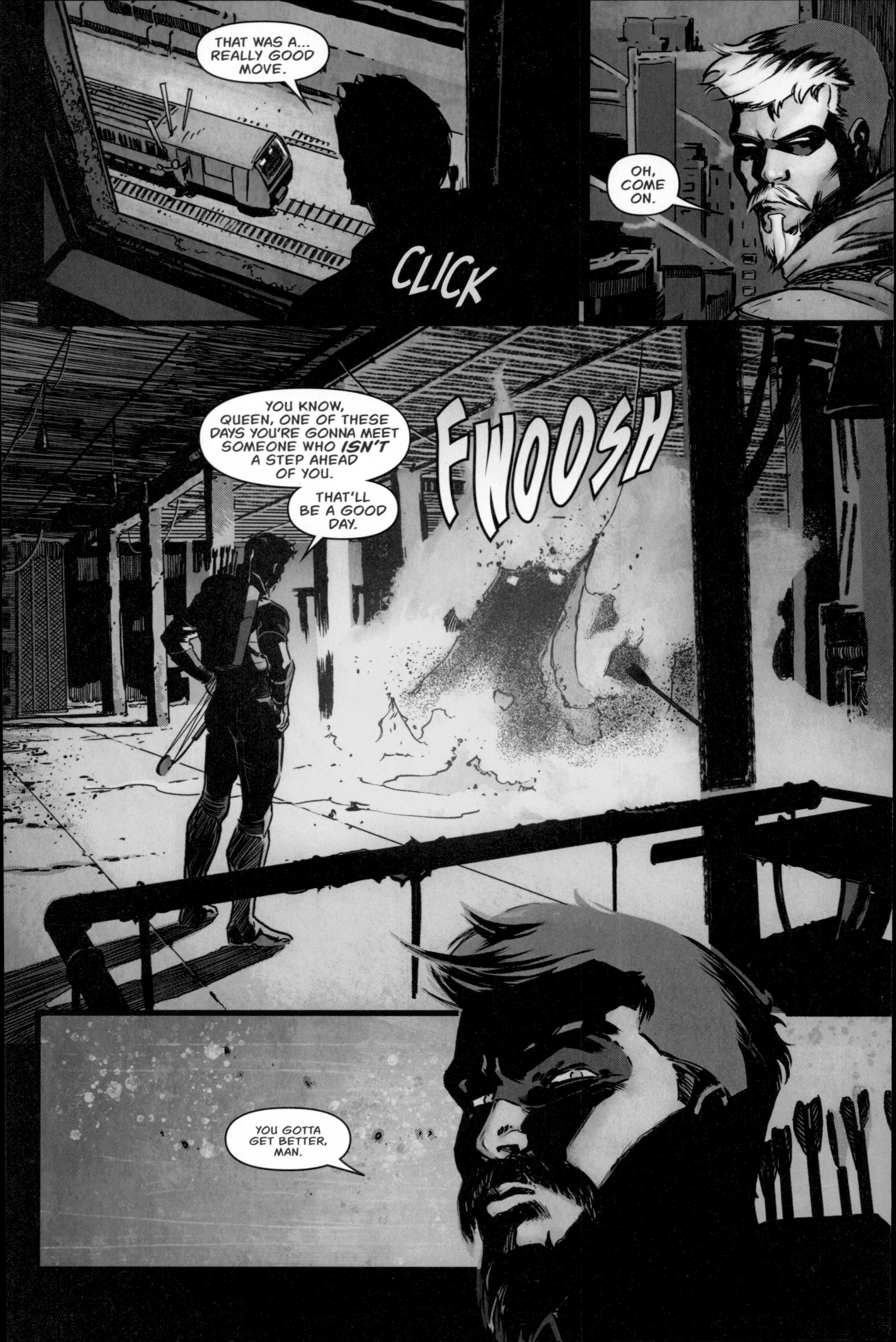
THAT WAS A... REALLY GOOD MOVE.
CLICK
OH, COME ON.
YOU KNOW, QUEEN, ONE OF THESE DAYS YOU'RE GONNA MEET SOMEONE WHO ISN'T A STEP AHEAD OF YOU.
THAT'LL BE A GOOD DAY.
FWOOSH
YOU GOTTA GET BETTER, MAN.

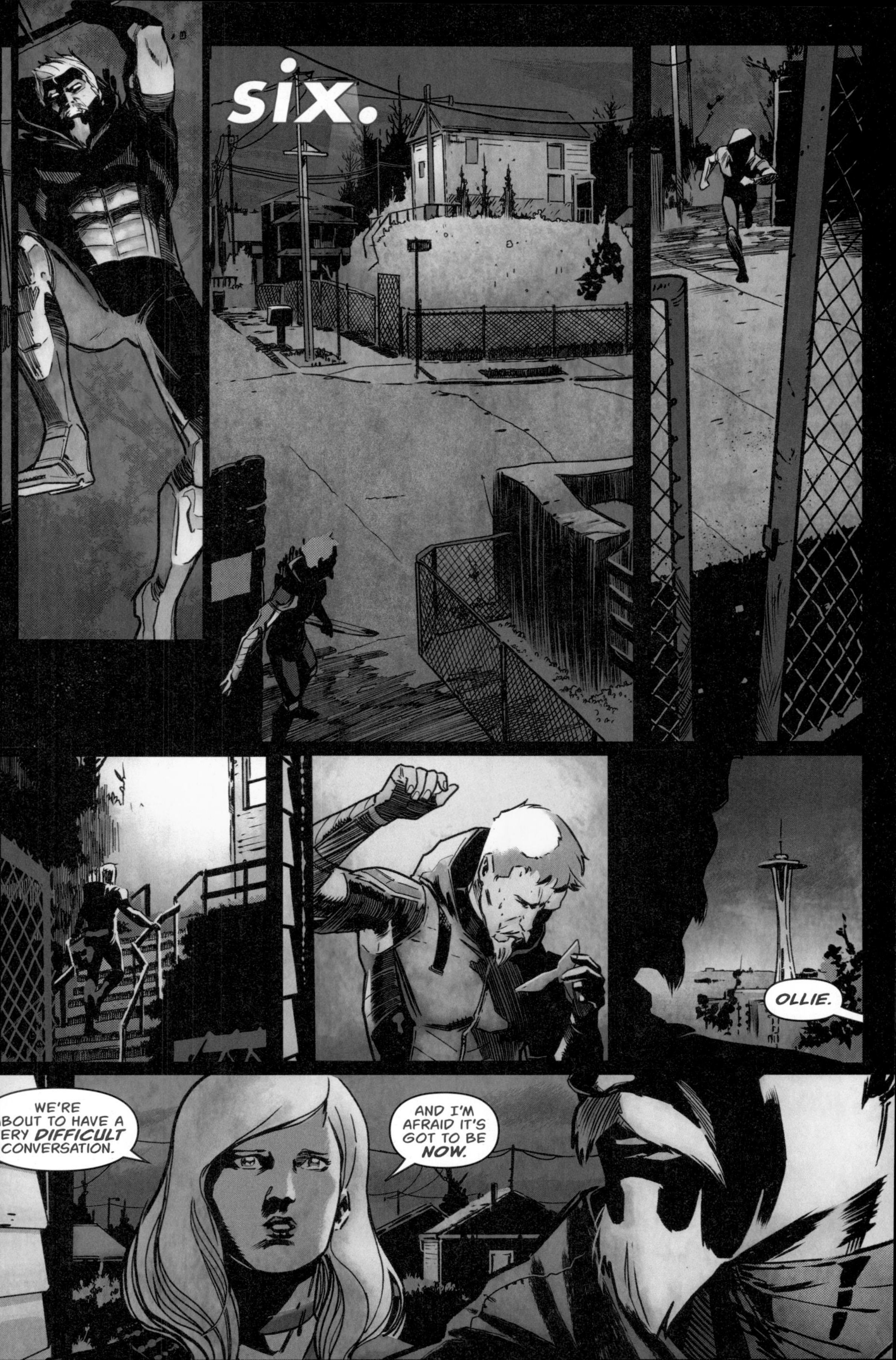
six.
OLLIE.
WE'RE ABOUT TO HAVE A VERY DIFFICULT CONVERSATION.
AND I'M AFRAID IT'S GOT TO BE NOW.

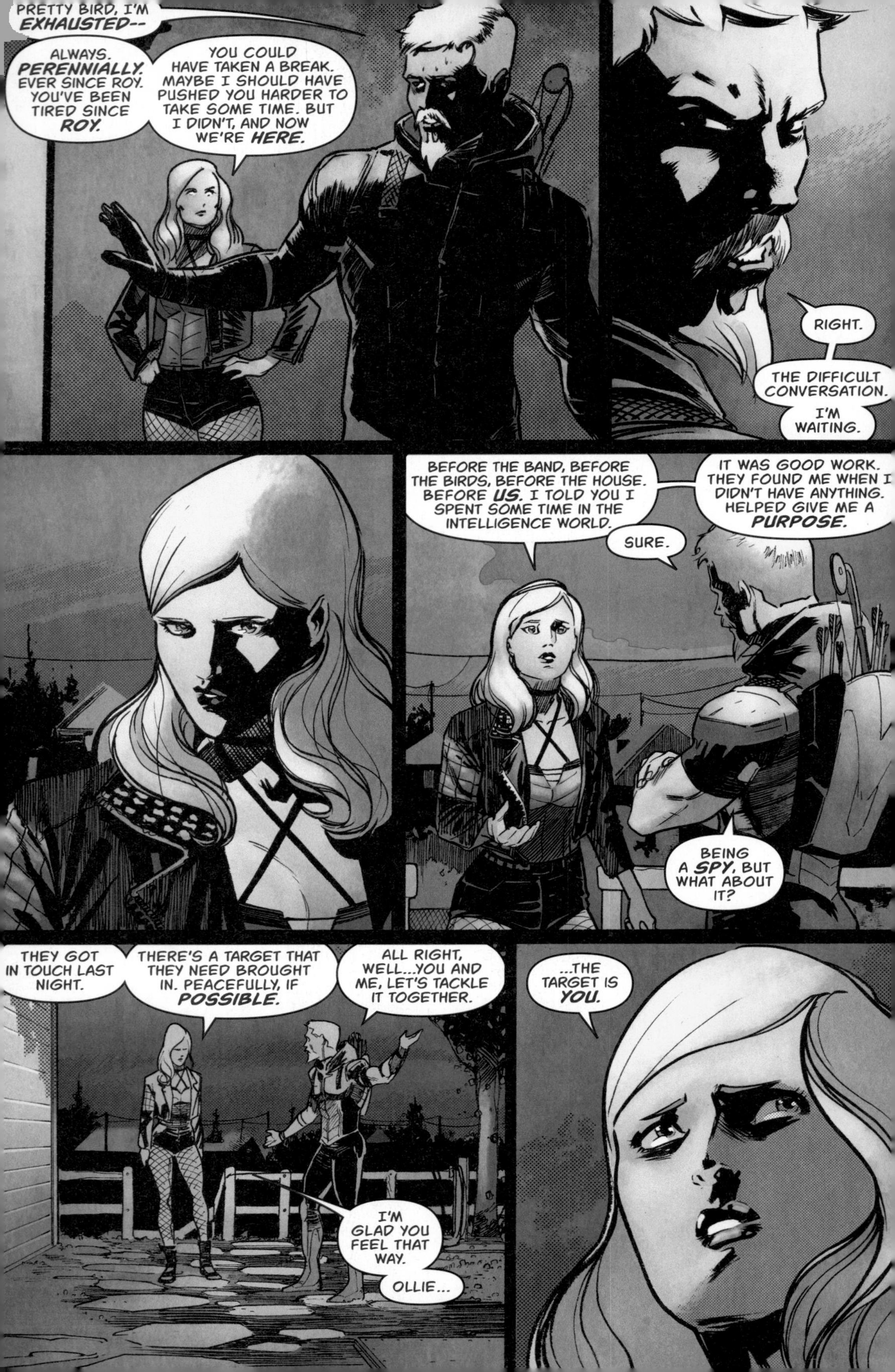
PRETTY BIRD, I'M EXHAUSTED--
ALWAYS. PERENNIALLY. EVER SINCE ROY. YOU'VE BEEN TIRED SINCE ROY.
YOU COULD HAVE TAKEN A BREAK. MAYBE I SHOULD HAVE PUSHED YOU HARDER TO TAKE SOME TIME. BUT I DIDN'T, AND NOW WE'RE HERE.
RIGHT.
THE DIFFICULT CONVERSATION.
I'M WAITING.
BEFORE THE BAND, BEFORE THE BIRDS, BEFORE THE HOUSE. BEFORE US. I TOLD YOU I SPENT SOME TIME IN THE INTELLIGENCE WORLD.
SURE.
IT WAS GOOD WORK. THEY FOUND ME WHEN I DIDN'T HAVE ANYTHING. HELPED GIVE ME A PURPOSE.
BEING A SPY, BUT WHAT ABOUT IT?
THEY GOT IN TOUCH LAST NIGHT.
THERE'S A TARGET THAT THEY NEED BROUGHT IN. PEACEFULLY, IF POSSIBLE.
ALL RIGHT, WELL...YOU AND ME, LET'S TACKLE IT TOGETHER.
I'M GLAD YOU FEEL THAT WAY.
OLLIE...
...THE TARGET IS YOU.

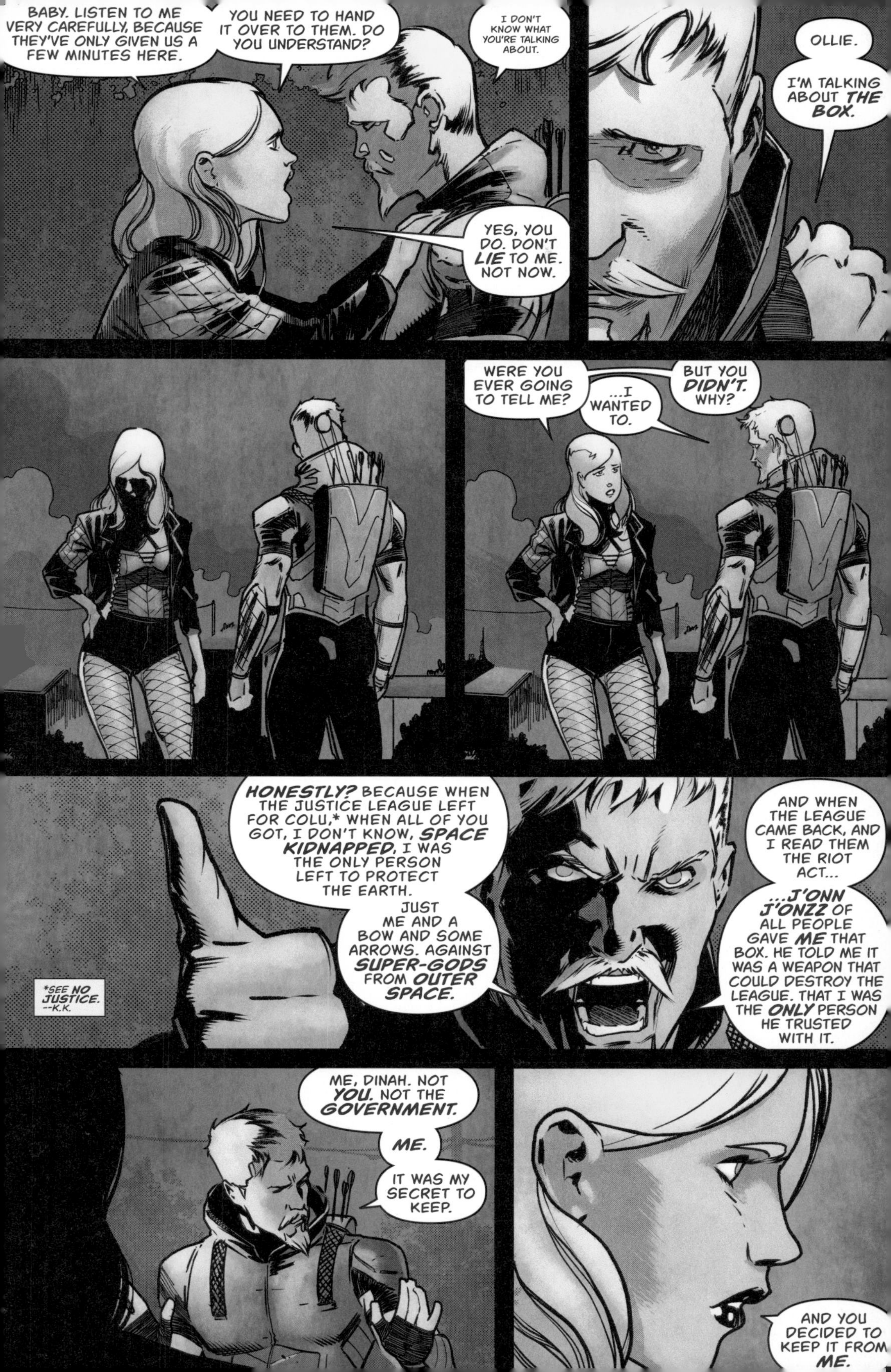
BABY. LISTEN TO ME VERY CAREFULLY, BECAUSE THEY'VE ONLY GIVEN US A FEW MINUTES HERE.
YOU NEED TO HAND IT OVER TO THEM. DO YOU UNDERSTAND?
I DON'T KNOW WHAT YOU'RE TALKING ABOUT.
YES, YOU DO. DON'T LIE TO ME. NOT NOW.
OLLIE.
I'M TALKING ABOUT THE BOX.
WERE YOU EVER GOING TO TELL ME?
...I WANTED TO.
BUT YOU DIDN'T. WHY?
HONESTLY? BECAUSE WHEN THE JUSTICE LEAGUE LEFT FOR COLU,* WHEN ALL OF YOU GOT, I DON'T KNOW, SPACE KIDNAPPED, I WAS THE ONLY PERSON LEFT TO PROTECT THE EARTH.
JUST ME AND A BOW AND SOME ARROWS. AGAINST SUPER-GODS FROM OUTER SPACE.
AND WHEN THE LEAGUE CAME BACK, AND I READ THEM THE RIOT ACT...
...J'ONN J'ONZZ OF ALL PEOPLE GAVE ME THAT BOX. HE TOLD ME IT WAS A WEAPON THAT COULD DESTROY THE LEAGUE. THAT I WAS THE ONLY PERSON HE TRUSTED WITH IT.
*SEE NO JUSTICE. --K.K.
ME, DINAH. NOT YOU. NOT THE GOVERNMENT.
ME.
IT WAS MY SECRET TO KEEP.
AND YOU DECIDED TO KEEP IT FROM ME.

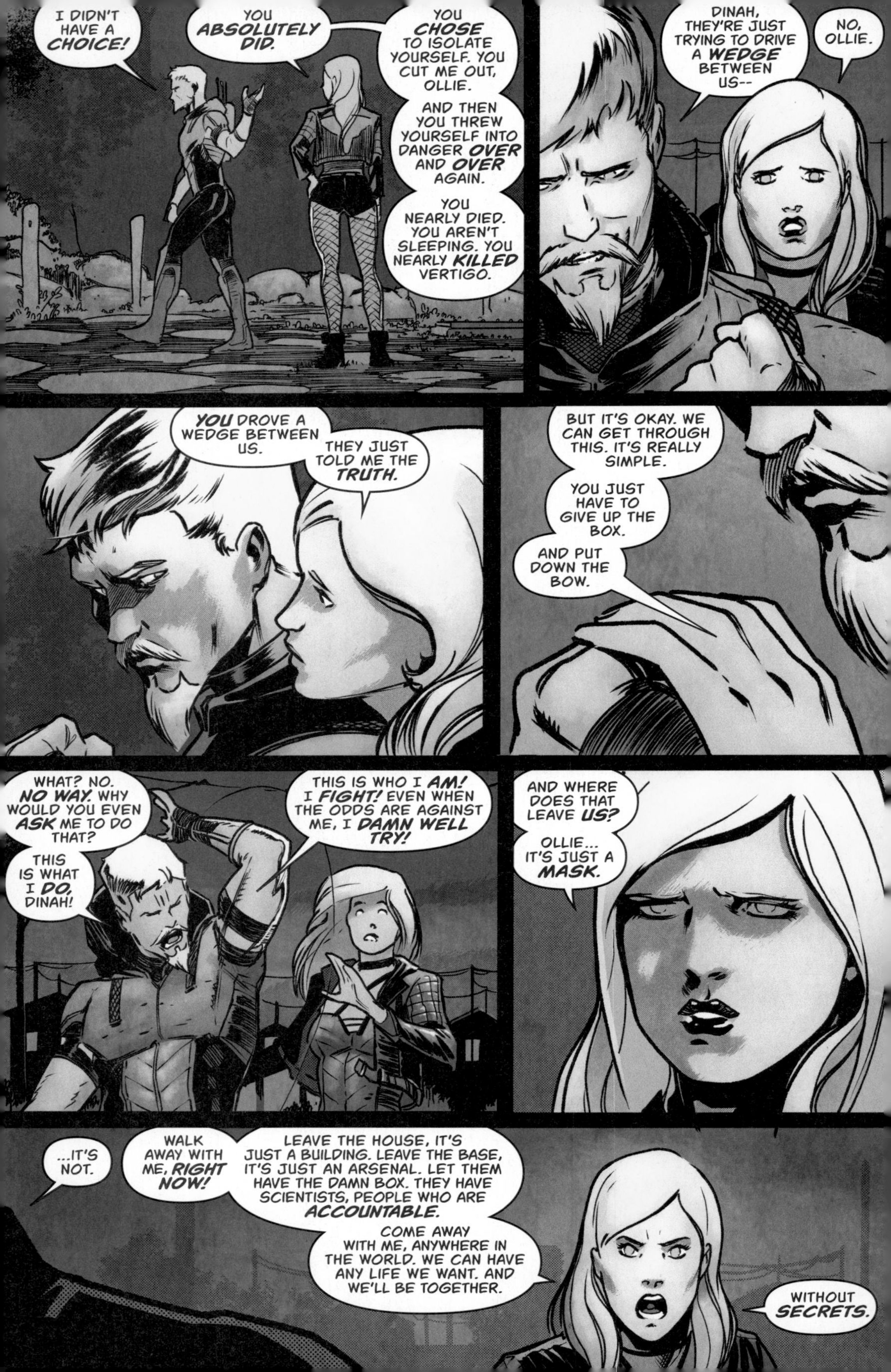
I DIDN'T HAVE A CHOICE!
YOU ABSOLUTELY DID.
YOU CHOSE TO ISOLATE YOURSELF. YOU CUT ME OUT, OLLIE.
AND THEN YOU THREW YOURSELF INTO DANGER OVER AND OVER AGAIN.
YOU NEARLY DIED. YOU AREN'T SLEEPING. YOU NEARLY KILLED VERTIGO.
DINAH, THEY'RE JUST TRYING TO DRIVE A WEDGE BETWEEN US--
NO, OLLIE.
YOU DROVE A WEDGE BETWEEN US.
THEY JUST TOLD ME THE TRUTH.
BUT IT'S OKAY. WE CAN GET THROUGH THIS. IT'S REALLY SIMPLE.
YOU JUST HAVE TO GIVE UP THE BOX.
AND PUT DOWN THE BOW.
WHAT? NO. NO WAY. WHY WOULD YOU EVEN ASK ME TO DO THAT?
THIS IS WHAT I DO, DINAH!
THIS IS WHO I AM! I FIGHT! EVEN WHEN THE ODDS ARE AGAINST ME, I DAMN WELL TRY!
AND WHERE DOES THAT LEAVE US?
OLLIE... IT'S JUST A MASK.
...IT'S NOT.
WALK AWAY WITH ME, RIGHT NOW!
LEAVE THE HOUSE, IT'S JUST A BUILDING. LEAVE THE BASE, IT'S JUST AN ARSENAL. LET THEM HAVE THE DAMN BOX. THEY HAVE SCIENTISTS, PEOPLE WHO ARE ACCOUNTABLE.
COME AWAY WITH ME, ANYWHERE IN THE WORLD. WE CAN HAVE ANY LIFE WE WANT. AND WE'LL BE TOGETHER.
WITHOUT SECRETS.

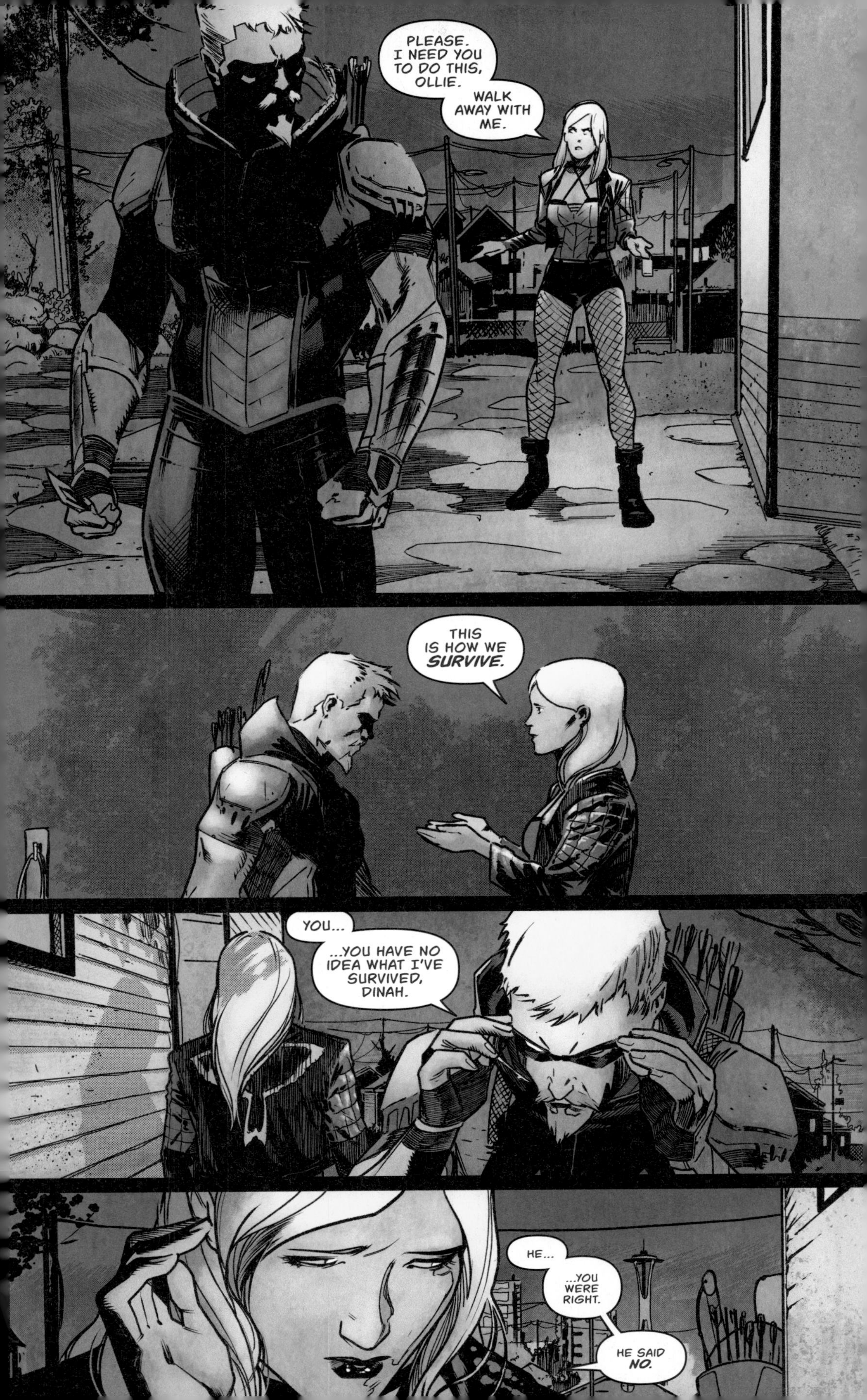
PLEASE. I NEED YOU TO DO THIS, OLLIE.
WALK AWAY WITH ME.
THIS IS HOW WE *SURVIVE.*
YOU...
...YOU HAVE NO IDEA WHAT I'VE SURVIVED, DINAH.
HE...
...YOU WERE RIGHT.
HE SAID *NO.*

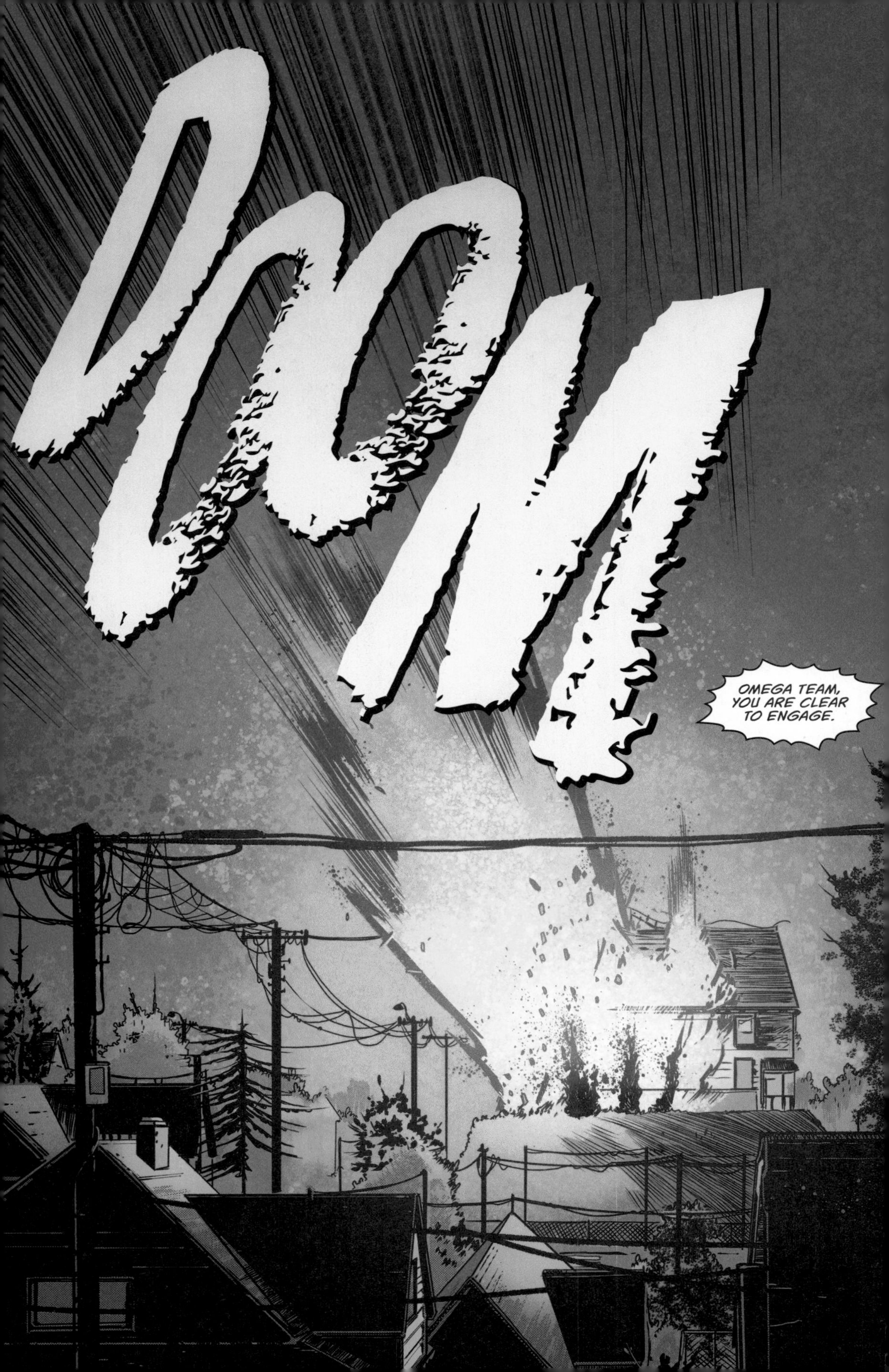
OMEGA TEAM, YOU ARE CLEAR TO ENGAGE.

# five.

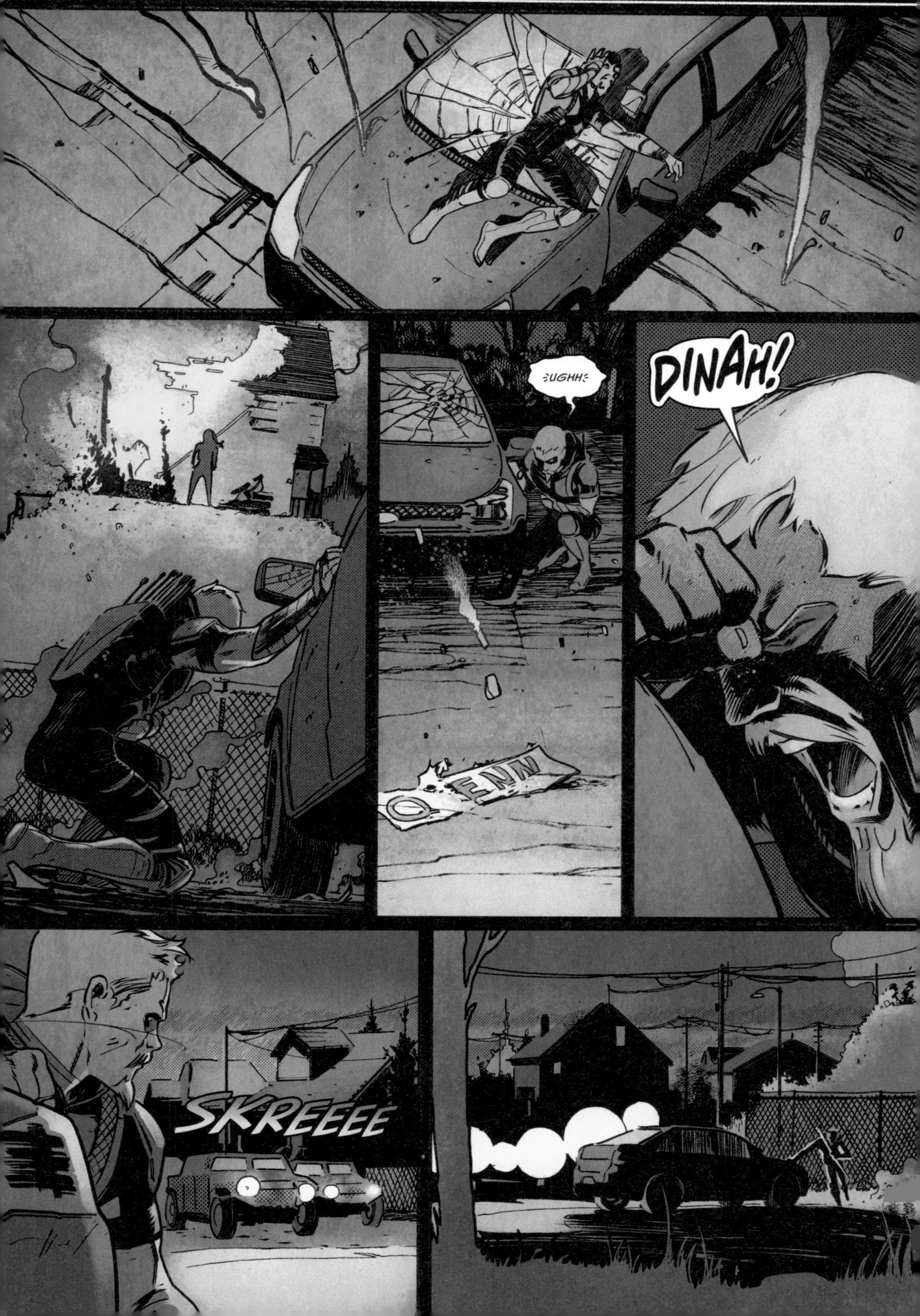

UGHH
DINAH!
SKREEEE

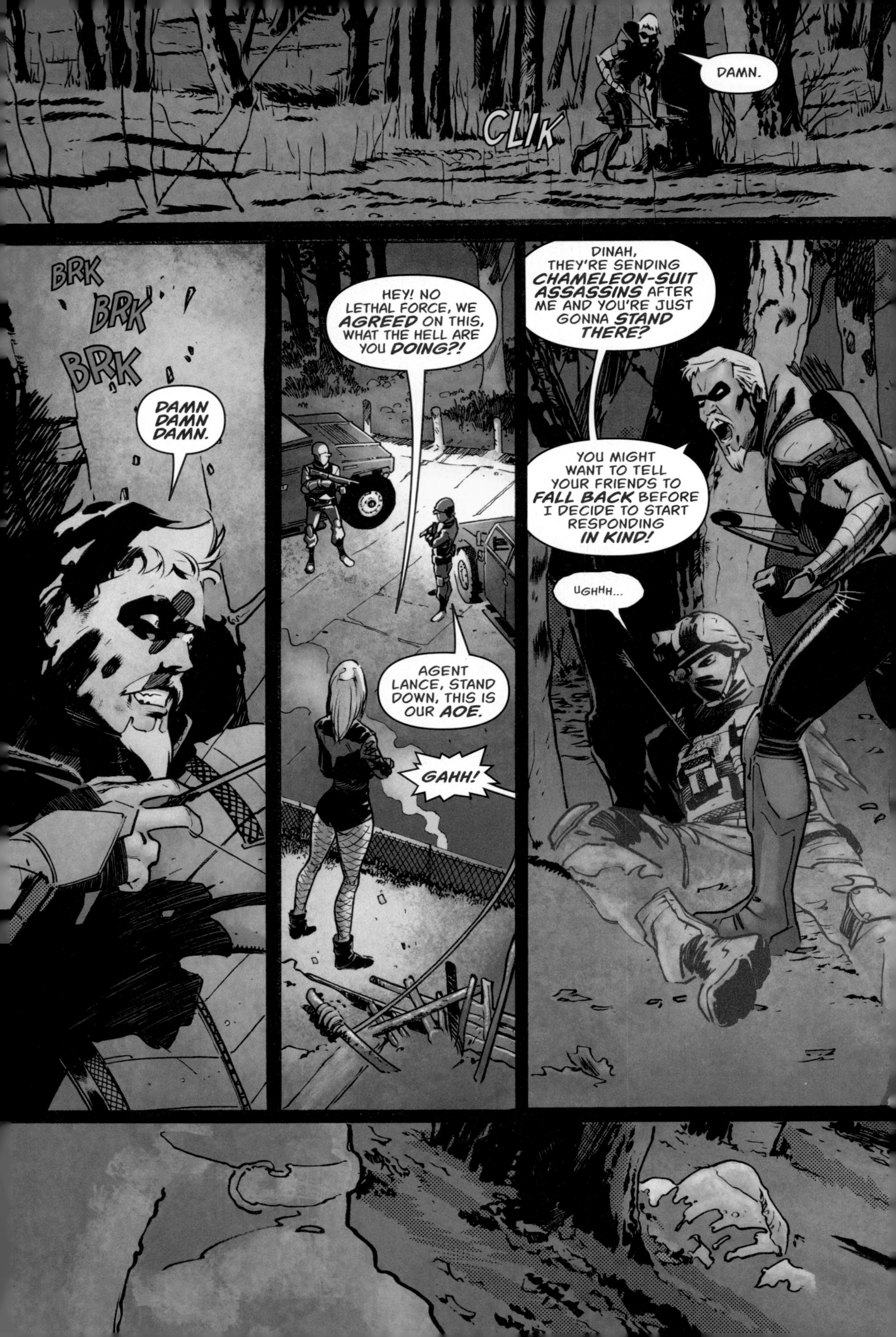
DAMN.
CLIK
BRK
BRK
BRK
DAMN DAMN DAMN.
HEY! NO LETHAL FORCE, WE AGREED ON THIS, WHAT THE HELL ARE YOU DOING?!
AGENT LANCE, STAND DOWN, THIS IS OUR AOE.
GAHH!
DINAH, THEY'RE SENDING CHAMELEON-SUIT ASSASSINS AFTER ME AND YOU'RE JUST GONNA STAND THERE?
YOU MIGHT WANT TO TELL YOUR FRIENDS TO FALL BACK BEFORE I DECIDE TO START RESPONDING IN KIND!
UGHHH...

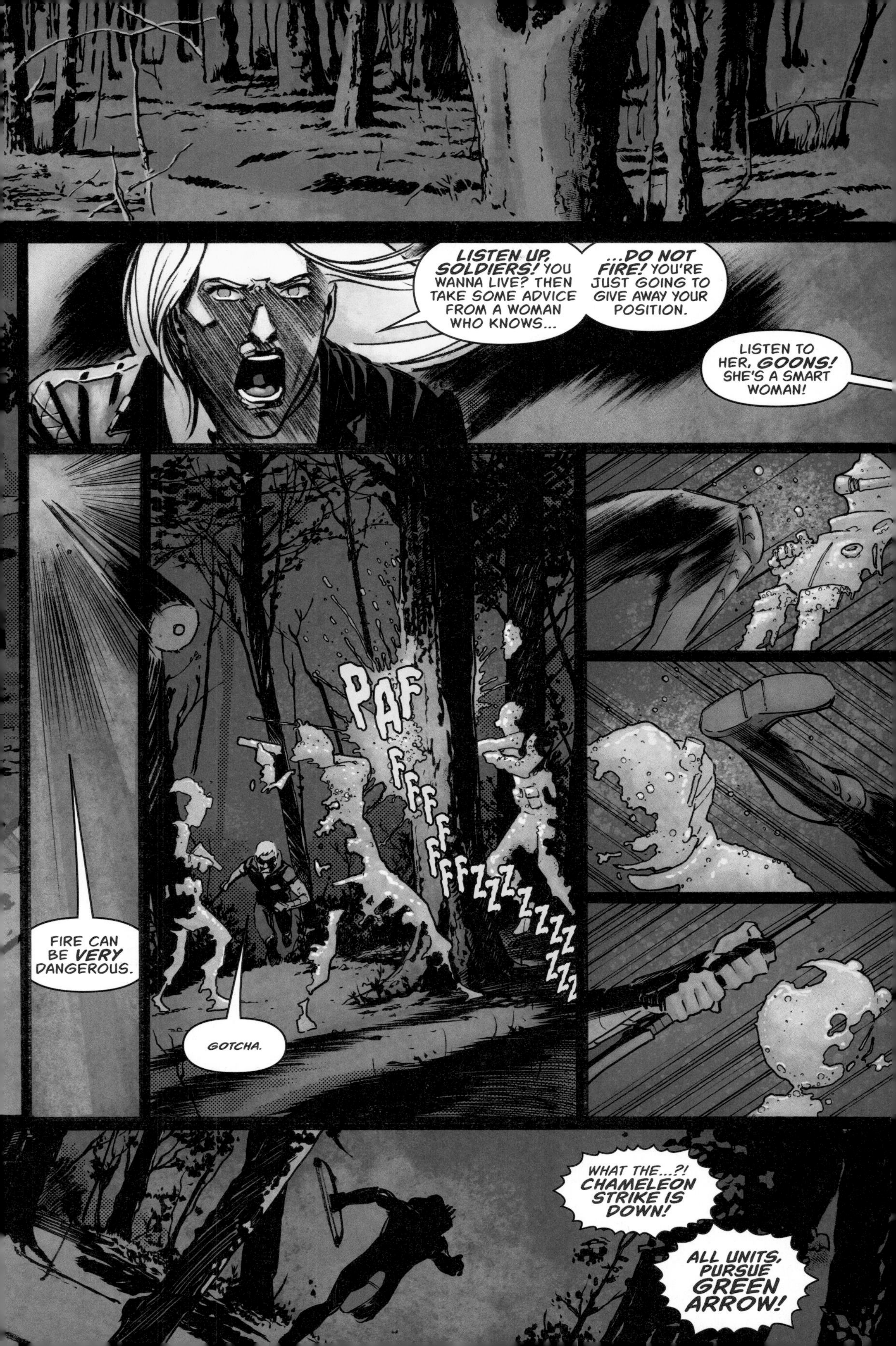
LISTEN UP, SOLDIERS! YOU WANNA LIVE? THEN TAKE SOME ADVICE FROM A WOMAN WHO KNOWS...
...DO NOT FIRE! YOU'RE JUST GOING TO GIVE AWAY YOUR POSITION.
LISTEN TO HER, GOONS! SHE'S A SMART WOMAN!
FIRE CAN BE VERY DANGEROUS.
PAF
FFFFFFFZZZZZZZZZZZ
GOTCHA.
WHAT THE...?! CHAMELEON STRIKE IS DOWN!
ALL UNITS, PURSUE GREEN ARROW!

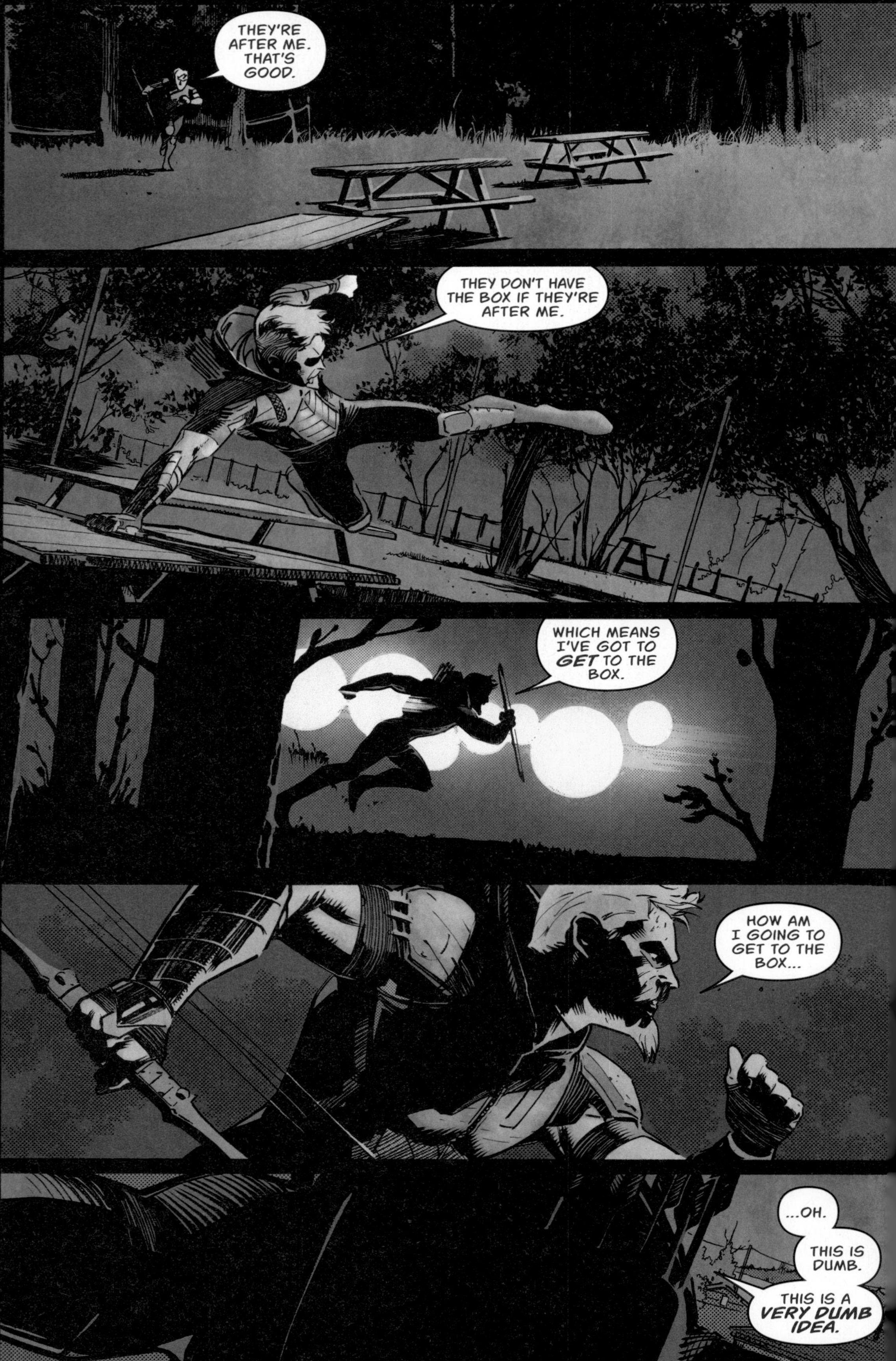
THEY'RE AFTER ME. THAT'S GOOD.
THEY DON'T HAVE THE BOX IF THEY'RE AFTER ME.
WHICH MEANS I'VE GOT TO *GET* TO THE BOX.
HOW AM I GOING TO GET TO THE BOX...
...OH.
THIS IS DUMB.
THIS IS A ***VERY DUMB IDEA.***

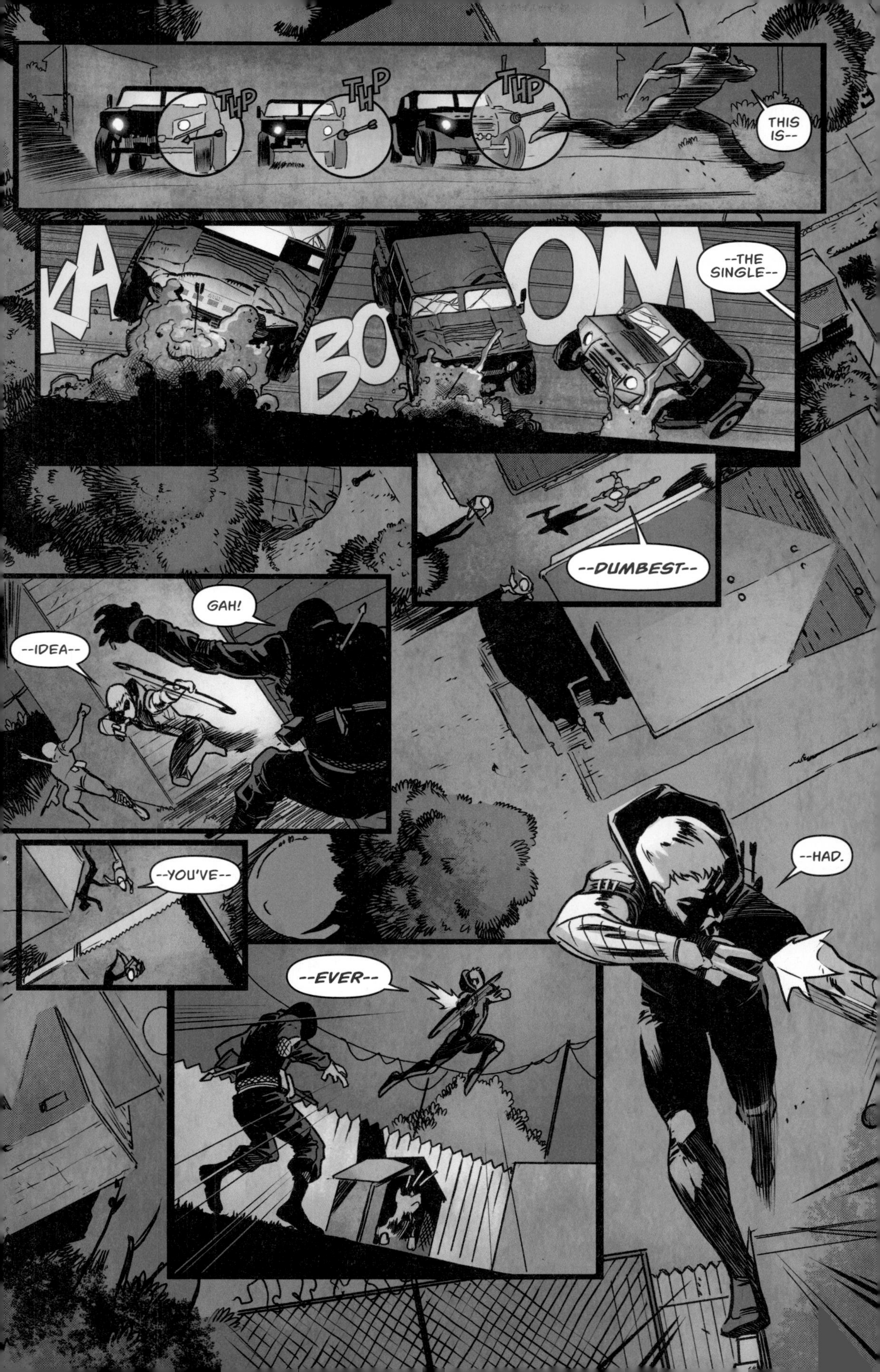
THP
THP
THP
THIS IS--
KA
BOOM
--THE SINGLE--
--DUMBEST--
GAH!
--IDEA--
--YOU'VE--
--EVER--
--HAD.

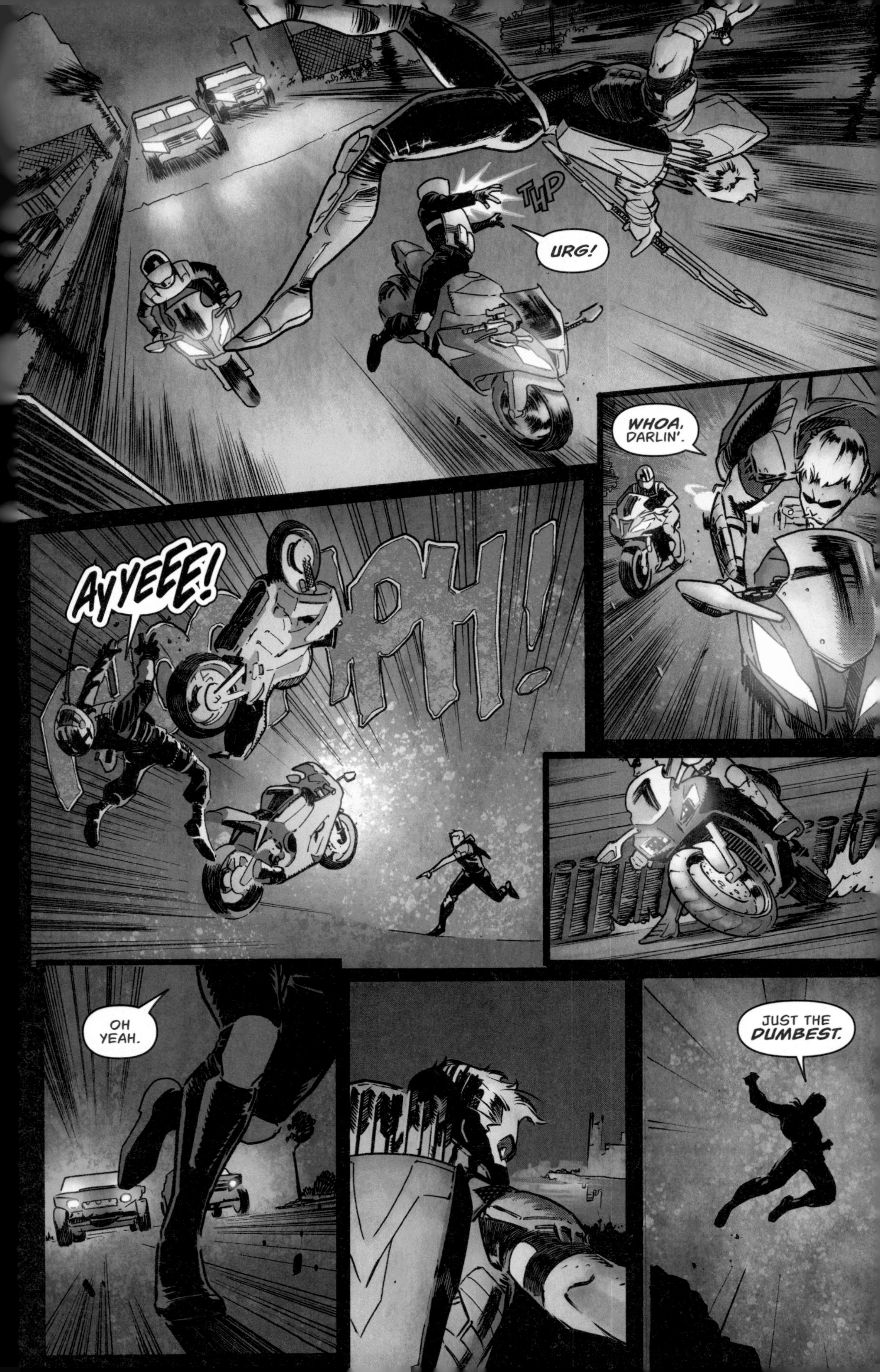
THP
URG!
WHOA, DARLIN'.
AyYEEE!
WAM!
OH YEAH.
JUST THE DUMBEST.

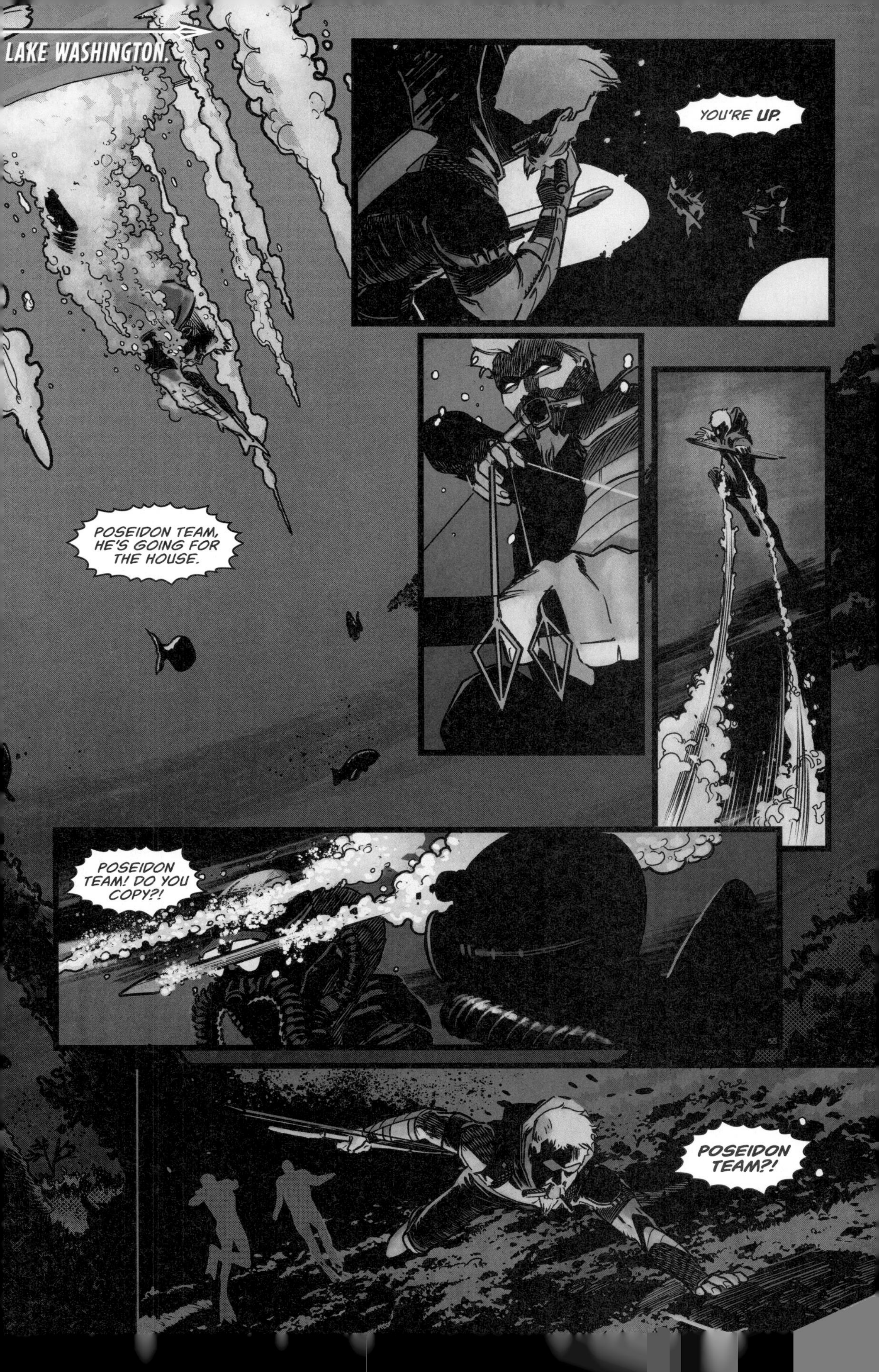
LAKE WASHINGTON.
YOU'RE UP.
POSEIDON TEAM, HE'S GOING FOR THE HOUSE.
POSEIDON TEAM! DO YOU COPY?!
POSEIDON TEAM?!

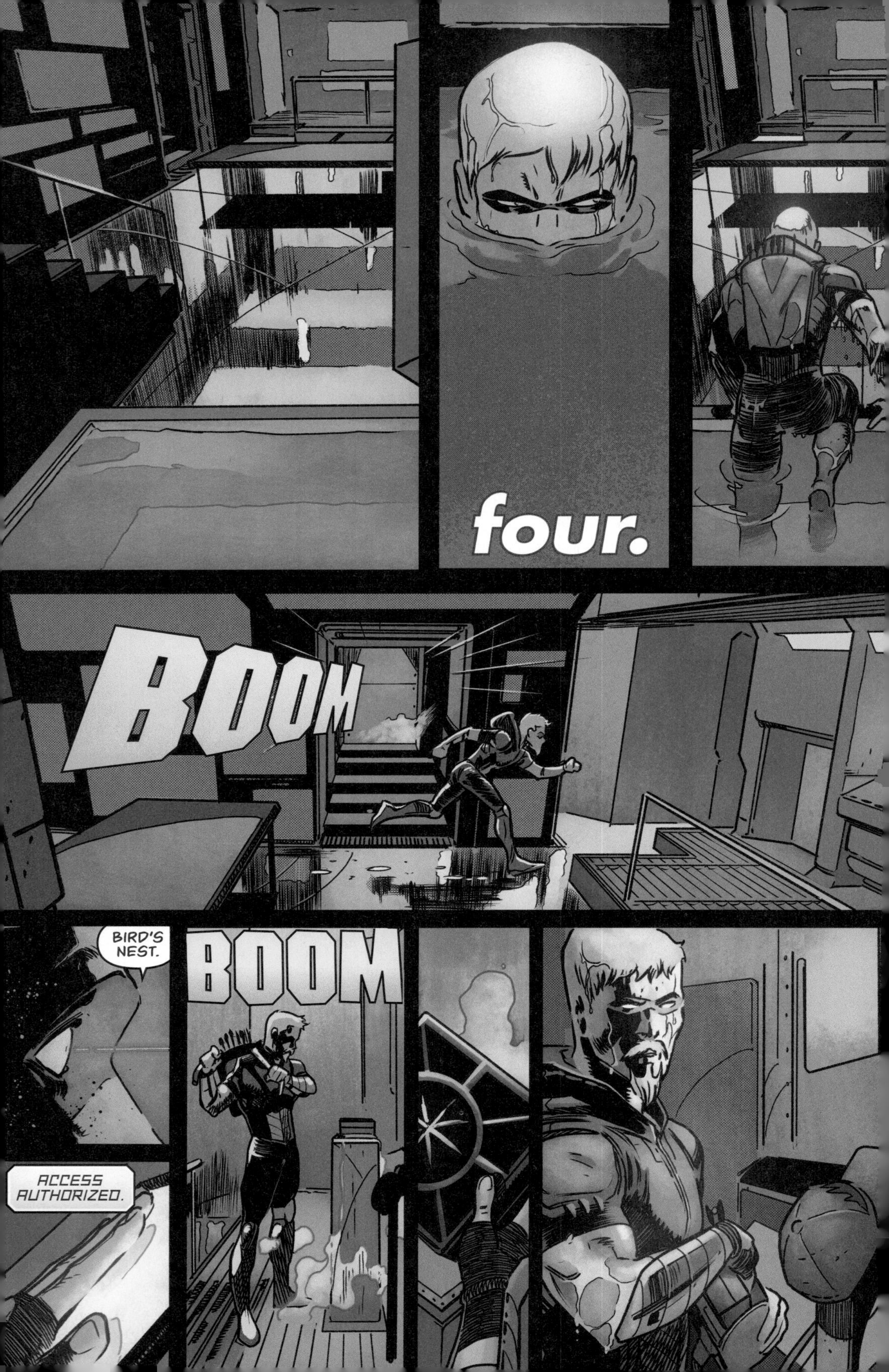
four.
BOOM
BIRD'S NEST.
ACCESS AUTHORIZED.
BOOM

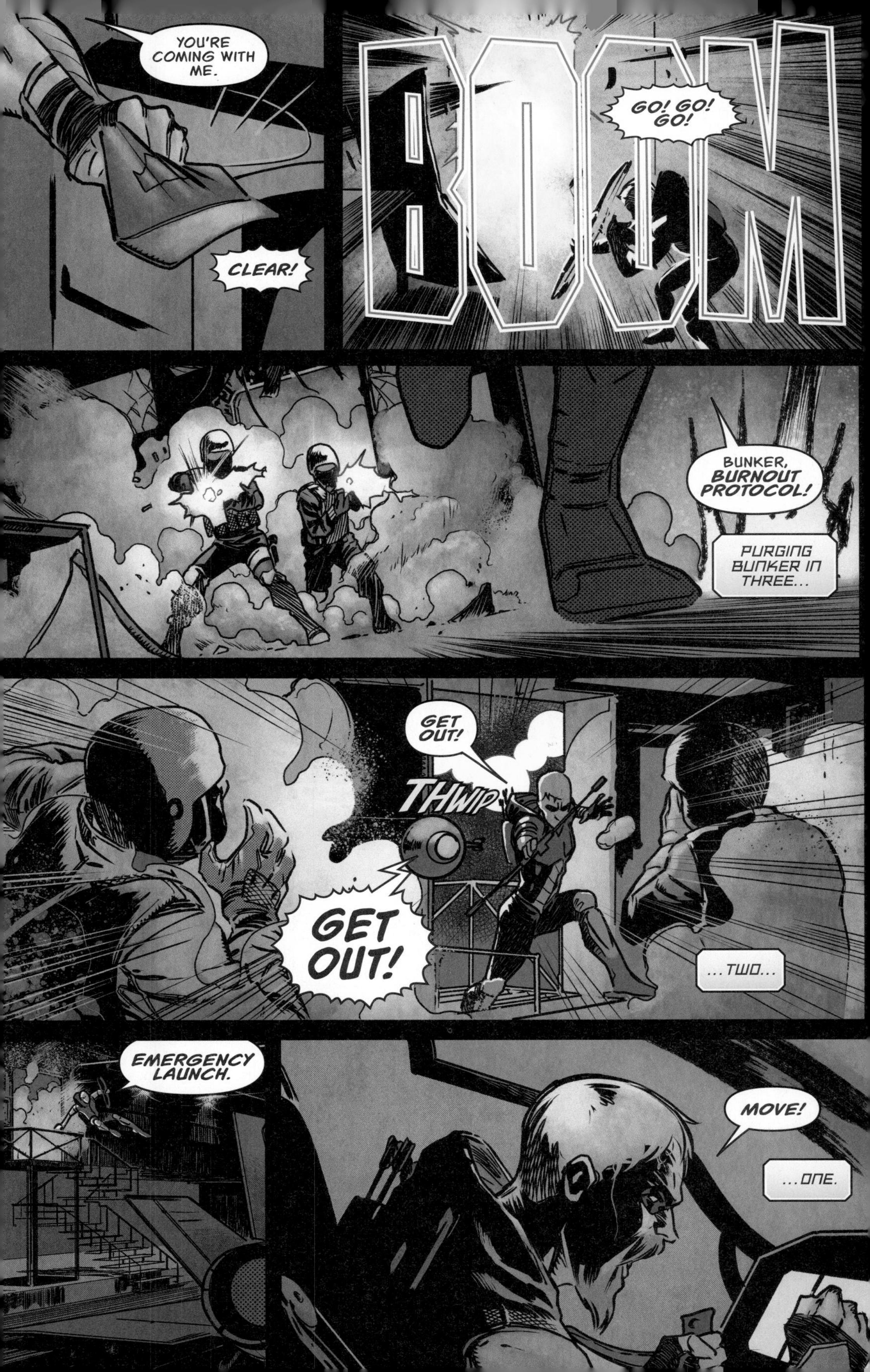
YOU'RE COMING WITH ME.
CLEAR!
BOOM
GO! GO! GO!
BUNKER, BURNOUT PROTOCOL!
PURGING BUNKER IN THREE...
GET OUT!
THWIP
GET OUT!
...TWO...
EMERGENCY LAUNCH.
MOVE!
...ONE.

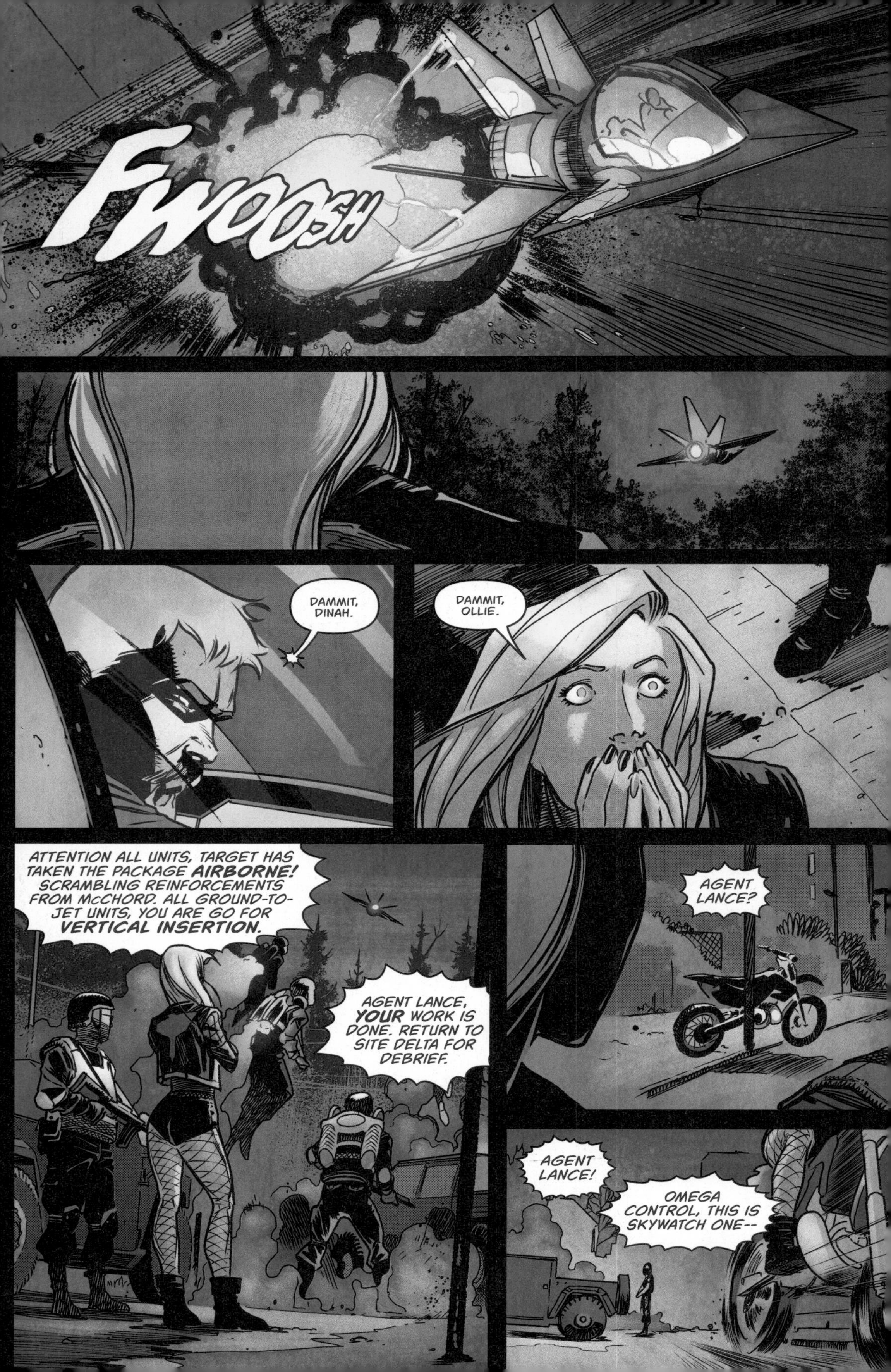
FWOOSH
DAMMIT, DINAH.
DAMMIT, OLLIE.
ATTENTION ALL UNITS, TARGET HAS TAKEN THE PACKAGE AIRBORNE! SCRAMBLING REINFORCEMENTS FROM McCHORD. ALL GROUND-TO-JET UNITS, YOU ARE GO FOR VERTICAL INSERTION.
AGENT LANCE, YOUR WORK IS DONE. RETURN TO SITE DELTA FOR DEBRIEF.
AGENT LANCE?
AGENT LANCE!
OMEGA CONTROL, THIS IS SKYWATCH ONE--

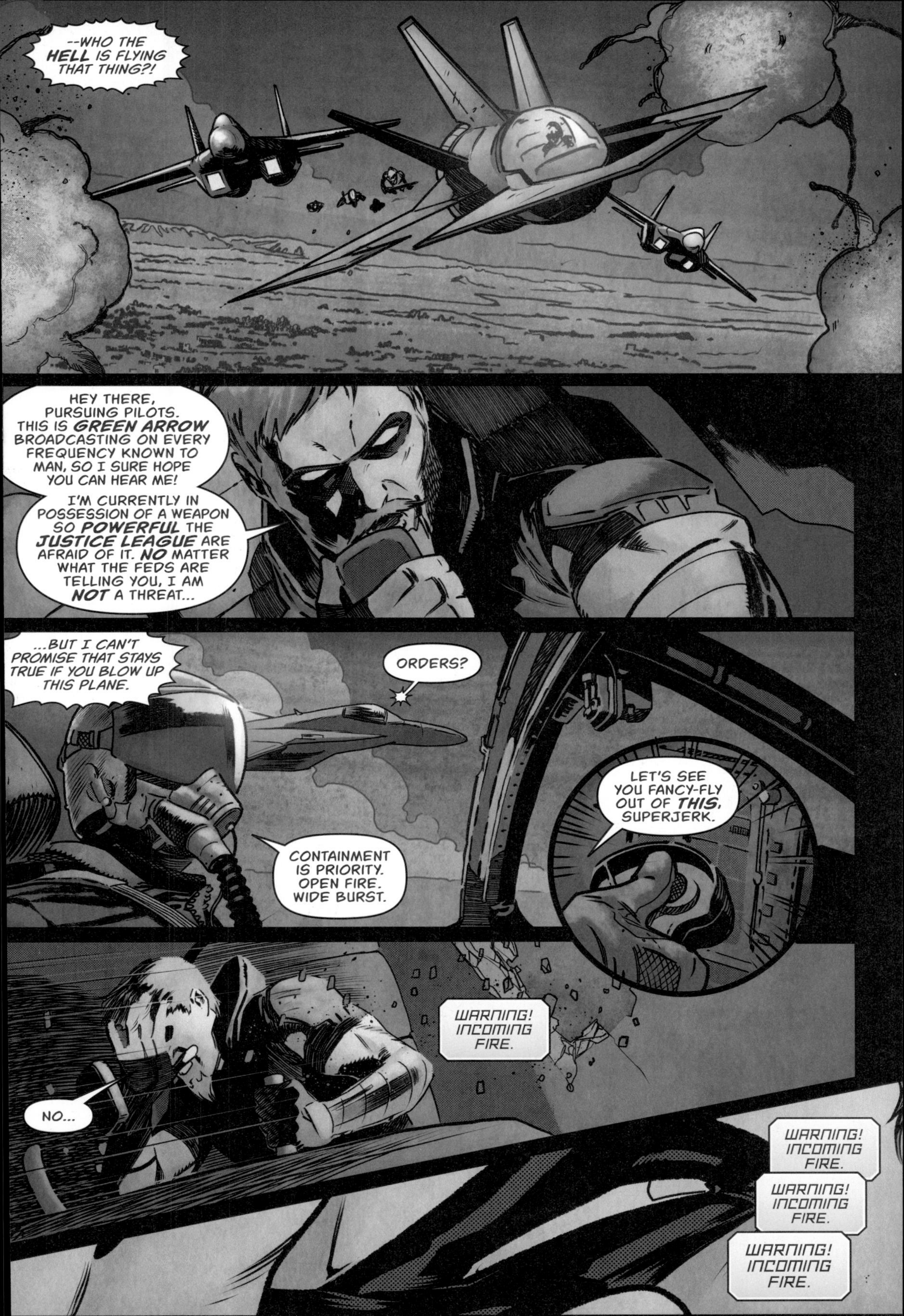
--WHO THE HELL IS FLYING THAT THING?!
HEY THERE, PURSUING PILOTS. THIS IS GREEN ARROW BROADCASTING ON EVERY FREQUENCY KNOWN TO MAN, SO I SURE HOPE YOU CAN HEAR ME!
I'M CURRENTLY IN POSSESSION OF A WEAPON SO POWERFUL THE JUSTICE LEAGUE ARE AFRAID OF IT. NO MATTER WHAT THE FEDS ARE TELLING YOU, I AM NOT A THREAT...
...BUT I CAN'T PROMISE THAT STAYS TRUE IF YOU BLOW UP THIS PLANE.
ORDERS?
CONTAINMENT IS PRIORITY. OPEN FIRE. WIDE BURST.
LET'S SEE YOU FANCY-FLY OUT OF THIS, SUPERJERK.
WARNING! INCOMING FIRE.
NO...
WARNING! INCOMING FIRE.
WARNING! INCOMING FIRE.
WARNING! INCOMING FIRE.

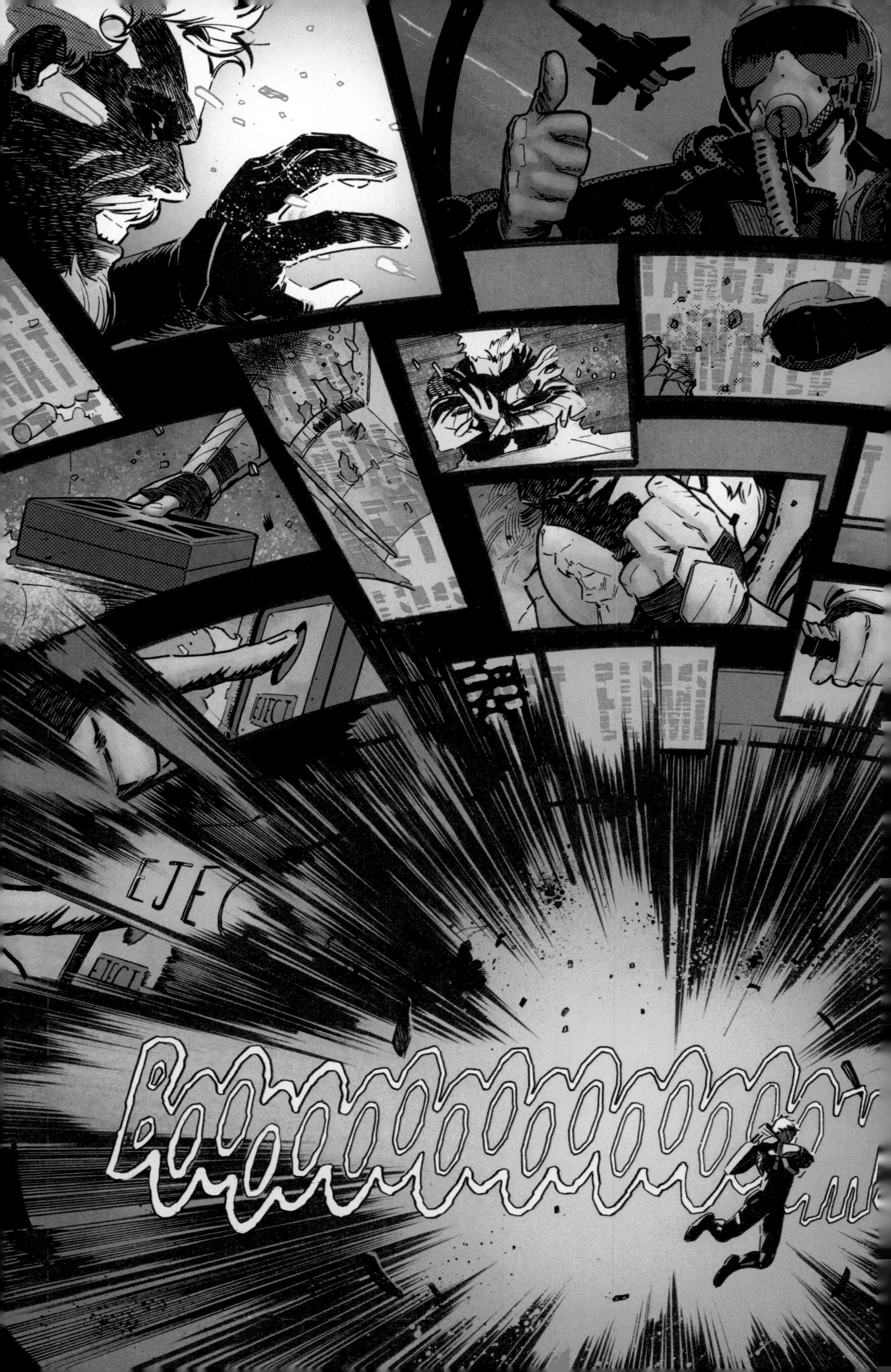
EJECT
EJEC
EJECT

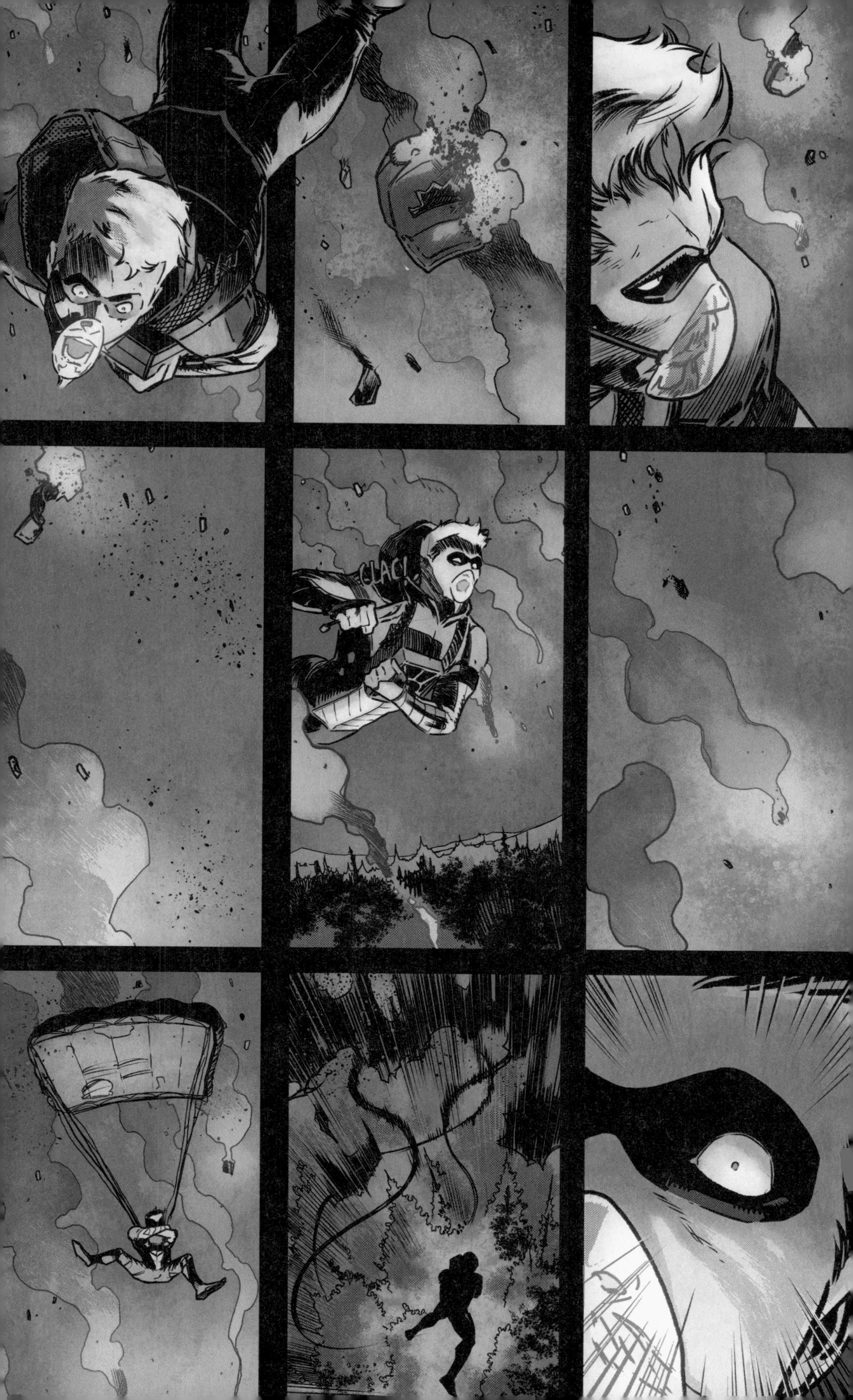

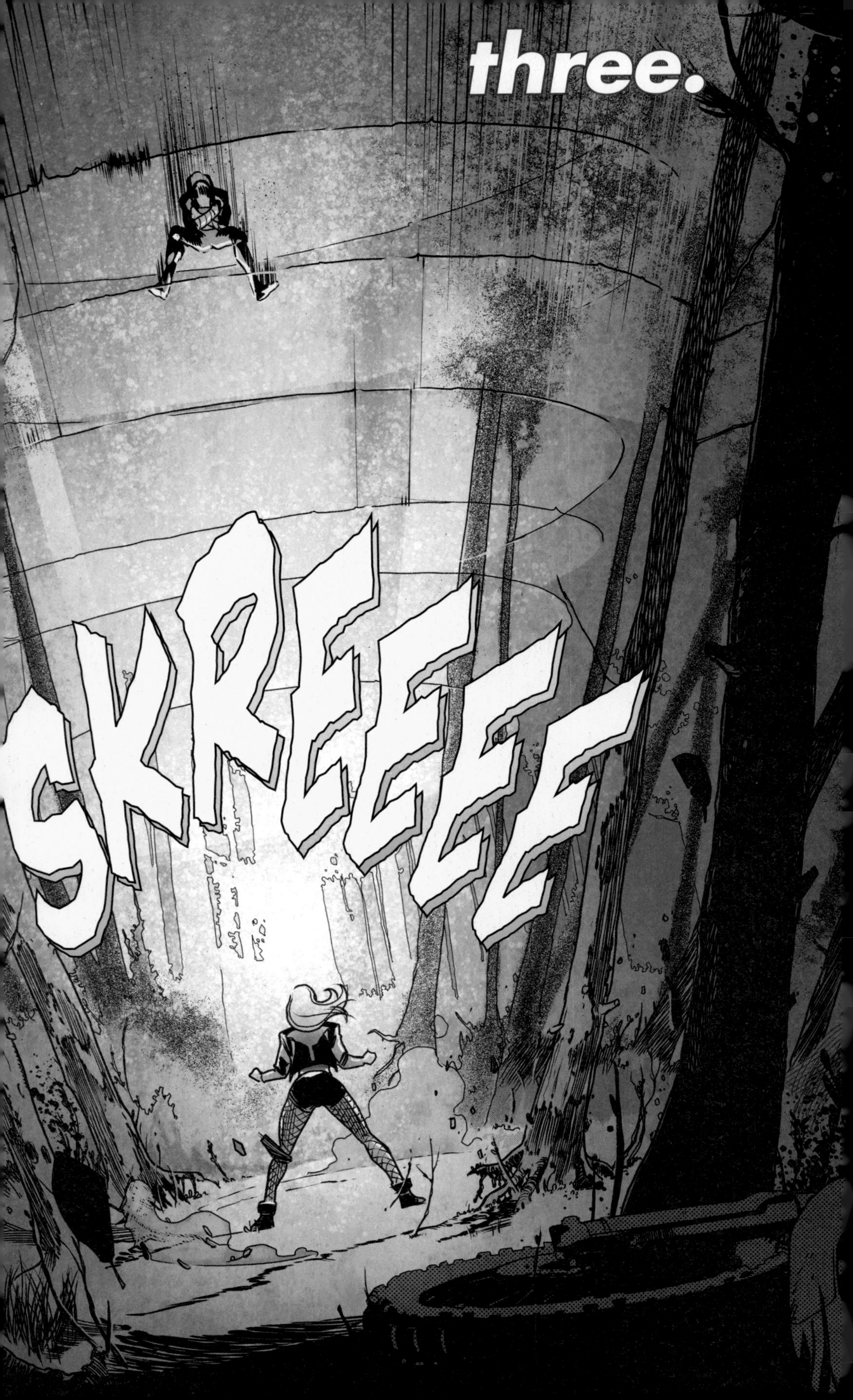
three.
SKREEEEE

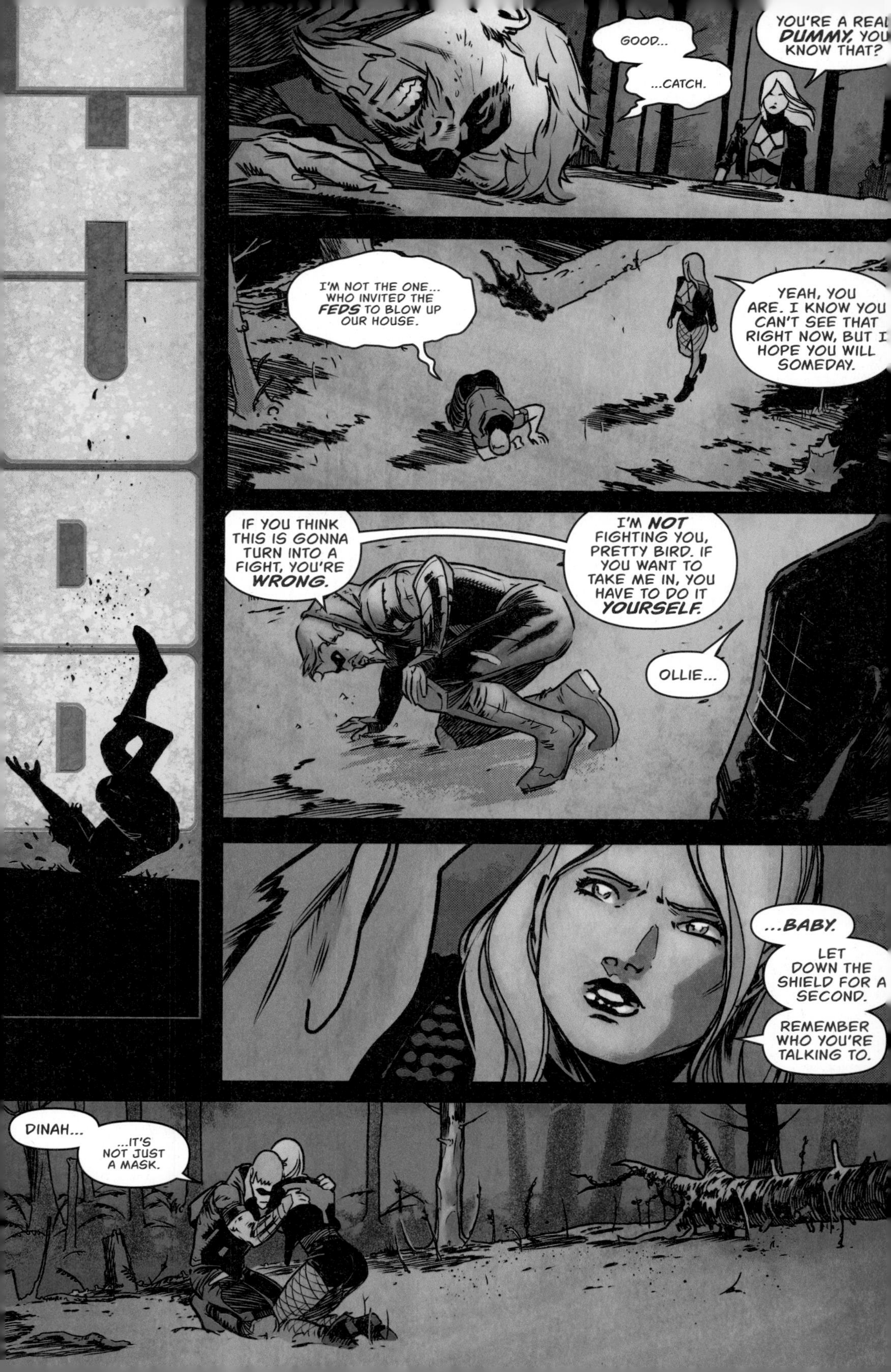
GOOD...
...CATCH.
YOU'RE A REAL DUMMY, YOU KNOW THAT?
I'M NOT THE ONE... WHO INVITED THE FEDS TO BLOW UP OUR HOUSE.
YEAH, YOU ARE. I KNOW YOU CAN'T SEE THAT RIGHT NOW, BUT I HOPE YOU WILL SOMEDAY.
IF YOU THINK THIS IS GONNA TURN INTO A FIGHT, YOU'RE WRONG.
I'M NOT FIGHTING YOU, PRETTY BIRD. IF YOU WANT TO TAKE ME IN, YOU HAVE TO DO IT YOURSELF.
OLLIE...
...BABY.
LET DOWN THE SHIELD FOR A SECOND.
REMEMBER WHO YOU'RE TALKING TO.
DINAH...
...IT'S NOT JUST A MASK.

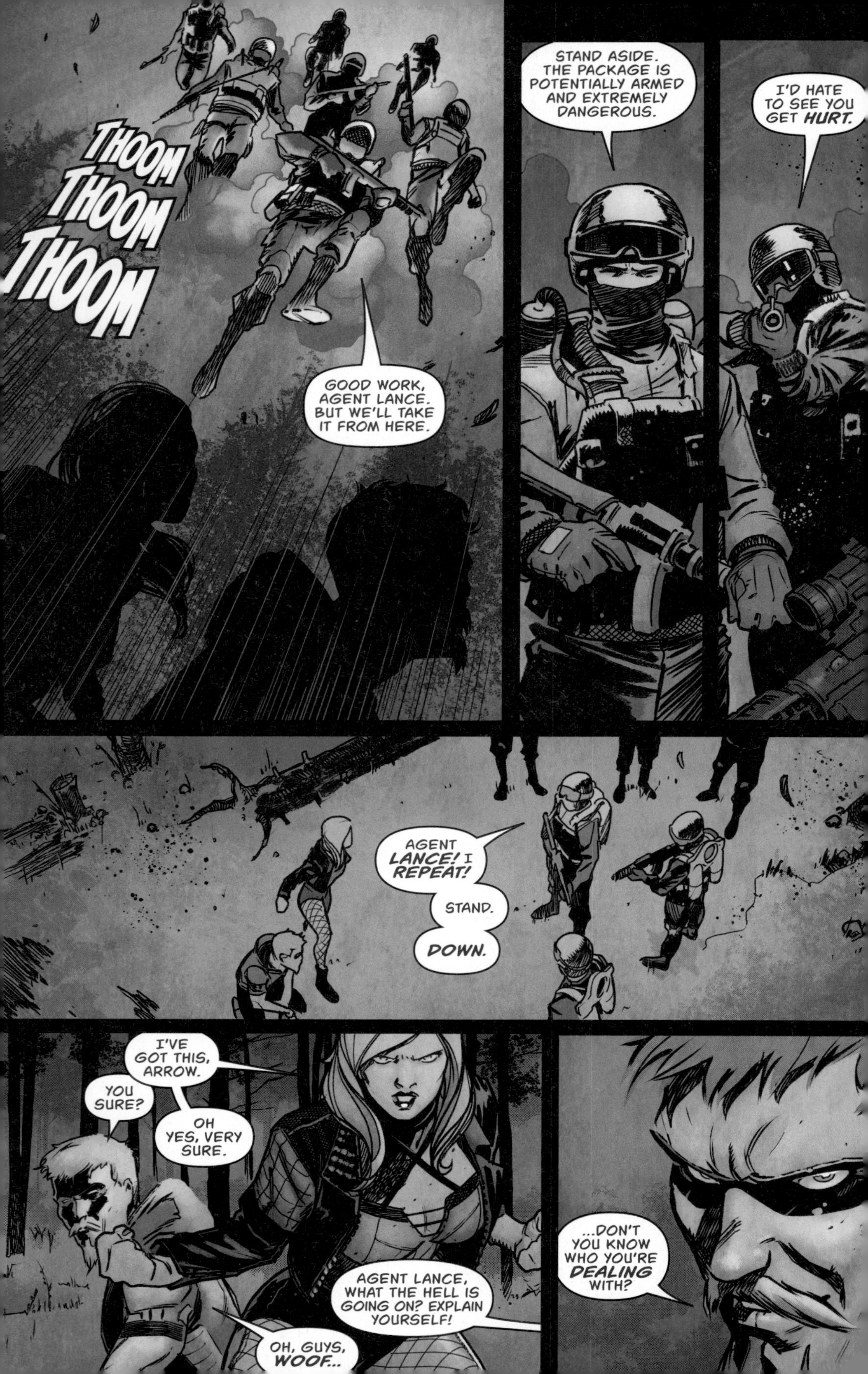
THOOM THOOM THOOM
GOOD WORK, AGENT LANCE. BUT WE'LL TAKE IT FROM HERE.
STAND ASIDE. THE PACKAGE IS POTENTIALLY ARMED AND EXTREMELY DANGEROUS.
I'D HATE TO SEE YOU GET HURT.
AGENT LANCE! I REPEAT!
STAND.
DOWN.
I'VE GOT THIS, ARROW.
YOU SURE?
OH YES, VERY SURE.
AGENT LANCE, WHAT THE HELL IS GOING ON? EXPLAIN YOURSELF!
OH, GUYS, WOOF...
...DON'T YOU KNOW WHO YOU'RE DEALING WITH?

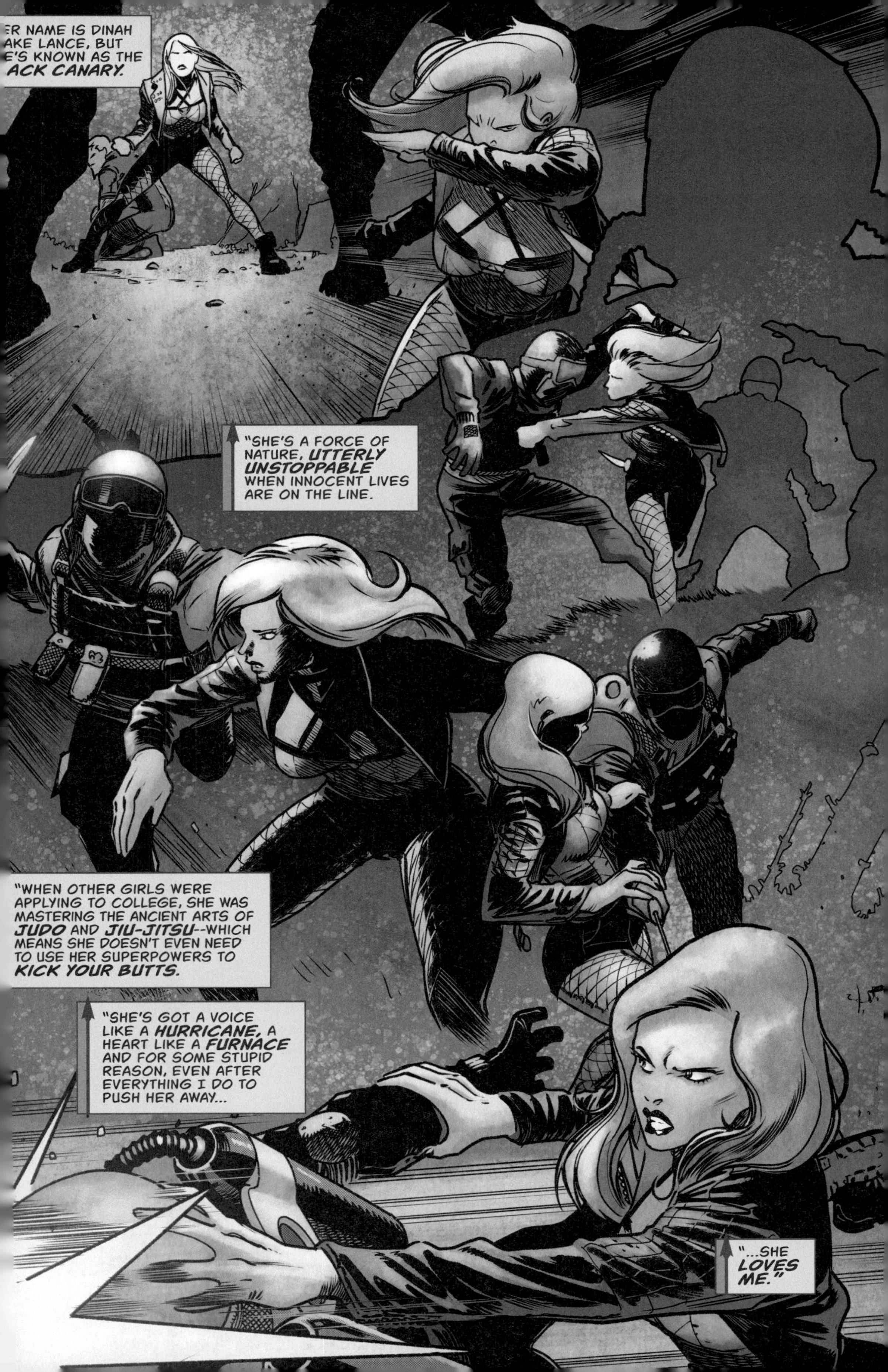
ER NAME IS DINAH
AKE LANCE, BUT
E'S KNOWN AS THE
ACK CANARY.
"SHE'S A FORCE OF NATURE, UTTERLY UNSTOPPABLE WHEN INNOCENT LIVES ARE ON THE LINE.
"WHEN OTHER GIRLS WERE APPLYING TO COLLEGE, SHE WAS MASTERING THE ANCIENT ARTS OF JUDO AND JIU-JITSU--WHICH MEANS SHE DOESN'T EVEN NEED TO USE HER SUPERPOWERS TO KICK YOUR BUTTS.
"SHE'S GOT A VOICE LIKE A HURRICANE, A HEART LIKE A FURNACE AND FOR SOME STUPID REASON, EVEN AFTER EVERYTHING I DO TO PUSH HER AWAY...
"...SHE LOVES ME."

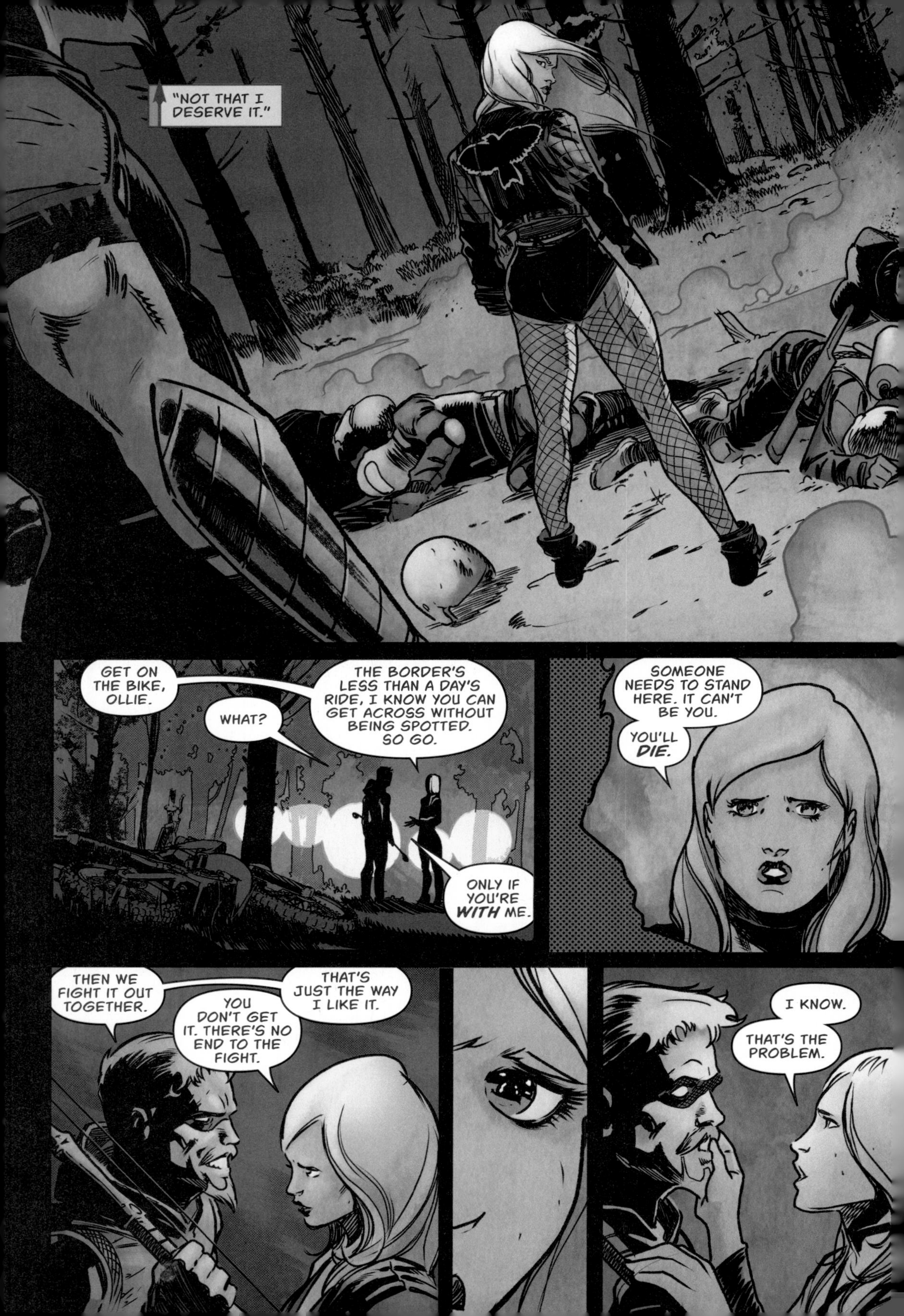
"NOT THAT I DESERVE IT."
GET ON THE BIKE, OLLIE.
THE BORDER'S LESS THAN A DAY'S RIDE, I KNOW YOU CAN GET ACROSS WITHOUT BEING SPOTTED. SO GO.
WHAT?
ONLY IF YOU'RE **WITH** ME.
SOMEONE NEEDS TO STAND HERE. IT CAN'T BE YOU.
YOU'LL **DIE.**
THEN WE FIGHT IT OUT TOGETHER.
THAT'S JUST THE WAY I LIKE IT.
YOU DON'T GET IT. THERE'S NO END TO THE FIGHT.
I KNOW.
THAT'S THE PROBLEM.

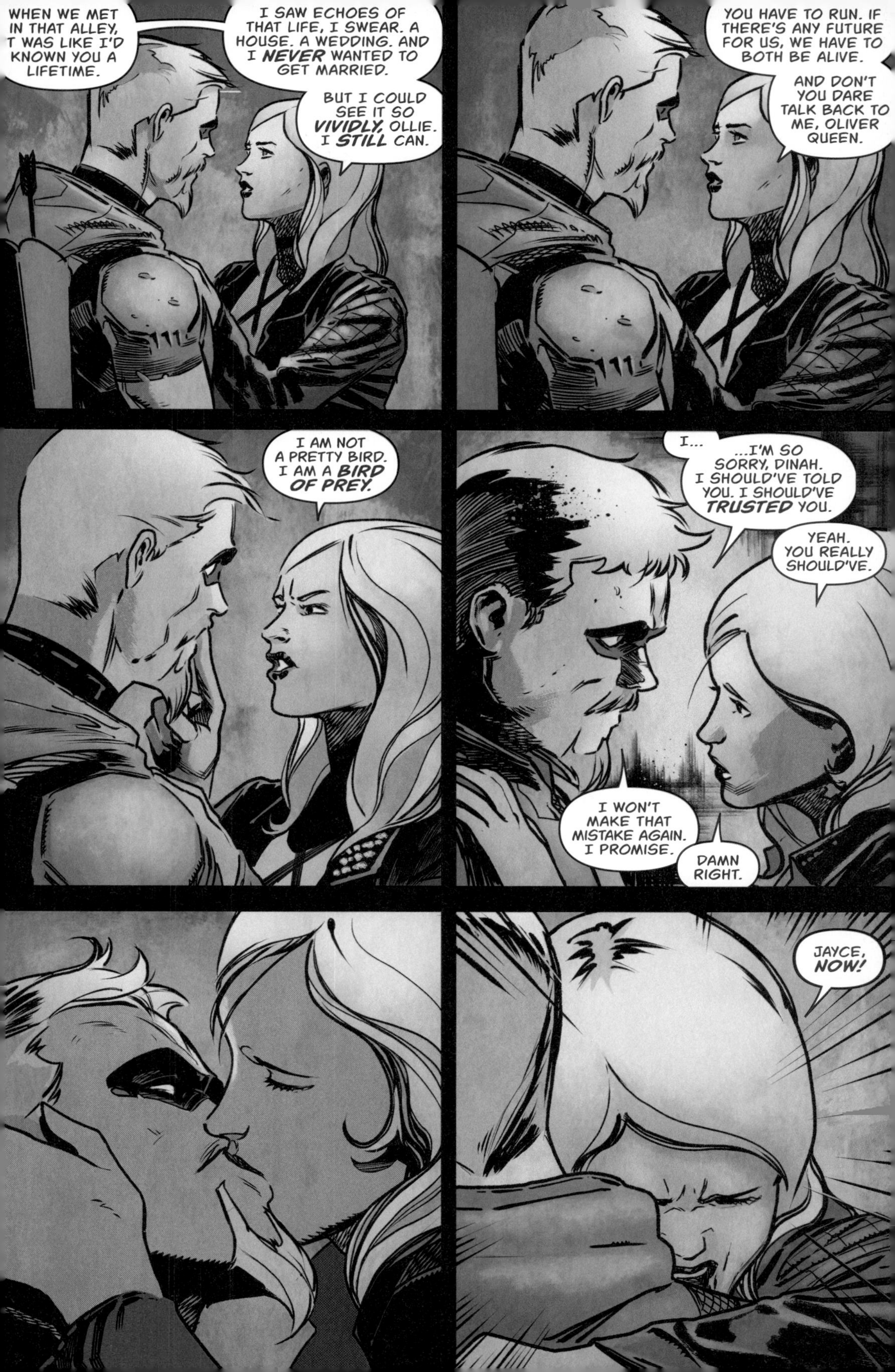
WHEN WE MET IN THAT ALLEY, IT WAS LIKE I'D KNOWN YOU A LIFETIME.
I SAW ECHOES OF THAT LIFE, I SWEAR. A HOUSE. A WEDDING. AND I NEVER WANTED TO GET MARRIED.
BUT I COULD SEE IT SO VIVIDLY, OLLIE. I STILL CAN.
YOU HAVE TO RUN. IF THERE'S ANY FUTURE FOR US, WE HAVE TO BOTH BE ALIVE.
AND DON'T YOU DARE TALK BACK TO ME, OLIVER QUEEN.
I AM NOT A PRETTY BIRD. I AM A BIRD OF PREY.
I...
...I'M SO SORRY, DINAH. I SHOULD'VE TOLD YOU. I SHOULD'VE TRUSTED YOU.
YEAH. YOU REALLY SHOULD'VE.
I WON'T MAKE THAT MISTAKE AGAIN. I PROMISE.
DAMN RIGHT.
JAYCE, NOW!

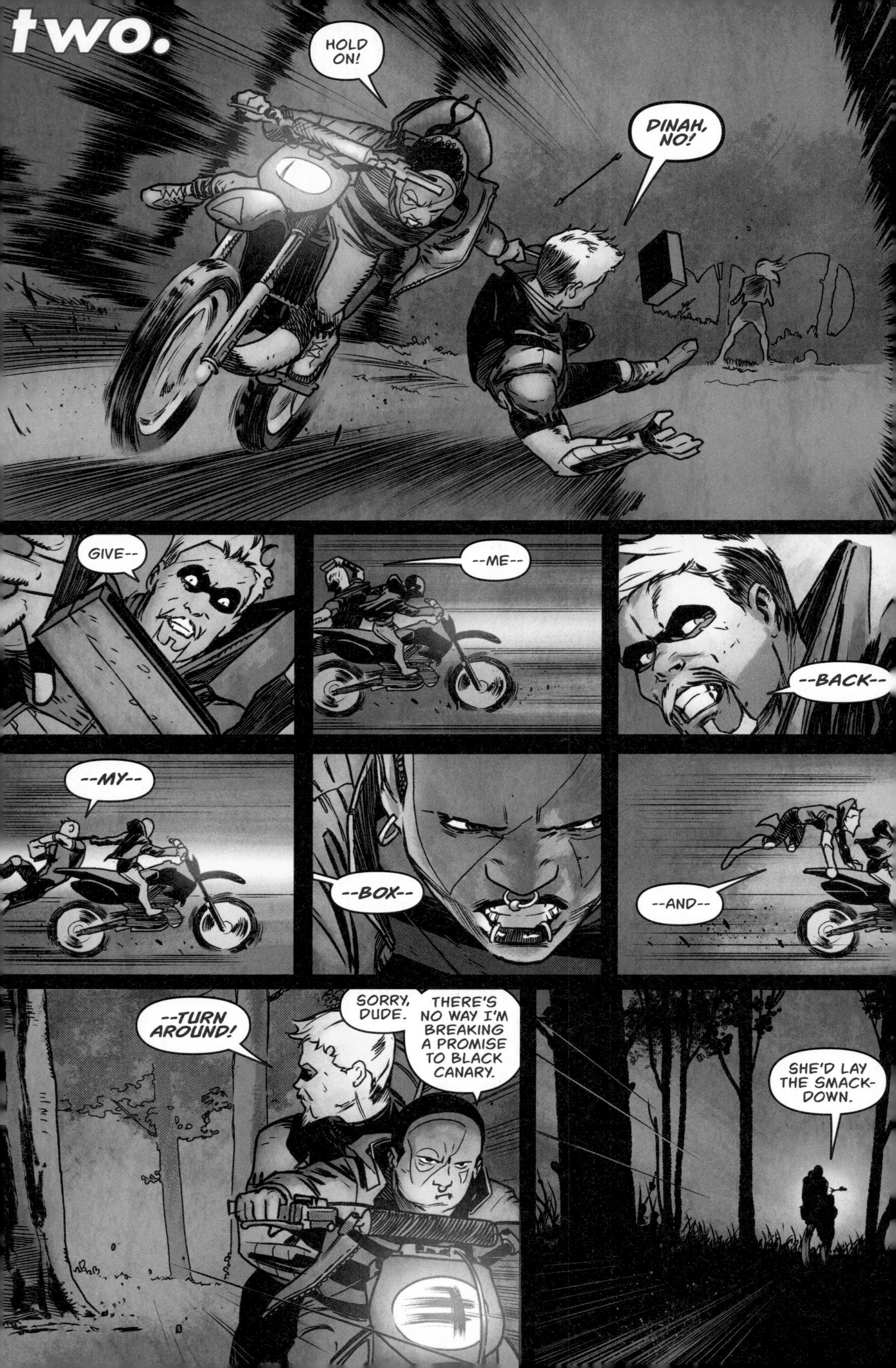
two.
HOLD ON!
DINAH, NO!
GIVE--
--ME--
--BACK--
--MY--
--BOX--
--AND--
--TURN AROUND!
SORRY, DUDE.
THERE'S NO WAY I'M BREAKING A PROMISE TO BLACK CANARY.
SHE'D LAY THE SMACK-DOWN.

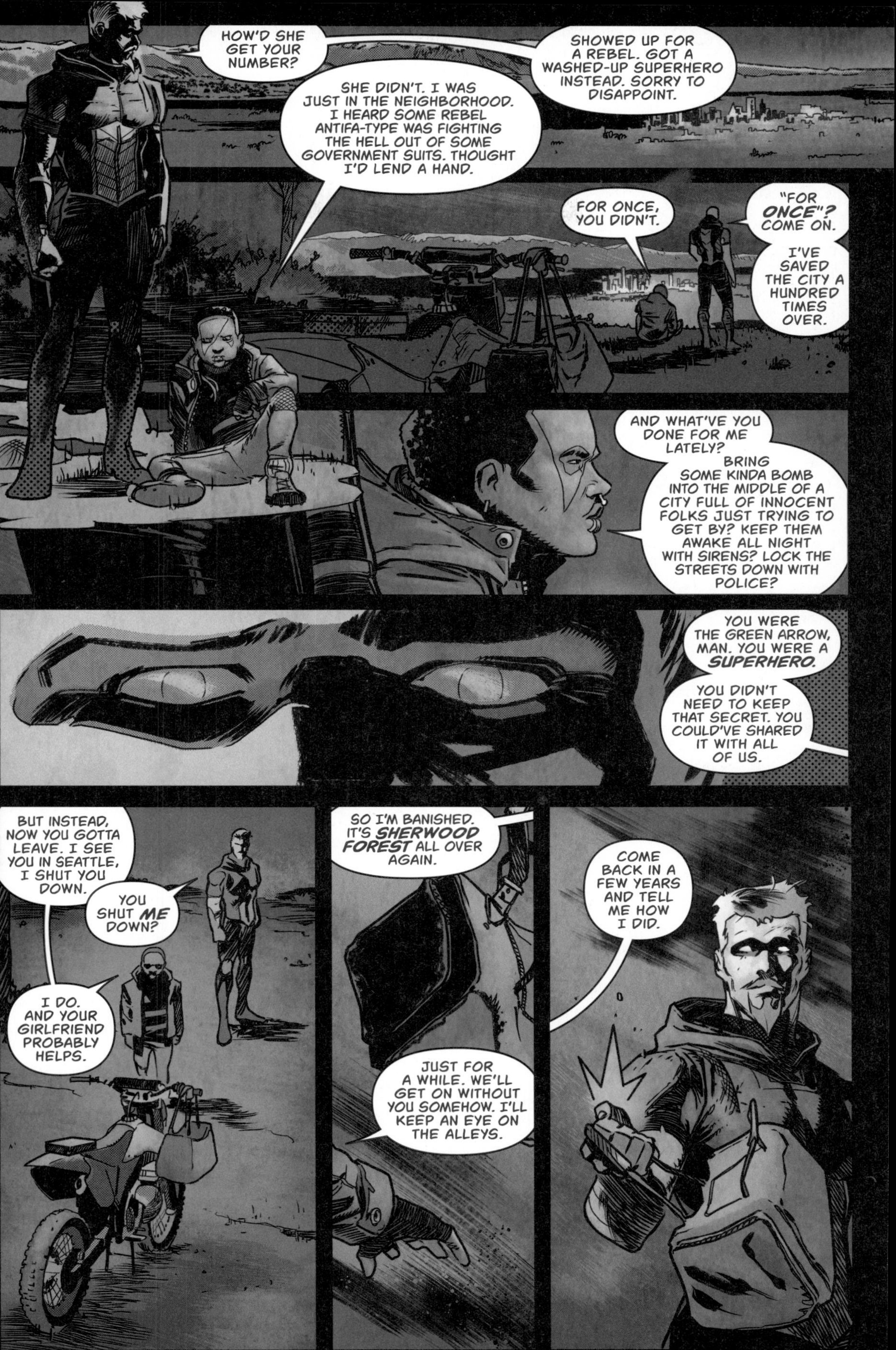
HOW'D SHE GET YOUR NUMBER?
SHOWED UP FOR A REBEL. GOT A WASHED-UP SUPERHERO INSTEAD. SORRY TO DISAPPOINT.
SHE DIDN'T. I WAS JUST IN THE NEIGHBORHOOD. I HEARD SOME REBEL ANTIFA-TYPE WAS FIGHTING THE HELL OUT OF SOME GOVERNMENT SUITS. THOUGHT I'D LEND A HAND.
FOR ONCE, YOU DIDN'T.
"FOR *ONCE*"? COME ON.
I'VE SAVED THE CITY A HUNDRED TIMES OVER.
AND WHAT'VE YOU DONE FOR ME LATELY?
BRING SOME KINDA BOMB INTO THE MIDDLE OF A CITY FULL OF INNOCENT FOLKS JUST TRYING TO GET BY? KEEP THEM AWAKE ALL NIGHT WITH SIRENS? LOCK THE STREETS DOWN WITH POLICE?
YOU WERE THE GREEN ARROW, MAN. YOU WERE A ***SUPERHERO.***
YOU DIDN'T NEED TO KEEP THAT SECRET. YOU COULD'VE SHARED IT WITH ALL OF US.
BUT INSTEAD, NOW YOU GOTTA LEAVE. I SEE YOU IN SEATTLE, I SHUT YOU DOWN.
YOU SHUT *ME* DOWN?
I DO. AND YOUR GIRLFRIEND PROBABLY HELPS.
SO I'M BANISHED. IT'S ***SHERWOOD FOREST*** ALL OVER AGAIN.
JUST FOR A WHILE. WE'LL GET ON WITHOUT YOU SOMEHOW. I'LL KEEP AN EYE ON THE ALLEYS.
COME BACK IN A FEW YEARS AND TELL ME HOW I DID.

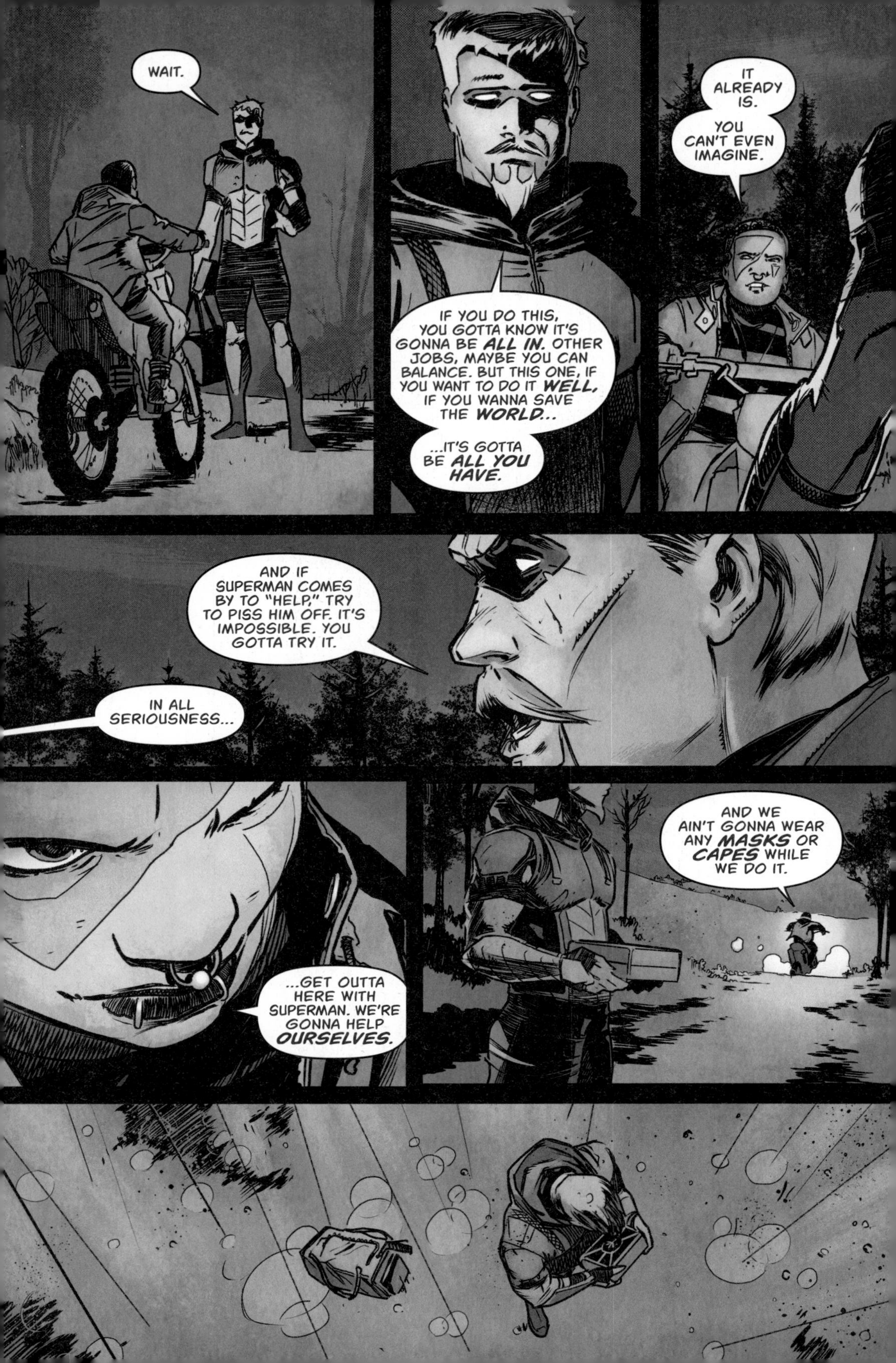
WAIT.
IF YOU DO THIS, YOU GOTTA KNOW IT'S GONNA BE ALL IN. OTHER JOBS, MAYBE YOU CAN BALANCE. BUT THIS ONE, IF YOU WANT TO DO IT WELL, IF YOU WANNA SAVE THE WORLD...
...IT'S GOTTA BE ALL YOU HAVE.
IT ALREADY IS.
YOU CAN'T EVEN IMAGINE.
AND IF SUPERMAN COMES BY TO "HELP," TRY TO PISS HIM OFF. IT'S IMPOSSIBLE. YOU GOTTA TRY IT.
IN ALL SERIOUSNESS...
...GET OUTTA HERE WITH SUPERMAN. WE'RE GONNA HELP OURSELVES.
AND WE AIN'T GONNA WEAR ANY MASKS OR CAPES WHILE WE DO IT.

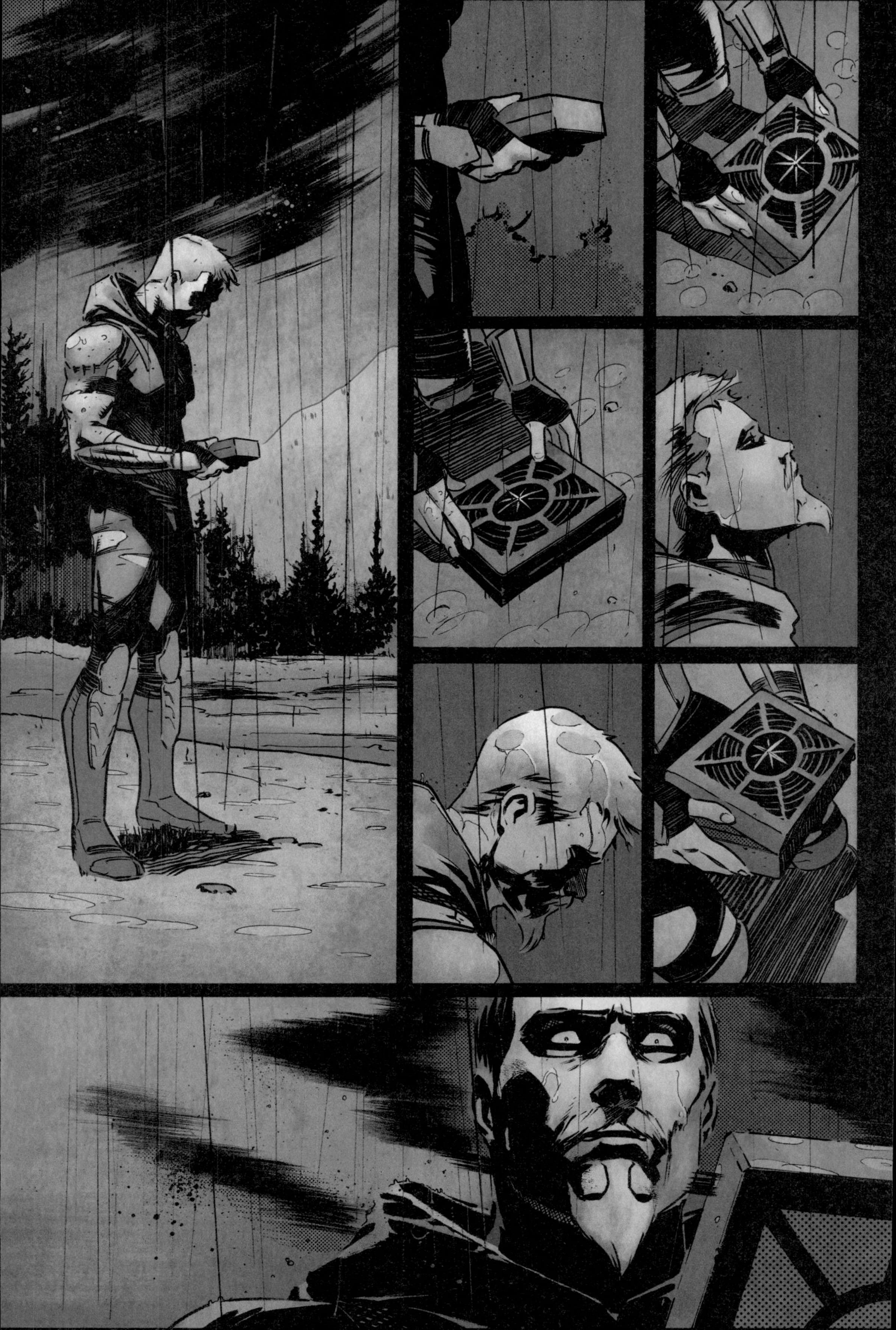

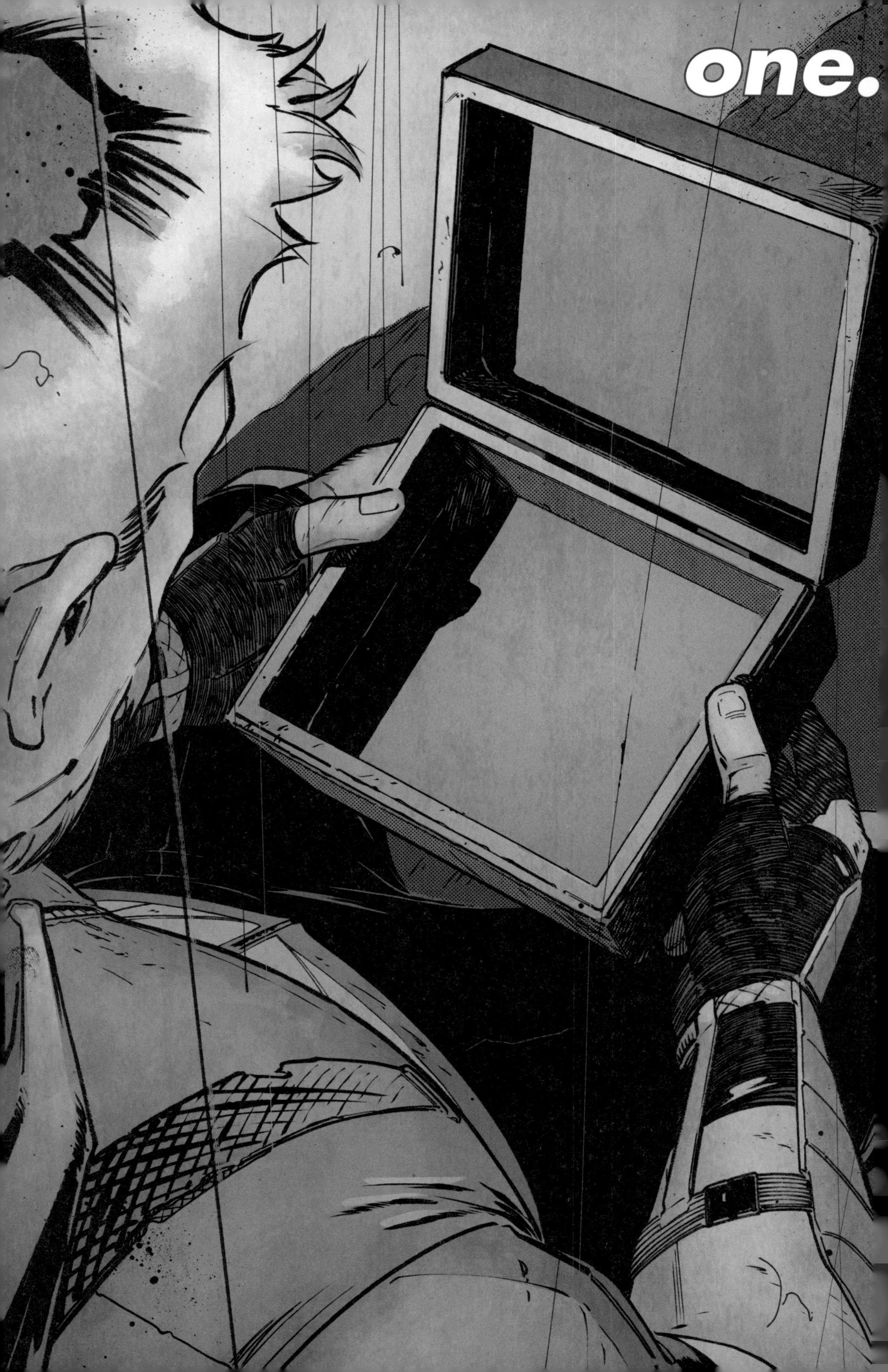
one.

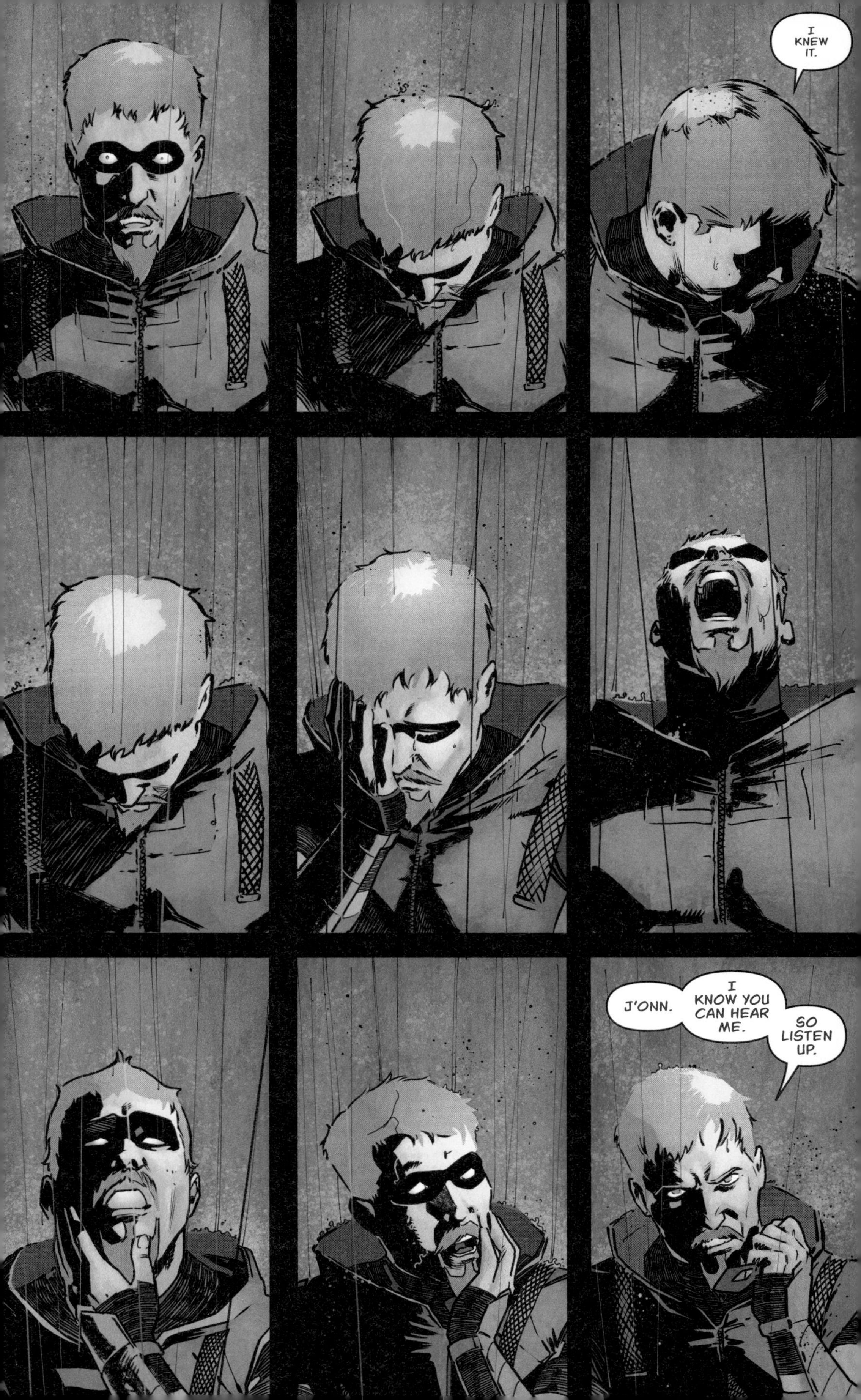
I KNEW IT.
J'ONN.
I KNOW YOU CAN HEAR ME.
SO LISTEN UP.

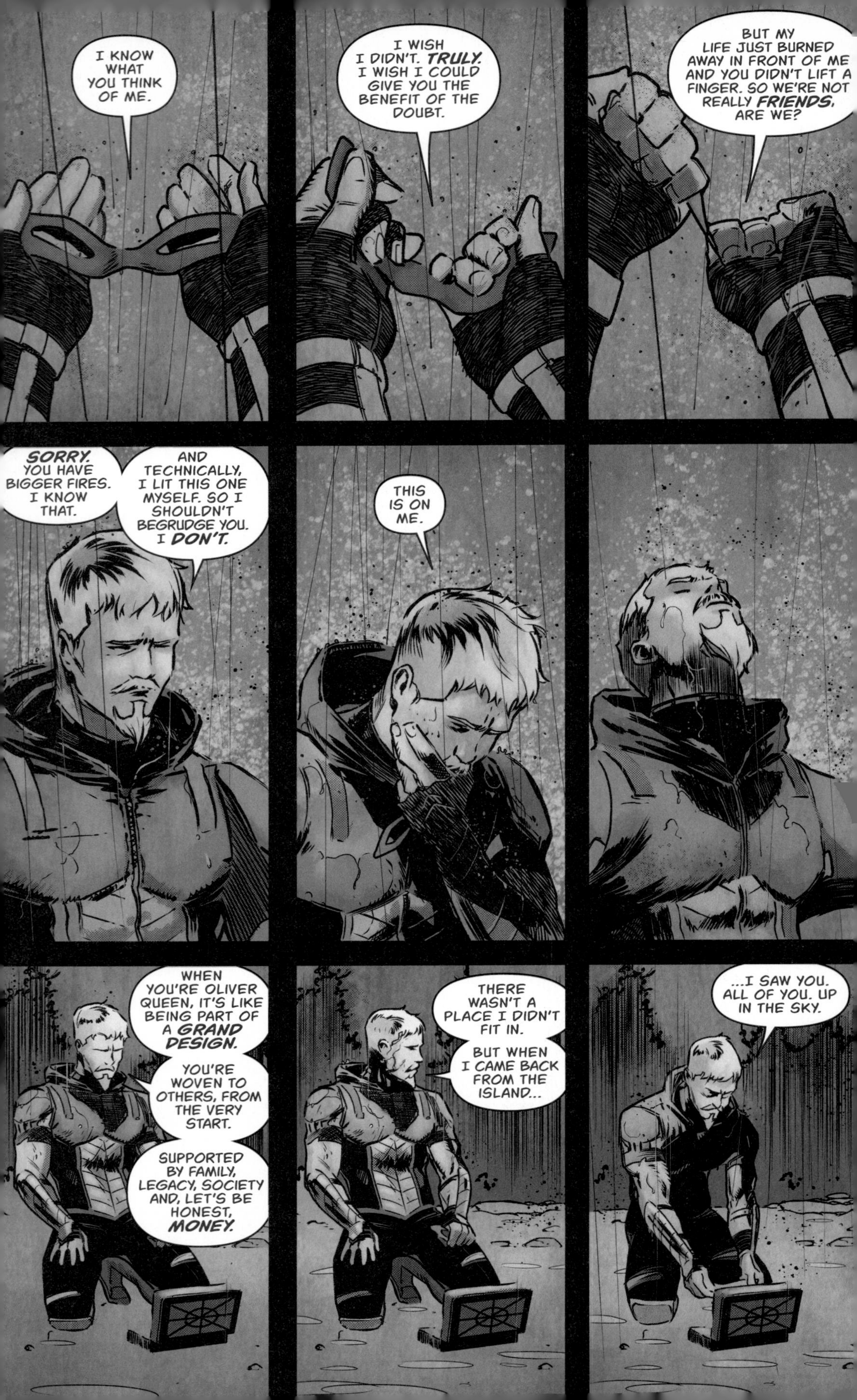
I KNOW WHAT YOU THINK OF ME.
I WISH I DIDN'T. TRULY. I WISH I COULD GIVE YOU THE BENEFIT OF THE DOUBT.
BUT MY LIFE JUST BURNED AWAY IN FRONT OF ME AND YOU DIDN'T LIFT A FINGER. SO WE'RE NOT REALLY FRIENDS, ARE WE?
SORRY. YOU HAVE BIGGER FIRES. I KNOW THAT.
AND TECHNICALLY, I LIT THIS ONE MYSELF. SO I SHOULDN'T BEGRUDGE YOU. I DON'T.
THIS IS ON ME.
WHEN YOU'RE OLIVER QUEEN, IT'S LIKE BEING PART OF A GRAND DESIGN.
YOU'RE WOVEN TO OTHERS, FROM THE VERY START.
SUPPORTED BY FAMILY, LEGACY, SOCIETY AND, LET'S BE HONEST, MONEY.
THERE WASN'T A PLACE I DIDN'T FIT IN.
BUT WHEN I CAME BACK FROM THE ISLAND...
...I SAW YOU. ALL OF YOU. UP IN THE SKY.

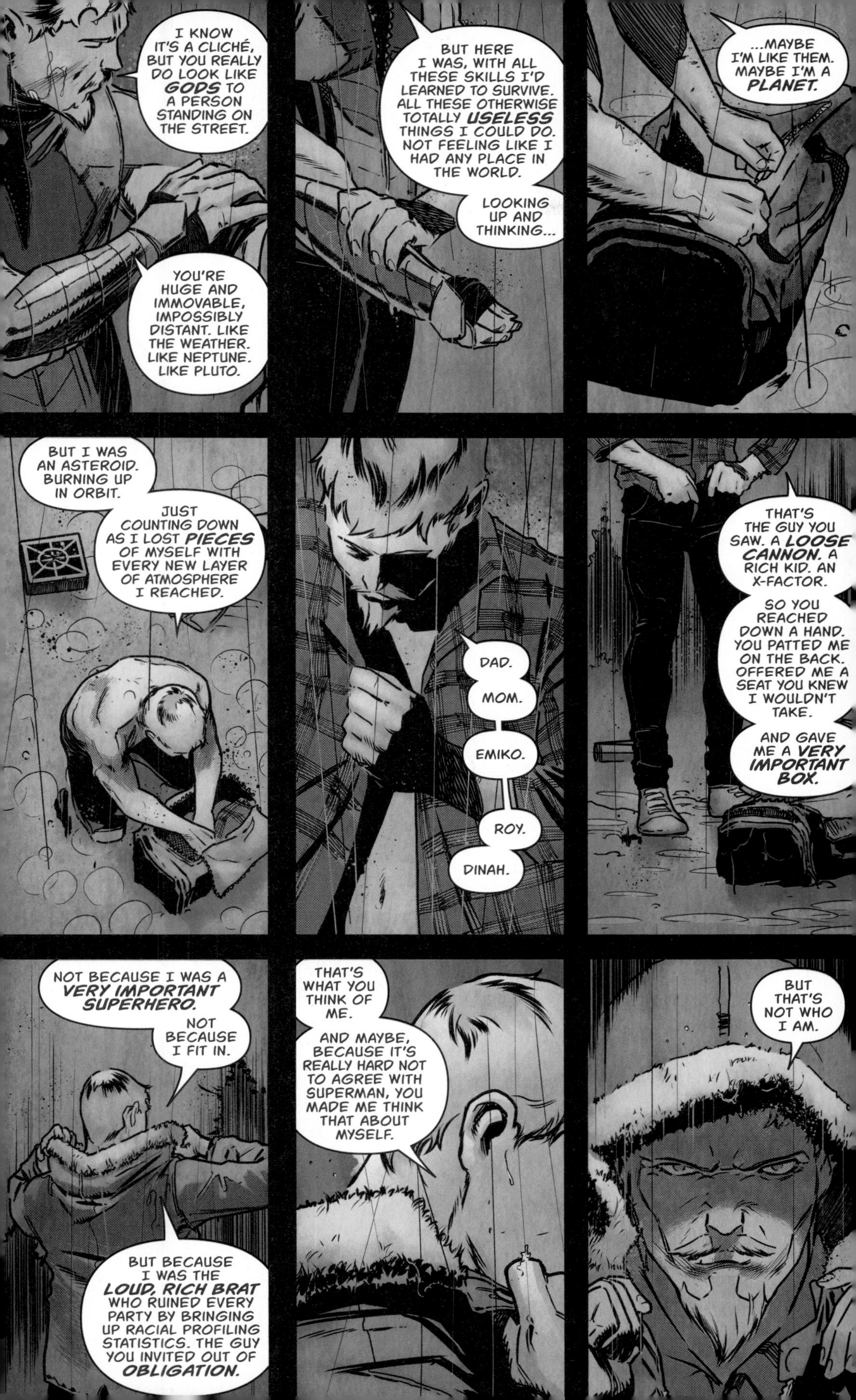
I KNOW IT'S A CLICHÉ, BUT YOU REALLY DO LOOK LIKE GODS TO A PERSON STANDING ON THE STREET.
YOU'RE HUGE AND IMMOVABLE, IMPOSSIBLY DISTANT. LIKE THE WEATHER. LIKE NEPTUNE. LIKE PLUTO.
BUT HERE I WAS, WITH ALL THESE SKILLS I'D LEARNED TO SURVIVE. ALL THESE OTHERWISE TOTALLY USELESS THINGS I COULD DO. NOT FEELING LIKE I HAD ANY PLACE IN THE WORLD.
LOOKING UP AND THINKING...
...MAYBE I'M LIKE THEM. MAYBE I'M A PLANET.
BUT I WAS AN ASTEROID. BURNING UP IN ORBIT.
JUST COUNTING DOWN AS I LOST PIECES OF MYSELF WITH EVERY NEW LAYER OF ATMOSPHERE I REACHED.
DAD.
MOM.
EMIKO.
ROY.
DINAH.
THAT'S THE GUY YOU SAW. A LOOSE CANNON. A RICH KID. AN X-FACTOR.
SO YOU REACHED DOWN A HAND. YOU PATTED ME ON THE BACK. OFFERED ME A SEAT YOU KNEW I WOULDN'T TAKE.
AND GAVE ME A VERY IMPORTANT BOX.
NOT BECAUSE I WAS A VERY IMPORTANT SUPERHERO.
NOT BECAUSE I FIT IN.
BUT BECAUSE I WAS THE LOUD, RICH BRAT WHO RUINED EVERY PARTY BY BRINGING UP RACIAL PROFILING STATISTICS. THE GUY YOU INVITED OUT OF OBLIGATION.
THAT'S WHAT YOU THINK OF ME.
AND MAYBE, BECAUSE IT'S REALLY HARD NOT TO AGREE WITH SUPERMAN, YOU MADE ME THINK THAT ABOUT MYSELF.
BUT THAT'S NOT WHO I AM.

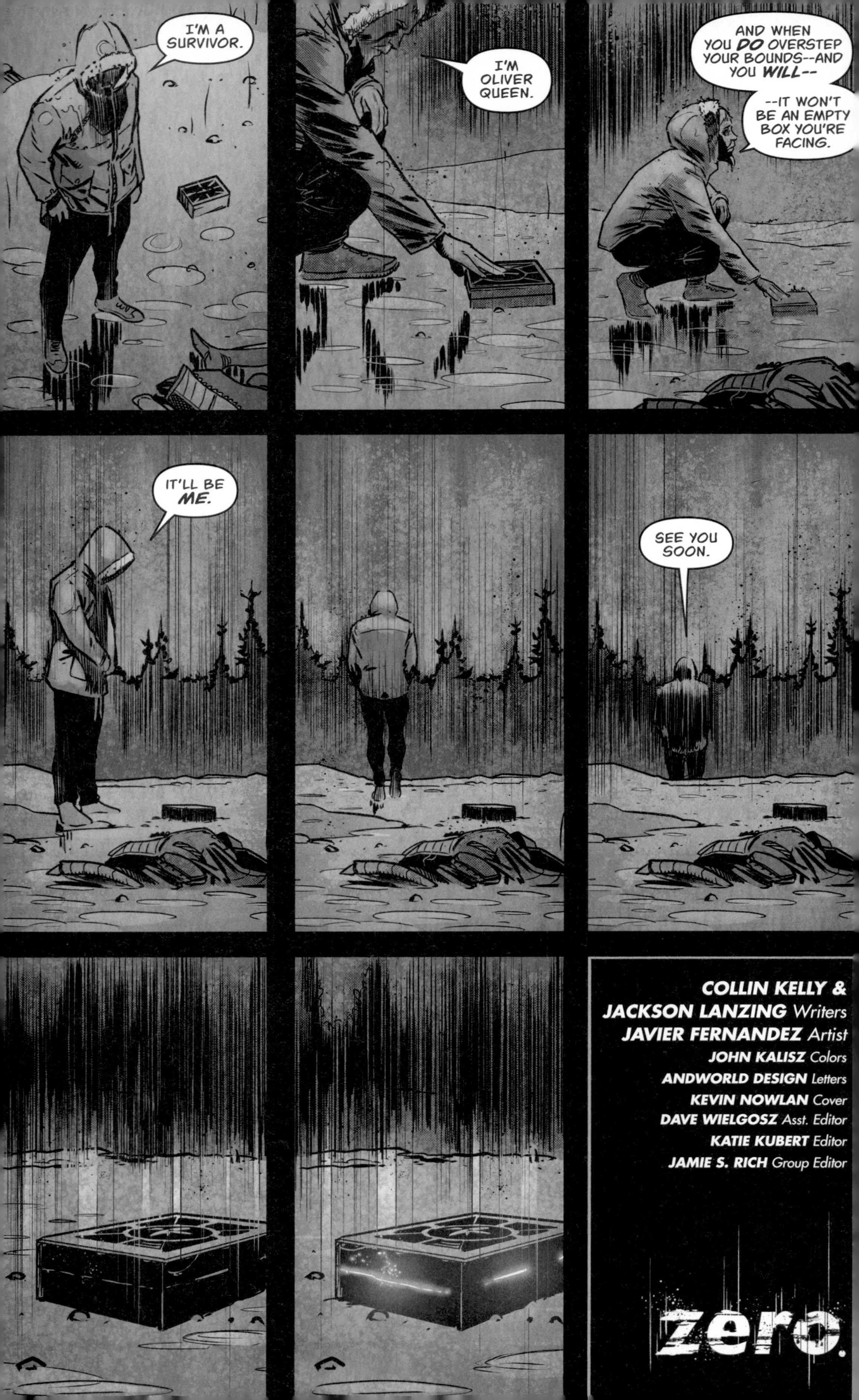
I'M A SURVIVOR.
I'M OLIVER QUEEN.
AND WHEN YOU *DO* OVERSTEP YOUR BOUNDS--AND YOU *WILL*--
--IT WON'T BE AN EMPTY BOX YOU'RE FACING.
IT'LL BE *ME.*
SEE YOU SOON.
**COLLIN KELLY & JACKSON LANZING** *Writers*
**JAVIER FERNANDEZ** *Artist*
**JOHN KALISZ** *Colors*
**ANDWORLD DESIGN** *Letters*
**KEVIN NOWLAN** *Cover*
**DAVE WIELGOSZ** *Asst. Editor*
**KATIE KUBERT** *Editor*
**JAMIE S. RICH** *Group Editor*
zero.

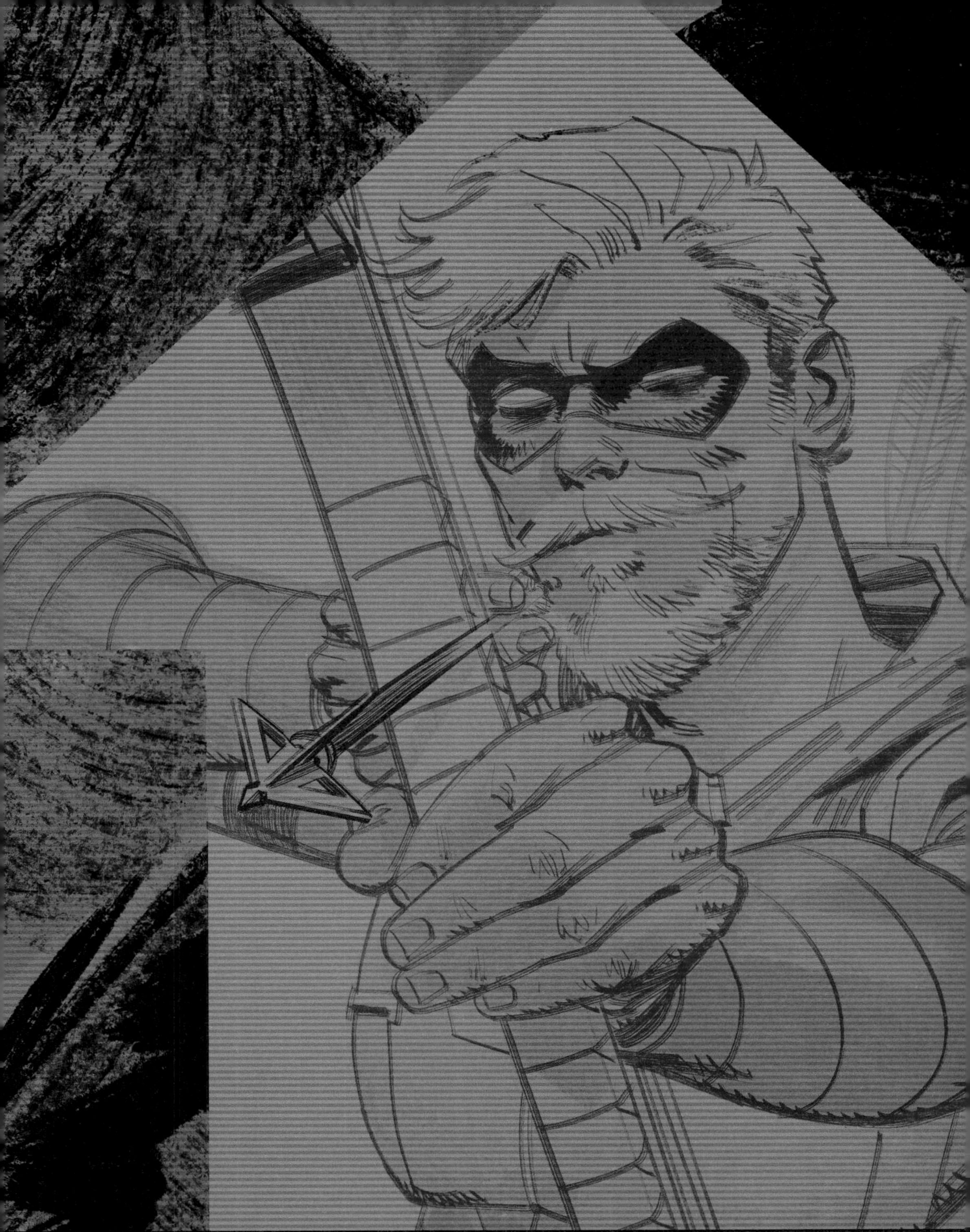

# VARIANT COVER GALLERY

***GREEN ARROW* #39** variant cover
by MIKE GRELL

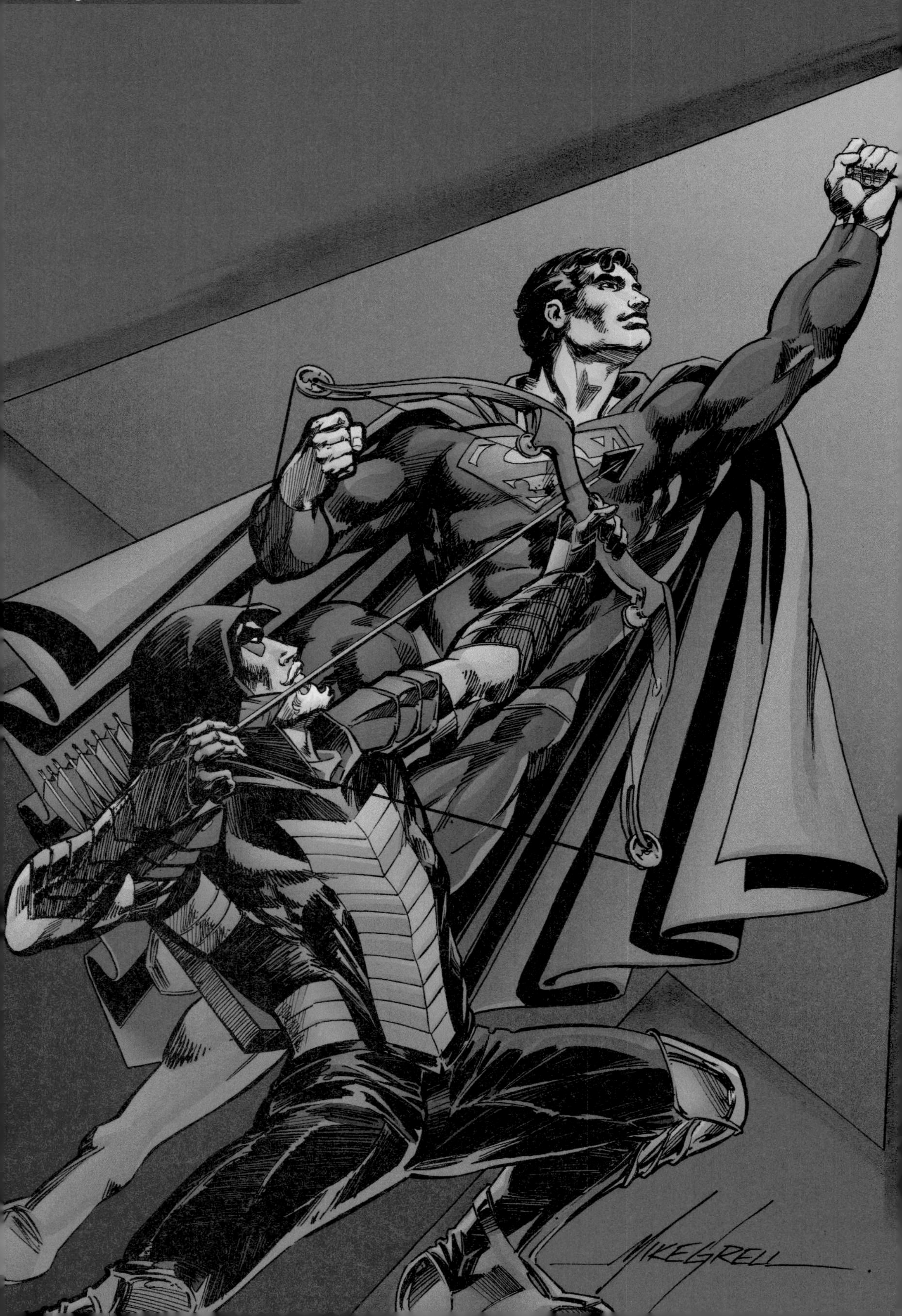
MIKE GRELL

GREEN ARROW #40 variant cover
by MIKE GRELL

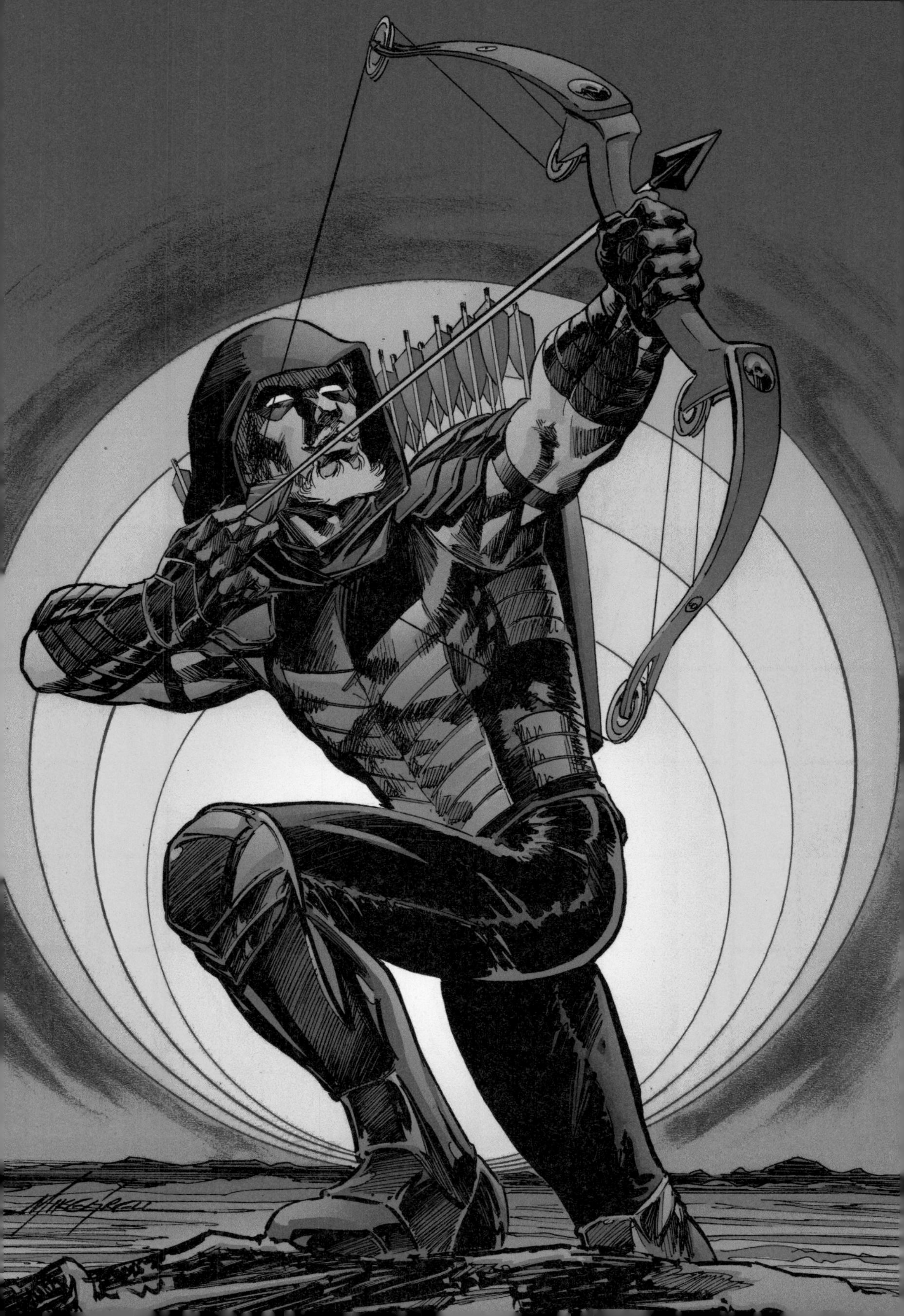

**_GREEN ARROW #41_** variant cover
by MIKE GRELL

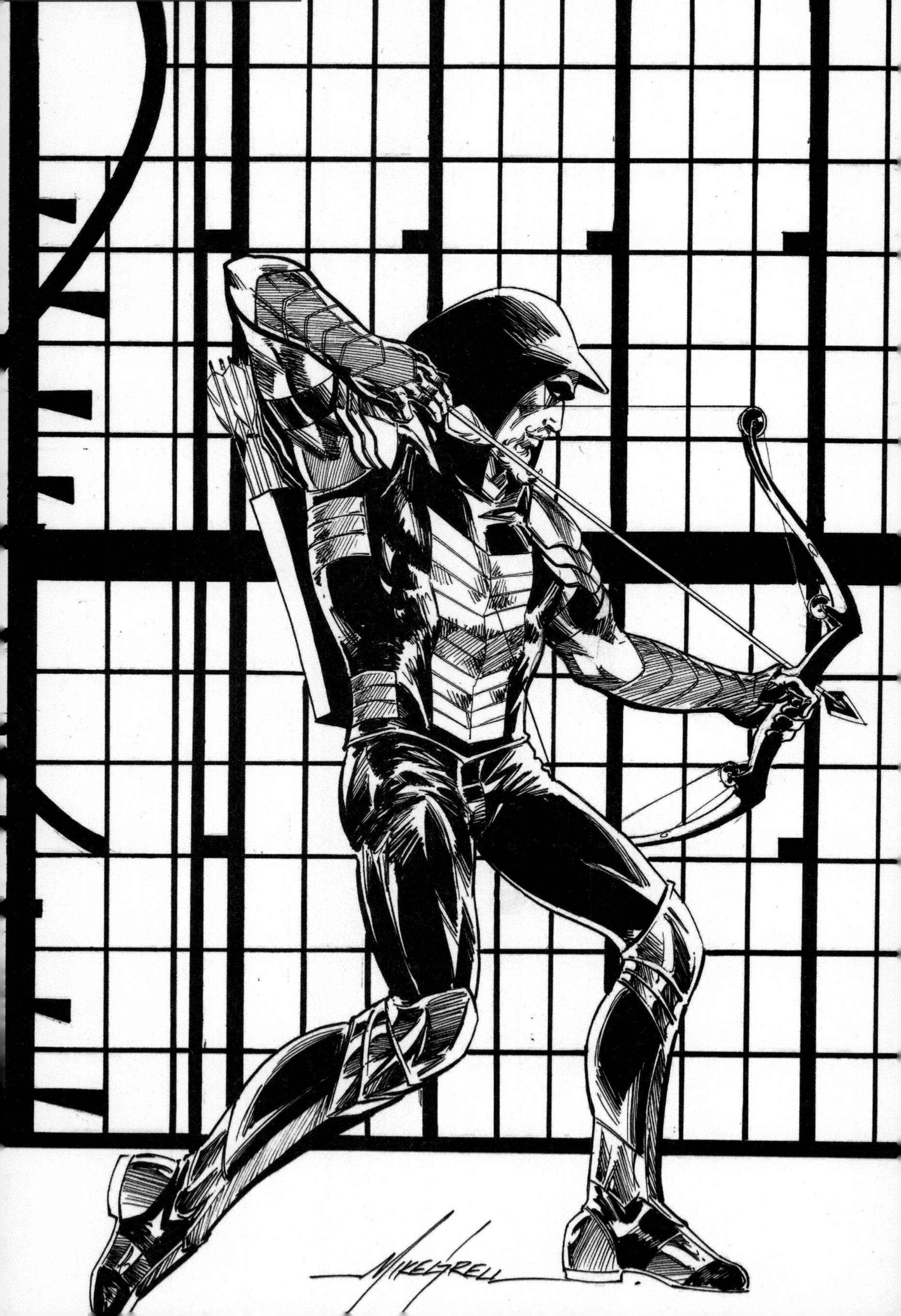
MIKE GRELL

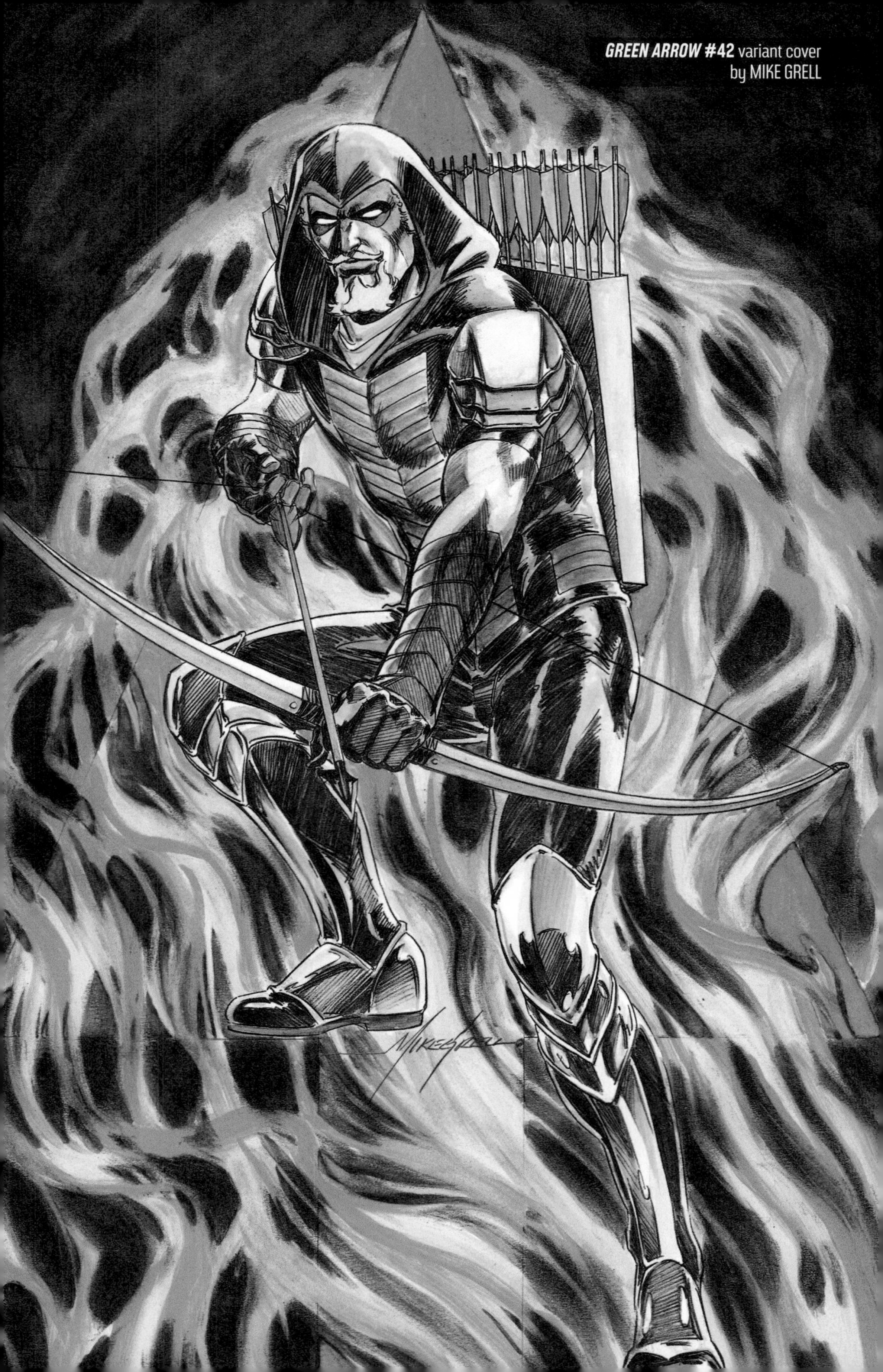

***GREEN ARROW* #42** variant cover
by MIKE GRELL

***GREEN ARROW* #48** variant cover
by NEAL ADAMS

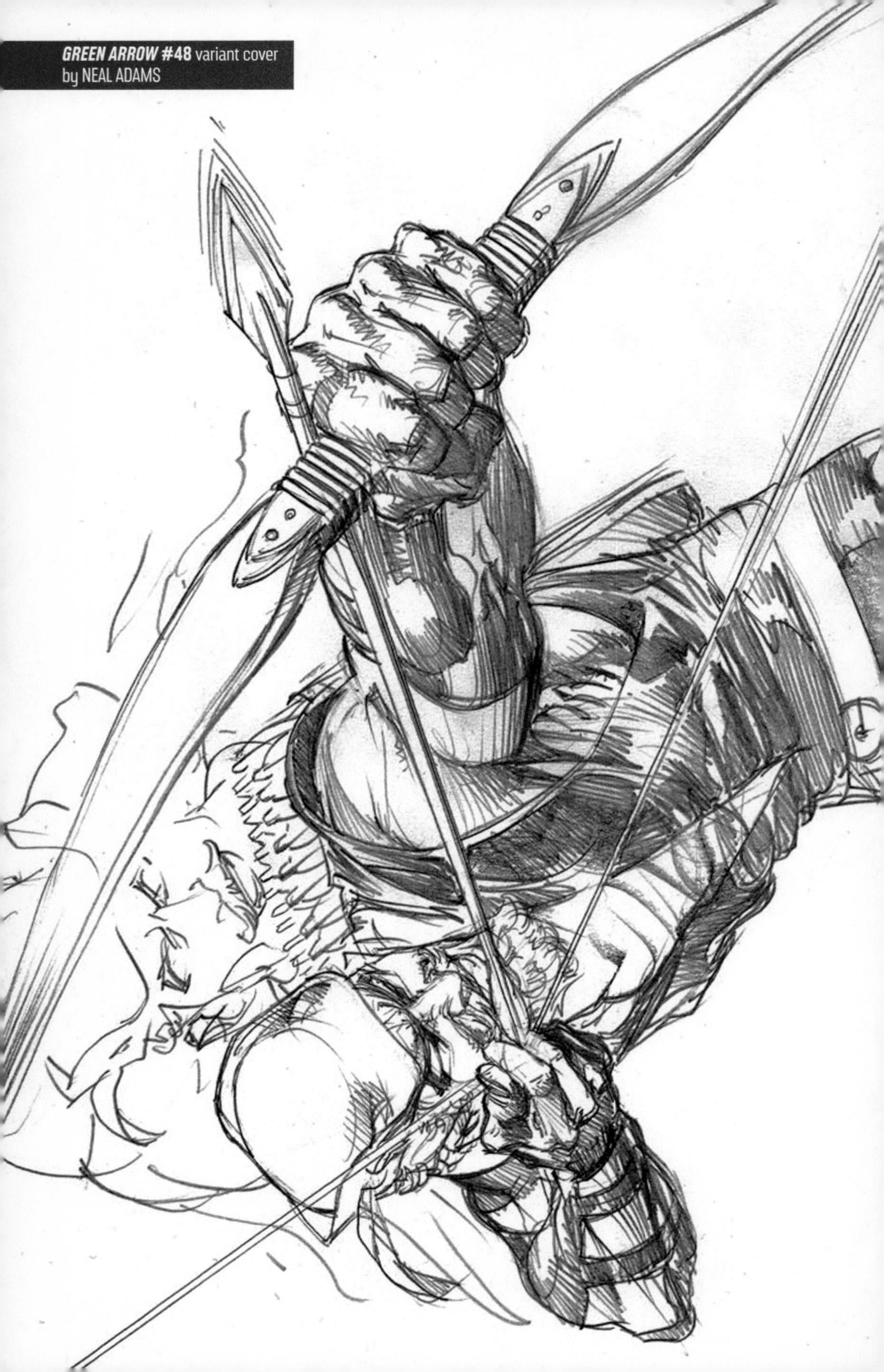

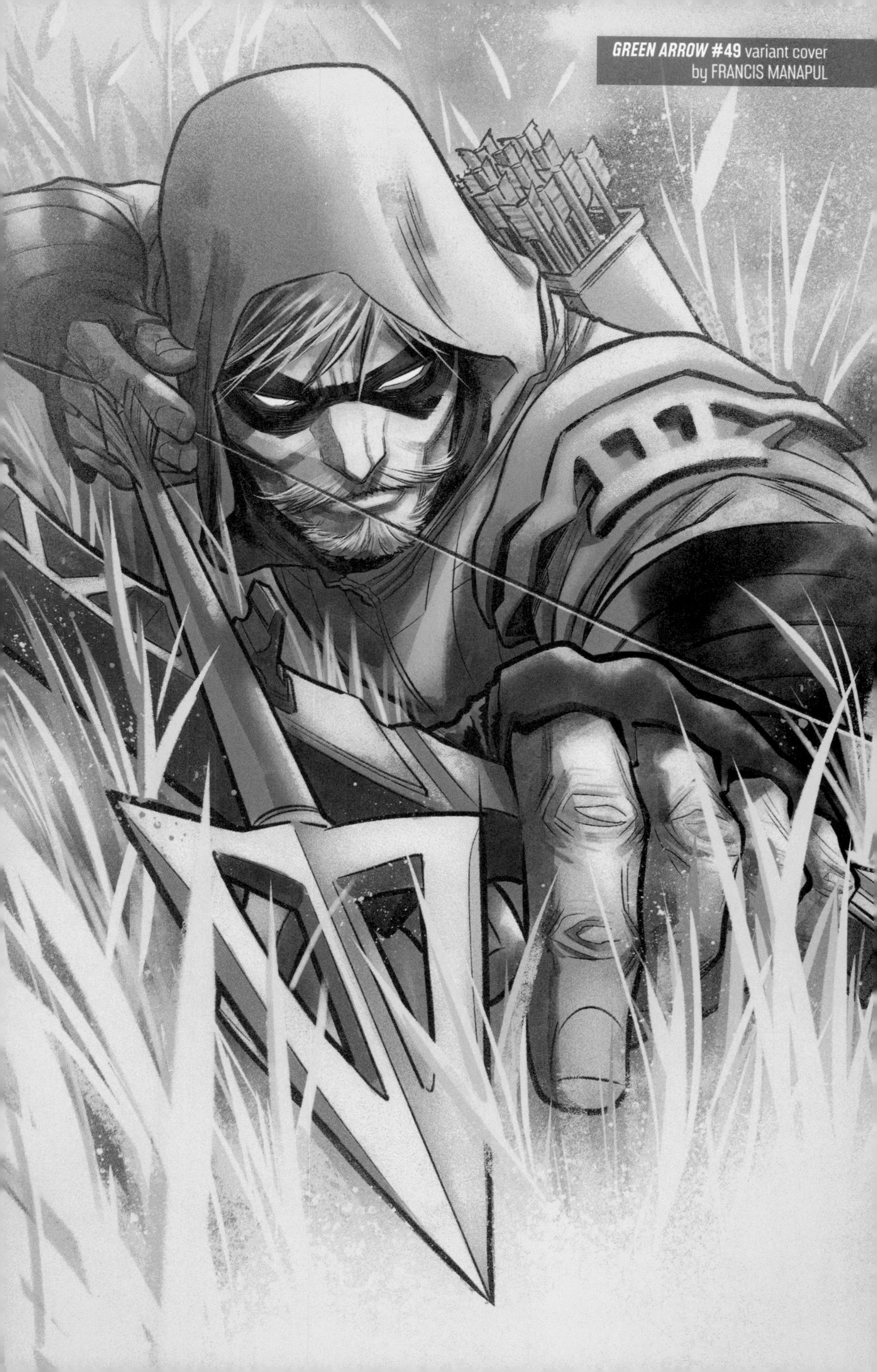

***GREEN ARROW* #49** variant cover
by FRANCIS MANAPUL

**GREEN ARROW #50** variant cover
by EVAN "DOC" SHANER

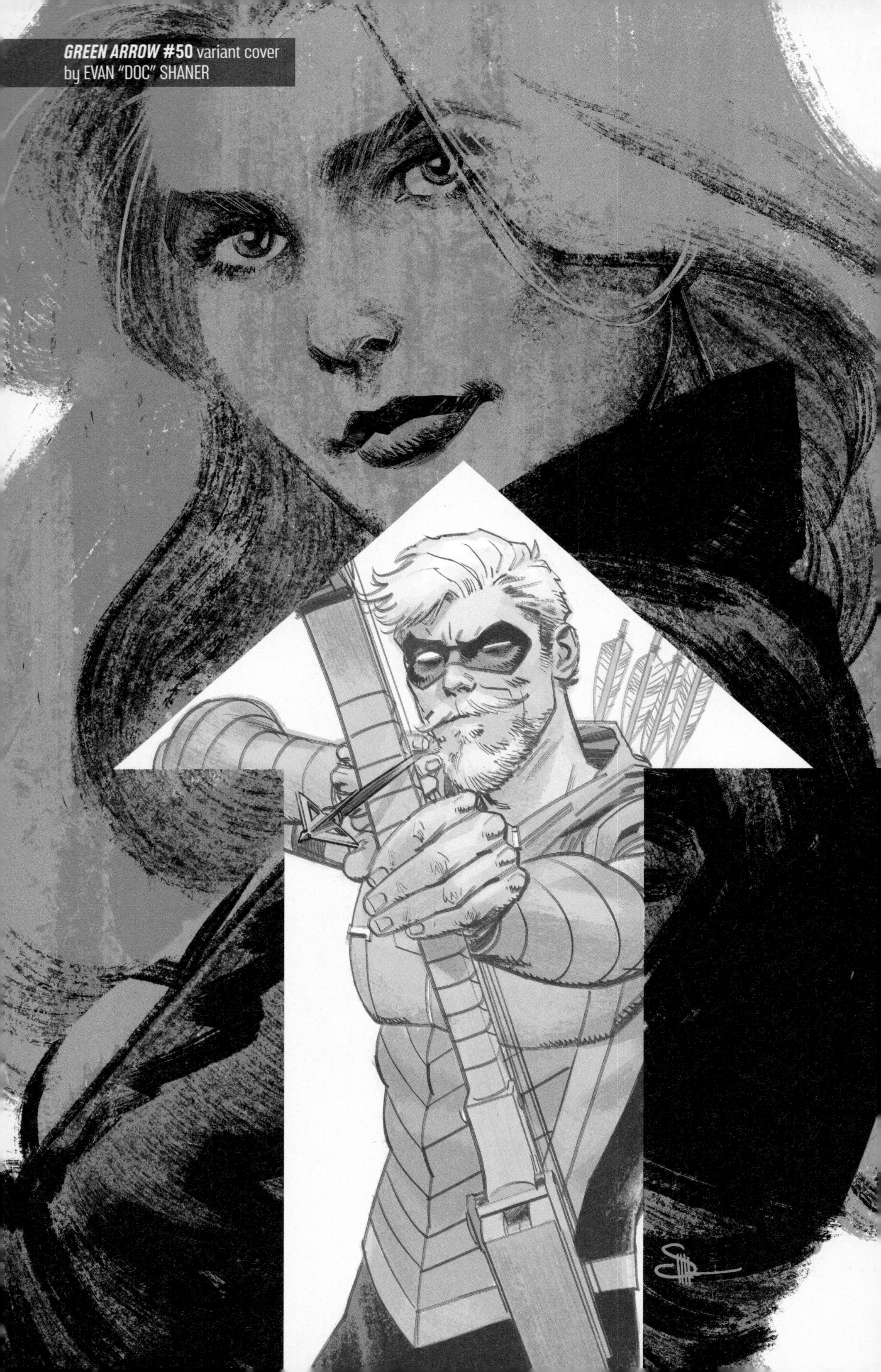

***GREEN ARROW* #41** page 1 line art by MATTHEW CLARK and SEAN PARSONS

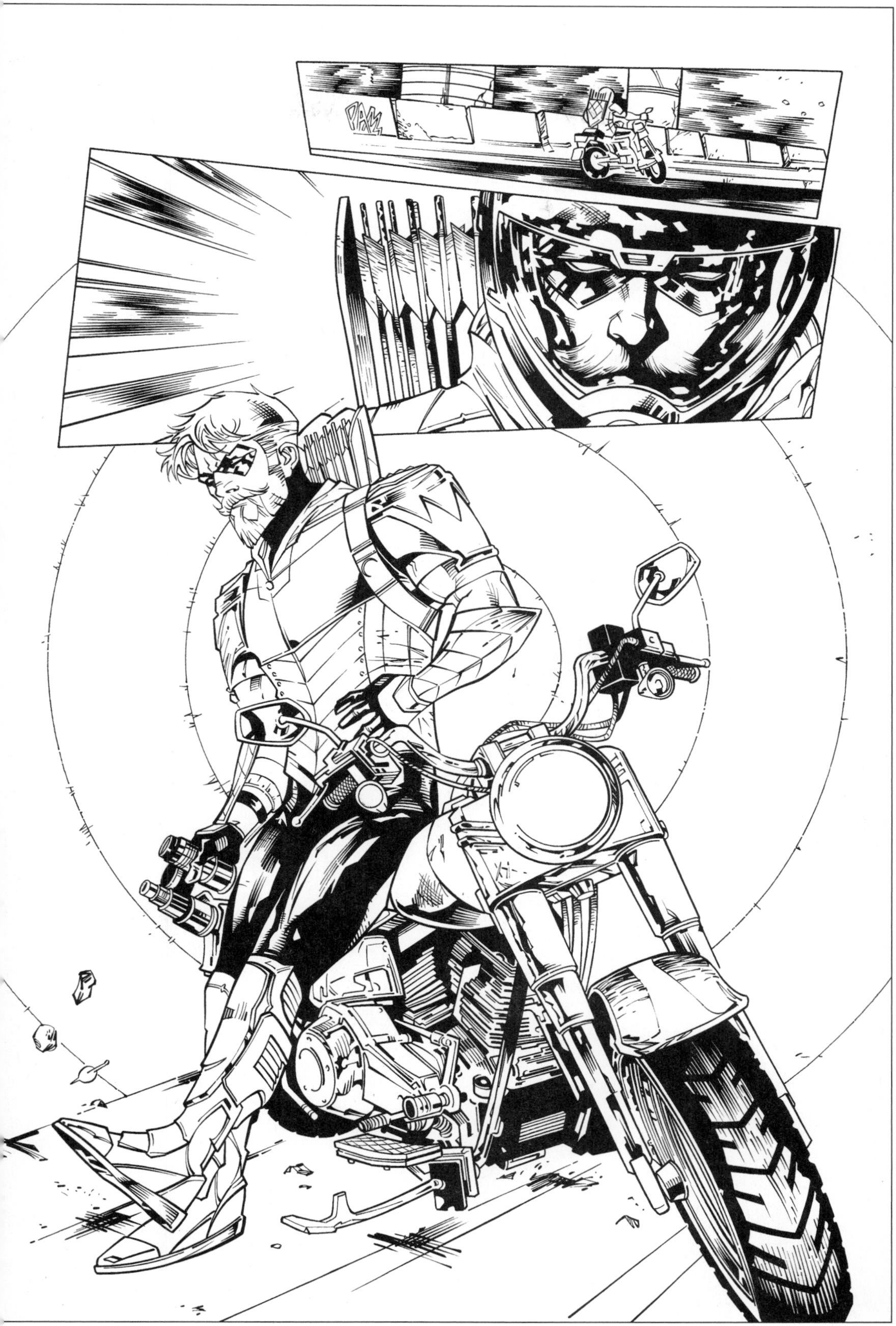
PAM

***GREEN ARROW* #41** page 20 line art by MATTHEW CLARK and SEAN PARSONS

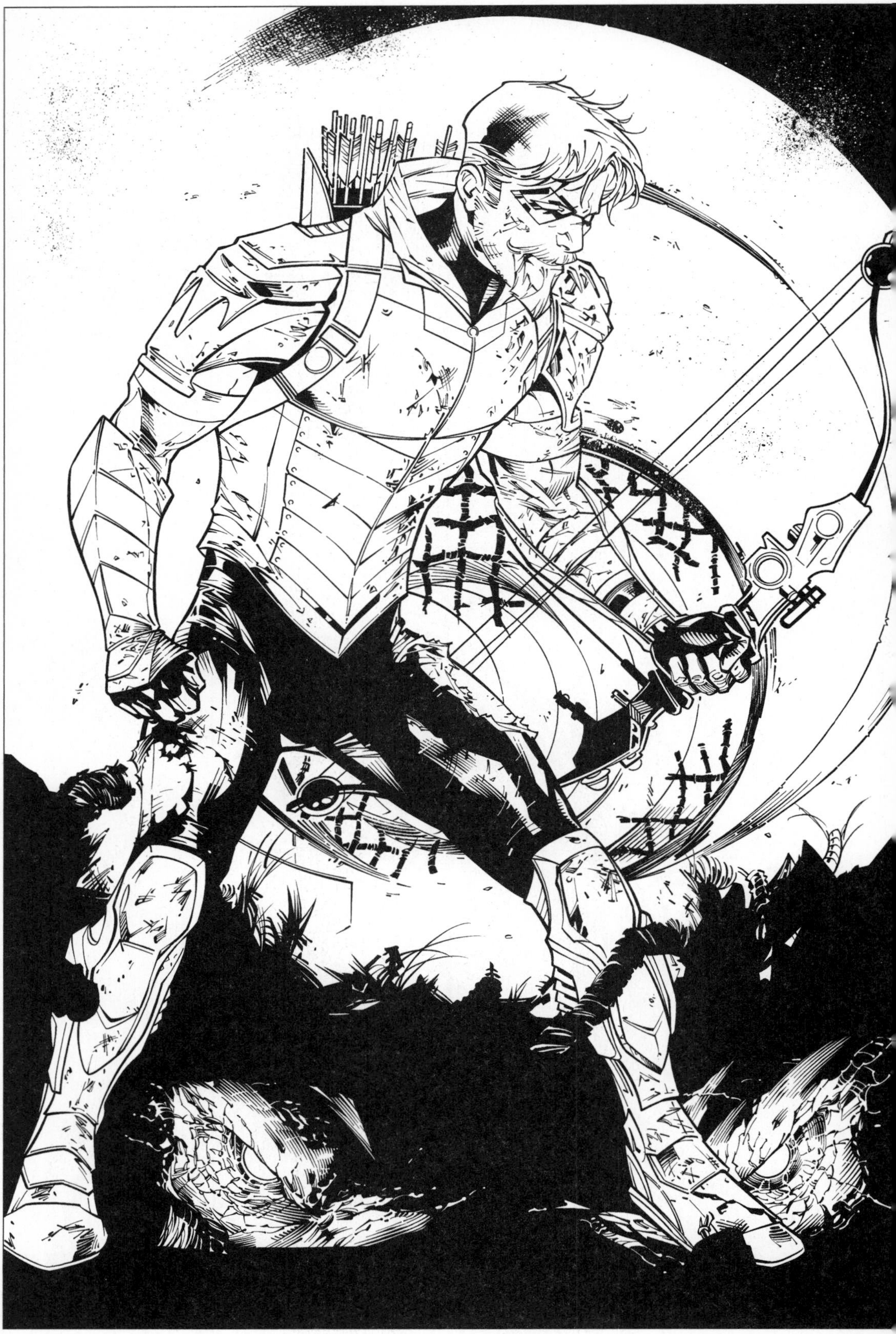

**GREEN ARROW #48** page 13 line art by JAVIER FERNANDEZ

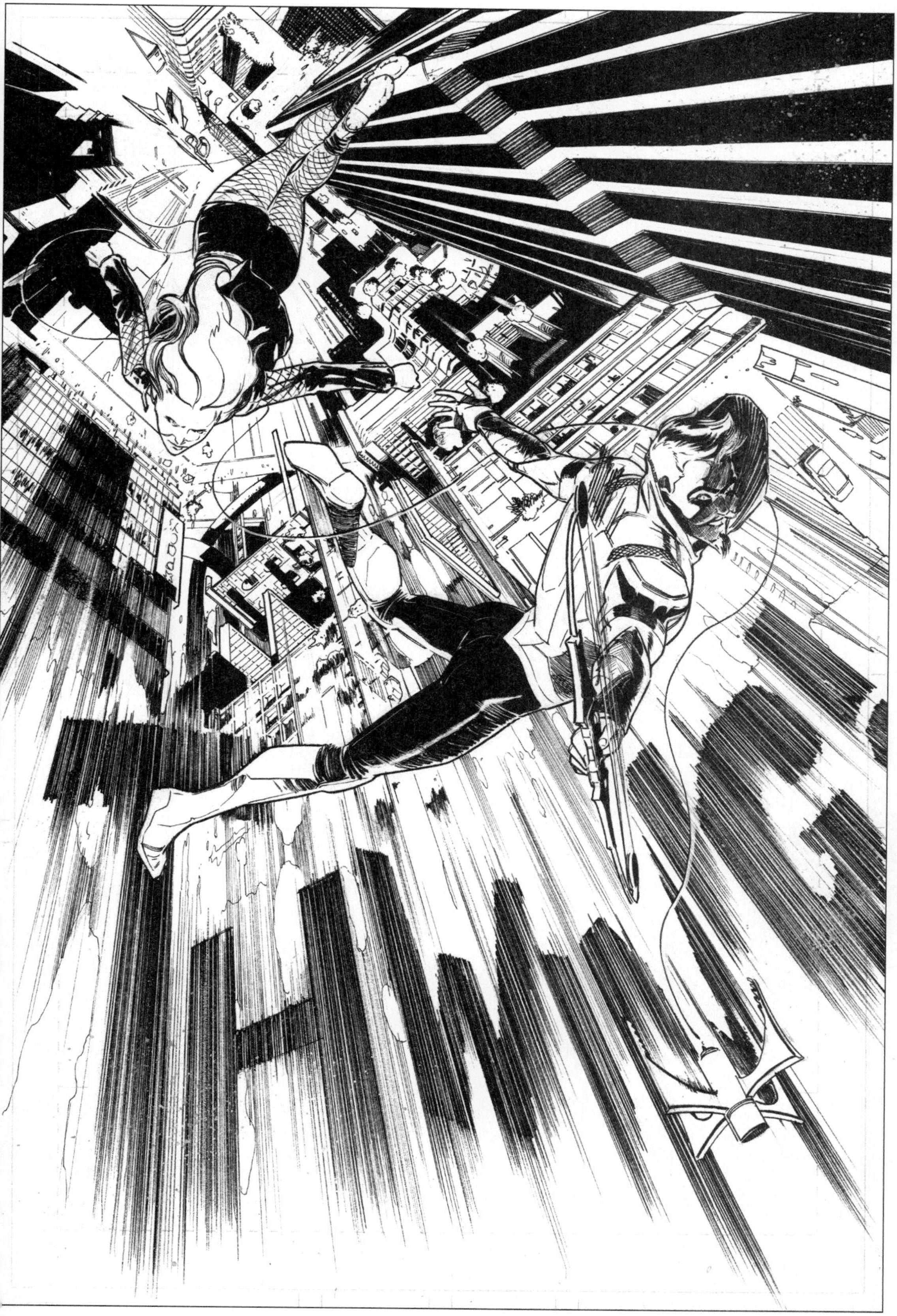

"Great writing, awesome artwork,
fun premise, and looks of cool action;
GREEN ARROW's got it all."
**–IGN**

"Sharply written and beautiful artwork."
**–CRAVE ONLINE**

# GREEN ARROW
## VOL. 4: THE KILL MACHINE
### JEFF LEMIRE with ANDREA SORRENTINO

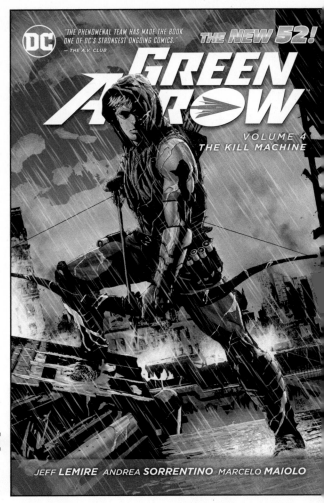

**GREEN ARROW
VOL. 5: THE OUTSIDERS WAR**

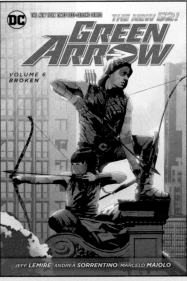

**GREEN ARROW
VOL. 6: BROKEN**

**READ THE ENTIRE EP**

GREEN ARR
VOL. 1: THE MIDAS TO

GREEN ARR
VOL. 2: TRIPLE THR

GREEN ARR
VOL. 3: HARP

GREEN ARR
VOL. 7: KING

GREEN ARR
VOL. 8: THE NIGHTBI

Get more DC graphic novels wherever comics and books are sold!

he world that Schmidt creates feels real and
'ed in."– **NEWSARAMA**

he artwork from Otto Schmidt is delightful and
irky."– **NERDIST**

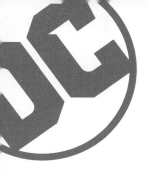

**C UNIVERSE REBIRTH**

# GREEN ARROW

**OL. 1: THE DEATH & LIFE OF OLIVER QUEEN**
ENJAMIN PERCY
ith OTTO SCHMIDT & JUAN FERREYRA

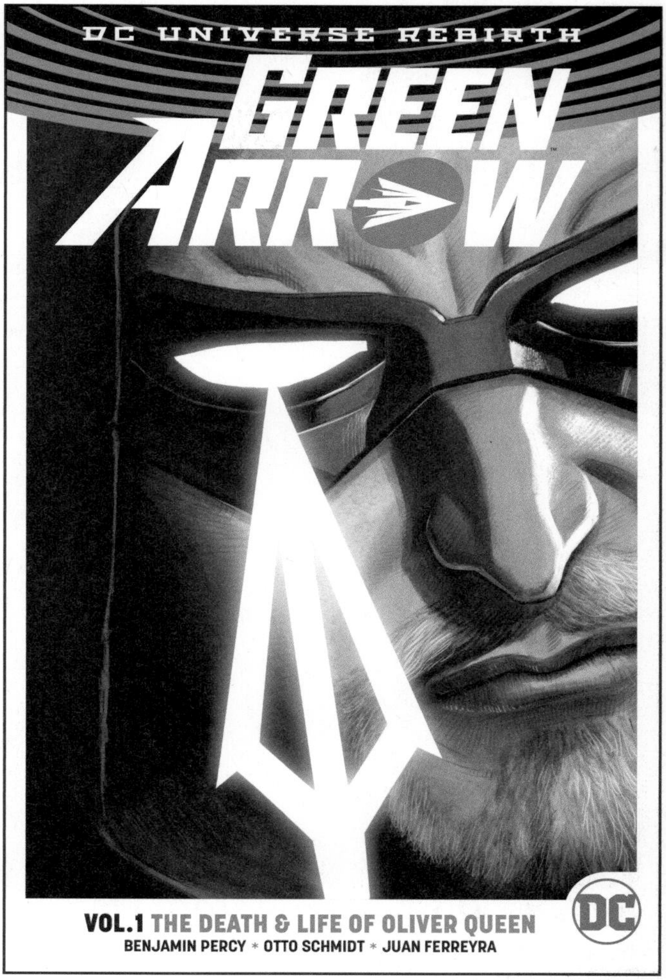
DC UNIVERSE REBIRTH
GREEN ARROW
VOL.1 THE DEATH & LIFE OF OLIVER QUEEN
BENJAMIN PERCY * OTTO SCHMIDT * JUAN FERREYRA

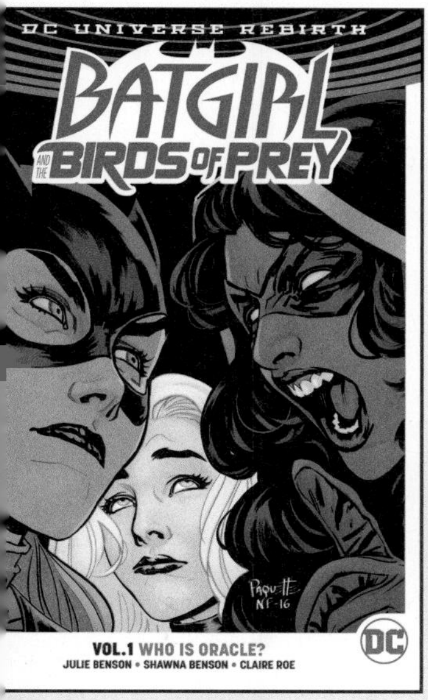
DC UNIVERSE REBIRTH
BATGIRL AND THE BIRDS OF PREY
VOL.1 WHO IS ORACLE?
JULIE BENSON • SHAWNA BENSON • CLAIRE ROE

BATGIRL AND
THE BIRDS OF PREY VOL. 1:
WHO IS ORACLE?

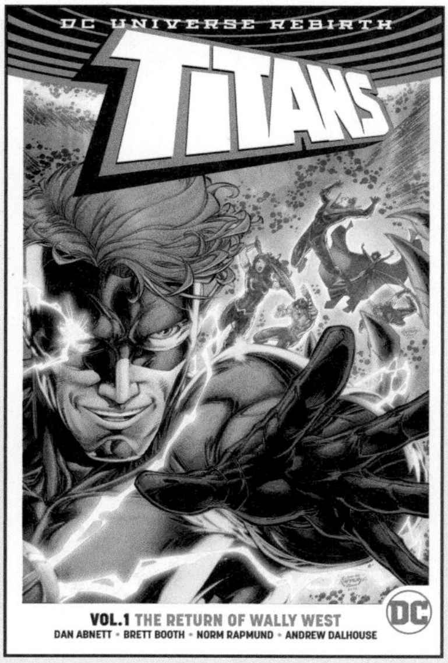
DC UNIVERSE REBIRTH
TITANS
VOL.1 THE RETURN OF WALLY WEST
DAN ABNETT • BRETT BOOTH • NORM RAPMUND • ANDREW DALHOUSE

TITANS VOL. 1:
THE RETURN OF WALLY WEST

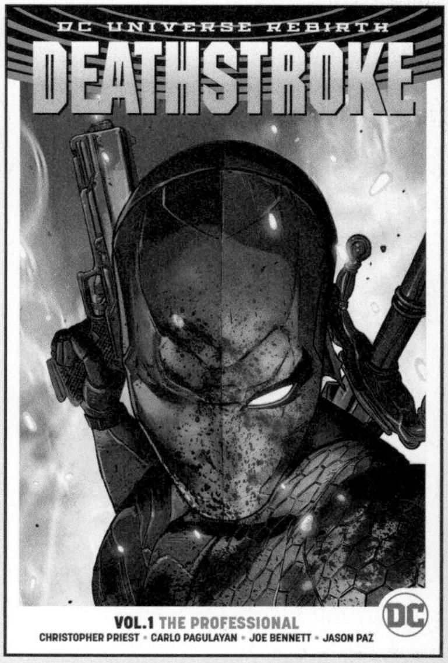
DC UNIVERSE REBIRTH
DEATHSTROKE
VOL.1 THE PROFESSIONAL
CHRISTOPHER PRIEST • CARLO PAGULAYAN • JOE BENNETT • JASON PAZ

DEATHSTROKE VOL. 1:
THE PROFESSIONAL

Get more DC graphic novels wherever comics and books are sold!

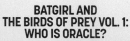

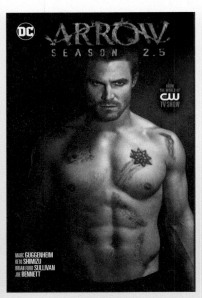